CHILDREN AND THE LAW

Children and the Law

Essays in Honour of Professor Nicholas Bala

SANJEEV ANAND, EDITOR

IRWIN LAW

Children and the Law: Essays in Honour of Professor Nicholas Bala

Published in 2011 by
Irwin Law Inc.
Suite 206, 14 Duncan Street
Toronto, ON
M5H 3G8

www.irwinlaw.com

ISBN: 978-1-55221-207-3
e-book ISBN: 978-1-55221-216-5

Library and Archives Canada Cataloguing in Publication

Children and the law : essays in honour of Professor Nicholas Bala / Sanjeev Anand, editor.

Includes bibliographical references.
Issued also in electronic format.
ISBN 978-1-55221-207-3

1. Children's rights—Canada. 2. Minors—Canada. 3. Children— Legal status, laws, etc.—Canada. 4. Teenagers—Legal status, laws, etc.—Canada. I. Bala, Nicholas, 1952– II. Anand, Sanjeev Singh, 1970–

KE512.C44 2011 342.7108'772 C2011-902042-4
KF479.C44 2011

The publisher acknowledges the financial support of the Government of Canada through the Canada Book Fund for its publishing activities.

We acknowledge the assistance of the OMDC Book Fund, an initiative of Ontario Media Development Corporation.

Printed and bound in Canada.

1 2 3 4 5 15 14 13 12 11

Contents

Preface

In 2009, I was working with Nicholas Bala, a distinguished professor of law at Queen's University, on a particularly difficult project: a book analyzing six years of jurisprudence under the *Youth Criminal Justice Act*. For us, the challenge lay not in the complex subject matter but in the precarious health in which Nick found himself that spring. Nick had been diagnosed with stage four metastatic melanoma. Because the cancer had spread to his liver, Nick's physicians recommended potentially dangerous surgery, to be followed by a year of chemotherapy. He advised me that even with this treatment, which he did undertake successfully, the median life expectancy statistics were not very encouraging. Nevertheless, Nick fervently desired to finish the book project that we had begun. Somehow he found the strength and will to complete the manuscript with me, and Irwin Law published the book in September 2009.

During my discussions about that book with Jeffrey Miller, the president of Irwin Law, Jeff suggested that the time was ripe to publish a collection of essays honouring Nick's massive contribution to the area of children and the law. When Jeff asked if I would solicit these essays, arrange for their peer review, and edit the collection, I readily agreed.

The impressive collection of essays contained in this volume mirrors much of Nicholas Bala's own vast scholarship. The papers address various issues concerning children within the context of criminal, family, evidence, health, and constitutional law. A number of the chapters go beyond traditional legal analyses and adopt social science perspectives to better understand the problems facing children and their families in the justice system. This book cannot claim to be a comprehensive treatment of the subject, but the authors of these essays, drawn from a number of different disciplines, present vital perspectives on key areas pertaining to children and the law, and it is hoped that their work will prompt further research and investigation.

Nick's passionate commitment to improving the lives of children is genuine and heartfelt. With Irwin Law's gracious support, he has requested that all royalties resulting from the sale of this volume be donated to UNICEF Canada.

The pedagogy and writing of Professor Bala have shed light on various and important aspects of children's experiences under the law. As this collection of essays demonstrates, Nick has also had a profound influence on the work of other scholars and professionals. Indeed, the name Nicholas Bala is synonymous with children's rights in academic, judicial, and public policy circles both within Canada and abroad. I am delighted that as this book goes to press, Nick reports that he is in good condition and remains very hopeful for the future. May his light continue to burn brightly and illuminate the way for others for many years to come.

Sanjeev Anand
Professor, Faculty of Law
University of Alberta
June 2010

Introduction: Paradoxes of Children's Rights

NICHOLAS BALA

A. THE "HOLISTIC STUDY" OF THE LEGAL STATUS OF CHILDHOOD

This is a fine collection of essays that individually and collectively address some of the most important and challenging issues related to the legal status of children, and the volume makes an important contribution to the growing but still small Canadian literature on children's rights. These essays are being published together to honour and, at least in part, reflect upon some of my scholarship written over the past three decades. As is fitting, some of the contributions are laudatory of my work, some barely mention it, some gently disagree with some of my ideas, while others are deeply critical of some of the controversial positions that I have taken on contentious issues. So it is both a pleasure and a challenge for me to provide some words of introduction to this volume.

I have devoted much of my career as a scholar to writing about a range of interrelated issues concerning children, their parents, and the law in Canada. As my good friend Cathy Lane Goodfellow observes in her contribution to this book, I have taken a holistic approach in my study of the legal status of children. I have written about children as both victims and offenders, and as the focus of disputes both between separated parents and between parents and state child welfare agencies; I also have considered the position of children both as subjects of litigation and as parties to court proceedings. In writing about this range of issues, I have covered a wider range of proceedings than most professionals deal with and written about a broader range of issues than most legal scholars consider in their study of children and adolescents. I have tried to understand legal issues in a broader social context, and have also appreciated the limitations of the law in addressing the problems of children and families; as a result, I have often collaborated with scholars and researchers from other disciplines. This interdisciplinary approach is reflected in the contributions to this book by scholars from outside of law.

B. TENSIONS AND PARADOXES

The study of the legal status of children and adolescents in Canada today contains many tensions and paradoxes, and the essays in this book explore some of the most challenging issues in this field.

The concept of "children's rights" is frequently invoked but often seems to lack traction; if children have the "right" to have their best interests promoted, can decisions be made to promote a child's best interests when they are contrary to the wishes of the child? In other words, does the child's right to "best interests decisions" take priority over the child's "right" to exercise his or her own right to make decisions? A number of papers in this collection address the question of when and how to give effect to a child's right to make decisions, or at least participate in decision making.

The best interests of the child is a central concept in legislation, caselaw, and the United Nations *Convention on the Rights of the Child*,[1] and the discussion of this concept is a central theme of this book, yet the Supreme Court in *Canadian Foundation for Children, Youth and the Law v. Canada (Attorney General)*[2] considered the term so vague and ill defined that it refused to treat it as a "principle of fundamental justice." A number of papers in this volume address the question of whether the concept of the best interests of the child has meaning, and if so, how it should be applied, and one directly challenges the conclusion of the Supreme Court on this issue.

One of the troubling questions in this area is whether making decisions that promote the best interests of children in general may sometimes be contrary to the best interests of a specific child. One context in which this ques-

---

1 Can. T.S. 1992 No 3.

2 2004 SCC 4 [*Foundation*].

tion may arise is in considering how a child is to be viewed in relation to his or her parents. If children's interests are usually promoted by strengthening their families, when and how should the state become involved in controlling parents? Does state regulation of parents sometimes undermine the interests of children?

Another contentious issue is whether the processes used in Canada for making decisions in the best interests of children are sometimes contrary to their best interests. Does the adversarial system, especially when used for making "best interests" determinations about the care of children, actually undermine their welfare by increasing animosity between caregivers? Is enough being done by the family justice system to promote the best interests of children, in terms of both the decisions made and the process adopted for making those decisions?

What are the capacities of children, and if they are generally less than adults, when and how should this relative incapacity be taken into account? Are child offenders entitled to some sort of a "discount" in accountability because of immaturity, and if so, should the evidence of child witnesses also be discounted due to their lack of adult capacities of perception, communication, and memory? A number of the essays in this book address from quite different perspectives questions related to how to protect children because of their limited capacity without losing respect for children and their capacity.

C. THE ESSAYS

The essays in this volume address a number of interrelated themes and could have been arranged in a number of different ways, but ultimately a decision was made to order them to reflect the organization of the justice system. The first five essays deal with situations in which children are alleged to be in need of protection from abuse or neglect, either in the context of child protection proceedings or in the criminal justice system. In this context, the rights of parents (or alleged abusers) and children must be balanced against the interests of the state in the protection of children. The next four papers address issues related to the youth justice system, whereby the state seeks to hold adolescents accountable for their criminal behaviour and the rights of a youth are most directly and obviously implicated. The last four papers deal with issues that arise when parents separate, and they disagree about what will do the most to promote the child's best interests, a context in which the rights of children sometimes seem totally subsumed to the rights of their parents.

Increasingly Canada's courts are being asked to struggle with the concepts of children's rights and the best interests of children. This collection begins with a provocative commentary by constitutional law scholar Mark Carter about the "children's trilogy," three decisions rendered by the Supreme Court between 2004 and 2009 that wrestle with the complex relationship of the rights of children and parents, and the powers and responsibilities of the state. The cases clearly recognize both childhood and adolescence as stages of life with constitutional significance; the developing capacity of a minor must be reflected in an evolving set of constitutional rights and limitations. However, each of the cases is challenging for readers, if for no other reason than the splits within the Court, with each case having strong dissents and two producing multiple judgments. Further, Carter argues that read together, the cases reflect an inconsistent, or perhaps evolving, approach to the relationship between the best interests of the child and constitutional law. In her 2004 majority judgment in *Foundation*,[3] McLachlin CJ upheld the validity of section 43 of the *Criminal Code*[4] and concluded that the "best interests of the child" is not a "principle of fundamental justice." Carter boldly argues that the 2009 majority judgment of Abella J in *A.C. v. Manitoba (Director of Child and Family Services)*[5] recognizes the "best interests of the child" as a constitutional principle and "an essential modern tool" for resolving debates about children. His argument has considerable force, and it may well be that at the Supreme Court, as elsewhere, context is very important. In the *Foundation* case, the Court refused to allow the "best interests principle" to be used to criminalize conduct of parents that is not clearly harmful to their children. In *A.C.*, the Court was dealing with the limits of the power of the state in imposing treatment on children and was, understandably, much more sympathetic to giving effect to the rights of children *against the state* and imposing an obligation on the state to promote their best interests. It seems likely that in future cases, the courts will be influenced by context and may well revisit the question of the extent to which the "best interests of the child" — a principle widely used in caselaw, legislation, and international law — should be given constitutional significance in Canada.

---

3 *Ibid.*

4 RSC 1985, c. C-46.

5 2009 SCC 30 [*A.C.*].

An essay by Gerald Robertson, one of Canada's leading health law scholars, follows the introductory chapter by Mark Carter and focuses on *A.C.*, one decision in the Supreme Court's children's trilogy. Robertson provides a critical and more detailed analysis of *A.C.*, set in the context of a broader examination of the right of children to consent to or refuse medical treatment. Robertson observes that the issue of the capacity of an adolescent to consent to treatment, which has arisen most frequently in regard to access to abortion and birth control, is very different from the question of capacity to refuse treatment, which has arisen most commonly in Canadian courts, as in *A.C.*, when a Jehovah's Witness youth, with the support of the parents, is refusing treatment for religious reasons. As Robertson points out, the judgment of Abella J in *A.C.* delicately balances children's right of decision making with their right to have decisions made in their best interests. He argues persuasively that the courts need to robustly assess not only the child's maturity and capacity to make an informed decision about medical issues in general but also whether the child's decision in this type of case is truly voluntary. He recognizes that if the threshold is met, the child's views ought to be determinative, but predicts that when the consequences of refusal of treatment are "severe," it is to be expected that courts will set a high threshold of capacity. One can also expect that the courts will take into consideration the intrusiveness and duration of the medical treatment; the courts seem more likely to order a blood transfusion when that relatively simple treatment will have a high likelihood of saving the child's life than to order a prolonged course of chemotherapy, even though recommended by physicians, when the likelihood of successful treatment may be uncertain.

In Chapter 3, law professor Anne McGillivray, a prominent defender of the rights of children, continues and deepens the critical examination of the Supreme Court children's trilogy, considering the Court's decision in the *Foundation* case, setting the discussion in the context of a broader consideration of corporal punishment. McGillivray graphically describes the horrific history of legalized abuse of children by parents, teachers, and other caregivers, exercising their "right of correction." As she acknowledges, the courts have gradually narrowed the scope of acceptable physical punishment, and the Supreme Court in *Foundation* attempted to further define and limit the scope of this authority over children. She correctly points out that almost nothing has been done to educate parents about the effect of this decision, and there continues to be significant variation in how trial judges are applying it, though it is clear that corporal punishment of children, which was common and legally acceptable a half century ago, is now less common, and in many cases punishment that was acceptable in the past would no longer be legally tolerated. McGillivray concludes her passionate essay with a critique of the position that I took as an expert witness, for the federal government, in the *Foundation* case. While my views were broadly consistent with those of the majority of the Court, and were quoted by Binnie J in his opinion, they were highly controversial with some of my colleagues and friends, such as McGillivray. Some of our disagreement may relate to differences in how we interpret the social science literature on corporal punishment; despite the large body of literature, there are significant ethical and practical constraints to the research that can be done. We may also disagree about the role that the criminal law should play in regulating parental conduct, and how much scope we would give to children to assert *constitutional rights* against their parents. I believe, however, that we share a common concern that too often angry, frustrated, or emotionally unbalanced parents end up causing serious physical and psychological harm or even permanent injury or death to their children, and a common hope that this type of abusive conduct can eventually be eliminated.

After the three essays by law professors, the next two chapters are contributed by social scientists who take a very different approach to understanding the rights and capacities of children. I have had the pleasure of collaborating with child psychologists Victoria Talwar and Kang Lee and forensic psychologist Rod Lindsay for over a decade in a program of research on the credibility and competency of child witnesses. In Chapter 4, these three researchers tell the story of how a series of studies that we did resulted in a significant piece of law reform that has facilitated the process of children testifying in Canadian criminal courts, most commonly in cases where they have been victims of or witnesses to abuse. Our program of research included traditional legal scholarship, analyzing caselaw and legislation, and surveys of professional practices and attitudes. For me, as a legal academic, the most foreign and interesting aspect of the research was a series of experiments we conducted in psychology laboratories, where we could test whether some traditional legal assumptions about children were valid. Specifically, we tested whether children's ability to establish competence to testify by "passing" the traditional legal inquiry and answering questions about the "promise to tell the truth" was in any way predictive of whether they were more likely to tell the truth. We found that ability to answer these questions was not related to truth-telling behaviour, though the fact that a child had promised to tell the truth did make it more likely that the child would tell the truth. The results of our research were shared with a House of Commons committee studying the *Canada Evidence Act*,[6] and the law was amended so that the test for competency of children now focuses on the child's ability to communicate meaningfully with the court. Children who are being qualified as witnesses are now not to be asked about their understanding of the "promise to tell the truth," although they are still required to make the promise. This of course treats children in a similar fashion to adults. Adults are required to give an oath or affirmation without being asked to explain its significance, and a substantial number of adults cannot explain these legal undertakings. The story that is told in this chapter is an important, albeit all too rare, instance of social science research affecting law reform in Canada; as discussed in a number of chapters in this book, especially those dealing with youth justice, too often it is politics rather than research that drives law reform.

Rod Lindsay, one of the world's leading researchers on eyewitness identification procedures, collaborated with three colleagues to write Chapter 5, summarizing work that he and others have undertaken on the accuracy of children's identification of adults whom they have previously seen but whom they do not know well. Such identifications can be extremely important in criminal prosecutions for child abuse or abduction. Consistent with other research about children, it has been established that children are more likely than adults to be influenced by social factors when asked to identify a person. While they are almost as accurate as adults in correctly identifying persons whom they have previously seen when those persons are placed in a lineup, children are more likely to feel social pressure to make a choice even if the person is not in the lineup; when confronted with a lineup without the target present, they are more likely than adults to identify one of them incorrectly as the previously observed person. The chapter discusses research on some innovative techniques for identification that may reduce the error rate of children. While steps can and should be taken to improve the testimony of children, the capacities of child and adult witnesses inevitably differ. This justifies taking steps to accommodate child witnesses, for example, by

6 RSC 1985, c. C-5.

allowing them to testify outside of the intimidating court environment via closed circuit television. However, the historical dismissal of testimony from children was not justified, and both violated their rights and contributed to their abuse and exploitation.

Canada's youth justice law was substantially reformed in 2003 when the *Youth Criminal Justice Act* (*YCJA*)[7] came into effect, resulting in a significant reduction in the number of youth being charged and placed in custody. The first two chapters on youth justice are by criminologists and present original research on the effects of the new law, while the next two chapters address some of the long-standing controversies of juvenile justice in Canada.

Carla Cesaroni, one of the bright young lights of Canadian criminology, presents some results of her research on the effect of the *YCJA* on Canada's youth corrections system in Chapter 6. While significantly fewer youth are being committed to custody, and some custody facilities have closed, the number in pre-trial remand has somewhat increased. Based on her interviews and research with youth and staff, Cesaroni reports that youth in the corrections system have higher levels of psychosocial needs than other youth. There are significant concerns about youth who are incarcerated, especially those in pre-trial detention, over peer-to-peer violence and victimization and consequent pressures to join a gang to gain protection. Overall, Cesaroni paints a disturbing picture of Canada's youth corrections system; while the *YCJA* has reduced the total number of incarcerated youth, the population is in many respects more challenging to work with, and its needs are too often not adequately addressed.

I have had the privilege of collaborating with criminologists Peter Carrington and Julian Roberts on a number of papers analyzing the effects of the *YCJA*. In Chapter 7, they provide the first published analysis of Deferred Custody and Supervision Orders (DCSOs), one of the new sentences created by the *YCJA* with the intent of reducing the use of custody by providing judges with a "last chance sanction" for youths who would otherwise be committed to custody. As always, Carrington and Roberts offer a sophisticated analysis, comparing youth and adult sanctions and sentencing principles, and concluding that the DCSO is more rehabilitative than the adult conditional sentence. While pointing out the limitations of current data and identifying the need for further research, they conclude that the introduction of the DCSO

7 SC 2002, c. 1.

has had a significant "decarcerating effect" and that the "failure rate" for DCSOs seems low, supporting the view that this was an important addition to Canada's youth justice regime.

Cathy Lane Goodfellow, one of Canada's most experienced lawyers for adolescent clients, works at the youth offender legal aid clinic in Calgary. While Alberta has a reputation as a conservative and "get tough on crime" jurisdiction, it is interesting that it also has the most sophisticated youth defender program in Canada, in which seasoned lawyers and social workers collaborate to advocate for and advise adolescent clients. It is apparent that those responsible for the administration of justice in Alberta recognize the social value of effective advocacy for youth. In Chapter 8, Goodfellow articulates the challenges and expectations for any lawyer providing representation for adolescent clients and describes the way in which her office fulfils its mandate. She also analyzes some of the conflicting caselaw about the provisions governing access to counsel for youth, concluding that the Alberta courts, perhaps influenced by the existence of clinics in their province, have taken an approach to the *YCJA* that facilitates access of adolescents to counsel.

Anthony Doob and Jane Sprott, the two Canadian criminologists who have done the most research on juvenile justice and offending over the past decade, provide a nuanced discussion in Chapter 9 of the issue of the minimum age of youth court jurisdiction, set within a broader philosophical discussion of the nature and purposes of the youth justice system. In this piece, they engage with another controversial position that I took, advocating a reduction, in certain limited circumstances, of the minimum age of youth court jurisdiction from twelve to ten years. Like a number of pieces in this book, Doob and Sprott explore the complex interaction of law reform, politics, and social science research. They elegantly explain our intellectual differences, though politely observing that my position could be (mis)used by "law and order" politicians to support a potentially ever-growing list of situations that would invite a criminal justice response for child offenders.

The last four chapters consider a number of issues that arise when parents separate. This is a legal context in which decisions are to be based solely on the "best interests of the child," though there is often bitter controversy about what this means, and in many cases it seems that judges must choose the "least detrimental alternative."

Dan Goldberg, one of Canada's most experienced lawyers for children, addresses the contentious issue of judicial interviewing of children in custody and access cases. As he discusses in Chapter 10, in these cases judges in Canada (outside of Quebec) have traditionally been very reluctant to interview or meet with children, and the idea of meeting with a child without the presence of their parents or counsel is not consistent with the traditional judicial role. In other jurisdictions, however, including Quebec and many American states,[8] judges not infrequently meet with children, and there is increasing interest in this practice in Canada. As Goldberg argues, it is important to be clear about the purpose of any judicial meetings with a child, and the focus should be on the opportunity for the judge and child to meet each other rather than any attempt to gain factual information. It is also crucial that a child not be placed in the position of feeling forced to "choose" between parents and must not be explicitly asked to express a preference for which parent they want to live with. Even without meeting the judge, in the cases that are commonly litigated, children are likely to feel considerable pressure from their parents to "take sides." Experience from other jurisdictions does not suggest that children are distressed by meeting with a judge, though the overall process of parental separation and litigation may be very stressful. As Goldberg recognizes, however, more empirical research is needed into the actual experiences of children in the family justice system, not only with judges but also with lawyers and mental health professionals.

In Chapter 11, two Calgary-based practitioners provide just such research, reporting on an innovative pilot program that provided integrated services of mental health professionals and lawyers to children experiencing domestic violence and parental separations. Dale Hensley, a highly experienced children's lawyer, and Jean Dunbar, a child therapist with extensive experience in working with children from families with a history of violence, were both involved in the *Speaking for Themselves* program. This program operated for three years, providing the services of both a trauma therapist and a lawyer to children exposed to confirmed or alleged domestic violence and high-conflict parenting disputes. The program partners provided services based on the premise that it is important to listen to what children have to say without imposing decision-making responsibility on them. The mental health professionals were responsible both for providing counselling services to the children and for preparing reports, based on their assessments of

8 See Rachel Birnbaum & Nicholas Bala, "Judicial Interviews with Children in Custody and Access Cases: Comparing Experiences in Ontario and Ohio" (2010) 24 Int'l JL Pol'y & Fam. 300.

a child's best interests. Only a few of the children disagreed with the recommendations of their therapists, and these reports contributed to a very high rate of resolution for these cases without a trial. Most of the parents and children also reported high levels of satisfaction with the program. The chapter clearly establishes the need of this very vulnerable population of children for services from both lawyers and mental health professionals. The manner of delivery requires more experimentation and research, however. This program was too expensive on a per case basis to sustain, although the costs reflect at least in part the fact that it was a pilot program.

In Chapter 12, Leslie D. MacRae, Shane D. Simpson, Joanne J. Paetsch, Lorne D. Bertrand, Sheryl Pearson, and Joseph P. Hornick provide a thorough and very instructive summary of their research into the implementation of Alberta's *Family Law Act*.[9] They use several different methodologies to assess the impact of the new law; interestingly, they include a study of the perceptions of self-represented litigants, an increasingly large but understudied population in the family courts. While Alberta has the reputation of being Canada's most conservative jurisdiction for family law matters (deserved for such issues as legal approaches to same-sex relationships), in some respects it is one of the most innovative jurisdictions. As discussed in the chapter, in enacting this statute, the province adopted new, more child-focused concepts for making parenting arrangements after separation and procedures intended to reduce the adversarial nature of decision making about children. According to this research, Alberta has succeeded in increasing the efficiency of its family justice process, improving access to justice (especially for the self-represented) and increasing the use of non-adversarial methods of dispute resolution. These Alberta reforms, and other innovations discussed in other chapters, clearly merit serious study in other jurisdictions.

Chapter 13 is a study of judicial approaches to joint custody by Susan Boyd, one of Canada's leading feminist scholars. As is typical of much of her work, she provides a sophisticated analysis of social trends and legal change. As some other contributors do, Boyd makes the important point that too often Canadian scholars focus on developments in Ontario and incorrectly assume that other provinces have similar responses to legal issues. She contrasts developments in the British Columbia and Ontario courts, suggesting that the Ontario courts may be taking a more cautious approach to awarding joint

9 SA 2003, c. F-4.5.

custody. Boyd offers a very helpful analysis of the more flexible approach that the British Columbia courts have taken to the making of parenting orders, with the possibility of both joint guardianship and joint custody. She wisely notes that inappropriate imposition of joint decision-making regimes may prejudice the welfare and safety of mothers and children, and that caution must be exercised about these regimes, especially in cases involving abuse concerns. On the other hand, given the gradual increase in the involvement of fathers in parenting their children in intact marital relationships, which Boyd notes, it is not surprising that there has also been a gradual increase in various forms of post-separation shared parenting.

D. EXPRESSIONS OF GRATITUDE

It is an honour for any scholar to have a Festschrift published in his life time, and it is an especial honour for one who is relatively young at the time of publication (fifty-nine). Unfortunately, I suspect that the genesis of this project was not the sense that I was particularly worthy of honour at this time but that it needed to be done soon if it was not to be done posthumously. The announcement that this project would be undertaken was put forward by Sanjeev Anand on the occasion of a conference and celebratory dinner held in my honour in May 2009 in Kingston. That event, known colloquially as the "Bala Gala," was quickly organized to coincide with my recovery from surgery for stage four metastatic melanoma, just as I was beginning what turned out to be a year of chemotherapy (pill based and fortunately relatively mild). I was deeply moved when the announcement was made, though not completely convinced that I would live to see the project to fruition, as the median life expectancy statistics for my condition suggested that I would be beating the odds to live into the spring of 2010. As I write this introduction, my treatment is over — at least for now — and I feel strong and optimistic. I can also report that "the median is not the message."[10]

I would like to conclude by expressing my deep gratitude to all the contributors to this book, and especially to my dear friend Sanjeev Anand for undertaking the challenging task of organizing the project and editing the

10 This is the title of an article written by the famous American biologist Stephen Gould for fellow cancer patients. He was diagnosed with an aggressive form of cancer and learned that the median life expectancy was eight months; he lived more than another twenty years: S.J. Gould, "The Median Is Not the Message" *Discover* (June 1985) at 40.

manuscript. I am also deeply indebted to Jeff Miller, president of Irwin Law, for publishing this work; it reflects both his commitment to Canadian legal scholarship and his warm and supportive approach to his authors. Most of all, I am deeply grateful for the support I have received from so many friends, colleagues, present and former students, and family members over the course of my illness. I feel very fortunate to have had the career and life that I have had.

Part One

CHAPTER 1

The Children's Trilogy: The Best Interests of the Child Principle and the Principles of Fundamental Justice

MARK CARTER

The "Bala perspective" on the constitutional status of children's rights demonstrates comprehensive legal knowledge and sophisticated analysis, but its most distinguishing characteristic is its compassion. Nicholas Bala's work on the constitutional dimensions of the criminal sentencing of youths bears all of these hallmarks. Employing precise legal analysis[1] and integrating important psychological research about the intellectual and emotional development of children and young people,[2] he has stood firmly against attempts to impose a "law and order" agenda upon children through the use of mandatory and presumptive adult sentencing.[3]

The constitutionality of the provisions in the *Youth Criminal Justice Act* (*YCJA*)[4] relating to presumptive adult sentencing of young people was central

1 See, for example, Nicholas Bala, "*Charter* Challenges to Presumptive Adult Sentences for Serious Youth Offenders" (2006), 37 CR (6th) 287.

2 See, for example, Carla Cesaroni & Nicholas Bala, "Deterrence as a Principle of Youth Sentencing: No Effect on Youth, but a Significant Effect on Judges" (2008) 34 Queen's LJ 447.

3 In an interview with the CBC's John Grey in September 2008 concerning the governing Conservative Party's election proposal to lower the age at which young people could be subjected to presumptive adult sentences, Professor Bala characterized the proposal as "seriously bad social policy." Asked by Grey why the Conservatives would advance the proposal, Grey reports, "Bala laughed: 'We're in the middle of an election campaign!'" John Grey, "The Uneasy Mix of Crime, Punishment, and Politics," online: www.cbc.ca/news/canadavotes/realitycheck/2008/09/the_uneasy_mix_of_crime_punish.html.

4 SC 2002, c. 1 [*YCJA*].

to the Supreme Court of Canada's decision in *R. v. D.B.*[5] Writing after the Ontario Court of Appeal's decision in the case,[6] Bala correctly predicted that the Supreme Court would find these provisions an unreasonable infringement of section 7 of the *Canadian Charter of Rights and Freedoms.*[7] At the time, however, he considered it "unwise to predict how the Supreme Court will resolve [the] controversial issue" of how the "best interests of the child" principle (the "best interests" principle) might inform the Court's interpretation of the "principles of fundamental justice" under section 7.[8]

The controversy at that time was rooted in opposing decisions by the Quebec and British Columbia courts of appeal on the constitutionality of the *YCJA* provisions. In finding that the presumptive adult sentencing of young people who have committed certain serious crimes infringes section 7, the Quebec Court of Appeal in *Québec (Ministre de la Justice) c. Canada (Ministre de la Justice)*[9] identified the best interests principle as one of the dimensions of fundamental justice with which the *YCJA* provisions were inconsistent. Subsequently, in *R. v. T. (K.D.)*[10] the British Columbia Court of Appeal upheld the same *YCJA* provisions. Among the reasons that the BC court gave for rejecting the Quebec Court of Appeal's approach was the Supreme Court's intervening decision in *Canadian Foundation for Children, Youth and the Law v. Canada (Attorney General).*[11] In upholding the constitutionality of the corporal punishment defence[12] in *Foundation,* the majority refused to recognize the best interests principle as a principle of fundamental justice. In *D.B.* itself, the Ontario Court of Appeal sided with the Quebec Court of Appeal as to the unconstitutionality of the *YCJA* provisions, while avoiding the Quebec court's suggestion that the best interests of the child principle is a principle of fundamental justice. The Supreme Court upheld the Ontario Court of Appeal's decision in *D.B.*

---

5 [2008] 2 SCR 3. [*D.B.*].

6 *R .v. D.B.* (2006), 37 CR (6th) 265 (ONCA).

7 Bala, above note 1 at 288–89; *Canadian Charter of Rights and Freedoms,* Part I of the *Constitution Act, 1982,* being Schedule B to the *Canada Act 1982* (UK), 1982, c. 11 [*Charter*]. Section 7 of the *Charter* reads: "Everyone has the right to life, liberty and security of the person and the right not to be deprived thereof except in accordance with the principles of fundamental justice."

8 Bala, *ibid.* at 297.

9 (2003), 10 CR (6th) 281 (QCCA).

10 2006 BCCA 60.

11 2004 SCC 4 [*Foundation*].

12 *Criminal Code,* RSC 1985, c. C-46, s. 43.

Most recently, *A.C. v. Manitoba (Director of Child and Family Services)*[13] has joined *Foundation* and *D.B.* to form a trilogy of important decisions by the Supreme Court on the relationship between the best interests of the child principle and the principles of fundamental justice. In *A.C.*, the Court considered the constitutionality of the provisions of Manitoba's *Child and Family Services Act* (*CFSA*)[14] that allow courts to order that children who are fifteen years of age or younger receive necessary medical treatment to which their parents or, in the *A.C.* case, the children themselves object. The *CFSA* provisions successfully withstood a challenge based on several sections of the *Charter*. In relation to the section 7 argument, the majority held that the *CFSA* provision was saved from being unconstitutionally arbitrary by the best interests of the child principle, which guides courts' decision making under the section.

In this article I argue that a close comparison of the Supreme Court's fundamental justice analysis in *Foundation* and *D.B.* indicates that the best interests principle's claim to constitutional status is at least as strong as — and in some respects stronger than — that of one of the principles recognized in the *D.B.* case: the "presumption of diminished moral blameworthiness or culpability" of young people. This comparison places in sharp relief the artificiality of the exclusion of the best interests principle from the scope of fundamental justice in the *Foundation* decision. I then examine the unique role played by the best interests principle in *A.C.* I argue that by relying on the best interests principle as it does in order to find that the *CFSA* section in question is not arbitrary, the Court must be held to have recognized the constitutional status of the best interests of the child principle. If this throws into doubt the status of the *Foundation* decision, suggesting, in fact, that the corporal punishment defence must be unconstitutional, then so much the worse for the defence, but so much the better for children.

A. THE BEST INTERESTS OF THE CHILD PRINCIPLE

In the majority decision in *Foundation*, McLachlin CJ employed a basic but useful definition of the best interests of the child principle: "[L]aws affecting children must be in their best interests."[15] A fuller definition is contained in Article 3(1) of the United Nations *Convention on the Rights of the Child*,[16] to

13 2009 SCC 30 [*A.C.* (SCC)].
14 *Child and Family Services Act*, CCSM c. C80 [*CFSA*].
15 *Foundation*, above note 11 at para. 7.
16 Can. T.S. 1992 No 3.

which Canada is a signatory: "In all actions concerning children, whether undertaken by public or private social welfare institutions, courts of law, administrative authorities or legislative bodies, the best interests of the child shall be a primary consideration."

The best interests of the child principle represents an important landmark in the evolving recognition of children as full and equal rights–bearing individuals in society, albeit ones who also require special care and guidance. Claire Breen connects the growth of the best interests principle to the emergence of the ideal of the "innocent child" that has dominated social and legal perceptions of children over the last 200 years.[17] This view — however romantic — carried with it an attention to, and a measure of respect for, children's status as individuals and, indeed, as human beings. The "radical" idea that children are people undermined the view, dominant prior to the eighteenth century, that children were "essentially . . . without identity . . . akin to animals or slaves . . . exchangeable and replaceable property" belonging to their parents or, more particularly, to their fathers.[18]

As a legal standard, the best interests principle developed primarily in the context of Anglo-American law concerning child custody proceedings following divorce, adoption, guardianship, and foster parenting law.[19] In the twentieth century, the principle became enshrined in international child welfare declarations[20] and, ultimately, in the *Convention on the Rights of the Child*.[21] Domestically, as indicated by McLachlin CJ in *Foundation*,[22] the principle is

17 Claire Breen, *The Best Interests of the Child: A Western Tradition in International and Comparative Law* (The Hague: Martinus Nijhoff, 2002) at 43. Breen writes (at 42):

> [T]hroughout the nineteenth century and into the early part of the twentieth century, reformers and philanthropists became deeply imbued with the Romantic belief that childhood should be happy. The belief was that adults should look back upon their childhood as being the best time of their lives, providing a sense of both nostalgia and inspiration.

18 *Ibid.* at 43.

19 In the opinion of at least one scholar, the principle is "genuinely and uniquely American" insofar as American courts developed the doctrine more robustly than British courts, which demonstrated an inclination to cling to such contrary doctrines as the paternal preference rule in the context of child custody proceedings. Lynne Kohm, "Tracing the Foundations of the Best Interests of the Child Standard in American Jurisprudence" (2008) 10 JL & Fam Stud 337 at 339 and 359.

20 *Declaration of the Rights of the Child*, GA Res 1386 (XIV), 14 UNGAOR, Supp No 16, UN Doc A/4354, (1959).

21 Above note 16.

22 *Foundation*, above note 11 at para. 9.

explicitly mentioned as a legal consideration in many federal statutes[23] and provincial family law statutes are "saturated with references to the 'best interests of the child' as a legal principle of paramount importance."[24]

Notwithstanding this level of recognition, the best interests principle resists precise or exhaustive definition, depending as it does upon a determination of what a child's interests may be in any given context and which of those interests is "best" in accordance with some standard of assessment. Indeed, as discussed in the following section, the fact that the best interests principle is "inevitably highly contextual and subject to dispute"[25] counted against its recognition as a principle of fundamental justice.

Doubts about our ability to determine the precise nature of the principle or how it should operate in every circumstance, however, should not detract from the relative precision with which the principle can be employed in many circumstances. In the *Foundation* case, for example, none of the parties denied that subjecting children to corporal punishment is against their best interests. The only question was whether that principle has constitutional status.[26] Indeed, the prevalence of the principle internationally and domestically provides evidence of the utility of the concept and, therefore, that "all hope of certainty need not be abandoned."[27]

---

23 *Immigration and Refugee Protection Act*, SC 2001, c. 27, ss. 25, 28, 60, 67, 68, & 69; *YCJA*, above note 4, ss. 25(8), 27(1), 30(3)–(4); *Divorce Act*, RSC 1985, c. 3 (2d Supp.), ss. 16(8) and (10), 17(5) and (9).

24 *Foundation*, above note 11 at para. 9. For example, *Family Relations Act*, RSBC 1996, c. 128, s. 24(1); *Child and Family Services Act*, RSO 1990, c. C.11, s. 1(a); *Children's Law Reform Act*, RSO 1990, c. C.12, s. 19(a).

25 *Foundation*, *ibid.* at para. 11.

26 Arguably, the consensus that the corporal punishment defence is inconsistent with the best interests of the child principle should have been far more determinative of the principle's constitutional status than the fact that principle defies precise definition. See Cass Sunstein, "Incompletely Theorized Agreements" (1995) 108 Harv L Rev 1733 at 1735–36:

> Participants in legal controversies try to produce incompletely theorized agreements on particular outcomes. They agree on the result and on relatively narrow or low-level explanations for it. They need not agree on fundamental principle. They do not offer larger or more abstract explanations than are necessary to decide the case. . . . The distinctive feature of this account is that it emphasizes agreement on (relative) particulars rather than on (relative) abstractions. This is an important source of social stability and an important way for diverse people to demonstrate mutual respect, in law especially but also in liberal democracy as a whole [footnotes omitted].

27 Stephen Parker, "The Best Interests of the Child — Principles and Problems" in Philip Alson, ed., *The Best Interests of the Child: Reconciling Culture and Human Rights* (Oxford: Clarendon, 1994) at 27.

As Stephen Parker argues, "communities of [legal] rule users" can draw upon local and national conventions in relation to the nature and application of the best interests of the child principle to provide guidance for its future application; "even if [the conventions] do not determine the exact result, they may well operate to confine the pool of possible results."[28] Little more than this can be said of almost any constitutional principle, including those that have been identified by the Supreme Court as principles of fundamental justice. Accordingly, there is no reason why the best interests of the child principle should be held to a higher standard.

B. THE BEST INTERESTS PRINCIPLE AND CHILDREN'S RIGHTS UNDER THE *CHARTER*

As I have argued elsewhere,[29] the lack of any formal age limits for the exercise of *Charter*-protected rights removes from the Canadian constitutional context any debate about whether or not children do or should have rights.[30] In the Canadian constitutional context, children are presumed to have the same range of constitutionally protected rights and freedoms as adults. The only debate is over the extent to which the exercise of these rights by children can be limited on account of age. Such limitations could be defended by the government in the context of section 1 of the *Charter*, the limitation clause. Limits can also be placed on the exercise of rights by qualifications that are part of the wording of some of the guarantees in the *Charter*. The qualifying concept that is the source of limitations on the enjoyment of section 7 rights to life, liberty, and security of the person is "fundamental justice."

---

28 *Ibid.* at 39.

29 Mark Carter, "'Debunking' Parental Rights in the Canadian Constitutional Context" (2008) 86 Can Bar Rev 479 at 483.

30 Theoretical arguments relating to the existence of children's rights arise from basic rights theory. According to the "will" or "choice" theory, rights are possessed by people who are capable of choosing whether or not to enforce the duty, which is the correlate of every right and which lies on someone or a government, to satisfy the rights claim. By this account, to the extent that children are unable to choose, their ability to possess rights is limited accordingly. The welfare or interest theory of rights, on the other hand, sees these rights as vehicles for protecting interests that are important enough to give rise to duties (which, again, lie on other people or governments) to satisfy that rights claim. Insofar as the welfare or interest theory does not require the exercise of choice, the problem of the immaturity of children does not arise. See David Archard, *Children, Rights and Childhood*, 2d ed. (London: Routledge, 1993) at 54–56.

The children's trilogy of cases demonstrates how the best interests of the child principle, as a principle of fundamental justice, could operate both to enhance the protection that section 7 affords to children's right to life, liberty, and security of the person — in *Foundation* and *D.B.* — and to justify restrictions on those rights in *A.C.* That the best interests principle should have this "double aspect" (to borrow a federalism term) does not undermine its potential to form part of the fundamental justice concept. This is precisely what the terms that define a qualification on a rights guarantee are expected to do. They represent standards against which laws will be compared and in relation to which some will measure up and some will not.

C. *CANADIAN FOUNDATION FOR CHILDREN, YOUTH AND THE LAW v. CANADA (ATTORNEY GENERAL)*

1) The Majority's Rejection of the Best Interests of the Child Principle

In *Foundation*, the section of the *Criminal Code* that provides a defence to assault charges for parents and teachers who use physical force to punish children (section 43) was challenged under several sections of the *Charter*.[31] The section 7 argument itself had three separate branches. The argument that concerns this discussion was that, given that corporal punishment deprives children of their right to security of the person — as the Crown conceded was the case — the corporal punishment defence offends section 7, since hitting children is not in their best interests and the best interests of the child must be a principle of fundamental justice.[32] While McLachlin CJ's majority decision did not deny that hitting children is contrary to their best interests, she rejected the argument that the best interests of the child principle is part of fundamental justice.

The best interests principle's candidacy for inclusion within the concept of fundamental justice was analyzed pursuant to what was, at the time, a

---

31 Along with the s. 7 arguments discussed below, the challengers argued that the corporal punishment defence discriminates on the basis of age contrary to s. 15 of the *Charter*, above note 7, and represents cruel and unusual punishment under s. 12.

32 Along with the best interests of the child argument, the challengers also argued that the principles of fundamental justice require higher procedural protections for children who have been subjected to corporal punishment, in situations when their attackers are raising the defence. The challengers also argued that the defence is unconstitutionally vague, which also offends fundamental justice.

newly minted framework for such considerations. In *R. v. Malmo-Levine; R. v. Caine*[33] — handed down one month before *Foundation* — the majority identified three criteria that the principles of fundamental justice must satisfy:

> [F]or a rule or principle to constitute a principle of fundamental justice for the purposes of s. 7, it must be a legal principle about which there is significant societal consensus that it is fundamental to the way in which the legal system ought fairly to operate, and it must be identified with sufficient precision to yield a manageable standard against which to measure deprivations of life, liberty or security of the person.[34]

In light of the recognition received by the best interests principle in the international conventions and domestic legislation mentioned above, McLachlin CJ accepted that the best interests of the child is a legal principle and that it therefore satisfies the first criterion.[35] The Chief Justice was not convinced, however, that global recognition of the best interests principle and its "saturation" in domestic child protection legislation indicate that it is "vital or fundamental to our societal notion of justice,"[36] which is the second criterion. Finally, the majority decision held that the best interests of the child principle could not satisfy the "precise and manageable" criterion for principles of fundamental justice because the application of the best interests principle is "highly contextual and subject to dispute."[37]

2) Critique of the Majority's Best Interests of the Child Analysis

As I have argued elsewhere,[38] among the most extraordinary aspects of the majority's reasoning in support of its conclusion that the best interests of the child principle is not fundamental to our societal notion of justice is that we have traditionally had — and continue to have — many laws that are not in the best interests of children. The Chief Justice stated:

> . . . [T]he "best interests of the child" may be subordinated to other concerns in appropriate contexts. For example, a person convicted of a crime may be

33 *R. v. Malmo-Levine; R. v. Caine*, [2003] 3 SCR 571 [*Malmo-Levine*].
34 *Ibid.* at para. 113.
35 *Foundation*, above note 11 at para. 9.
36 *Ibid.* at para. 10.
37 *Ibid.* at para. 11.
38 Mark Carter, "The Constitutional Validity of the Corporal Punishment Defence in Canada: A Critical Analysis of *Canadian Foundation for Children, Youth and the Law versus Canada (Attorney General)*" (2005) 12 Int'l J Victimology 189 [Carter, "Constitutional Validity"].

> sentenced to prison even where it may not be in his or her child's best interests. Society does not always deem it essential . . . that the "best interests of the child" trump all other concerns in the administration of justice.[39]

In McLachlin CJ's analysis, the fact that the law has for centuries tolerated certain regressive practices can be used as evidence of the lack of a constitutional principle of justice that is offended by such practices.[40]

Furthermore, if taken seriously, the Chief Justice's indication that a principle of fundamental justice has to be able to "trump all other concerns in the administration of justice" would invalidate all the principles that have already been recognized under section 7.[41] Again, as I have argued elsewhere, rather than being expected to "trump" all other principles, the principles of fundamental justice are in a necessary and ongoing tension with the many competing standards that comprise the complex character of the concept of justice.[42]

D. *R. v. D.B.*

1) The "Presumption of Diminished Moral Blameworthiness" Principle

D.B. involved a constitutional challenge of two groups of provisions under the *YCJA*. These groups of provisions concerned the sentencing and privacy of young persons who are at least fourteen years old[43] and who have been convicted of certain serious ("presumptive") offences. These offences include murder, attempted murder, manslaughter, aggravated sexual assault,[44] or other serious violent offences for which adults are liable to prison terms of more than two years.[45] According to the first group of provisions, young people convicted of presumptive offences have to justify why a youth sentence

---

39 *Foundation*, above note 11 at para. 10.

40 See Mark Carter, "'Black*stoned*' Again: Common Law Liberties, the Canadian Constitution, and the Principles of Fundamental Justice" (2007) 13 Tex Wesleyan L Rev 343, in which I argue that this is a form of rights analysis that reflects the common law naturalism of William Blackstone, a method of analysis that, I also argue, is inconsistent with the existence of a constitutionally entrenched bill of rights.

41 Carter, "Constitutional Validity," above note 38 at 200.

42 *Ibid.*

43 Or older "in a province where the lieutenant governor in council has fixed an age greater than fourteen years." *YCJA*, above note 4, s. 2(1).

44 *Ibid.*, definition of *presumptive offence*.

45 *Ibid.*

should be imposed rather than an adult sentence.[46] The second group of provisions concerns the privacy of young persons who are convicted of presumptive offences. As a general matter the *YCJA* bans the publication of the name or other information that would identify someone as a young person who has been dealt with under the Act. This identity protection does not apply, however, to young persons who have received adult sentences. Furthermore, when a young person convicted of a presumptive offence succeeds in persuading a court that, notwithstanding this conviction, a youth sentence is appropriate, no publication ban will be ordered unless the young person applies for one and satisfies the court that a ban is appropriate.[47]

In *D.B.*, the Crown conceded that the *YCJA*'s presumptive sentencing provisions — dealing as they do with possible imprisonment or the threat of imprisonment — engage the liberty interests of young persons under section 7 of the *Charter*. Accordingly, the inquiry in the case focused on whether this deprivation is in accordance with the principles of fundamental justice.[48] As indicated in the introduction to this article, *D.B.* arrived at the Supreme Court of Canada with opposing courts of appeal decisions concerning the constitutionality of the *YCJA* provisions. The Ontario Court of Appeal in *D.B.* had sided with the Quebec Court of Appeal, finding that the *YCJA* provisions are unreasonable infringements of section 7 of the *Charter*.[49] The Ontario court did not, however, rely on the Quebec Court of Appeal's recognition of the best interests of the child principle in its fundamental justice analysis.[50] The British Columbia Court of Appeal upheld the *YCJA* provisions.[51]

In her decision for five of the justices of the Supreme Court,[52] Abella J recognized that the Quebec Court of Appeal's analysis of the same issue relied on the best interests of the child principle[53] but that this principle had subsequently been rejected as a principle of fundamental justice in *Foundation*.[54] In fairly short order, however, Abella J, speaking for the entire Court on this

---

46 *Ibid.*, ss. 62, 63, 64(1) and (5), 70, 72(1)–(2), 73(1).

47 *Ibid.*, ss. 75(1), 110(1)–(2).

48 *D.B.*, above note 5 at paras. 38–39.

49 *Québec (Ministre de la Justice) c. Canada (Ministre de la Justice)*, above note 9.

50 *R. v. D.B.*, above note 6.

51 *R. v. T. (K.D.)*, above note 10.

52 Chief Justice McLachlin and Binnie, LeBel, and Fish JJ concurred with Abella J. In dissent, Bastarache, Deschamps, and Charron JJ concurred with Rothstein J's reasons.

53 *D.B.*, above note 5 at para. 32.

54 *Ibid.* at para. 34.

issue,[55] identified an alternative principle of fundamental justice — articulated for the first time in the *D.B.* decision — that served to invalidate the presumptive sentencing and publicity provisions in the *YCJA*: the "*presumption* of diminished moral blameworthiness or culpability"[56] ("diminished" or "reduced responsibility" principle).

In Abella J's analysis, the constitutional status of the presumption of diminished responsibility is evinced, in significant part, by the existence of the *YCJA* itself: "This presumption . . . has resulted in the entire youth sentencing scheme, with its unique approach to punishment"[57] and its "preoccupation with ensuring that sentencing reflects the reduced maturity and moral sophistication of young persons."[58] Ultimately, the "legal principle" criterion for a principle of fundamental justice was satisfied by this degree of contemporary and historic[59] statutory respect for the presumption of diminished responsibility principle. This first step in the *Malmo-Levine* framework was also satisfied by international recognition of the presumption of diminished responsibility, as evidenced by the wording of the *Convention on the Rights of the Child*. Justice Abella emphasized the wording of Article 40, paragraph 1, of the Convention which requires that, in criminal proceedings against a child who is "alleged as, accused of, or recognized as having infringed the penal law" a state party will "take . . . into account the child's age and the desirability of promoting the child's reintegration and the child's assuming a constructive role in society."[60]

In relation to the second criterion of the *Malmo-Levine* framework, the Court again relied on the existence of a separate justice system for youths as strong evidence of the existence of a societal consensus that the presumption of diminished responsibility for young people is fundamental to the operation of a fair legal system.[61] Justice Abella also supported her finding of a

---

55 Rothstein J accepted that the presumption of diminished moral blameworthiness is a principle of fundamental justice. His Lordship's dissent was based on his disagreement that this principle leads to a further presumption of a youth sentence or a publication ban. *D.B., ibid.* at paras. 106–7.

56 *Ibid.* at para. 41.

57 *Ibid.*

58 *Ibid.* at para. 44.

59 *Ibid.* at paras. 48–56, discussing the development of a "distinct criminal justice system" in Canada, beginning with the *Juvenile Delinquents Act,* SC 1908, c. 40, which consistently reflected the presumption of diminished moral culpability

60 *D.B.*, above note 5 at para. 60.

61 *Ibid.* at para. 61.

consensus with reference to caselaw and academic commentary, in the context of which Professor Bala's work figures most prominently.[62]

In Abella J's decision, the presumption of diminished responsibility very quickly passed the final criterion for a principle of fundamental justice. In fact, the decision for the Court on this issue is presented in terms that suggest that the principle's "precise and manageable" characteristics are self-evident:

> This is not a difficult criterion to satisfy in this case. The principle that young people are entitled to a presumption of diminished moral culpability throughout any proceedings against them, including during sentencing, is readily administrable and sufficiently precise to yield a manageable standard. It is, in fact, a principle that has been administered and applied to proceedings against young people for decades in this country.[63]

Having recognized the presumption of diminished responsibility as a principle of fundamental justice, Abella J for the majority held that the reverse onus aspect of presumptive sentencing of youths was inconsistent with it.[64] The majority also held that maintaining the Crown's burden to prove that an adult sentence is warranted is consistent with the principle of fundamental justice that the Crown must prove beyond a reasonable doubt any aggravating factors that it may rely on in sentencing.[65] In relation to the publication ban provisions, the majority held that this, too, infringes section 7 in that it "renders the sentence more severe" and therefore, the diminished responsibility principle requires that the Crown justify the enhanced severity of the sentence.[66] Neither group of provisions was upheld as reasonable infringements of section 7 under section 1 of the *Charter.*[67]

2) Comparing the Diminished Responsibility Principle to the Best Interests of the Child Principle

A comparison of the best interests of the child principle with the presumption of diminished responsibility provides no "bright line" to indicate why the former was rejected as a principle of fundamental justice in *Foundation*

62 *Ibid.* at paras. 63–67.

63 *Ibid.* at para. 69.

64 *Ibid.* at para. 76.

65 *Ibid.* at para. 78.

66 *Ibid.* at para. 87. Section 75(4) of the *YCJA*, above note 4, recognizes publication bans as part of the sentence.

67 *D.B.*, above note 5 at para. 91.

while the latter sailed through the *Malmo-Levine* framework in *D.B.* Since both principles satisfied the first "legal principle" criterion, such a comparison can begin with the second "societal consensus" step of the test. Global recognition of a principle provides some evidence of consensus in relation to its status as a vital or fundamental part of our societal notion of justice. That being the case, it must be assumed that the respective claims for consensus of the diminished responsibility and best interests principles are about even, but with a slightly better claim for the best interests principle.

The most significant source of international recognition for both principles is the *Convention on the Rights of the Child.* In this context the best interests of the child principle is specifically mentioned in Article 3(1): "All legal proceedings against children and all actions in relation to them taken by government officials, the best interests of the child shall be a primary consideration."[68] The diminished responsibility principle, on the other hand, has to be imputed from the reference in Article 4 to a party state's obligation to "take . . . into account the child's age and the desirability of promoting the child's reintegration and the child's assuming a constructive role in society." Here, the characteristics of clarity and precision that the Supreme Court has otherwise valued in its fundamental justice jurisprudence[69] seem clearly to be on the side of the best interests principle.

The reference in the *Convention* to the best interests principle being "a" consideration — rather than "the" only one — counted against it at the societal consensus stage of fundamental justice analysis in *Foundation.*[70] In the majority's analysis, this indicates that the best interests principle can be subordinated to other considerations in certain contexts. It might be suggested that in matters involving children's welfare, the majority's strict textualist approach — allowing its analysis to turn on the use of "a" rather than "the" — should have been relaxed. Regardless of this concern, whatever the majority might say about the best interests principle in this respect would apply equally to the diminished responsibility principle. A state party's obligation to "take . . . into

68 Above note 16.

69 See *Malmo-Levine,* above note 33 at para. 113. A principle of fundamental justice "must be identified with sufficient precision to yield a manageable standard against which to measure deprivations of life, liberty or security of the person."

70 *Foundation,* above note 11 at para. 10: "The 'best interests of the child' is widely supported in legislation and social policy, and is an important factor for consideration in many contexts. It is not, however, a foundational requirement for the dispensation of justice. Article 3(1) of the *Convention on the Rights of the Child* describes it as '*a* primary consideration' rather than '*the* primary consideration'" [emphasis added].

account the child's age" is a far weaker directive than the obligation to treat the best interests principle as a primary consideration. Accordingly, if the vague way in which the diminished responsibility principle in the *Convention* is framed does not undermine its status as a principle that enjoys societal consensus, then the more precise and directive framing of the best interests of the child principle certainly should have counted in its favour.

Using the domestic legal context as evidence of consensus, the respective claims of the best interests and diminished responsibility principles to being part of our societal notion of justice are, again, at least even. As indicated, in *D.B.* Abella J — for the entire Court on this point — emphasized that the separate youth justice system is a kind of monument to the diminished responsibility principle. This fact supported the principle's claim to being the subject of consensus in relation to its place in our societal notion of justice. By comparison, the best interests principle enjoys pride of place in several federal statutes and, as McLachlin CJ indicated in *Foundation*, "saturates" provincial child welfare legislation.[71] Indeed, as demonstrated by the *A.C.* decision, which will be discussed in the next section, legislation such as Manitoba's *Child and Family Services Act* and similar legislation existing in every province is at least as much of a monument to the best interests principle and the consensus that exists in relation to it, as the *YCJA* is to the diminished responsibility principle. The *A.C.* decision demonstrates, in fact, that the constitutionality of important provisions of child welfare legislation depends upon the extent to which the legislation is administered in accordance with the best interests principle.

Finally, in relation the "precise and manageable" criterion of the *Malmo-Levine* framework for principles of fundamental justice, the best interests of the child principle also compares favourably to Abella J's indication in *A.C.* that the diminished responsibility principle is "readily administrable and sufficiently precise." Although the best interests principle was characterized as "highly contextual and subject to dispute"[72] in *Foundation*, there was no dispute about its applicability in the case at hand. In *Foundation* none of the justices could bring themselves to deny that the corporal punishment defence is inconsistent with children's best interests. Accordingly, in relation to a specific and important issue, the Court itself demonstrated that the best interests of the child principle is every bit as administrable and precise as the diminished responsibility principle. Furthermore, the fact that the

71 *Ibid.* at para. 9.

72 *Ibid.* at para. 11.

applicability of the best interests principle may be contextual and disputatious in some hypothetical situations is something that could be said about the diminished responsibility principle, or any others that have been identified as principles of fundamental justice.[73]

This close comparison of the treatment of the best interests and the diminished responsibility principles in *Foundation* and *D.B.* respectively indicates that the best interests principle is as worthy of recognition as a principle of fundamental justice as is the diminished responsibility principle, which received that status. In fact, in many respects the best interests principle emerges as a stronger candidate for constitutional status than the diminished responsibility principle. The Supreme Court may have conceded this fact in *A.C.* where, as I will argue, the Court seems to acknowledge that section 7 analysis of laws that relate to children cannot be adequately analyzed without reliance on the best interests principle. In *D.B.* the invocation of the diminished moral responsibility principle was an indirect way of doing this.

E. *A.C. v. MANITOBA (DIRECTOR OF CHILD AND FAMILY SERVICES)*

1) Overview

A.C. involved a constitutional challenge to the provisions of Manitoba's *Child and Family Services Act* that allow children to be apprehended when the children themselves or their parents on their behalf refuse medical treatment that has been deemed essential for them. Upon completion of a hearing, section 25(8) of the Act allows a court to order "a medical examination or any medical or dental treatment that the court considers to be *in the best interests of the child*.[74] Section 25(9) limits the court's jurisdiction in relation to children who are sixteen or older, requiring that consent to court-ordered procedures be obtained from children of this age.

In the words of Abella J for the plurality,[75] the best interests of the child "standard" is the "conceptual cornerstone" of the *CFSA*.[76] The best interests of children is identified as a "fundamental responsibility[y] of society" in the

---

73 See Carter, "Constitutional Validity," above note 38 at 200.

74 *CFSA*, above note 14, s. 25(a) [emphasis added].

75 LeBel, Deschamps, and Charron JJ concurred with the reasons of Abella J. McLachlin CJ and Rothstein J provided separate concurring reasons. Binnie J dissented.

76 *A.C.* (SCC), above note 13 at para. 32.

Act's Declaration of Principles, and section 2(1) indicates that "[t]he best interests of the child shall be the paramount consideration . . . in all proceedings under this Act affecting a child." Section 2(1) goes on to specify that in determining the best interests of the child "all relevant matters shall be considered" including a list of eight specific factors.[77]

A.C. was a fourteen-year-old girl who was apprehended under the Act to allow a medically necessary blood transfusion that was ordered pursuant to section 25(8). A.C. is a follower of the Jehovah's Witness faith who believes that her religion does not allow blood transfusions.[78] A.C. had signed an advance medical directive prior to her hospitalization indicating that she did not want to receive a blood transfusion under any circumstances. A.C.'s parents supported her decision.[79]

Along with *Charter* section 7 arguments that will be focused on below, A.C. and her parents also challenged sections 25(8)–(9) as unreasonable infringements of A.C.'s freedom of religion under section 2(a) of the *Charter* and as age discrimination under section 15. All of these arguments had been unsuccessful on the appeal[80] of Kaufman J's original order. Based upon its interpretation of the best interests principle, which involves "tak[ing] into increasingly serious account the young person's views in accordance with his or her maturity in a given treatment case" — including children younger than sixteen — the plurality decision held that the sections of the *CFSA* do not violate religious freedom or discriminate on the basis of age.[81] In accompanying reasons for herself and Rothstein J, McLachlin CJ held that the distinction drawn by the Act on the basis of age was ameliorative, not invidious, and therefore not discriminatory under section 15 of the *Charter*.[82] The Chief Justice and Rothstein J also held that the provisions of the *CFSA* are reasonable infringements of freedom of religion under section 2(a).[83]

---

77 *CFSA*, above note 14, s. 2(1)(a)–(h). Of particular significance to the plurality were (b) "the mental, emotional, physical and educational needs of the child and the appropriate care or treatment, or both, to meet such needs"; (c) "the child's mental, emotional and physical stage of development"; (f) "the views and preferences of the child where they can reasonably be ascertained"; and (h) "the child's cultural, linguistic, racial and religious heritage."

78 *A.C.* (SCC), above note 13 at para. 5.

79 *Ibid.* at para. 6.

80 *A.C.* (SCC), above note 13; *Manitoba (Director of Child and Family Services) v. A.C.*, 2007 MBCA 9 [*A.C.* MBCA). The original order of Kaufman J, dated 16 April 2006, is unreported.

81 *A.C.* (SCC), *ibid.* at para. 98.

82 *Ibid.* at para. 152.

83 *Ibid.* at para. 156.

2) The Section 7 Argument

It is well established that the liberty and security of the person interests in section 7 of the *Charter* are engaged by government activity that limits or denies the ability of people to make decisions relating to medical treatment and bodily integrity.[84] Accordingly, the entire Court in *A.C.* conceded that the *CFSA* provisions need to satisfy the principles of fundamental justice.

In contrast with the *Foundation* and *D.B.* cases, *A.C.* did not involve an attempt to have the Supreme Court recognize a new principle of fundamental justice. The core of the *Charter* section 7 argument was that insofar as section 25(8) of the *CFSA* establishes an irrebuttable presumption[85] that children under sixteen years of age lack the capacity to direct their medical treatment — which was the basis upon which Kaufman J made the treatment order[86] — it draws an arbitrary distinction. In *Chaoulli v. Quebec (Attorney General)*, the Supreme Court has recognized that the principles of fundamental justice are offended by laws that "arbitrarily limit . . . citizens' rights to life, liberty, and security of the person."[87] Chief Justice McLachlin, writing for the plurality, indicated that "[i]n order not to be arbitrary, the limit on life, liberty and security requires not only a theoretical connection between the limit and the legislative goal, but a real connection on the facts."[88]

While coming to the same conclusion as Steel JA for the Manitoba Court of Appeal as to the constitutionality of the *CFSA* provisions, Abella J disagreed with Steel JA's position that section 25(8) treats all children under sixteen years old the same way. In Steel JA's analysis, section 25(8) represents a "complete and exclusive code for dealing with refusal of medical treatment" by children who are fifteen years of age or younger.[89] According to Steel JA,

---

84 *Ibid.* at paras. 100–1.

85 "Irrebuttable presumptions" have received considerable attention in American constitutional law. They have been identified as statutory vehicles that limit rights on the basis of overbroad stereotypes that fail to consider the actual characteristics and situation of a rights claimant. See Mary Anne Case, "The Very Stereotype the Law Condemns: Constitutional Sex Discrimination Law as a Quest for Perfect Proxies" (2000) 85 Cornell L Rev 1447.

86 The original order of Kaufman J, dated 16 April 2006, is unreported. Justice Kaufman's analysis was referred to by Abella J in *A.C.* (SCC), above note 13, at para. 119: "Kaufman J. proceeded based on his view that the question of A.C.'s capacity was ultimately irrelevant under the Act, concluding that when a child is under 16, there are no restrictions on the court's ability to authorize medical treatment on his or her behalf."

87 [2005] 1 SCR 791 at para. 129.

88 *Ibid.* at para. 131.

89 *A.C.* (MBCA), above note 80 at para. 61.

section 25(8) ousts the common law "mature minor" rule, which accords deference to adolescents' treatment wishes to a degree that is "reflective of [their] evolving maturity."[90] On appeal to the Supreme Court, this was the position of McLachlin J for the minority as well.[91]

In Abella J's analysis, the constitutionality of section 25(8) rests on the best interests of the child principle being applied in a manner that is sensitive to the mature minor rule. Justice Abella states: "If, after a careful and sophisticated analysis of the young person's ability to exercise mature, independent judgment, the court is persuaded that the necessary level of maturity exists, it seems to me necessarily to follow that the adolescent's views ought to be respected."[92] Justice Abella reasons that treating children's views as increasingly determinative as their individual maturity increases is not in tension with the best interests of the child principle but is part of it: "[I]t is, by definition, in a child's best interests to respect and promote his or her autonomy to the extent that his or her maturity dictates."[93]

Having established that the best interests of the child principle, as it has evolved in Canada, in other national jurisdictions, and at the international level, embraces the mature minor principle, Abella J determined that its application in section 25(8) is not arbitrary. The best interests principle, when properly applied, allows children under the age of sixteen an opportunity to prove that they are sufficiently mature to make medical treatment decisions.[94] The arbitrariness of the fixed age of sixteen is therefore undermined by the fact that, although people of that age or older will be presumed to have the capacity to make treatment decisions, younger people can rebut the presumption that they do not: "Given the significance we attach to bodily integrity, it would be arbitrary to assume that no one under the age of 16 has capacity to make medical treatment decisions. It is not, however, arbitrary to give them the opportunity to prove that they have sufficient maturity to do so."[95]

90 As defined by Abella J in *A.C.* (SCC), above note 13 at para. 23.

91 *Ibid.* at para. 126.

92 *Ibid.* at para. 87.

93 *Ibid.* at para. 88.

94 *Ibid.* at para. 107.

95 *Ibid.* In relation to the age discrimination claim, Abella J held that the application of the best interests principle in a manner that allows adolescents under sixteen to prove that they are sufficiently mature to make medical decisions calibrates the application of s. 25(8) of the *CFSA*, above note 14, in response to maturity rather than age. Justice Abella therefore found no disadvantage, prejudice, or stereotyping based on age (*ibid.* at para. 111). In relation to the freedom of religion argument, Abella J again found no

Chief Justice McLachlin's decision for the minority, which held that the mature minor rule is ousted by section 25(8),[96] seems to be commendably motivated by a concern that an inclusion of the rule within the best interests standard could result in a judge "declin[ing] to order medical treatment for a child under the age of 16 where the result would be probable death."[97] The Chief Justice held that, even without the mature minor rule, section 25(8) avoided being unconstitutionally arbitrary, however, by the extent to which the age of sixteen represents a reasonable proxy for maturity. Sixteen years of age roughly corresponds with the legal ability to drive, to work, and to become independent from parents in other respects.[98] In McLachlin CJ's estimation, this establishes that the sixteen-year threshold has an adequate connection to the *CFSA*'s objectives of balancing "society's interest in ensuring that children receive necessary medical care on the one hand, with the protection of minors' autonomy interest to the extent this can be done, on the other."[99] Furthermore, the statute incorporates some of the considerations that would be part of the mature minor analysis mandated by Abella J. The Chief Justice emphasizes, for example, that the *CFSA* requires judges to take account of the treatment preferences of minors who are under sixteen in assessing their "best interests."[100] The difference between Abella J's and the Chief Justice's perspectives in this respect is that, according to the latter, the under-sixteen minor's preferences would never receive the presumptive weight of a youth who is sixteen years old or more, whereas this might occur under Abella J's best interests framework.

3) The Best Interests of the Child Principle as a Principle of Fundamental Justice

As indicated above, in order to respect the rule against arbitrariness, a law that infringes section 7 rights has to have "a real connection on the facts" to the purpose that the law serves.[101] As this formulation of the rule suggests, it

infringement of s. 2(a) of the *Charter*, above note 7, because the young person is able to lead evidence of maturity. Furthermore, the reference to "religious heritage" as a factor for consideration in determining best interest also prevents s. 25(8) of the *CFSA* from infringing s. 2(a) of the *Charter*. (*A.C.* (SCC), *ibid.* at para. 113).

96 *A.C.* (SCC), *ibid.* at para. 126.

97 *Ibid.* at para. 133.

98 *Ibid.* at para. 145.

99 *Ibid.* at para. 141.

100 *Ibid.* at para. 147.

101 *Ibid.* at para. 103.

is axiomatic that the purpose the law serves must itself be constitutionally valid. The purpose of a law that prevents it from imposing arbitrary restrictions on entrenched rights and liberties is not necessarily itself a constitutional principle, but it could be. For example, in *Rodriguez v. British Columbia (Attorney General)*,[102] a majority of the Supreme Court held that section 241(b) of the *Criminal Code*, which makes it an offence to aid suicides, does not arbitrarily restrict the *Charter* section 7 right to security of the person of those who are physically incapable of ending their own lives.[103] While not speaking in the precise terms of the more recent *Chaoulli* decision, Sopinka J's analysis nonetheless indicates that the *Criminal Code* provision has a connection on the facts to the purpose of the legislation, which, ultimately, is to respect the sanctity of life. Furthermore, the sanctity of life is a principle of fundamental justice. Justice Sopinka stated that the purpose of section 241(b) "is grounded in the state interest in protecting life and reflects the policy of the state that human life should not be depreciated by allowing life to be taken . . . . This is not only a policy of the state . . . [It] is part of our fundamental conception of the sanctity of human life."[104]

Later Sopinka J concluded:

> The principles of fundamental justice . . . are concerned with . . . principles which are "fundamental" in the sense that they would have general acceptance among reasonable people . . . . To the extent that there is a consensus [in this area of the criminal law], it is that human life must be respected and we must be careful not to undermine the institutions that protect it.[105]

A majority of the Supreme Court in *A.C.* was satisfied that section 25(8) of the *CFSA* evinces the kind of "real connection on the facts" between the infringement of *Charter* section 7 rights and a valid purpose that the rule

---

102 [1993] 3 SCR 519 [*Rodriguez*].

103 *Criminal Code*, above note 12, s. 241.

104 *Rodriguez*, above note 102 at 595.

105 *Ibid.* at 608. If Sopinka J stops slightly short of specifically identifying the sanctity of life as a principle of fundamental justice under s. 7, then this is the conclusion that was drawn by the Manitoba Court of Appeal in *A.C.* (MBCA) (above note 80 at para. 69). Academics have also concluded that *Rodriguez* stands for the proposition that sanctity of life is a principle of fundamental justice. See Cheryl Milne, "Religious Freedom: At What Age?" (2008) 25 NJCL 71 at 74. Milne was summarizing the analysis of Steel JA of the Manitoba Court of Appeal in *A.C.*, *ibid.* See also Edward Keyserlingk, "Assisted Suicide, Causality, and the Supreme Court of Canada" (1994) 39 McGill LJ 708 at 714; Isabel Grant, "Developments in Criminal Law: The 1993–94 Term" (1995) 6 Sup Ct L Rev 209 at 274.

against arbitrary laws requires. For Abella J, the constitutionality of the section 25(8) — its non-arbitrary nature — depends on the operation of the best interests of the child principle, which, in her estimation, reflects the mature minor rule. Chief Justice McLachlin similarly emphasized how the best interests principle, as defined by the *CFSA* to include some elements of what would otherwise be part of the mature minor rule, prevents the section in question from being arbitrary. It is difficult to escape the conclusion, therefore, that the majority decision in *A.C.* is committed to the position that the best interests principle operates in the child welfare context (at least) as a constitutional principle. Without it, it would be impossible to impose medical treatment on non-consenting young people in a manner that respects section 7 of the *Charter.*

Although ushered into the constitutional analysis in *A.C.* by the non-arbitrary laws principle, the best interests of the child principle essentially takes over as the only explanation for the kinds of infringements upon the right to life and security of the person of young people that can be imposed under the *CFSA* and similar child welfare legislation in other provinces. These infringements are allowed because they are (as section 7 states) "in accordance with the principle . . . of fundamental justice" that allows children to be treated differently from adults when it is in children's best interests to be treated in such a manner. Whatever the content of the best interests principle may be in abstract terms, high up on any list of possible characteristics must be that it allows the state to save children from the worst consequences of some of their self-destructive decision making. In *A.C.*, the best interests of the child principle supported an order that erred on the side of the life and physical well-being of a child, and (only temporarily) against the child's decision to reject life-saving treatment. In doing so, the best interests principle demonstrated the kind of manageability and applicability to "real" situations that have become a hallmark of the analysis of fundamental justice principles in the caselaw applying the *Malmo-Levine* framework.

Chief Justice McLachlin's majority decision in *Foundation* excluded the best interests of the child principle from section 7. It is ironic, therefore, that the Chief Justice's minority decision in *A.C.* provides some of the firmest rooting of the best interests of the child principle in the Constitution. Without, perhaps, recognizing the full implications of her comments, the Chief Justice almost equated the best interests principle with the "reduced maturity and moral capacity principle" that the entire Court in *D.B.* accepted as a principle of fundamental justice. The Chief Justice stated:

> The danger of excessive parental and peer influence overwhelming free and voluntary choice is ever-present. Similarly, in the youth criminal law context, it is recognized as a principle of fundamental justice that young persons must generally be treated differently from adults by virtue of their "reduced maturity and moral capacity": *R. v. D.B.* . . . The *CFSA* acknowledges these realities and therefore places the final decision-making power with the courts *in accordance with the best interests of the child.*[106]

The Chief Justice's comments suggest not only that the reduced moral responsibility principle articulated in *D.B.* is consistent with the best interests principle but that the two are part of the same concept.

F. CONCLUSION

The children's trilogy of cases chronicles the recent constitutional journey of the best interests of the child principle. Although the principle was banished from the fundamental justice concept in *Foundation,* it operated as a kind of *eminence grise* in *D.B.*, where its absence required the Court to define an alternative principle that would do the same kind of work. Finally, in *A.C.*, the best interests of the child principle returned to do the work itself. The trilogy demonstrates that the best interests of the child principle is an essential modern tool for focusing debates about why laws may insufficiently protect children's rights to life, liberty, and security of the person, and why limitations of those rights may be justified. With the *A.C.* decision the best interests principle has been given the constitutional recognition that will allow it to play this crucial role most effectively.

---

106 *A.C.* (SCC), above note 13 at para. 145 [emphasis added].

CHAPTER 2

Children's Rights and Health Law: The "Mature Minor" Rule Revisited

GERALD B. ROBERTSON, QC

This essay discusses the rights of children in the context of consent to medical treatment. It focuses in particular on the recent decision of the Supreme Court of Canada in *A.C. v. Manitoba (Director of Child and Family Services)*,[1] in which the Court examined the parameters of the right of a child to refuse medical treatment (including potentially life-saving procedures) and the corresponding power of the courts to override that refusal and order the treatment. A detailed analysis of the *A.C.* decision is especially important given that there appears to be considerable uncertainty over what the Supreme Court actually decided in that case.

A. THE RIGHT TO REFUSE MEDICAL TREATMENT

Reflecting the fundamental importance of personal autonomy and medical self-determination, the law recognizes that mentally competent adults have the right to refuse medical treatment.[2] Nowhere is this legal principle more eloquently captured than in the judgment of Robbins J of the Ontario Court of Appeal in the leading case of *Fleming v. Reid*:

1 2009 SCC 30 [*A.C.*].

2 See, generally, Ellen I. Picard & Gerald B. Robertson, *Legal Liability of Doctors and Hospitals in Canada*, 4th ed. (Toronto: Thomson Canada, 2007) at 44–49 [Picard & Robertson].

> The right to determine what shall, or shall not, be done with one's own body, and to be free from non-consensual medical treatment, is a right deeply rooted in our common law. This right underlies the doctrine of informed consent. With very limited exceptions, every person's body is considered inviolate, and, accordingly, every competent adult has the right to be free from unwanted medical treatment.[3]

It is important to note that this right applies even when the treatment is potentially life saving. As the Supreme Court of Canada has stated, "[t]he fact that serious risks or consequences may result from a refusal of medical treatment does not vitiate the right of medical self-determination."[4] Indeed, it is exactly in this type of case that the strength of the courts' commitment to protect the right of medical self-determination is truly tested, and Canadian courts have withstood that test. Consequently, the right of a mentally competent adult to refuse life-saving treatment has been upheld in a number of Canadian cases, including *Malette v. Shulman*[5] (refusal of potentially life-saving blood transfusions) and *Nancy B. v. Hôtel-Dieu de Québec*[6] (discontinuation of respiratory life support).

Another very important aspect of the right to refuse medical treatment is that it applies regardless of the patient's reasons for the decision (assuming that the patient's competence is not in question),[7] and regardless of whether other people view the decision as reasonable. Once again, this is a key test of the robustness of the right of medical self-determination. If it were to mean only that the patient has a right to make decisions that other people agree with and consider reasonable (including the patient's physician and family, and ultimately the court), it would be reduced to a meaningless and impotent right. As Robins J noted in *Malette v. Shulman*, "For this freedom to be meaningful, people must have the right to make choices that accord with

---

3 (1991), 4 OR (3d) 74 at 85 (CA) [*Fleming*].

4 *Ciarlariello v. Schacter*, [1993] 2 SCR 119 at para. 40 [*Ciarlariello*], quoting from *Fleming*, *ibid.* at 85. See also *Rodriguez v. British Columbia (Attorney-General)*, [1993] 3 SCR 519 at para. 156 [*Rodriguez*]; *A.C.*, above note 1 at para. 40.

5 (1990), 72 OR (2d) 417 (CA).

6 [1992] JQ no 1(SC).

7 The reasons for the refusal may be relevant if they indicate that the patient may lack the mental capacity to make the decision. However, the Supreme Court of Canada has cautioned against using the patient's disagreement with the diagnosis or proposed treatment plan as evidence of incapacity. See *Starson v. Swayze*, 2003 SCC 32 at para. 19 [*Starson*].

their own values regardless of how unwise or foolish those choices may appear to others."[8]

These principles have been well entrenched in the common law for many years, as can be seen from the frequent support they are accorded by reference to the statement of Cardozo J in 1914, that "[e]very human being of adult years and sound mind has a right to determine what shall be done with his own body."[9] The right to refuse unwanted medical treatment has been affirmed by the Supreme Court of Canada on numerous occasions,[10] including its recent decision in *Starson v. Swayze*, in which the Court stated that the "right to refuse unwanted medical treatment is fundamental to a person's dignity and autonomy."[11] It has also been held to be a constitutionally protected right, in the sense that legislation that infringes it will be struck down under the *Charter of Rights and Freedoms* unless it can be justified under a section 1 analysis.[12]

B. CHILDREN AND THE MATURE MINOR RULE

The position is somewhat less clear with respect to children. What *is* clear is that at common law a child, regardless of age, has the power to consent to medical treatment if he or she is capable of appreciating the nature and purpose of the proposed treatment and the consequences of consenting to it.[13]

---

8 Above note 5 at 424.

9 *Schloendorff v. New York Hospital*, 105 NE 92 at 93 (NYCA 1914). This statement was quoted with approval by the Supreme Court of Canada in *Reibl v. Hughes*, [1980] 2 SCR 880 at 890.

10 See, for example, *Parmley v. Parmley*, [1945] SCR 635 at 645–46; *Hopp v. Lepp*, [1980] 2 SCR 192 at 196; *Ciarlariello*, above note 4 at paras. 39–40; *Rodriguez*, above note 4 at para. 156; *Starson*, above note 7 at para. 19. This was also recognized in *A.C.*, above note 1 at paras. 40–45 and at para. 196.

11 Above note 7 at para. 75.

12 *Canadian Charter of Rights and Freedoms*, Part I of the *Constitution Act, 1982*, being Schedule B to the *Canada Act 1982* (UK), 1982, c. 11; *Fleming*, above note 3. This is also clear from the decision in *A.C.*, above note 1.

13 *A.C.*, *ibid.* at para. 46. See also Picard & Robertson, above note 2 at 82–85; David C. Day, "The Capable Minor's Healthcare: Who Decides?" (2007) 86 Can Bar Rev 379 [Day]; Lucinda Ferguson, *The End of an Age: Beyond Age Restrictions for Minors' Medical Treatment Decisions* (Ottawa: Law Commission of Canada, 2004) [Ferguson]; Joan M. Gilmour, "Children, Adolescents, and Health Care" in Jocelyn Downie, Timothy Caulfield, & Colleen Flood, eds., *Canadian Health Law and Policy*, 2d ed. (Toronto: Butterworths, 2002) at 205; Joan M. Gilmour, "Death, Dying and Decision-Making about End of Life Care" in Jocelyn Downie, Timothy Caulfield, & Colleen Flood, eds., *Canadian Health Law and Policy*, 3d ed. (Toronto: LexisNexis Canada, 2007) at 437; Manitoba Law Reform

Canadian caselaw affirming a minor's right to consent to medical treatment dates back to at least 1910,[14] but its recognition in English common law has much earlier roots. Indeed, support for it can be found in *Blackstone's Commentaries*, published in 1765.[15] In early Canadian cases, a minor's ability to consent was premised on evidence of emancipation from parental control,[16] including factors such as whether the minor was working and taking care of himself.[17] However, the focus eventually shifted from emancipation to maturity,[18] and it is now well established that the latter is the key to capacity to consent; that is, the minor's ability to appreciate the nature and purpose of the proposed treatment and the consequences of consenting to it.[19] As the Manitoba Law Reform Commission points out, the "mature minor rule focuses less on the minor's lifestyle and more on the minor's physical, emotional and intellectual development."[20]

Some provinces have enacted legislation that sets an age of consent to medical treatment (in some provinces, a presumptive age).[21] However, this does not affect the mature minor rule, because the legislation recognizes that

---

Commission, *Minors' Consent to Health Care*, Report No 91 (Winnipeg: The Commission, 1995).

14 *Booth v. Toronto General Hospital*, [1910] OJ No 379 (H Ct J) [*Booth*]. See also *Johnston v. Wellesley Hospital*, [1970] OJ No 1741 (H Ct J) [*Johnston*].

15 William Blackstone, *Commentaries on the Laws of England* (Oxford: Clarendon Press, 1765) Book 1, c. 16 and 17. The equivalent passages from the 17th edition (1830) are discussed in *Gillick v. West Norfolk and Wisbech Area Health Authority*, [1986] 1 AC 112 at 185 (HL), Lord Scarman [*Gillick*]. See also Bernard M. Dickens, *Medico-Legal Aspects of Family Law* (Toronto: Butterworths, 1979) at 94.

16 See *Booth*, above note 14.

17 *Ibid.* at paras. 11 and 12.

18 The first indication of this change was probably *Johnston*, above note 14. As Joan Gilmour has pointed out, this shift from emancipation to maturity is especially relevant (and necessary) nowadays given that children tend to enter the workforce later, and live with their parents longer, than in the past: see Gilmour, "Children, Adolescents, and Health Care," above note 13 at 211.

19 See, for example, *A.C.*, above note 1 at para. 46. For other appellate-level decisions recognizing the mature minor rule in Canada, see *B.H. v. Alberta (Director of Child Welfare)*, 2002 ABQB 371 [*B.H.*], aff'd on other grounds 2002 ABCA 109, leave to appeal to SCC refused, [2002] 3 SCR vi; *C.(J.S.) v. Wren*, [1986] AJ No 1166 (CA) [*Wren*]; *C.U. v. McGonigle*, 2003 ABCA 66 [*C.U.*]; *Van Mol v. Ashmore*, 1999 BCCA 6 [*Van Mol*], leave to appeal to SCC refused (2000), [1999] SCCA 117; *Region 2 Hospital Corp. v. Walker*, [1994] NBJ No 242 (CA) [*Walker*].

20 Above note 13 at 4. See also Ferguson, above note 13 at 11–12.

21 *Infants Act*, RSBC 1996, c. 223, s. 17; *Medical Consent of Minors Act*, SNB 1976, c. M-6.1, ss. 2 and 3(1); *Health Care Directives Act*, CCSM, c. H27, s. 4(2); art 14 CCQ. For caselaw interpreting these provisions, see *Ney v. Canada (Attorney General)*, [1993] BCJ No 993 (SC) [*Ney*]; *Van Mol*, above note 19; *Walker*, above note 19.

someone under the prescribed age may consent to treatment if they have the mental capacity to do so.[22] Therefore, although this consent legislation may affect the onus of proof by creating a presumption of capacity,[23] in essence it does not detract from the mature minor rule, namely, that regardless of age, a minor has the power to consent to medical treatment if he or she is capable of appreciating the nature and purpose of the proposed treatment and the consequences of consenting to it.[24]

The decision of the Alberta Court of Appeal in *C. (J.S.) v. Wren*[25] is a useful example of the mature minor principle. In that case, a sixteen-year-old girl who was pregnant arranged to have an abortion. Her parents objected to her decision, so much so that they applied to the court for an injunction to prevent her from going ahead with the procedure. However, they were unsuccessful because their daughter was held to have sufficient maturity to understand the nature and consequences of her decision to consent to an abortion and hence the legal right to do so.[26]

Likewise, in *Van Mol*,[27] the British Columbia Court of Appeal held that if a child is competent to consent to treatment, the child's consent *must* be obtained; the parents' consent is insufficient. Moreover, the doctor's duty to obtain informed consent means that the risks and other material information

---

22 However, legislation in some provinces applies a "welfare principle" to children under the prescribed age, whereby the child may consent only if the physician considers the treatment to be in the child's best interests: see, for example, *Infants Act*, RSBC 1996, c. 223, s. 17; *Medical Consent of Minors Act*, above note 21. For an excellent discussion of the applicable legislation and its relationship with the common law, see Ferguson, above note 13; Day, above note 13.

23 See Gilmour, "Children, Adolescents, and Health Care," above note 13 at 210.

24 Legislation in Ontario, Prince Edward Island, and Yukon applies this principle to all patients, regardless of age: see *Health Care Consent Act, 1996*, SO 1996, c. 2, Sch. A, s. 4(1); *Consent to Treatment and Health Care Directives Act*, RSPEI 1988, c. C-17.2, s. 7(1); *Care Consent Act*, SY 2003, c. 21, Sch. B, s. 6(2).

25 Above note 19.

26 In *A.C.*, above note 1 at para. 58, the Supreme Court of Canada interpreted *Wren* as deciding "not that a 'mature minor' was essentially an adult for medical treatment purposes, but rather that courts must give adolescents room to exercise their autonomy to the extent that their maturity allows." This interpretation is difficult to understand and flies in the face of the very clear conclusion of the Alberta Court of Appeal that the girl had the capacity to understand the nature and consequences of her decision and hence had the legal right to make that decision. This is not to equate her with being "essentially an adult for medical treatment purposes"; it is merely an assessment that, *for the particular purposes of the treatment in question*, she had the necessary mental capacity to give valid consent.

27 Above note 19.

associated with the treatment must be disclosed *to the child,* not to the parents. Speaking for the majority of the court, Lambert JA stated:

> At common law, without any reference to statute law, a young person, still a minor, may give, on his or her own behalf, a fully informed consent to medical treatment if he or she has sufficient maturity, intelligence and capability of understanding what is involved in making informed choices about the proposed medical treatment .... [O]nce the required capacity to consent has been achieved by the young person reaching sufficient maturity, intelligence and capability of understanding, the discussions about the nature of the treatment, its gravity, the material risks and any special or unusual risks, and the decisions about undergoing treatment, and about the form of the treatment, must all take place with and be made by the young person whose bodily integrity is to be invaded and whose life and health will be affected by the outcome. At that stage, the parent or guardian will no longer have any overriding right to give or withhold consent. All rights in relation to giving or withholding consent will then be held entirely by the child. The role of the parent or guardian is as advisor and friend. There is no room for conflicting decisions between a young person who has achieved consenting capacity, on the one hand, and a parent or guardian, on the other.[28]

C. OVERRIDING THE MATURE MINOR'S DECISION

The *Wren* and *Van Mol* cases are important in emphasizing that a decision by a competent minor to consent to treatment cannot be overridden by the parents. Their refusal of consent is immaterial and of no legal consequence if the child is competent and consents to the treatment.[29] But what if a mature minor *refuses* treatment? Can that decision be overridden by the parents?

English law on this issue is unclear. In particular, while some court of appeal cases suggest that parents do indeed have the power to override a mature minor's refusal of consent,[30] this seems to contradict the earlier decision

28 *Ibid.* at para. 75.

29 Indeed, the physician's duty of confidentiality means that the parents have no right to be advised that their child is seeking the proposed treatment: see Picard & Robertson, above note 2 at 18.

30 *Re R (a minor) (wardship: medical treatment),* [1991] 4 All ER 177 at 186–87 (CA), Lord Donaldson; *Re W (a minor) (medical treatment),* [1992] 4 All ER 627 at 639–40 (CA), Lord Donaldson, and at 643–44, Balcombe LJ. For a critique of these decisions, see Jane Fortin, *Children's Rights and the Developing Law* (London: LexisNexis UK, 2003) at 83–87.

of the House of Lords in *Gillick*.[31] Compared to English law, however, Canadian law is fairly settled on this issue: a mature minor's decision to refuse consent to medical treatment cannot be vetoed by the child's parents.[32] As is apparent from the passage quoted above, the British Columbia Court of Appeal's decision in *Van Mol* was unequivocal on this; if the child is competent, the parents "no longer have any overriding right to give or withhold consent."[33] In other words, a physician faced with a competent minor who is refusing consent to treatment cannot simply turn to the parents and obtain their consent instead. The child's consent is essential (otherwise the treatment constitutes a battery), and parents' consent does not override the child's refusal if the child is competent.[34]

What is less clear is whether the *court* has the power to override a competent minor's refusal of consent. Such a power could arise in one of two ways — first, as part of the court's inherent *parens patriae* jurisdiction over children,[35] and second, as part of the powers conferred by provincial child welfare legislation in relation to children who are found to be in need of protection. Child welfare legislation typically defines a "child in need of protection" as including one whose parent or guardian has refused to provide or consent to essential medical treatment for the child,[36] and this refusal then triggers the powers of apprehension under the legislation.[37]

---

31 *Gillick*, above note 15.

32 This was also the position adopted by the High Court of Australia: see *Secretary, Department of Health and Community Services v. JWB* (1992), 106 ALR 385 (HC). See also New South Wales Law Reform Commission, *Young People and Consent to Health Care*, Report No 119 (Sydney, New South Wales: The Commission, 2008).

33 Above note 19 at para. 75. See also *ibid.* at para. 89: "The capacity of the parents to consent on behalf of the child does not coexist with the child's own capacity to consent or to refuse to consent. It could not be otherwise." In a concurring judgment, Huddart JA agreed with this view (see *ibid.* at paras. 140–45), and in so doing she clarified her earlier comments (expressed as a trial judge) in *Ney*, above note 21.

34 See also *Chmiliar v. Chmiliar*, 2001 ABQB 525, 295 AR 140; *Walker*, above note 19. The issue was left open in *C.U.*, above note 19.

35 For a detailed discussion of the history and scope of the *parens patriae* jurisdiction, see *E. (Mrs.) v. Eve*, [1986] 2 SCR 388 [*E. (Mrs.)*]; Day, above note 13.

36 See, for example, *Child, Youth and Family Enhancement Act*, RSA 2000, c. C-12, s. 1(2.1). See also Nicholas Bala, "Child Welfare Law in Canada: An Introduction" in Nicholas Bala *et al.*, eds., *Canadian Child Welfare Law: Children, Families and the State*, 2d ed. (Toronto: Thompson Educational Publishing, 2004) at 1; Picard & Robertson, above note 2 at 89–90.

37 Even after the decision in *A.C.*, above note 1, it is not entirely clear how this legislation is engaged in the case of minors who at common law have the capacity to make their own treatment decisions. If the minor has capacity, the parents have no legal power to veto

Leading up to the Supreme Court of Canada's decision in *A.C.*, there was some uncertainty on this issue. On the one hand, some cases had held[38] (or at least acknowledged the possibility)[39] that a court cannot exercise its inherent *parens patriae* jurisdiction to override the refusal of consent by a competent minor.[40] The rationale for this view is that the courts' *parens patriae* jurisdiction is exercised only over those who lack capacity to make their own decisions,[41] and a mature minor (by definition) does not lack this capacity. On the other hand, some courts endorsed the use of the *parens patriae* jurisdiction even in cases of a mature minor,[42] and this is certainly the position adopted by English courts.[43]

At the same time, however, most courts had held that the position is clear with respect to child welfare legislation.[44] That legislation was construed as giving the court the authority (and indeed, the duty) to override a competent minor's refusal and to order the treatment, if the court considered this to be in the child's best interests.[45] This interpretation then raises the issue of the

their child's decision. See above notes 31 to 33. Hence, if the minor is competent the parents should not be consulted and therefore this should not be a case in which the parents have "refused consent"; they have no legal right to do so. How, then, can the child be apprehended? Indeed, the same would be true even if the parents consented. The child could not be apprehended under the legislation because the parents have not refused, yet the child could not be treated because the child has refused consent and is competent to do so.

38 *Walker*, above note 19. See also Ferguson, above note 13.

39 *C.U.*, above note 19 at para. 33.

40 There are also many other cases in which treatment has been ordered by the court but the child was held to not be a mature minor. Hence, these cases are not relevant in determining whether the court has the power to override the refusal of a mature minor. See, for example, *Children's Aid Society of Metropolitan Toronto v. S.H.*, [1996] OJ No 2578 (Gen Div); *T.T.D. (Re)*, [1999] SJ No 143 (QB); *B.H.*, above note 19. These cases are discussed in *A.C.*, above note 1 at paras. 59–61.

41 See *E. (Mrs.)*, above note 35.

42 See, for example, *Ney*, above note 21; *Van Mol*, above note 19 at para. 143, Huddart, JA. See also *P.H. v. Eastern Regional Integrated Health Authority*, 2010 NLTD 34 (SC)[*P.H.*].

43 See *Re W (a minor) (medical treatment)*, above note 30; *Re M (medical treatment: consent)*, [1999] 2 FLR 1097 (Fam Div). See also *A.C.*, above note 1 at paras. 54–57.

44 There are some cases, in the context of child welfare legislation, where the court has refused to order treatment for a child whom it considered to be a "mature minor," but in these cases the court determined that the treatment was not in the child's best interests. See, for example, *Children's Aid Society of Metropolitan Toronto v. L.D.K.*, [1985] OJ No 803 (Prov Ct (Fam Div)) (court refusing to order chemotherapy and blood transfusions for a twelve-year-old girl suffering from acute myeloid leukemia); *A.Y. (Re)*, [1993] NJ No 197 (SC (Fam Div)) (court refusing to order chemotherapy and blood transfusions for a fifteen-year-old boy).

45 See, for example, *C.U.*, above note 19; *Ney*, above note 21; *S.J.B. v. British Columbia (Director of Child, Family and Community Services)*, 2005 BCSC 573 [*S.J.B.*]; see also *P.H.*, above note 42. For a critique of this position, see Day, above note 13.

constitutional validity of the legislation: can the statutory power to override a competent minor's refusal of medical treatment withstand *Charter* scrutiny? Prior to *A.C.*, some courts had upheld the constitutional validity of the legislation,[46] while others had left the question open.[47]

These were the issues that confronted the Supreme Court of Canada in the case of *A.C.*, which was heard by the Court in May 2008, with judgment being issued in June of the following year.

D. THE SUPREME COURT'S DECISION IN *A.C.*

1) Background

The case involved a young girl (identified throughout the proceedings as A.C.) who was admitted to hospital suffering from lower gastrointestinal bleeding, associated with an underlying condition of Crohn's disease. At the time of her admission to hospital, A.C. was almost fifteen years old. Although her condition was initially relatively stable, she began to experience more internal bleeding and her physicians decided that she should be given a blood transfusion. However, she declined it, in keeping with her faith as a Jehovah's Witness. Indeed, a few months prior to her hospital admission she had completed an advance medical directive requesting that she not be given blood transfusions under any circumstances. In addition, her parents fully supported her decision to refuse consent to the blood transfusion.

A mental capacity assessment of A.C. was conducted by three psychiatrists shortly after her admission to hospital, and they concluded that the "patient understands the reason why a transfusion may be recommended, and the consequences of refusing to have a transfusion."[48]

Following A.C.'s refusal of consent she was apprehended under the authority of the Director of Child and Family Services, as being a child in need of protection pursuant to Manitoba's child welfare legislation.[49] An application was then made to the Court of Queen's Bench for an order authorizing the blood transfusion. The application was heard by Kaufman J, who at the request of counsel proceeded on the basis that A.C. had the necessary mental capacity to make her own medical decisions. Nonetheless, Kaufman J ultimately held

---

46 See, for example, *S.J.B.*, *ibid.*

47 See, for example, *C.U.*, above note 19.

48 *A.C.*, above note 1 at para. 6.

49 *Child and Family Services Act*, CCSM c. C80.

that A.C.'s capacity was irrelevant because in his view the legislation empowers the court to authorize treatment in the best interests of the child regardless of whether the child has capacity at common law. Justice Kaufman concluded that it was in A.C.'s best interests to have the blood transfusion, and he granted an order authorizing it. The treatment was successful, and A.C. recovered.[50]

Justice Kaufman's decision was upheld by the Manitoba Court of Appeal.[51] It agreed that the issue of A.C.'s capacity was irrelevant because in its opinion the child welfare legislation ousts the common law mature minor doctrine. Like Kaufman J, the Court of Appeal took the view that the legislation empowers the court to authorize the proposed treatment, regardless of the child's capacity, if the treatment is in the child's best interests. In addition, the Court of Appeal held that the legislation does not infringe the *Charter* and hence is constitutionally valid.[52]

2) The Majority's Decision

The Supreme Court of Canada (Binnie J dissenting) upheld the decision (though not all of the reasons) of the Manitoba Court of Appeal, and concluded that the legislation is constitutionally valid. The judgment of the majority was written by Abella J, with McLachlin CJ and Rothstein J issuing a separate, concurring judgment.

The specific statutory provisions that were the subject of the constitutional challenge are as follows:

> 25(8) Subject to subsection (9), upon completing a hearing, the court may authorize a medical examination or any medical or dental treatment that the court considers to be in the best interests of the child.
>
> 25(9) The court shall not make an order under subsection (8) with respect to a child who is 16 years of age or older without the child's consent unless the court is satisfied that the child is unable
>
> (a) to understand the information that is relevant to making a decision to consent or not consent to the medical examination or the medical or dental treatment; or

50 *A.C.*, above note 1 at para. 13.

51 2007 MBCA 9.

52 For a critique of the Court of Appeal's decision, see Day, above note 13. Mr. Day acted as counsel for A.C. in the Supreme Court of Canada.

(b) to appreciate the reasonably foreseeable consequences of making a decision to consent or not consent to the medical examination or the medical or dental treatment.[53]

At the heart of the constitutional challenge was the argument that the legislation draws a bright line at age sixteen and provides that mental capacity is relevant only if the child has crossed that line. Hence, the constitutional challenge was linked to a specific interpretation of the legislation, namely, that it provides that if the child is under the age of sixteen the court may authorize the medical treatment if it considers it to be in the child's best interests, *regardless of the child's capacity.*

Justice Abella rejected this interpretation, and in so doing found the legislation to be constitutionally valid. Specifically, she interpreted the legislation as meaning that an assessment of the child's best interests (in the case of a minor under the age of sixteen) "requires that sufficient account be taken of a particular adolescent's maturity in any given medical treatment context."[54] She described this as involving a "sliding scale of scrutiny," with the child's views "becoming increasingly determinative depending on his or her ability to exercise mature, independent judgment."[55] Justice Abella also emphasized that the more serious the consequences that flow from the child's decision to refuse treatment, the greater the degree of scrutiny of the child's maturity that is required.

Based on this interpretation — that the child's capacity and maturity are not irrelevant but rather form an integral part of the best interests assessment — the majority concluded that the legislation is not arbitrary or discriminatory, nor does it violate religious freedom.

3) Justice Binnie's Dissent

As indicated at the outset of this essay, in my opinion there is considerable uncertainty as to what was actually decided by the Supreme Court in *A.C.* In that regard, the dissenting reasons of Binnie J provide a useful starting point. His interpretation of the majority's decision is clear: for children under the age of sixteen, the court has the power to order the treatment if it considers this to be in the child's best interests, even if at common law the child is a

---

53 *Child and Family Services Act*, above note 49, ss. 25(8)–(9).

54 *A.C.*, above note 1 at para. 21.

55 *Ibid.* at para. 22.

mature minor with capacity to consent. This is what, in Binnie J's opinion, rendered the legislation unconstitutional: that it enables a court to order treatment over the objections of a competent, mature minor.[56]

It is also clear that Binnie J interpreted Abella J's reasons as meaning that although the court must take into account the child's wishes in applying the best interests test, these wishes are never determinative. This interpretation is particularly evident from the following passage from Binnie J's judgment:

> In this case, the majority's interpretation of the *CFSA* does not render rebuttable the presumption that persons under 16 lack the capacity to refuse medical treatment. Under their interpretation of the *CFSA*, even if a minor under 16 demonstrates his or her capacity, he or she is still not treated in the same manner as a minor who is 16 and over. His or her demonstrated capacity remains one consideration among others (however much its weight increases in correspondence with the maturity level and the nature of the treatment decision to be made), and is in no way determinative.[57]

If this interpretation of the majority's decision is correct, *A.C.* does no more than reaffirm a well-established principle that has been applied in numerous previous cases: namely, that in assessing a child's best interests the wishes of the child must be taken into consideration,[58] and the weight to be attached to those wishes will depend on the child's level of maturity (among other things). This was the approach taken by the English Court of Appeal in *Re W*,[59] in emphasizing that the child's wishes, though not determinative, are an important factor for the court to consider, and their importance increases with the child's maturity. As in *A.C.*, the Court of Appeal in *Re W* also linked the concepts of *best interests* and *autonomy* by noting that it will normally be in the best interests of adolescent children for the court to respect the autonomy and integrity of their decisions.

4) What Did the Supreme Court Actually Decide?

Despite the views expressed by Binnie J, in my opinion it is by no means clear that the majority did in fact decide that the wishes of a mature minor

56 See, in particular, *ibid.* at para. 177.

57 *Ibid.* at para. 194.

58 Indeed, this is a statutory requirement under child welfare legislation. See, for example, *Child and Family Services Act*, above note 49, ss. 2(2)–(3). See generally Bala, above note 36 at 17.

59 Above note 30.

are not determinative. Indeed, a strong argument can be made for the opposite interpretation.[60] In particular, a number of passages in Abella J's reasons strongly indicate her opinion that if a court is satisfied that the child is sufficiently mature to make the decision, the child's views *must* be respected. For example, Abella J stated:

> The more a court is satisfied that a child is capable of making a mature, independent decision on his or her own behalf, the greater the weight that will be given to his or her views when a court is exercising its discretion under s. 25(8). In some cases, courts will inevitably be so convinced of a child's maturity that *the principles of welfare and autonomy will collapse altogether and the child's wishes will become the controlling factor.* If, after a careful and sophisticated analysis of the young person's ability to exercise mature, independent judgment, the court is persuaded that the necessary level of maturity exists, *it seems to me necessarily to follow that the adolescent's views ought to be respected.* Such an approach clarifies that in the context of medical treatment, young people under 16 should be permitted to attempt to demonstrate that their views about a particular medical treatment decision reflect a sufficient degree of independence of thought and maturity.[61]

Admittedly some of the language in this passage (especially in the first sentence) is ambiguous. Indeed, it could easily be taken to refer to the issue of standard of proof — that is, how "satisfied" or "convinced" the court must be with respect to the child's maturity — but this would be inconsistent with the Supreme Court's own recent decision that in civil matters, there is only one standard of proof, namely, proof on a balance of probabilities, regardless of the seriousness of the issue before the court.[62] Despite this ambiguity, in my opinion the remainder of the passage is sufficiently clear to infer that Abella J's position was that the child's views are indeed determinative, as long as the court is satisfied that the child is mature enough to make the decision.

Justice Abella's reference in the above passage to the point at which the principles of welfare and autonomy "collapse" is of particular interest. She used this same term later in her judgment when discussing the fact that the legislation prohibits the court from authorizing treatment for children over

---

60 This of course raises the question of why, if Binnie J were incorrect in his interpretation of the majority's judgment, Abella J did not point this out in her reasons, presumably having seen a draft of Binnie J's dissent.

61 *A.C.*, above note 1 at para. 87 [emphasis added].

62 *F.H. v. McDougall*, 2008 SCC 53, [2008] 3 SCR 41.

the age of sixteen, unless they lack capacity.[63] According to Abella J, "the distinction between promoting autonomy and protecting welfare is presumed to collapse at age 16, subject to evidence to the contrary."[64] In this passage she is clearly using the term *collapse* to describe the point at which the child's wishes become determinative. It is reasonable to conclude that she intended the same meaning earlier in her judgment when using the term to describe the position with respect to children under the age of sixteen.

This interpretation is not inconsistent with the fact that A.C.'s appeal of the treatment order was dismissed despite the case having proceeded on the basis that A.C. was competent. Justice Abella held (1) that the issue of A.C.'s competence and maturity had not been properly determined by the lower courts, nor had they assessed her best interests in light of her maturity, and (2) that in any event, the validity of the treatment order was now moot.[65]

Elsewhere in her judgment, Justice Abella stated:

> If ss. 25(8) and 25(9) did in fact grant courts an unfettered discretion to make decisions on behalf of all children under 16, despite their actual capacities, while at the same time presuming that children 16 and over were competent to veto treatment they did not want, I would likely agree that the legislative scheme was arbitrary and discriminatory. A rigid statutory distinction that completely ignored the actual decision-making capabilities of children under a certain age would fail to reflect the realities of childhood and child development. However, this is not the effect of ss. 25(8) and 25(9). As the foregoing analysis demonstrates, a child's maturity and corresponding interest in self-determination will factor significantly into any determination of his or her "best interests" under s. 25(8) of the Act, *with the child's views becoming increasingly determinative as his or her maturity increases.*[66]

Once again this seems to support the interpretation that if the child is judged to be sufficiently mature to make the decision, the child's wishes are determinative. So, too, does the following passage:

---

63 *Child and Family Services Act*, above note 49, s. 25(9).

64 *A.C.*, above note 1 at para. 111.

65 See *ibid.* at paras. 118–22.

66 *Ibid.* at para. 116 [emphasis added]. This reference to the child's views "becoming increasingly determinative" as maturity increases is repeated elsewhere in Abella J's judgment: see *ibid.* at para. 22.

> Given the significance we attach to bodily integrity, it would be arbitrary to assume that no one under the age of 16 has capacity to make medical treatment decisions. It is not, however, arbitrary to give them the opportunity to prove that they have sufficient maturity to do so.[67]

In my opinion, the key to understanding Abella J's reasons lies in her emphasis on the need for a proper, thorough, and robust assessment of the child's competence and maturity. Citing an abundance of literature on the point, Abella J noted that while adolescents "may have the technical ability to make complex decisions, this does not always mean they will have the necessary maturity and independence of judgment to make truly autonomous choices."[68] The major thrust of her reasons, in my opinion, is that there needs to be a much more probing and robust assessment than has typically occurred in the past, not only of the child's maturity and capacity to make an informed decision, but also of whether the child's decision is truly a voluntary one[69] (that is, an independent decision free from the undue influence of others, such as parents).[70] This view was endorsed by McLachlin CJ and Rothstein J in their concurring judgment, in calling for a "more robust conception of capacity"[71] and in emphasizing that capacity is not to be interpreted in a narrow intellectual sense but rather includes issues of maturity and independent judgment.[72]

Once capacity is understood in this more robust, rigorous sense, it seems entirely reasonable and acceptable to conclude that if the child meets that test, his or her wishes should be determinative. Though by no means entirely clear, it is certainly arguable that this is indeed what was decided by the majority in *A.C.*

---

67 *Ibid.* at para. 107.

68 *Ibid.* at para. 71.

69 The distinction between the two issues of whether the child has capacity to make the decision and whether the child's decision is a voluntary one is often blurred in the caselaw. See Picard & Robertson, above note 2 at 62.

70 But note the point made by Day, above note 13 at 395, that considerable caution should be exercised when dealing with an allegation that the child's decision, based on religious beliefs shared by the family, is not voluntary.

71 *A.C.*, above note 1 at para. 147.

72 *Ibid.* at para. 159. On the question of whether the concurring judgment supports the interpretation that if the child is sufficiently mature, his or her wishes are determinative, the answer is not clear. Some passages in the judgment appear to support this interpretation — such as paras. 133 and 144 — whereas others appear contrary, for example, para. 152.

5) Subsequent Caselaw

Only two subsequent cases have applied *A.C.*, and neither is conclusive in its interpretation of the decision. In the first case, *P.H. v. Eastern Regional Integrated Health Authority*,[73] an application was made to the court for an order authorizing psychiatric treatment for a sixteen-year-old girl who had refused consent to the treatment. Justice LeBlanc held that the girl was not mentally competent to make the decision because she did not have the ability to appreciate the reasonably foreseeable consequences of her decision to refuse the treatment. However, referring to *A.C.*, LeBlanc J also held that even if he had concluded that the girl was mentally competent, he would have ordered the treatment because he considered this to be in her best interests.

Justice LeBlanc interpreted *A.C.* as requiring the court to assess the child's level of maturity (even when the child has been found to be mentally competent) in deciding whether to authorize the treatment, as part of the best interests assessment. He noted, "The more the young person is found to be mature in his or her thinking process and in life, the greater regard that must be given to that person's choice."[74] Applying this principle, LeBlanc J concluded that the girl was not sufficiently mature to make her own health care decisions.

Whereas this decision can certainly be interpreted as supporting the conclusion that the wishes of a mentally competent child are not determinative, the decision must be read in light of the judge's determination that the girl was not sufficiently mature to make her own decisions. Justice LeBlanc appears to have regarded competence and maturity as two separate issues, whereas in my view it is more in keeping with the decision in *A.C.* to view them as two aspects of the same concept.

The other case that has interpreted *A.C.* is *K. (Re)*,[75] in which the court concluded that the fifteen-year-old girl in question was not a mature minor but that her views were nonetheless entitled to some weight. The court offered no view on whether her wishes would have been determinative if she had been assessed as being a mature minor.

---

73 Above note 42.

74 *Ibid.* at para. 52.

75 2010 NLUFC 6.

E. CONCLUSION

One of the key questions in *A.C.* was, does the court have the power to override the refusal of medical treatment by a mentally competent minor? It is unfortunate that the answer remains unclear. I have attempted to show that the majority's decision can be interpreted as denying the courts this power by making the views of the competent minor determinative, but with the important proviso that "capacity" must now be understood in a much broader, robust sense, taking account of the child's maturity to make a truly informed and independent decision. Particularly in cases in which the consequences of refusal of treatment are severe, it is to be expected that courts will set a high threshold of capacity. However, if that threshold is met, the child's views ought to be determinative.

CHAPTER 3

Nowhere to Stand: Correction by Force in the Supreme Court of Canada

ANNE McGILLIVRAY

> Chasten thy son while there is hope, and let not thy soul spare for his crying.
>
> — Proverbs 19:18[1]

> Every school teacher, parent or person standing in the place of a parent is justified in using force by way of correction toward a pupil or child, as the case may be, who is under his care, if the force does not exceed what is reasonable in the circumstances.
>
> — *Criminal Code*[2]

> . . . it's just
> A family tradition
> The strength of this land
> Where what's right and wrong
> Is the back of a hand
> Turns girls into women
> A boy to a man
> But the rights of the children
> Have nowhere to stand.
>
> — k.d. lang, 1989[3]

---

1 The verse "has probably been responsible for more physical pain than any other sentence ever written." Northrop Frye, *The Great Code: The Bible and Literature* (Toronto: Harcourt Brace Jovanovich, 1986) at 21. Twelve verses exhort corporal punishment but "spare the rod" is not among them. It comes from Samuel Butler's sexual satire *Hudibras* (1660): "Love is a boy by poets stil'd; Then spare the rod, and spoil the child."

2 *Criminal Code*, RSC 1953–54, c. 51, s. 43.

3 k.d. lang and The Reclines, "Nowhere to Stand," *Absolute Torch and Twang* (Prod. Greg Penny, Ben Mink, and k.d. lang. Sire Records, May 1989).

The 1989 United Nations *Convention on the Rights of the Child* requires that the child be protected from "all forms of physical or mental violence" and from "cruel, inhuman or degrading treatment or punishment."[4] The *Charter* guarantees equal protection and equal benefit of the law to everyone, children included.[5] Consistent and cumulative research shows the inutility of corporal punishment. Canada's constitutionally frail "spanking law," section 43 of the *Criminal Code*,[6] was ripe for challenge. The Canadian Foundation for Children, Youth and the Law challenged the law by way of stated case in the Ontario courts and the Supreme Court of Canada, arguing that section 43 breaches children's rights to security of the person, freedom from cruel or unusual punishment, and freedom from age-based discrimination.[7] In 2004, McLachlin CJ found that section 43 violates no right of the child. The decision in *Canadian Foundation for Children, Youth and the Law v. Canada (Attorney General)* was vigorously denounced in dissenting judgments by Binnie, Arbour, and Deschamps JJ and in numerous academic articles.[8]

---

4 Can. T.S. 1992 No 3, arts. 19(1) and 37. See also the *Convention on the Elimination of All Forms of Discrimination against Women*, Can. T.S. 1982 No 31; and the *International Covenant on Civil and Political Rights*, Can. T.S. 1976 No 47.

5 *Canadian Charter of Rights and Freedoms*, Part I of the *Constitution Act, 1982*, being Schedule B to the *Canada Act 1982* (UK), 1982, c. 11, s. 15(1) [*Charter*]: "Every individual is equal before and under the law and has the right to the equal protection and equal benefit of the law without discrimination and, in particular, without discrimination based on race, national or ethnic origin, colour, religion, sex, age or mental or physical disability." Section 15(2) makes an exception for programs whose object is to ameliorate conditions of inequality arising from disadvantages such as age.

6 RSC 1985, c. C-46.

7 *Canadian Foundation for Children, Youth and the Law v. Canada (Attorney General)*, 2004 SCC 4 [*Foundation*], aff'g (2002), 57 OR (3d) 511 (CA), aff'g (2000), 49 OR (3d) (SCJ). Appeal dismissed, Binnie J dissenting in part and Arbour and Deschamps JJ dissenting. The Foundation operates the Toronto law clinic Justice for Children and Youth, which provides legal services to children, advocates for law and system reform, and seeks "to further Canada's compliance with its obligations to children under international law, in particular with the United Nations *Convention on the Rights of the Child*," Mission statement, online: www.jfcy.org. The Court Challenges Program provided start-up funding on the application of Dr. Ailsa Watkinson, Faculty of Social Work, University of Regina.

8 Among others, see Joan E. Durrant *et al.*, "Protection of Children from Physical Maltreatment in Canada: An Evaluation of the Supreme Court's Definition of Reasonable Force" (2009) 18:1 J Aggression, Maltreatment & Trauma 64 [Durant *et al.*, "Protection of Children"]; Rory O'Connell, "The Role of Dignity in Equality Law: Lessons from Canada and South Africa" (2008) 6:2 Int'l J Constitutional L 267; Joan E. Durrant *et al.*, "What Did the Canadian Public Learn from the 2004 Supreme Court Decision on Physical Punishment?" (2008) 16:2 Int'l J Child Rts 229; Mark Carter, "'Debunking' Par-

The weird constitutional interpretation and flawed empiricism of *Foundation* have been widely reviewed. This essay examines other assertions for which the Supreme Court offers little or no support. In what sense was it "Parliament's decision" to give parents and teachers special protection from the law of assault? What does Canadian jurisprudence disclose about section 43? Without section 43, will parents go to jail? As this book honours the work of Professor Nicholas Bala, his comments on the defence are discussed in the concluding remarks.

A. PARLIAMENT'S DECISION

"The issue in this case is the constitutionality of Parliament's decision to carve out a sphere within which children's parents and teachers may use minor corrective force in some circumstances without facing criminal sanction," McLachlin CJ writes for the majority of the Supreme Court.[9] Did Parliament "decide"? That children cannot learn without being beaten, broken

ents' Rights in the Canadian Constitutional Context" (2007) 86 Can Bar Rev 479; Joan E. Durrant, "Corporal Punishment" in R. Brian Howe & Katherine Covell, *A Question of Commitment: Children's Rights in Canada* (Waterloo, ON: Wilfrid Laurier University Press, 2007); Anne McGillivray & Joan Durrant, "Child Corporal Punishment: Violence, Law and Rights" in Ramona Alaggia & Cathy Vine, *Cruel but Not Unusual: Violence in Canadian Families* (Waterloo, ON: Wilfrid Laurier University Press, 2006); Katie Sykes, "Bambi Meets Godzilla: Children's Rights and Parents' Rights in *Canadian Foundation for Children, Youth and the Law v. Canada*" (2006) 51:1 McGill LJ 131; Marvin M. Bernstein, "The Decision of the Supreme Court of Canada Upholding the Constitutionality of Section 43 of the *Criminal Code* of Canada: What This Decision Means to the Child Welfare Sector" (2006) 44:1 Fam Ct Rev 104; Robert Leckey, "Embodied Dignity" (2005) 5:1 OUCLJ 63; Mark Carter, "The Constitutional Validity of the Corporal Punishment Defence in Canada: A Critical Analysis of *Canadian Foundation for Children, Youth and the Law* versus *Canada (Attorney-General)*" (2005) 12:2 Int'l J Victimology 189; Judith Mosoff & Isabel Grant, "Upholding Corporal Punishment: For Whose Benefit?" (2005) 31 Man LJ 177; Martha Bailey, "The Corporal Punishment Debate" (2005) 41:4 2005 Fam Ct Rev 508; Joan Small, "*Canadian Foundation for Children, Youth and the Law* v. *Canada (Attorney General)*: The Supreme Court of Canada Gives Children's Human Rights a Hiding" (2005) 3 JL & Equality 209; Sanjeev Anand, "Reasonable Chastisement: A Critique of the Supreme Court of Canada's Decision in the 'Spanking' Case" (2004) 41:4 Alta L Rev 871; Sonja Grover, "A Commentary on *Canadian Foundation for Children, Youth and the Law* v. *Canada (Attorney-General)*" (2004) 11:2 Murdoch UEJL; Anne McGillivray, "Child Physical Assault: Law, Equality and Intervention" (2004) 30 Man LJ 133 [McGillivray, "Child Physical Assault"]; Tim Quigley, "Correction of Children: The Supreme Court Divided" (2004), 16 CR (6th) 286.

9 *Foundation*, above note 7 at para. 1. Also see among others, paras. 45, 51, 54, 59, and 65.

to obedience like horses or hawks, was a strongly held belief for some 3,500 years. *Ius corrigendi*, or the right of chastisement — corporal punishment, correction by force, the infliction of pain for the purpose of correction — is a magisterial power valued for its degrading effect and used to reinforce hierarchy and compel obedience. Its use with children was considered both necessary and virtuous.[10] It once belonged to masters of households, schools, pupils, ships, courts, prisons, apprentices, slaves, servants, and colonies as well as to fathers.[11] Only children remain legally subject to it in Canada today.[12] Parliament's "decision" begins with Roman law.

The Roman *pater familias* held an "absolutely despotic personal authority" over wives, children, relatives, servants, and slaves, "often exercised with merciless cruelty."[13] *Pater potestas*, the power of the father, included infanticide, the sale and surrender of children, banishment, execution, emancipation of sons and slaves, and corporal punishment.[14] *Potestas* was reduced by

---

10 Corporal punishment was used "not only a means of inducing [children] to conduct themselves well and tell the truth, but also as an aid to education itself." George Ryley Scott, *The History of Corporal Punishment: A Survey of Flagellation in Its Historical, Anthropological and Sociological Aspects* (London: T. Werner Laurie, 1938) at 16.

11 The legal chastisement of slaves ended with the *Slavery Abolition Act* (1833); of wives with the English Court of Appeal decision in *R. v. Jackson*, [1891] 1 QB 671 (the court claimed this never was legal); of apprentices with the renovated 1955 Canadian *Criminal Code*, SC 1953–54, c. 51; of offenders and prisoners with the *Criminal Law Amendment Act, 1972*, SC 1972, c. 13, s. 59, repealing s. 668 of the *Criminal Code*; of persons aboard ships with the *Canada Shipping Act, 2001*, SC 2001, c. 26, s. 294, repealing s. 44 of the *Criminal Code*; and of schoolchildren in 2004 with *Foundation*, above note 7 at paras. 38 and 40.

12 By August 2010, 29 states had enacted prohibitions against the corporal punishment of children and the supreme courts of two more had declared it unlawful. End Physical Punishment of Children (EPOCH), "States with Full Abolition," online: www.endcorporalpunishment.org/pages/progress/prohib_states.html.

13 Samuel Parsons Scott, ed., preface to *The Code of Justinian: The Civil Law* (Cincinnati: The Central Trust Company, 1932) [Scott, *Justinian's Code*]. See also Charles Phineas Sherman, *Roman Law in the Modern World*, 3d ed. (New York: Baker, Voorhis, 1937); and M.C.J. Olmesdahl, "Paternal Power and Child Abuse" in John M. Eekelaar & Sanford N. Katz, eds., *Family Violence: An International and Interdisciplinary Study* (Toronto: Butterworths, 1978) at 253.

14 "Subject to paternal ownership, children in the early days of Rome were treated with no more consideration than domestic animals. It was entirely optional with the father whether his offspring should be spared and brought up, or abandoned . . . [I]nfanticide was frequently practised to avoid expense . . . . A child, like a slave or an ox, could be surrendered by its father by way of reparation for any damage it had caused . . . [N]either marriage nor the attainment of majority, had any effect, so far as the release of paternal authority was concerned." Scott, *Justinian's Code*, *ibid.*

imperial edict in the latter days of the empire.[15] The emperor Severus prohibited corporal punishment exceeding moderate flogging and ordered that fathers who killed sons be subject to the penalty for sons who killed fathers — "sewed up in a sack with a dog, a cock, a viper, and a monkey, and, enclosed with these wild animals and associated with serpents, thrown into the sea."[16] In AD 365, co-emperors Valentinian and Valens issued an edict on "domestic correction" to prohibit "extremely severe castigation," limit the use of castigation to "minors" and remove paternal jurisdiction over "atrocious crime" to the courts of justice.[17] An early annotation to the AD 365 edict states: "The motive: for example, flogging, which goes unpunished if administered by a magistrate or parent, because it is inflicted for the purpose of correction not for the sake of insult; but it is punished when someone has been beaten up in anger by an outsider." Canon law and the rediscovery of Justinian's works strongly influenced the development of common law doctrine. *Bracton on the Laws and Customs of England* (c. 1230) restates the Roman annotation as the law of England: "Motive, as in whippings, which are not punishable if imposed by a master or parent (unless they are immoderate) since they are taken to be inflicted to correct not injure."[18]

The *pater familias* was resurrected in the Protestant Reformation, a nucleated father-headed family being both metaphor for the king as *pater patriae* and more amenable to state control than the feudal open-kinship family with its complex political allegiances. Manuals and broadsheets equated obedience to the father with obedience to god and king.[19] Filial, state, and religious obedience was inculcated through obligatory beating. "More children were being beaten in the sixteenth and early seventeenth centuries, over a longer age span, than ever before."[20] Apprentices sued their masters "for almost

15 Alan Watson, ed., *The Digest of Justinian*, English translation, Latin text edited by Theodor Mommsen with the aid of Paul Krueger (Philadelphia: University of Pennsylvania Press, 1985) at 48.19.16 [*Justinian's Digest*]. References are, respectively, 37.12.5 (Trajan, 98–117); 48.9.5 (Hadrian, 117–38); *Justinian's Code*, above note 13 at 9.17 (Constantine, 318–19); and see Anne McGillivray, "'He'll Learn It on His Body': Disciplining Childhood in Canadian Law" (1998) 5 Int'l J Child Rts 193 [McGillivray].

16 *Justinian's Code, ibid.*, 8.46 at 227.

17 *Ibid.*, Book IX.

18 Samuel E. Thorne, ed., *Bracton on the Laws and Customs of England*, vol. 2 (Cambridge, MA: Belknap Press, 1968) at 298–300. Affront to dignity — degradation — is the purpose of corporal punishment. The text draws heavily on Roman and canon law.

19 Lawrence Stone, *The Family, Sex and Marriage in England 1500–1800* (Harmondsworth, UK: Penguin, 1979) at 27. See also c. 5 and pp. 408–11.

20 *Ibid.* at 117.

limitless sadism" and children hated parents for their harsh discipline.[21] The ecclesiastical courts held jurisdiction over family matters. As judges were concerned with enforcing filial piety rather than protecting children from parents, no child assault case is found in court records from 1400 to 1600.[22] The magistrates' handbook *Eirenarcha* (1581) explains that "some are allowed to have privately, a *natural,* and some a *civile* power (or authoritie) over others, so that they may be excused themselves if but (in reasonable manner) they correct and chastise them for their offenses."[23] Fathers had a "natural" authority and masters a "civil" authority to chastise children under their charge.

By the close of the 1700s, a handful of criminal prosecutions for extreme cruelty had been brought against parents.[24] As Blackstone explains, the father's power is absolute ("a mother, as such, is entitled to no power, but only to reverence and respect") and his power of correction, while "much more moderate" than in ancient Rome, is "still sufficient to keep the child in order and obedience. He may lawfully correct his child, being under age, in a reasonable manner; for this is for the benefit of his education."[25] The power of teachers was tested in 1860 in *R. v. Hopley.*[26] Thomas Hopley, master of an Eastbourne private school, wrote to the father of thirteen-year-old Reginald Cancellor, "a dull boy," for permission to "chastise him severely" to cure his obstinacy and "that if necessary he should do it again and again" and "continue it at intervals even if he held out for hours." The father agreed. Hopley beat his pupil for two and a half hours with an inch-thick, brass-tipped stick.

21 *Ibid.* at 120–21.

22 R.H. Helmholz, "And were there children's rights in early modern England? The canon law and 'intra-family violence' in England, 1400–1640" (1993) 1 Int'l J Child Rts 23–32.

23 Maeve E. Doggett, *Marriage, Wife-Beating and the Law in Victorian England* (Columbia, SC: University of South Carolina Press, 1993) at 5. Chastisement of children was a natural power. Wives disappeared from later editions of the handbook.

24 This resulted from the rise of the public prosecutor and changing ideas of childhood. From 1785 to 1860, *The Times* reported 385 physical and sexual assault cases in which children were victims, nine in ten of whom were children of the accused. Linda A. Pollock, *Forgotten Children: Parcel Child Relation from 1500 to 1900* (Cambridge and New York: Cambridge University Press, 1983).

25 William Blackstone, *Commentaries on the Law of England* (1769) Book I, c. 16, online: www.lonang.com/exlibris/blackstone/bla-000.htm. See also *R. v. Greenhill* (1836), 4 Ad & E 624, 111 ER 922, asserting that "when a father has the custody of his children, he is not to be deprived of it except under particular circumstances . . . any doubts left on the minds of the public as to the right to claim the custody of children might lead to dreadful disputes, and even endanger the lives of persons at the most helpless age." Only in proven cases of extreme cruelty would paternal rights be severed.

26 (1860) 2 F&F 202 [*Hopley*].

The boy died. In convicting Hopley of manslaughter for "excessive chastisement," Cockburn CJ writes: "By the law of England, a parent or a schoolmaster . . . may for the purpose of correcting what is evil in the child inflict moderate and reasonable corporal punishment, always, however, with this condition, that it is moderate and reasonable." Punishment in "passion" or "rage" or "immoderate or excessive in its nature or degree" or "protracted beyond the child's powers of endurance, or with an instrument unfitted for the purpose and calculated to produce danger to life or limb" exceeds the limits of the defence.

The question for nineteenth-century jurists and educators was not the legality or desirability of chastising children, but its severity.[27] Quebec judge Henri Elzéar Taschereau's annotation to the *Criminal Law Consolidation and Amendments Acts of 1869* reflects *Hopley*. Under "Killing by correction," he writes: "Moderate and reasonable correction may properly be given by parents, masters and other persons, having authority in *foro domestico*, to those who are under their care, but if the correction be immoderate or unreasonable, either in the measure of it, or in the instrument made use of for that purpose, it will be either murder or manslaughter, according to the circumstances of the case."[28] The English judge James Fitzjames Stephen cites *Hopley* in his 1887 formulation of a general defence of chastisement which would, like Taschereau's defence, apply to all under the control of a master: "It is not a crime to inflict bodily harm by way of lawful correction . . . to the person of another; but if the harm inflicted on such an occasion is excessive the act,

27 Although debate was beginning to shift from how severe school corporal punishment should be to whether it should be used at all, Canadian education reformer Egerton Ryerson defends use of the rod: "The regulations established by law provide that each master (or mistress) of a school is '*to practise such discipline as would be exercised by a judicious parent in his family*.'" That a judicious parent uses corporal punishment is supported by "scripture and common sense." Department of Public Instructors for Upper Canada, *Reports of the Local Superintendents of Common Schools, and of the Inspector of Grammar Schools* (Toronto, July 1865) 24–26 [emphasis in original]. This fits with the decision in *Hopley*, above note 26.

28 32–33 Victoria for the Dominion of Canada (1874), vol. 1: "In Grey's case . . . says the report, if a father, master, or school-master will correct his child, servant or scholar, he must do it with such things as are fit for correction, and not with such instruments as may probably kill them" (177). "If it be done with a dangerous weapon, likely to kill or maim, due regard being always had to the age and strength of the party, it will be murder, but if with a cudgel or other thing not likely to kill, although unsuitable for the purpose of correction, it will be manslaughter" (203).

which inflicts it is unlawful."[29] Somewhat grudgingly, Stephen's fourth edition references "the correction of children and servants" to section 66 of the *Draft Code,* appended to the report of the Royal Commission on the Law Relating to Indictable Offences.[30] It was not Stephen, a member of the Commission and considered the architect of the *Draft Code,* but Lord Blackburn, Commission chair, who drafted the defences. Blackburn's draft of section 66, "Correction and Preservation of Discipline," does not include servants. By comparison to his ornate defences of person and property which set out detailed circumstances and limits, the simplicity of section 66 is remarkable: "It is lawful for every parent or person in the place of a parent, schoolmaster or master to use force by way of correction towards any child pupil or apprentice under his care: Provided that such force is reasonable under the circumstances." A similar defence for assault by masters of ships "for the purpose of maintaining good order and discipline" was included in the section.[31]

The *Draft Code* was rejected in England but purchased for Canada, where Blackburn's section 66 was adopted verbatim and without debate. It was renumbered section 55 in the 1892 Canadian *Criminal Code* and retitled "Discipline of Minors and on Ships."[32] The haste to promulgate a federal code in the wake of Confederation resulted in "serious defects" due to "too much reliance on Sir James Stephen's draft" and "too light an estimate of the difficulties that lie in the drafting of a code," Taschereau, now on the Supreme

---

29 James Fitzjames Stephen, *A Digest of the Criminal Law (Crimes and Punishments),* 4th ed. (London: Macmillan, 1887) at 138 and 183. This is repeated verbatim in George Wheelock Burbidge, *A Digest of the Criminal Law of Canada (Crimes and Punishments) founded by permission on James Fitzjames Stephen's* Digest of the Criminal Law (Toronto: Carswell, 1890) s.257.

30 *Criminal Code (Indictable Offences Bill) 1878; Report of the Royal Commission Appointed to Consider the Law relating to Indictable Offences: With an Appendix Containing a Draft Code Embodying the Suggestions of the Commissioners* (London, 1879); Appendix to the Report of the Commissioners, 1879, online: www.lareau-legal.ca/EnglishDraftCodeTWO.pdf. The *Draft Code* was adopted by Canada with modifications (though none to s. 55), and by Queensland, West Australia, and New Zealand (which repealed its identical statutory defence in 2007), British territories in East and West Africa, Cyprus, and Palestine. The Israeli defence, which remained in the common law, was abolished by the Supreme Court in 2000. See *State of Israel v. Plonit,* [2000] Cr. App. 4596/98 44 PD 145; and Rhona Shuz, "'Three Years On': An Analysis of the Delegalization of Physical Punishment of Children by the Israeli Courts" (2003) 11 Int'l J Child Rts 235.

31 See above note 11.

32 Henri Elzéar Taschereau, *The Criminal Code of the Dominion of Canada as amended in 1893,* 3d ed. (Toronto, Carswell, 1893) at v, noting that ss. 16–60 (the defences) were "Drawn by Lord Blackburn for Imperial draft."

Court of Canada, told Justice Minister Sir John Thompson in 1893.[33] Deputy Justice Minister Robert Sedgewick, drafter of the *Criminal Code*'s Canadian content, prepared a memorandum for his minister in which he reminds him, "One of the principal objects of the Code was to place in short and sustainable compass the existing law . . . . We are not law reformers, and therefore the Bill as submitted contained as far as possible the existing law."[34] There was no parliamentary consideration of the discipline of minors. Taschereau's annotation of section 55 of the new 1892 *Criminal Code* states: "A parent may in a reasonable manner chastise his child, or a master his servant, or a schoolmaster his scholar, or a gaoler his prisoner, and a captain of a ship any of the crew . . . . As to homicide by correction : see *R.* v. *Hopley*."[35] In 1906, the title became "Correction of child by force."[36] In the 1953–54 renovations of the *Code*, the section was renumbered 43, "justified" replaced "it is lawful," "teachers" replaced "schoolmasters" and were placed before parents, "masters and apprentices" disappeared, and ship masters were given their own section, section 44, since repealed.[37]

The history of section 43 discloses no substantive change to the AD 365 Roman edict on domestic correction in over 1,600 years. Contra McLachlin CJ, no "decision" worthy of the name was made by Parliament other than adopting existing common law defences as drafted by Lord Blackburn and, over fifty years ago, modernizing the language. Nor can its purpose fairly be stated as "to carve out a sphere within which children's parents and teachers may use minor corrective force." Its purpose is to recognize and preserve a status quo in which assaulting children was a necessary and virtuous tutorial duty. For most of its history, criminal sanctions were irrelevant.

B. A CANADIAN JURISPRUDENCE?

In a central area, *Foundation* is curiously silent. This is the analysis of the pre-existing caselaw. Chief Justice McLachlin explains that "judicial inter-

33 Letter by Judge Taschereau to the Attorney General of Canada with Comments and Suggestions (20 January 1893), online: www.lareau-law.ca/TaschereauLetter1893.pdf. Taschereau proposed no change to s. 55.

34 Memorandum as to Mr. Justice Taschereau's Open Letter on the Criminal Code (13 February 1893) at 26, online: www.lareau-legal.ca/Sedgewick.pdf.

35 Taschereau, above note 32.

36 RSC 1906, c. 146.

37 RSC 1953–54, c. 51. Section 44 was repealed in 2001. *Canada Shipping Act*, SC 2001, c. 26.

pretation may assist in defining 'reasonable under the circumstances'" but "judicial decisions on s. 43 in the past have sometimes been unclear and inconsistent, sending a muddled message as to what is and is not permitted."[38] Judges "failed to acknowledge the evolutive nature of the standard of reasonableness," "gave undue authority to outdated conceptions of reasonable correction," and "erroneously applied their own subjective views on what constitutes reasonable discipline — views as varied as different judges' backgrounds."[39] Cases were "seldom viewed as sufficiently serious to merit in-depth research and expert evidence or the appeals which might have permitted a unified national standard to emerge." That legislation may be "open to varying interpretations," she concludes, "is not fatal."

The failure of Canadian courts to establish a coherent and defensible standard in well over a century suggests otherwise. An abortive attempt was made in 1903, when the Nova Scotia Supreme Court ordered the retrial of a teacher who had bloodied, bruised, and lamed a truant student. In acquitting the teacher, the magistrate had "applied a [permanent injury] test taken from an American decision ... for which ... there is no warrant in our Code."[40] The Canadian standard is: "If ... he went beyond the limit of moderate castigation, and, either in the mode or degree of correction, was guilty of any unreasonable and disproportionate violence of force, he was clearly liable for such excess." But the "permanent injury" test was resurrected in a 1927 Saskatchewan District Court decision which wrongly cites *R. v. Gaul* in support.[41] While permanent injury is out, pain and bruising are to be expected. "That the punishment naturally may cause pain hardly needs to be stated," the Quebec Court of King's Bench observed in 1951.[42] "Bruises or contusions alone will not be unreasonable" but one who "so far forgets himself as to strike

38 *Foundation*, above note 7 at para. 39.

39 On the "judicial childhood test," see McGillivray, above note 15.

40 *R. v. Gaul*, [1904] 8 CCC 178. The precedent applied in magistrate's court is *State v. Pendergrass* (1837), 19 NC 365 (SC), which states that parental duty "cannot be effectually performed without the ability to command obedience [and] to enable him to exercise this salutary sway he is armed with the power to administer moderate correction." Punishment "which may seriously endanger life, limbs, or health, or shall disfigure the child, or cause any other permanent injury, may be pronounced in itself immoderate." The Nova Scotia appeal court followed *Commonwealth* v. *Randall*, 4 Gray 36, "which is practically the same as our Code."

41 *R. v. Metcalfe*, [1927] 49 CCC 260 (Sask Dist Ct).

42 *Campeau v. R.* (1951), 103 CCC 355 (Qc KB). The force used must be "proportioned to the offenses committed" and "any punishment exceeding this limit, or motivated by arbitrariness, caprice, anger or bad humour constitutes an offence."

a child in any part of the body where permanent damage may be caused must take the consequences." The Saskatchewan Court of Appeal ruled in 1985 that a "severe" belt-lashing to prevent a learning-impaired boy from growing up to be "a bum on 20th Street" was corrective and that the deep bruising caused, while excessive, was not bodily harm.[43] The Saskatchewan court's list of factors to be considered was rarely considered in subsequent cases. Courts have excused assaults of children incapable of correction, stemming from anger and malice, resulting in broken teeth and eardrums, and committed with belts, straps, sticks, hairbrushes, and harnesses.[44] Community standards are referenced by some courts, rejected by others. Precedent is rarely cited. Standards are seldom articulated.

Judicial maps of the punishable body are an indecipherable maze of lines drawn around injury, gender, age, correctability, weapons, and body parts.[45] That the deciding factor is the judge's personal opinion of corporal punishment may be explicit, as in a 1992 Manitoba Court of Appeal decision: "The discipline administered to the boy in question in these proceedings was mild indeed compared to the discipline I received in my home. There were times when I thought my parents were too strict, but in retrospect I am glad that my parents were not subjected to prosecution or persecution for attempting to keep the children in my family in line."[46] Chief Justice McLachlin sought to clean up the judicial mess by articulating yet another standard. The result is worthy of Dr. Seuss:

> When you're under twelve and over two
> It doesn't matter what you do,

---

43 *R. v. Dupperon* (1985), 16 CCC (3d) 453 at 86 (Sask CA). Chief Justice McLachlin rejects "the nature of the offence calling for correction" as a factor (*Foundation*, above note 7 at para. 35): "[I]t is improper to retrospectively focus on the gravity of a child's wrongdoing, which invites a punitive rather than corrective focus" (*Foundation, ibid.*). Surely the sole vestige of fairness in corporal punishment is the relationship between the seriousness of the conduct and the severity of punishment.

44 On pre-*Foundation* law, McGillivray, above note 15, and *Foundation*, above note 7, Arbour J dissenting at paras. 151ff.

45 Sexual assault further confuses the body map. Children who breach sexual boundaries are punished by sexual assault or in sexually suggestive ways. Assaults that are objectively sexual have been justified under s. 43 of the *Criminal Code*, above note 6. See McGillivray, above note 15; Mark Carter, "The Corrective Force Defence (section 43) and Sexual Assault" (2000) 6 Can Crim L Rev 53; and Nigel King *et al.*, "Spanking and the Corporal Punishment of Children: The Sexual Story" (2003) 11 Int J Child Rts 199.

46 *R. v. K.(M.)*, 1992 CanLII 2765 (MBCA), O'Sullivan JA for the court.

The judge says they can beat on you.
But not on the head or if they're mad
And not with a stick and not too bad
And just if they're your mom and dad.[47]

Children over twelve and under two years of age cannot be hit and, although the punishment must be corrective, the child's conduct is irrelevant. The head cannot be hit, punishment cannot be in anger, no implement can be used, injury must be transitory and trifling, and only parents and those *in loco parentis* can use corporal punishment. Teachers are restricted to restraint. Punishment cannot be "degrading, inhuman or harmful." But these criteria are not defined. The Court cites no judicial or empirical evidence for these criteria.[48] Will this cure the vagueness of section 43?

A review of post-*Foundation* cases shows the futility of redefining the indefinable.[49] A father who shoved his son in the face, causing him to stumble and bruise his head, was acquitted, as "minor corrective force of a transitory and trifling nature" is not corporal punishment and anger is "part and parcel of correcting a child"[50] A bus driver who tied a six-year-old learning-impaired boy to his seat with surgical tape and taped a sock in his mouth was given the

47 With apologies to the spirit of Theodor Geisel.

48 *Foundation*, above note 7 at paras. 35–40. The "comprehensive and consistent expert evidence on what is reasonable presented in this appeal gives clear content to s. 43" (para. 2). This is contradicted in the affidavits of expert witnesses from Canada, the United States, and the United Kingdom. Consistent and cumulative research findings show that, irrespective of type, severity, or the age of the child, corporal punishment risks impaired mental health, physical injury, increased aggression, delinquency, poor parent–child relations, and assault of partners and children in adulthood. See Elizabeth T. Gershoff, "Corporal Punishment by Parents and Associated Child Behaviors and Experiences: A Meta-analytic and Theoretical Review" (2002) 128 Psychological Bulletin 359; Joan Durrant, Ron Ensom, & the Coalition on Physical Punishment of Children and Youth, *Joint Statement on Physical Punishment of Children and Youth* (Ottawa: Children's Hospital of Eastern Ontario, 2004), online: www.cheo.on.ca/english/pdf/joint_statement_e.pdf; and Elizabeth T. Gershoff, *Report on Physical Punishment in the United States: What the Research Tells Us about Its Effects on Children* (Columbus, OH: Centre for Effective Discipline, 2008), online: www.phoenixchildrens.com/PDFs/principles_and_practices-of_effective_discipline.pdf.

49 Adapted from summaries of forty-seven cases; see Repeal 43, online: www.repeal43.org/the-law.html; and Anne McGillivray & Cheryl Milne, "Canada: Two Steps Forward, One Step Back" in Anne Smith & Joan Durrant, eds., *Realizing the Rights of Children: Global Progress towards Ending Physical Punishment* (London: Routledge, 2010).

50 *R. v. Demelo*, [2009] OJ No 2387 (Ct J) at paras. 44 and 66. *Foundation*, above note 7, bars anger and blows to the head.

benefit of section 43.[51] For good measure, the court considered the hostility requirement of the English law of assault, citing this to Arbour J's comments on the common law.[52] A father who threw his fifteen-year-old daughter into his truck was acquitted on appeal.[53] The force was for restraint, not correction, the court found; paradoxically, it was reasonable "in light of the offence calling for correction." A teacher charged with fourteen counts of common assault and four of assault with a weapon for hitting learning-impaired first and second graders with books and rulers, pushing their faces into desks, and shoving them to the floor was acquitted.[54] While the force was "beyond the absolute minimum required," the court states, *Foundation* permits touching and the children were not hurt. A father who burned his seven-year-old son with a cigarette lighter to teach him not to set fires was acquitted at trial, the court finding the assault to be both unintentional and educational in intent.[55] The father was convicted of assault with a weapon on appeal. A mother who hit her thirteen-year-old daughter on the face for refusing to turn off the television was acquitted. The court noted that *Foundation* permits "minor corrective force of a transitory and trifling nature" and only slaps to the head that can be characterized as corporal punishment are unreasonable; as this slap was not corporal punishment, it was not unreasonable.[56] The only *Foundation* factor consistently applied by the courts is the ban on using objects, but this was already an established judicial trend.

The claim that the renovated section 43 "sets real boundaries and delineates a risk zone for criminal sanction"[57] does not hold. Judges use ever-stran-

---

51 *R. v. Morrow*, [2009] ABPC 114. *Foundation, ibid.*, bars objects and uncorrectable children. Also see *R. v. T.M.D.*, [2008] AJ No 900 (Prov Ct), extending the defence to an institutional care worker deemed *in loco parentis* for the purpose; and *R. v. D.L.M.*, [2009] BCJ No 1288 (Prov Ct), denying the defence to a biological father with joint custody: he had not assumed all the obligations of parenthood and there was no evidence that the mother had delegated her authority to use corporal punishment. *Foundation* restricts corrective assault to parents.

52 *Foundation*, above note 7, Arbour J dissenting at para. 136.

53 *R. v. Swan* (13 March 2008) Picton, (ON Sup Ct J). If the force used is corrective, it falls under s. 43 of the *Criminal Code*, above note 6. *Foundation*, above note 7, bars children over twelve.

54 *R. v. Persaud*, [2007] OJ No 1752 (Sup Ct J) [*Persaud*]. *Foundation*, above note 7, bars objects, uncorrectable children, and teachers.

55 *R. v. T.E.*, [2006] NSJ No 61 (SC). *Foundation*, above note 7, bars objects and degrading or harmful punishment.

56 *R. v. D.K.*, [2004] OJ No 4676 (Ct J). *Foundation, ibid.*, bars children over twelve.

57 *Foundation*, above note 7 at para. 42.

ger twists of logic to seek what is, in their view, a just result. The failure lies not with the courts but with the defence. There are too many circumstances, too many ideas about what is reasonable, too many forms of punishment, too many "subjective views" too deeply rooted in childhood experience, for legislative capture or an "evolutive" impact on standards. The defence is a lightning rod for values associated with authority and religion, values that in a pluralistic society are far too diverse, vague, and idiosyncratic to control the application of the criminal law.[58]

C. WILL PARENTS GO TO JAIL?

"The reality is that without s. 43, Canada's broad assault law would criminalize force falling far short of what we think of as corporal punishment, like placing an unwilling child in a chair for a five-minute 'time-out.'"[59] Will parents be jailed for time-outs or, for that matter, for wrapping a child in *Jobidon*'s ugly scarf?[60] "That absurd consequence could not have been intended by Parliament," the Supreme Court states in *Jobidon*. "Rather its intention must have been for the courts to explain the content of the offence, incrementally and over the course of time."[61] To claim that section 43 protects parental acts of care and nurture or anything other than physical punishment is, in the *Jobidon* sense, absurd.[62] Nurture, which requires touching and restraint, is

58 Anne McGillivray, "*R. v. K.(M.)*: Legitimating Brutality" (1993) 16 CR (4th) 125 at 132.

59 *Foundation*, above note 7 at para. 62. See also paras. 19, 51, and 60–61.

60 *R. v. Jobidon*, [1991] 2 SCR 714 at para. 63, Gonthier J for the majority.

> Assault has been given a very encompassing definition in s. 265 . . . [which] says nothing about the degree of harm which must be sustained. Nor does it refer to the motives for the touching. If taken at face value, this formulation would mean that the most trivial intended touching would constitute assault. As just one of many possible examples, a father would assault his daughter if he attempted to place a scarf around her neck to protect her from the cold but she did not consent to that touching, thinking the scarf ugly or undesirable. (Even an argument for implied consent would not seem to apply in a case like this.)

61 *Ibid.*

62 *R. v. A.E.*, [2000] OJ No 2984 at para. 29 (CA) [*A.E.*]. "[I]t is in the public interest that an infant be deemed to consent to applications of force by a parent done 'for the good of the child and, indeed, for the survival of the child.'" "Here, as in s. 43, the common law exception that allows a parent to touch a child in order to care for the child both protects the parent and removes a protection from the child" (*ibid.* at para. 33). The court's "defence of deemed consent" (para. 53) can be traced to Thomas Hobbes's dictum that the child's "absolute subjugation" to the parent "derives from the Childs Consent, either expresse, or by some other sufficient means declared" and extends to the child's consent

both a right of the child and a parental fiduciary duty. Corporal punishment is neither nurture nor duty. Conflating assault with restraint ignores the necessary, routine, and legal use of restraint by institutional care workers, who are not protected by section 43.[63] *Foundation*'s portrayal of the defence as a child protection measure — stating that it "does not devalue or discriminate against children, but responds to the reality of their lives by addressing their need for safety and security in an age-appropriate manner" — is misleading.[64]

As fiduciaries of their children, parents enjoy privileges necessary to carrying out their fiduciary duties.[65] These privileges necessarily include touch. A parent who did not touch her child would lose her fiduciary standing to the state's *parens patriae* jurisdiction and face criminal charges. Neither section 43 nor its common law "act of nurture" shadow is required to justify parental touch. As fiduciaries, parents can do things for, with, and to their children that others cannot. If touch risks or causes harm to the child, parental privilege is lost.[66] Assault — in its real sense, not its fictive *Foundation* sense — is such a harm.

Chief Justice McLachlin's redrawn body map is meant to delineate risk zones to guide both parents and the justice system.[67] "Again, the issue is not whether s. 43 has provided enough guidance in the past, but whether it expresses a standard that can be given a core meaning in tune with contemporary

---

to death; see *Leviathan* (1651), Part 2, c. 20, and *The Elements of Law* (1640). The Ontario Court of Appeal heard argument in *Foundation* the following year. The appeal court does not cite *A.E.*, *ibid.*

63 *R. v. Ogg-Moss*, [1984] 2 SCR 173.

64 *Foundation*, above note 7 at para. 51. "The decision not to criminalize such conduct is not grounded in devaluation of the child, but in a concern that to do so risks ruining lives and breaking up families — a burden that in large part would be borne by children and outweigh any benefit derived from applying the criminal process" (*ibid.* at para. 62 and see para. 1).

65 *R.B. v. Children's Aid Society of Metropolitan Toronto*, [1995] 1 SCR 315. As children's fiduciaries, "parents bear responsibilities . . . [and] must enjoy correlative rights to exercise them." Theirs is "a privileged role" within "a protected sphere of parental decision-making" (*ibid.* at para. 85).

66 *K.L.B. v. British Columbia*, [2003] 2 SCR 403 at para. 42, recognizing a parental fiduciary duty to refrain from inflicting personal injury on a child. On state duty, see Anne McGillivray, "Childhood in the Shadow of *Parens Patriae*" in Sally Ross *et al.*, eds., *Multiple Lenses, Multiple Images: Perspectives on the Child across Time, Space and Disciplines* (Toronto: University of Toronto Press, 2004).

67 *Foundation*, above note 7 at paras. 15–19, 22, 26, 27–29, 39–42, and 62.

consensus."[68] But a 2006 survey shows that most Canadians know nothing of the case or its limiting criteria, and most think that corporal punishment is against the law.[69] *Foundation* criteria fail to distinguish reasonable force from child abuse. In a 2009 study, the criteria were mapped onto 25,257 cases in which physical abuse was substantiated by Canadian child protection agencies.[70] In over 90 percent of cases, parents were perpetrators. Two-thirds of abused children were between two and twelve, permissible targets of assault according to *Foundation*. Assault of learning-impaired children is prohibited, and just 12.7 percent of abused children were learning impaired. The force used was minor in almost half the abuse cases, no object was used in over four in five cases, and the intent was corrective in over three in four cases. "Degrading, inhuman or harmful" could not be operationalized for analysis. If the criteria have value as indicators of excessive force and, therefore, as predictors of child abuse, then every case should violate at least one criterion. But almost one in four cases violates none. Only 0.1 percent of cases violate all. The use of non-minor disciplinary force, the study concludes, is the most reliable predictive variable of physical abuse. Spanking is second.

"When these considerations are taken together, a solid core of meaning emerges for 'reasonable under the circumstances,' sufficient to establish a zone in which discipline risks criminal sanction," McLachlan CJ concludes. But no "core of meaning" emerges — not for judges, police, or parents. The risk lies, simply, in the use of corporal punishment.

Is there a legislative solution to the problem? Can a defence for parents also protect the rights and bodies of children? Senate Bill S-209, purportedly a repeal bill, passed second reading in June 2009 but died on prorogation of

---

68 *Ibid.* at para. 39.

69 A national telephone survey of 2,451 French- and English-speaking adults conducted January to March 2006, two years after *Foundation*, showed that the majority (66 percent) had not heard of the Supreme Court decision. A minority (37 percent) knew that parents were allowed to physically punish children. Of these, fewer than one in five knew the limits set on its use; see PR Exchange, *National Survey of Canadians' Knowledge of the Law on Physical Punishment of Children* (Toronto: Toronto Public Health, 2007), online: www.toronto.ca/health/pdf/summary_report_200703.pdf.

70 Durrant *et al.*, "Protection of Children," above note 8. The data are taken from Nico Trocmé *et al.*, *Canadian Incidence Study of Reported Child Abuse and Neglect — 2003: Major Findings* (Ottawa: Minister of Public Works and Government Services Canada, 2005). The study examined cases of reported abuse seen by child protection agencies across the country, excepting Quebec, in the fall of 2003.

Parliament.[71] Under the title "Control of Child," section 43 would provide that "reasonable force other than corporal punishment" by teachers and parents is justified if the purpose is to prevent injury to the child or others, prevent the child from engaging "in conduct that is of a criminal nature," or prevent the child "from engaging or continuing to engage in excessively offensive or disruptive behaviour." As this conduct most frequently triggers corporal punishment and as the Bill fails to specify the kind of force that may be used, it retains the essence of section 43. The problem is not solved.

D. CONCLUDING REMARKS — IN REPLY TO PROFESSOR BALA

No judicial or legislative tinkering can fix section 43. Given its deep violation of the child's *Charter* rights and Canada's treaty obligations under the *Convention on the Rights of the Child*,[72] and the chaos that lies at its "reasonable" heart, all that is left is unmodified repeal. One who assaults a child should be prepared to defend it on the grounds established by the ordinary defences — although it may be that none apply to after-the-fact assault, as McLachlin CJ observes of the defence of necessity.[73] There are other ways to keep parents out of jail. One, of course, is not to take the risk of assaulting a child. Another is *de minimis non curat lex*. Although McLachlin CJ rejects this as "equally or more vague and difficult in application than the reason-

71 Canada, Bill S-209, *An Act to amend the Criminal Code (protection of children)*, 2nd Sess., 39th Parl., 2007–8. Canada, Bill S-204, *An Act to amend the Criminal Code (protection of children)*, 3rd Sess., 40th Parl., 2010 — which repeals section 43 without qualification, received second reading 10 June 2010.

72 In its 2003 *Concluding Observations*, the UN Committee on the Rights of the Child expressed "deep concern" that Canada has taken "no action to remove section 43 of the Criminal Code." The Committee called for "legislation to remove the existing authorization of the use of 'reasonable force' in disciplining children and explicitly prohibit all forms of violence against children, *however light*, within the family, in schools and in other institutions where children may be placed" [emphasis added]; see *Consideration of Reports Submitted by State Parties under Art. 44 of the Convention*, 34th Sess., CRC/C/15/Add. 215 (2003) at paras. 32–33. This is cited by Arbour J in dissent (*Foundation*, above note 7 at para. 188). Chief Justice McLachlin relies on an earlier UN Committee call for repeal, which she interprets as permitting "mild corporal punishment" (*ibid.* at para. 33). For UN Committee statements on corporal punishment laws, see online: www.endcorporalpunishment.org/pages/hrlaw/crc_session.html.

73 *Canadian Foundation*, above note 7 at para. 44.

ableness defence offered by s. 43,"[74] *de minimis* is alive and well in the courts.[75] Police and prosecutorial discretion already operate to shield trivial (and not-so-trivial) assaults from prosecution.[76] Child assault cases are routinely rerouted from the justice system to the child protection system in some jurisdictions, not always a good thing.[77] Contra *Foundation*, nurturing touch is neither assault in law nor in the working definition of assault used by police, prosecutors, and judges.

Professor Nicholas Bala, in whose honour this essay is written, supports section 43. His affidavit for Canada in *Foundation* states: "Children do not have the full range of rights afforded adults."[78] But the *Charter* says they do. The *Charter* further demands that limits on rights and freedoms be demonstrably justified, not presumptively asserted on the enumerated basis of age. To say that "these laws are not, in my view, discriminatory" begs the constitutional question. That "it is essential for families to enjoy a 'zone of privacy' so that they can make parenting decisions to reflect their personal values, experiences and beliefs" conjures up the sorry history of paternal power and private childhood.[79] That "there is no clear agreement on whether a parent's

74 *Ibid.* at para. 44, responding to Arbour J's assertion in dissent that "the defence of necessity and the '*de minimis*' defence, will suffice to ensure that parents and teachers are not branded as criminals for their trivial use of force to restrain children when appropriate" (para. 132) and would "adequately protect parents and teachers from excusable and/or trivial conduct" (para. 195); see also paras. 200ff.

75 For *de minimis* applied in s. 43 cases after *Foundation*, see *R. v. D.P.*, [2004] JQ no 10753 (CQ (Crim & Pen Div)); *R. v. Galliani*, [2004] OJ No 2978 (SCJ); and *Persaud*, above note 54. On *de minimis* generally, see *R. v. Freedman*, [2006] QJ No 1248 (CQ (Crim & Pen Div)).

76 Mark Carter, "Corporal Punishment and Prosecutorial Discretion in Canada" (2004) 12 Int'l J Child Rts 41.

77 Tammy Landau, "Policing the Punishment: Charging Practices under Canada's Corporal Punishment Laws" (2005) 12 Int'l Rev Victimology 121. Toronto police laid charges in half of cases in which children were injured, while Winnipeg police laid charges in just 13 percent of injury cases.

78 Ontario Court (General Division), Canadian Foundation for Children, Youth and the Law and the Attorney-General of Canada, Affidavit of Nicholas Bala, sworn 4 May 1999 at para. 72. The affidavit includes a historical review of s. 43. Professor Bala served on the Board of the Canadian Foundation for Children, Youth and the Law at the time the decision to challenge s. 43 was made. He opposed the decision and later resigned.

79 *Ibid.* at para. 95. See, among others, Anne McGillivray & Brenda Comaskey, *Black Eyes All of the Time: Intimate Violence, Aboriginal Women and the Justice System* (Toronto: University of Toronto Press, 1999); Anne McGillivray, "Abused Children in the Courts: Adjusting the Scales after Bill C-15" (1990) Man L Rev 549–79; Anne McGillivray, "Reconstructing Child Abuse: Western Definition and Non-Western Experience" in M.D.A.

use of reasonable force for the purpose of correcting a child is harmful or beneficial" is contradicted by a wealth of empirical data, much of it submitted in *Foundation*. These data show with an exceptionally high degree of reliability that corporal punishment does precisely the opposite of what it is thought to do.[80] It makes children and the adults they become more, not less, violent. It makes them less, not more, functional and contributing members of society. It weakens parents' relationships with their children. It is not distinguishable from physical abuse. Its severity escalates in imperceptible stages as children and adults become habituated to its use.

"There are lots of things many parents do that are much worse than corporal punishment that are not regulated by criminal law," Professor Bala asserts elsewhere; nor is the criminal justice system "a particularly good way of educating parents around optimal parenting."[81] Exposing parents to the justice system is more "traumatizing" for children than abuse, some children are not traumatized by corporal punishment, and "some immigrant communities are more likely to use corporal punishment and would be disproportionately affected by criminalization."[82] Factually debatable though these propositions are, substituting "husband" for "parent" and "wife" for "child" shows their inherent fallacy. "The evolution of the case law represents the evolution of society's values" and some day section 43 may be repealed. But where is the tipping point? Now, over six in ten adult Canadians think corporal punishment is illegal,[83] while seven in ten, when told of the law, think it should be repealed if this reduces child abuse.[84] Professor Bala suggests that repeal would undermine parental authority and "a parent's authority to remove a disruptive child from a situation against a child's will comes from

---

Freeman & P. Veerman, eds., *The Ideologies of Children's Rights* (Dordrecht, Boston, London: Martinus Nijhoff, 1992); Anne McGillivray, "Governing Childhood: Introduction" in McGillivray, ed. *Governing Childhood* (Aldershot: Dartmouth, 1997); Anne McGillivray, "Why Children Do Have Equal Rights: In Reply to Laura Purdy" (1994) 2 Int'l J Child Rts 243.

80 Anne McGillivray, "Child Physical Assault," above note 8.

81 Margaret Philip, "Spare the Rod — or Face Jail?" *The Globe and Mail* (7 June 2003), online: www.nospank.net/n-k48.htm.

82 Nicholas Bala, "The Supreme Court: Striking a Balance on Corporal Punishment" *Queen's Gazette* (23 February 2004) at 8.

83 PR Exchange, above note 69. Canadians under thirty-five were most strongly in support of repeal.

84 Decima Research, *National Survey of Canadians' Attitudes on Section 43 of the Criminal Code*, commissioned by Toronto Public Health, 2003 online: www.toronto.ca/health/pdf/ssl_survey.pdf.

s. 43."[85] It does not. It is a form of touch, which is a parental privilege arising from parental fiduciary duty.[86]

The issue is not what comes from section 43, but what section 43 comes from: the magisterial power of chastisement, a power now gone from every other arena in which it once ran. "This is the law as we must take it in order to assess its constitutionality," Arbour J states in her dissenting judgment.[87] "To essentially rewrite it before validating its constitutionality is to hide the constitutional imperative." By changing in midstream the boundaries and purpose of section 43 and concealing evidence of its history and harm, the Supreme Court hid the constitutional imperative and upheld a dangerous legal anachronism. If a law that allows children to be hit at will offends no right of the child, then it is true that "the rights of the children have nowhere to stand."[88]

85 John Hoffman, "One Strike and You're Out: In the Absence of Spank-o-Meters, How Can a Court Decide What Is Going Too Far?" *Today's Parent* (May 2000), online: www.todaysparent.com/lifeasparent/article.jsp?content=880&page=1.

86 Anne McGillivray, "Children's Rights, Paternal Power and Fiduciary Duty: From Roman Law to the Supreme Court of Canada" (2010) 18 Int'l J Child Rts 1.

87 *Foundation*, above note 7, Arbour J dissenting at para. 139.

88 k.d.lang, above note 3.

CHAPTER 4

The Child Witness Project: Examining the Assessment of the Competence of Child Witnesses

VICTORIA TALWAR, ROD LINDSAY, AND KANG LEE

Prior to the late 1980s, there was a general belief that child witnesses were inherently unreliable. Due to this prevailing attitude, child witnesses rarely appeared in court. However, over the last three decades, court cases involving child witnesses have increased dramatically and children are now regularly called to testify.[1] Yet in this period, controversy remained about children's testimony.[2] One critical challenge to children testifying in court was the competency inquiry or *voir dire*. In many countries, including Canada, a child was permitted to testify only if the judge was satisfied that the child was "competent." This was ascertained through an inquiry, often carried out by judges or prosecutors. Child witnesses often found these inquiries confusing and intimidating. If the judge was not satisfied with the answers and the child was not permitted to testify, a person guilty of abusing the child might be acquitted. The difficulty that the questioning posed and children's inability to give satisfactory answers sometimes prevented those who would potentially have been capable of giving important evidence from testifying. This chapter discusses research conducted by the Child Witness Project under

---

We would like to thank Nicholas Bala for his generous support and his insightful comments.

1 See Nicholas Bala, "Double Victims: Child Sexual Abuse and the Criminal Justice System" (1990) 15 Queen's LJ 3.

2 See David M. Paciocco, "The Evidence of Children: Testing the Rules against What We Know" (1996) 21 Queen's LJ 345.

the leadership of Nicholas Bala. The project examined the issues posed by the competence inquiry and ultimately led to reforms in the law.

A. HISTORICAL BACKGROUND

In 1893, Canada enacted its first law concerning child witnesses.[3] Prior to these reforms, testimony could be given only if an oath was taken, and children could swear an oath only if they answered questions demonstrating an understanding of the "nature and consequences of an oath." Children who could not explain the meaning of an oath were deemed less likely to tell the truth as witnesses and thus not permitted to testify. This proviso usually meant that children younger than ten could not be witnesses. After the new statutory provisions of 1893, children were permitted to give unsworn evidence if they "possessed sufficient intelligence" and understood "the duty to speak the truth." Judges were required to ask all children about their understanding of oaths. If children did not give satisfactory answers, they could give unsworn testimony provided they could correctly answer questions about "the duty to speak the truth." Nevertheless, a child's unsworn testimony continued to be viewed with suspicion and required corroboration.

Children were often questioned about their religious beliefs and practices in order to establish if they understood the consequences of an oath. However, by the middle of the twentieth century, emphasis on the need for religious answers regarding the meaning of an oath declined.[4] Children did not have to demonstrate an understanding of God or promise to God to tell the truth or understand that there were divine sanctions for failing to tell the truth. Appellate caselaw in the 1980s established that children did not have to demonstrate an understanding of the spiritual consequences of an oath to be permitted to testify providing that they understood the "social significance" of the oath. However, despite legal precedents, children were still commonly questioned about their religious beliefs.[5]

In general the courts were suspicious of child witnesses. There was a perception that children were not trustworthy as witnesses, reflecting wide-

3 *Canada Evidence Act*, SC 1893, c. 31, s. 25.

4 See *R. v. Bannerman* (1966), 55 WWR 257 (Man CA); *R. v. Budin* (1981), 32 OR (2d) 1 (CA).

5 See Nicholas Bala *et al.*, "A Legal and Psychological Critique of the Present Approach to the Assessment of the Competence of Child Witnesses" (2000) 38 Osgoode Hall LJ 409, [Bala *et al.*, "A Legal and Psychological Critique"].

spread contemporary beliefs. Psychiatric, medical, and psychological opinions of the late nineteenth and early twentieth century reinforced these beliefs. Children (especially girls) were considered inherently unreliable witnesses and prone to fantasy and fabrication. Crimes such as sexual abuse were believed to be rare occurrences.[6] This general wariness regarding child witness testimony lasted well into the second half of the twentieth century. Indeed, in 1967 the Supreme Court of Canada cautioned that even if a child was sworn as a witness, judges were obliged to warn juries of the "inherent frailties" of a child's evidence.[7] Due to this prevailing attitude, few reports of child victimization were made, and police or courts often dismissed those that were. In such an environment, it was very difficult to get a conviction for sexual abuse on the uncorroborated testimony of a child victim and as a result there were few prosecutions, which served to confirm the perception that child abuse was rare. However, by the 1980s the social environment had changed and more media reports covered shocking disclosures of abuse as adults came forward to disclose what had occurred to them as children. In 1984 this prompted the Royal Commission on Sexual Offences against Children on the extent of child sexual abuse in Canada.[8] The resulting report (the Badgley Report) documented major problems in how the legal and social services systems dealt with victims of abuse and made many recommendations to improve how society responds to child abuse.

These changes in the social consciousness led to a more receptive environment and increased reports by children of abuse they had experienced. More children were brought forward as witnesses. This trend also prompted new psychological research into the reliability of child witnesses. Psychological research has found that when questioned in an appropriate way, children can be reliable witnesses.[9] Even young children can distinguish fantasy from reality. However, the courts were still insensitive to the needs and capacities

6 See, for example, Carol Smart, "A History of Ambivalence and Conflict in the Discursive Construction of the 'Child Victim' of Sexual Abuse" (1999) 8 Soc & Leg Stud 391.

7 *R. v. Horsburgh*, [1967] SCR 746.

8 Canada, Royal Commission on Sexual Offences against Children, *Report*, 2 vols. (Ottawa: Minister of Supply and Services Canada, 1984) (Chair: Robin Badgley) [Badgley Report].

9 See, for example, Maggie Bruck, Stephen J. Ceci, & Helene Hembrooke, "Reliability and Credibility of Young Children's Reports from Research to Policy and Practice" *American Psychologist* (February 1998) 136; John E.B. Myers, Karen Saywitz, & Gail S. Goodman, "Psychological Research on Children as Witnesses: Practical Implications for Forensic Interviews and Courtroom Testimony" (1996) 28 Pac LJ 1.

of children. Fundamental legal reforms were required. In response to the Badgley Report, Parliament enacted law reforms on child testimony in 1988.

B. 1988 *CANADA EVIDENCE ACT*

The 1988 *Canada Evidence Act*[10] was amended to allow children who did not understand the nature of the oath to be able to testify if they had the ability to communicate as well as "promising to tell the truth." Thus, children could testify even if they did not understand the nature of an oath. Most important, the statutory requirement for corroboration of unsworn testimony was abolished.

The 1988 legislation did not explicitly require an inquiry into a child's understanding of such concepts as "truth," "lie," and "promise"; however, judges interpreted the law to still require children to answer questions about the meaning of these abstract terms.[11] The judicial practice of questioning children about their understanding of a "promise to tell the truth" remained. This questioning was premised on the view that if children could not demonstrate such an understanding, they were less likely to tell the truth. Adults were not expected to meet such standards and not subjected to intrusive and potentially embarrassing questions before being permitted to testify.

The type of questioning involved in the competency inquiry created a challenge for young children testifying in court. Young children think in concrete terms and have difficulty answering questions about abstract concepts. Such inquiries could be long, confusing, and onerous to the young child. For example, in British Columbia a five-and-a-half-year-old girl was subjected to a long inquiry process. Ultimately the judge allowed her to testify and the accused was convicted for sexual harassment. However, the British Columbia Court of Appeal overturned the conviction after reviewing the transcript on the basis that while the child gave satisfactory answers demonstrating an understanding of the concepts of "truth" and "lies," she did not demonstrate an understanding of the meaning of a "promise." Naturally, after this already traumatic experience with the courts, the parents felt that the child had been through enough and the prosecution did not pursue a new trial.[12]

---

10 *Canada Evidence Act*, RSC 1985, c. C-5, s. 16.

11 See, for example, *R. v. Marquard*, [1993] 4 SCR 223; and *R. v. Rockey*, [1996] 3 SCR 829.

12 *R. v. M.A.M.*, 2001 BCCA 6. For a critical commentary on this decision, see Nicholas Bala, Kang Lee, & R.C.L. Lindsay, "*R. v. M. (M.A.)*: Failing to Appreciate the Testimonial Capacity of Children" (2001), 40 CR (5th) 93.

The 1988 *Canada Evidence Act* reforms were significant. However, there were still fundamental concerns about this legislation. A 1999 consultation paper from the Department of Justice suggested:

> The competency test, and its interpretation by the courts, appears to add unnecessary complexity. The unintended effects of [the 1988] reform may have made the experience of child witnesses more rather than less traumatic and made it more difficult for their evidence to be heard. Preliminary proceedings for child witnesses are becoming more common and complex. A stigma continues to attach to evidence that is unsworn or given on a promise to tell the truth.[13]

C. CHILD WITNESS PROJECT

In 1999, the Child Witness Project was formed under the leadership of Nicholas Bala at the Queen's University Faculty of Law. The project brought together a number of professionals and researchers from different disciplines to examine issues related to child witness testimony. One of the first issues this interdisciplinary research team addressed was the effectiveness and experience of competence inquiries for child witnesses. This research included surveys of judicial attitudes as well as a number of psychological laboratory experiments with children.

1) Judicial Attitudes of Child Witnesses

Although the 1988 reforms allowed children who did not understand the nature of an oath to testify if they had the ability to communicate and "promised to tell the truth," a decade later the Child Witness Project survey of Canadian judicial practice found that many judges continued to ask child witnesses questions about such understanding. Some 86 percent of judges who participated in the survey reported that children were routinely questioned during the competence examination regarding religious beliefs and practices in order to assess their moral capacity to testify under oath.[14] Judges gave examples of questions such as "Do you go to Sunday school?"; "Is the Bible a special book?"; "Do you understand the importance of God and why

13 Canada, Department of Justice, "Child Victims and the Criminal Justice System: A Consultation Paper" (Ottawa, November 1999) at 17.

14 Bala *et al.*, "A Legal and Psychological Critique," above note 5.

it is important not to lie to God?" Such questions seem based on the assumption that children with religious backgrounds are less likely to lie or that an oath has a significant impact on children's testimony only if they demonstrate a belief in God. However, the purpose of competence inquiries is not to determine if children are religiously trained in order to assess whether they are committed to telling the truth as witnesses. Such a focus may have little bearing on the child's ability to tell the truth and may serve only to confuse the child. Indeed some of the questions asked would have confused theologians.

The 1988 legislation did not explicitly require an inquiry into a child's understanding of concepts such as "truth," "lie," or "promise," but the courts interpreted the law as still requiring children to answer questions about the meaning of these abstract concepts. In the survey, 34 percent of judges said they sometimes asked children to define a promise when determining whether they could give unsworn testimony. Also, 38 percent of judges reported that they often asked children whether it was good or bad to tell a lie; 51 percent asked children whether they knew it was very important to tell the truth; and 46 percent asked children if they knew the consequences of telling a lie in court.[15] Such questions could lead to long and confusing inquiries for children, who have short attention spans and are prone to confusion. Indeed, many judges expressed discomfort with the intrusive nature of questions asked in the competency inquiry, questioning whether the process assisted the search for truth.

In another survey, examining thirty-eight judges' perceptions of child witnesses and their capacity to give reliable testimony, the judges revealed that they believed children were significantly more likely to be honest than adult witnesses.[16] The judges believed that children are generally more likely than adults to make errors due to limitations of their memory or communication skills or to the effects of suggestive questions. However, they questioned the need to prevent children from testifying on the basis that they may not be honest. They also believed that children are often asked developmentally inappropriate questions in court, especially by defence counsel.

---

15 *Ibid.*

16 Nicholas Bala *et al.*, "Judicial Assessment of the Credibility of Child Witnesses" (2005) 42 Alta L Rev 4 [Bala *et al.*, "Judicial Assessment"].

2) Psychological Research on Lying

The Child Witness Project also conducted a number of laboratory experiments with hundreds of children to examine whether the legal test then used in Canada for assessing the competency of child witnesses had any validity for identifying children who are more or less likely to tell the truth.

In particular, researchers were interested in examining the influence of asking children about "truth," "lie," and "promise" on their actual truth-telling behaviour. The project examined whether children could provide appropriate answers to such questions and the impact on their reports of events after responding to such questions. Questioning children about their understanding of such terms and the moral consequences of lying is based on two major assumptions: (1) that children with appropriate understanding of truth and lie telling are more likely to tell the truth[17]; and (2) that assessing children's conceptual understanding of lying and truth telling and having them promise to tell the truth promotes truth telling in court.[18]

Prior to this project, most psychological research had examined children's understanding and moral evaluation of lying and truth telling.[19] These studies found that children show rudimentary conceptual and moral understanding of lying at around three years of age but take more than a decade to reach maturity (e.g., being able to consider intention when categorizing a statement as a lie and to evaluate moral values). However, even young children rate truthful statements about rule violations positively and judge lying in order to conceal rule violations negatively. A few studies found that children as young as three are able to lie intentionally to deceive another.[20]

---

17 Bala *et al.*, "A Legal and Psychological Critique," above note 5.

18 Bala, Lee, & Lindsay, above note 12; M.L. Huffman, A.R. Warren, & S.M. Larson, "Discussing Truth and Lies in Interviews with Children: Whether, Why, and How?" (1999) 3 Applied Developmental Science 6.

19 See, for example, Kay Bussey, "Lying and Truthfulness: Children's Definitions, Standards and Evaluative Reactions" (1992) 63 Child Development 129; Kang Lee *et al.*, "Chinese and Canadian Children's Evaluations of Lying and Truth-Telling: Similarities and Differences in the Context of Pro- and Anti-Social Behaviors" (1997) 68 Child Development 921; M. Siegal & C.C. Peterson, "Pre-schoolers' Understanding of Lies and Innocent and Negligent Mistakes" (1998) 34 Developmental Psychology 332; A.F. Strichartz & R.V. Burton, "Lies and Truth: A Study of the Development of the Concept" (1990) 61 Child Development 211. For a review, see K. Lee, "Lying as Doing Deceptive Things with Words: A Speech Act Theoretical Perspective" in Janet Wilde Astington, ed., *Minds in the Making: Essays in Honor of David Olsen* (Oxford: Blackwell, 2000) 177–96.

20 See, for example, M. Lewis, C. Stanger, & M.W. Sullivan, "Deception in 3 Year Olds" (1989) 25 Developmental Psychology 439; A. Polak & P.L. Harris, "Deception by Young Children

Despite extensive research on children's conceptual knowledge of lying and truth telling and, to a lesser extent, on lie- and truth-telling behaviour, no study had directly examined the relation between the two. This raised questions about the validity of the two major assumptions underlying the use of such types of question in court competence examinations.

Three experiments tested these assumptions.[21] Experiment 1 assessed 123 children between three and seven years of age. The experiment tested their conceptual understanding of truth telling and lying and placed them in a situation in which they might be motivated to lie. This design allowed an examination of the relation between children's conceptual knowledge and their actual behaviour. Children played a peeking game in which they were told not to look at toys while left alone in a room. The situation was very tempting and of the 123 children, 101 (82 percent) peeked. Thus, the majority committed a transgression, behaviour that was captured on a hidden video camera. Later, the researcher returned to the room and asked the children whether they had peeked when they were alone. Of the 101 children who peeked, 74 percent lied. Furthermore, older children were more likely to lie than younger children. Younger children were also poor lie tellers and more likely to incriminate themselves when asked follow-up questions.

In addition to examining children's lying, the project examined their conceptual and moral understanding of truth and lies. A moral assessment procedure used questions commonly used in competence examinations.[22] Some 87 percent of children could correctly identify a lie, and 73 percent said lying was "bad." Furthermore, when asked about a hypothetical situation in which they had transgressed, the majority of children said they would tell the truth about their behaviour. Nevertheless, a comparison of children's actual lying or truth-telling behaviour with their answers to these questions revealed that lying or truth telling was not statistically related to whether they could identify a lie or

---

Following Noncompliance" (1999) 35 Developmental Psychology 561; Victoria Talwar *et al.*, "Children's Conceptual Knowledge of Lying and Its Relation to Their Actual Behaviors: Implications for the Court Competence Examination" (2002) 26 Law and Human Behavior 395 [Talwar *et al.*, "Children's Conceptual Knowledge"]; Victoria Talwar & Kang Lee, "Development of Lying to Conceal a Transgression: Children's Control of Expressive Behaviour during Verbal Deception" (2002) 26:5 International Journal of Behavioral Development 436.

21 Talwar *et al.*, "Children's Conceptual Knowledge," *ibid.*

22 See Bala *et al.*, "A Legal and Psychological Critique," above note 5; Huffman *et al.*, above note 18; T.D. Lyon & K.J. Saywitz, "Young Maltreated Children's Competence to Take the Oath" (1999) 3 Applied Developmental Science 16.

evaluate lying as morally bad. Indeed, the majority of children who had said it was "bad" to lie and that they would confess a transgression lied about their own transgression. Thus, children's truth-telling behaviour is not related to knowing the "correct" answers to questions about truth and lies. These results cast into doubt the premise that children with appropriate understanding of truth telling and lying are more likely to tell the truth. In fact, the youngest children in this study (three-year-olds) had the greatest difficulty giving appropriate answers and were also the most likely to tell the truth.

A second study was conducted to reflect the competence examination more closely and to examine the second assumption underlying the examination: that discussing lying and truth telling and having children promise to tell the truth makes them more likely to tell the truth. In this study, eighty-six children between three and seven years of age played the peeking game. As in Experiment 1, they were told not to peek at a toy when they were left alone. Again the majority of children peeked (84 percent). However, before they were questioned about their behaviour, the children were given the moral understanding assessment questions to determine their understanding of the importance of telling the truth and then asked to promise to tell the truth. After they had promised, they were interviewed about their behaviour when left alone in the room and specifically asked about the transgression. This time the rate of lying dropped to 57 percent, compared to 74 percent in Experiment 1. Significantly fewer children lied. Furthermore, the greatest increase in truth telling was in the youngest children, who were also the ones who had the greatest difficulty "correctly" answering questions about truth and lying. Similarly to Experiment 1, children's answers to the moral assessment questions were not related to their actual truth- or lie-telling behaviour.

To examine the reasons for the significant drop in children's lying in Experiment 2 further, a third study was conducted, this time with 177 children between three and seven years of age. Experiment 3 was designed to examine whether it was the moral assessment procedure or the promise to tell the truth that significantly influenced children's truth-telling behaviour about their transgression. As in the previous two studies, children were told not to peek at a toy while the researcher was out of the room. Once again, the majority of children transgressed (77 percent). Before being questioned about their behaviour, however, approximately half (seventy-one children) were given the moral assessment procedure only, and the other half (sixty-six children) were asked only to promise to tell the truth. Then children were asked about their behaviour. When children engaged in a discussion about truth telling or lying in the moral assessment procedure (but did not promise to tell the truth), 75 percent of the seventy-one lied about their behaviour. However, most significantly, when asked only to promise to tell the truth prior to questioning about the transgression, only 59 percent of sixty-six children lied. While promising to tell the truth does not eliminate the possibility that the child will lie, it does significantly reduce the frequency of lying.

Since these studies were completed, the results have been replicated a number of times. For instance another study examined children's lying or truth-telling behaviour on behalf of another transgressor.[23] Children who testify in court may be coached by another individual with whom they have an important relationship (such as a family member), and they are also frequently called as witnesses to testify about events perpetrated by trusted adults. Central issues for the justice system are whether a child is lying to protect a parent who is alleged to have abused the child by falsely denying that abuse occurred, or whether a child is fabricating an allegation at the behest of a parent (perhaps against the other parent during a custody dispute). The study examined children's lying or truth telling about a parent's transgression and its relation to their moral and conceptual understanding of lies, truth, and promises. It involved sixty-four children between three and eleven years of age and their parents. Children and their parents were left alone in a room. While there, the parent would break a toy. Parents had been instructed to ask their children to keep the transgression a secret. Children were later questioned about the broken toy. Half the children had a moral discussion and promised to tell the truth. These children were more likely to tell the truth and expose their parents' transgressions. Furthermore, similarly to the previous studies, children's ability to identify lies and evaluate lying as wrong was unrelated to whether they told the truth or lied about their parents' transgressions.

Promising to tell the truth appears to highlight the importance of telling the truth to children and increases the likelihood that they will be truthful in their subsequent statements. Others have reported similar findings. For instance, one study examined 198 maltreated children between four and seven years of age.[24] These children were coached by an adult to keep secret that

23 Victoria Talwar *et al.*, "Children's Lie-Telling to Conceal a Parent's Transgression: Legal Implications" (2004) 28 Law and Human Behavior 411 [Talwar *et al.*, "Children's Lie-Telling"].

24 T.D. Lyon *et al.*, "Coaching, Truth Induction, and Young Maltreated Children's False Allegations and False Denial" (2008) 79 Child Development 914.

they played with a forbidden toy with the adult. Children were later questioned about what they did with this adult. The study found that when children promised to tell the truth they were significantly more likely to do so. Similarly, the ability to answer questions about the negative consequences of lying was not consistently related to truth telling. Thus, the failure to establish a strong relation between children's appropriate answers to questions about truth and lies and their actual behaviour raised serious questions about the validity of court competence examinations and the appropriateness of using such questions to screen out untruthful, unreliable child witnesses.

The relation between understanding truth and lies and lying would not matter if children were not effective liars. In addition to examining children's truth telling and lying, the Child Witness Project examined adults' abilities to assess the veracity of children's reports. One study examined the ability of university students, customs officers, and police officers to detect whether a child was lying or telling the truth.[25] There were three conditions. In one condition, they saw children answering questions in the moral assessment procedure; in the second, they saw children promising to tell the truth; and in the third, they saw children answering neutral questions unrelated to understanding truth, lies, or promises. They were shown video clips of children being questioned about whether or not they had committed a minor transgression. We found that adults were significantly more accurate in identifying whether a child was lying if the child had promised to tell the truth or engaged in a moral discussion about truth telling than if the child was simply asked questions about the transgression. Notably, customs officers and police, whose jobs require assessment of the truth of people's statements, were not better at detecting true and false statements than were undergraduate students. However, it may be that engaging in a moral discussion or being asked to promise to tell the truth increased children's arousal when they lied, making them easier to detect.

However, another study investigated adult judgments of the honesty of children's coached true and fabricated mock testimony.[26] Adults saw video clips of children testifying in a mock court about a true or fabricated event in their lives. They were asked to make an assessment of the truthfulness of the

---

25 Amy-May Leach *et al.*, "'Intuitive' Lie Detection of Children's Deception by Law Enforcement Officials and University Students" (2004) 28 Law and Human Behavior 661.

26 Victoria Talwar *et al.*, "Adults' Judgements of Children's Coached Reports" (2006) 30 Law and Human Behavior 561.

testimony and respond to questions about their perception of the children's credibility. Half of the adults saw children testifying after a competence examination and the other half saw children testifying without a competence examination. Overall, girls were rated as more competent than boys, and their testimony was more likely to be believed. Younger children were more likely to be rated as incompetent than older children. Overall, adults were no better than chance at detecting children's truth and lies. Adults tended to rate children as telling the truth. Viewing the competence examination did not help adults distinguish accurately between children's true and false testimony. Thus it appears that seeing children answer questions about truth and lies in the competence examination does not increase the likelihood of an accurate assessment of truthfulness.

Overall research raised serious doubts about the utility of asking children about their understanding of the concepts of lies, truth, and promises before permitting them to testify. Children's answers to such questions had no bearing on their ability to give truthful, accurate testimony and did not necessarily enhance the ability of others to assess the veracity of the children's testimony. Requiring children to demonstrate understanding of an oath actually required more of children than is expected of adults, since adults are not asked to define abstract concepts like "oath" before being permitted to testify, yet they may lie when testifying. The question of the credibility and veracity of adult testimony was a matter to be judged by the court during the court case.

Therefore, asking children these types of questions required putting them through onerous and lengthy examination that had no bearing on their ability to testify. Such a practice prevented children who were able to give truthful and useful testimony from testifying. Furthermore, the assumption that children who were unable to answer such questions would be less likely to give accurate, truthful statements was also proved false. However, the findings did show that asking children to promise to tell the truth has some real value and alerts children to the importance of telling the truth. A number of studies have found that when children promise to tell the truth they are more likely to do so.[27] This is a robust conclusion based upon the psychological literature.

---

27 For example, A. Evans, *The Development of Deceptive Behaviours in 8- to 16-year-olds* (PhD Dissertation, University of Toronto, 2009) [unpublished]; Lyon *et al.*, above note 24; Talwar *et al.*, "Children's Conceptual Knowledge," above note 20, and Talwar *et al.*, "Children's Lie-Telling," above note 23.

D. CANADIAN LAW REFORMS

In 2004, the House of Commons Committee on Justice and Human Rights considered new legislation dealing with a range of issues relating to child victimization and child witnesses in the criminal justice system. They received a number of written briefs and heard a range of witnesses from professional groups. This included only one brief on competency inquiries prepared by the Child Witness Project.[28] Representing the project, Nicholas Bala testified in front of the committee about psychological research in Canada and elsewhere on child competency issues. As a result of the brief and Bala's presentation, amendments were made to ensure that new legislation was consistent with the research findings. Under the *Canada Evidence Act*, section 16.1, a new approach for qualifying children under the age of fourteen as witnesses and securing their commitment to tell the truth to the best of their ability came into effect in January 2006, as follows:

> *Person under fourteen years of age*
> 16.1(1) A person under fourteen years of age is presumed to have the capacity to testify.
>
> *No oath or solemn affirmation*
> (2) A proposed witness under fourteen years of age shall not take an oath or make a solemn affirmation despite a provision of any Act that requires an oath or solemn affirmation.
>
> *Evidence shall be received*
> (3) The evidence of a proposed witness under fourteen years of age shall be received if they are able to understand and respond to questions.
>
> *Burden as to capacity of witness*
> (4) A party who challenges the capacity of a proposed witness under fourteen years of age has the burden of satisfying the court that there is an issue as to the capacity of the proposed witness to understand and respond to questions.
>
> *Court inquiry*
> (5) If the court is satisfied that there is an issue as to the capacity of a proposed witness under fourteen years of age to understand and respond to questions, it shall, before permitting them to give evidence, conduct an inquiry to determine whether they are able to understand and respond to questions.

28 Bala *et al.*, "A Legal and Psychological Critique," above note 5.

> *Promise to tell the truth*
> (6) The court shall, before permitting a proposed witness under fourteen years of age to give evidence, require them to promise to tell the truth.
>
> *Understanding of promise*
> (7) No proposed witness under fourteen years of age shall be asked any questions regarding their understanding of the nature of the promise to tell the truth for the purpose of determining whether their evidence shall be received by the court.
>
> *Effect*
> (8) For greater certainty, if the evidence of a witness under fourteen years of age is received by the court, it shall have the same effect as if it were taken under oath.[29]

Under these new reforms, there is now a presumption that children are competent to testify, and the burden is placed on those who challenge their capacity to "satisfy the court that there is an issue as to the capacity" of the child to "understand and respond to questions." Section 16.1(8) provides that if a child testifies after giving a promise to tell the truth, this will have the same effect as if the child had testified under oath. Thus evidence cannot be rejected because children gave no oath and there is no distinction between sworn and unsworn testimony.

Subsection 16.1(6) requires children to make a "promise to tell the truth" before they testify. The psychological research has clearly demonstrated that promising to tell the truth appears to have symbolic importance for children and reminds them of the importance of telling the truth. However, also congruent with the psychological research findings and a significant change from practice under 1988 law, subsection 16.1(7) specifies that children will not be asked any questions regarding their understanding of the promise to tell the truth in order to determine if they can give evidence. This prevents questions about the definition or meaning of abstract terms. The provisions that children under fourteen do not need to testify under oath but shall give "a promise to tell the truth" removes the possibility that children will be asked about the nature of an oath or be subjected to intrusive questions about religious understanding or observance by judges or counsel.

---

29 *Canada Evidence Act*, RSC 1985, c. C-5, enacted as SC 2005, c. 32, s. 27.

Now the sole test of the competency inquiry is whether the child has the basic cognitive, social, and language abilities to be able to answer questions. Judges or counsel who call children as witnesses should ask them brief preliminary questions about such matters as their name, age, school, and residence and then questions about events not related to the case (such as a holiday) to see if the children are "able to understand and respond to questions" and to understand their linguistic abilities. Children are no longer expected to demonstrate that they understand the duty to speak the truth. Judges can instruct children about the role of the witness in court, a process that could include simple statements about the importance of telling the truth. Finally, the onus has shifted from a responsibility to demonstrate competence before children can testify to an assumption of the competence of children and a requirement that those who oppose their testimony convince the court that they are not competent. Thus, in terms of competency, children and adults are now treated in a similar manner.

Recently, in a number of decisions, courts have upheld the constitutionality of the new section 16.1 of the *Canada Evidence Act*.[30] Each of the decisions discussed Canadian social science research, including research from the Child Witness Project about the soundness of the reform and its promotion of the search for the truth, and cited the work brief of Nicholas Bala and his colleagues. Most recently, in *R. v. J.S.*, the Canadian Supreme Court upheld the constitutionality of the new law.[31] It also appears that Canadian

30 The first decision upholding the constitutionality of this provision was *R. v. S.(M.)* (31 August 2006) Port Coquitlam, No 7740 (BC Prov Ct), Antifaev J. See also *R. v. Persaud*, [2007] OJ no 432 (Sup Ct), Epstein J. In *R. v. J.F.*, 2006 ABPC 198 at para. 39 (police asked questions in a video-recorded interview), Ho J said, "[N]ot being able to provide a satisfactory definition of the difference between a truth and a lie does not negate the ability of C.S. [the complainant] to provide reliable evidence to the Court."

31 The most complete constitutional decision about s. 16.1 is the British Columbia Court of Appeal in *R. v. J.Z.S.*, 2008 BCCA 401 in which the court concluded that s. 16.1 reflects the procedural and evidentiary evolution of Canada's criminal justice system, in order to facilitate the testimony of children as a necessary step in its "truth-seeking goal." Justice D.M. Smith wrote:

> I do not accept the . . . argument that if a moral obligation to tell the truth is not established, the testimony of the witness should be inadmissible. Parliament . . . has decided that a promise to tell the truth is sufficient to engage the child witness's moral obligation to tell the truth. Section 16.1 . . . discards the imposition of rigid pre-testimonial requirements which often prevented a child from testifying because of their inability to articulate an understanding of abstract concepts that many adults have difficulty explaining. It reflects the [research] findings . . . that the accuracy of a

judges are satisfied with the changes to the laws governing the assessment of child witness competency and believe that they do not interfere with the rights of an accused to a fair trial but facilitate the search for the truth. In a survey of thirty-four judges in four Canadian jurisdictions, 96 percent of the respondents agreed that the reform of the competency provision is "useful."[32] As a result of these reforms, Canada now has one of few legal regimes in the world in which assessing the competence of children is based upon sound psychological research. These reforms have significantly improved the conditions for permitting child witness testimony and pursuing cases involving child witnesses.

The work by the Child Witness Project team headed by Nicholas Bala is a rare instance of empirical research designed to test the implicit premises in a legal regime and the use of the results to advocate for a sounder legal regime. Some critics of the reforms question the significance of research carried out in psychology laboratories for the "real world" of child abuse investigations and the courts. However, the research has been regarded as highly persuasive by legislators and judges, who recognize that only in a controlled laboratory setting is it possible to be sure whether children are actually telling the truth. Further, the consistency of the results with child development theory and the similarity of results in a number of different studies made the conclusions robust. Many other laws should be subjected to such empirical scrutiny, and, if appropriate, reformed.

---

child's evidence is of paramount importance, not the ability of a child to articulate abstract concepts.

On 19 January 2010, the Supreme Court of Canada heard argument in *R. v. J.Z.S.*, 2010 SCC 1 and, in an unusual procedure, dismissed the appeal of the accused without even hearing from the respondent Crown, summarily adopting the decision of the British Columbia Court of Appeal in a very brief oral decision and upholding the constitutional validity of s. 16.1 of the *Canada Evidence Act*, above note 29.

32 N. Bala, A. Evans, & E. Bala, "Hearing the Voices of Children in Canada's Criminal Justice System: Recognizing Capacity and Facilitating Testimony" (2010) 22 Child and Family Law Quarterly (UK) 21.

CHAPTER 5

Factors Influencing the Eyewitness Identification Accuracy of Child Witnesses

NATALIE KALMET, ROD LINDSAY,
MICHELLE I. BERTRAND, AND JAMAL K. MANSOUR

Children are sometimes involved in the criminal justice system as eyewitnesses to, or direct victims of, criminal behaviour. As is the case with adults, child witnesses can play an important role during both criminal investigations and trials. For example, some children will be asked to identify the person(s) who committed the criminal act(s). However, the accuracy of such identifications is a critical issue for both adult and child eyewitnesses. Correct identifications (identifying guilty suspects) can lead investigations in useful directions, but false identifications (identifying innocent suspects) can lead investigators away from the actual perpetrator and result in the conviction and incarceration of innocent people. Of the DNA exonerations handled by the Innocence Project in the United States (over 220 cases), 75 percent have involved misidentifications by eyewitnesses.[1] Thus, concerns about eyewitness identification accuracy, including identifications given by children, are well founded.

Two research paradigms have investigated children's ability to accurately recognize faces.[2] One paradigm, face recognition, is less obviously applicable

---

1 Innocence Project, "Eyewitness Identification Reform," Fact sheet, online: www.innocenceproject.org/Content/165.php.

2 J.D. Pozzulo, "Person Description and Identification by Child Witnesses" in R.C.L. Lindsay *et al.*, eds., *Memory for People*, vol. 2 of *The Handbook of Eyewitness Psychology* (Mahwah, NJ: Lawrence Erlbaum, 2007) [Pozzulo].

to the situations faced by eyewitnesses when making identifications. In this paradigm, participants are presented with a set of faces to be remembered (the exposure phase). Later, they are presented with a second set of faces, which includes both faces seen during exposure and new faces, and asked to state which faces are new and which were seen before (the testing phase). In contrast, the specific tasks and pressures faced by eyewitnesses are better approximated by the eyewitness identification paradigm. Generally, participants are exposed to a target individual (the perpetrator) in person or via videos or photos. Later, participants are presented with an identification procedure (a lineup) and are asked to make an identification decision, such as stating who the target is or stating that the target is not there.

Admittedly, the eyewitness paradigm is not an exact replication of actual eyewitness situations. For example, laboratory delays between exposure to the target and identification are normally much shorter and the events evoke less stress or distress than can occur with real crimes.[3] Despite these differences from actual crimes, the eyewitness paradigm yields results that are more directly applicable to the forensic setting than does the face recognition paradigm. As well, though facial recognition studies can produce results similar to eyewitness studies, differences between the paradigms do exist.[4] This chapter describes only studies in which children made decisions using identification methods relevant to police officers.

A. IDENTIFICATION PROCEDURES

1) Naming

Police use a variety of procedures in an attempt to determine who committed a crime. The most straightforward is to ask witnesses whether they know the perpetrator, though neither adults nor children should be asked leading questions (such as "Was it your Uncle Bob who hurt you?"[5]). However, as-

---

3 See, for example, J. Gross & H. Hayne, "Eyewitness Identification by 5- to 6-Year-Old Children" (1996) 20 Law & Human Behavior 359, where exposure to targets was during a class field trip to a fire hall.

4 J.D. Pozzulo & R.C.L. Lindsay, "Identification Accuracy of Children versus Adults: A Meta-analysis" (1998) 22 Law & Human Behavior 549 [Pozzulo & Lindsay, "Identification Accuracy"].

5 S.J. Ceci & M. Bruck, "Suggestibility of the Child Witness: A Historical Review and Synthesis" (1993) 113 Psychological Bulletin 403; L. Melnyk, A.M. Crossman, & M.H. Scullin, "The Suggestibility of Children's Memory" in M.P. Toglia *et al.*, eds.,

suming unbiased questioning and no "coaching" (e.g., parents suggesting to children that Uncle Bob was the culprit prior to the identification procedure), there is no reason to question the reports of children more than those of adults when they name someone as the perpetrator of a crime. Most research relevant to this topic has examined children's suggestibility. The subject of suggestion and false memory in child witnesses is beyond the scope of this chapter, but excellent reviews are available elsewhere.[6]

2) Descriptions

Frequently there are no witnesses who are familiar with the perpetrator of a crime. Under this circumstance, police first must find a suspect. Initial attempts to find suspects normally start with a description of the perpetrator. Description studies generally indicate that child witnesses provide less information than adult witnesses.[7] Research examining whether children are less accurate than adults, however, is mixed.[8]

3) Mug Shots

Witnesses also are sometimes asked to search mug shots in an attempt to find a suspect.[9] We are unaware of any research examining the ability of children to find a single, previously seen person in a very large pool of photos. On the other hand, we are equally unaware of cases in which children have been asked to search through mug shots.

4) Showups

Once a suspect has been determined, identification procedures are used to test the hypothesis (obtain evidence indicating) that the suspect is the criminal. One such procedure is the showup. Showups involve showing a single

---

Memory for Events, vol. 1 of *The Handbook of Eyewitness Psychology* (Mahwah, NJ: Lawrence Erlbaum, 2007).

6 Melnyk, Crossman, & Scullin, *ibid.*

7 C.A. Meissner, S.L. Sporer, & J.W. Schooler, "Person Descriptions as Eyewitness Evidence" in R.C.L. Lindsay *et al.*, eds., *Memory for People*, vol. 2 of *The Handbook of Eyewitness Psychology* (Mahwah, NJ: Lawrence Erlbaum, 2007).

8 Meissner, Sporer, & Schooler, *ibid.*

9 H.A. McAllister, "Mug Books: More Than Just Large Photo Spreads" in R.C.L. Lindsay *et al.*, eds., *Memory for People*, vol. 2 of *The Handbook of Eyewitness Psychology* (Mahwah, NJ: Lawrence Erlbaum, 2007).

suspect to witness(es) either live or via photograph, and asking whether or not the person shown is the criminal. Police often argue that showups are used only shortly after a crime has occurred, in order to quickly eliminate innocent people from suspicion. However, the showup can be a dangerous procedure, as all identifications when the perpetrator (target) is absent will necessarily be false identifications, as only the one photo is shown.[10]

5) Simultaneous Lineups

The most studied identification procedure is the simultaneous lineup (the traditional method, whereby all lineup members are shown at the same time). A lineup presents the suspect along with additional people or photos, who are generally referred to as foils or fillers. Witnesses are asked if they recognize any lineup members and if so, from where. If the suspect is the criminal ("target-present" lineup), witnesses can choose the suspect (correct identification), select a foil (incorrect selection[11]), or select no one (incorrect rejection). If the suspect is innocent ("target-absent" lineup), witnesses can choose the suspect (false identification), select a foil (incorrect selection), or select no one (correct rejection[12]). In real-world cases, police often refer to lineup rejections as "*failures* to identify" the suspect, a phrase suggesting that police operate under a presumption of guilt.

An issue with the simultaneous lineup, however, is that it generates high rates of identification attempts (i.e., incorrect selections) from target-absent lineups.[13] Wells speculated that the high rate of target-absent selections was because many witnesses used a "relative judgment strategy"[14] when confronted with a lineup. By this he meant that some people would select the

---

10 J.E. Dysart & R.C.L. Lindsay, "Show-up Identifications: Suggestive Technique or Reliable Method?" in R.C.L. Lindsay *et al.*, eds., *Memory for People*, vol. 2 of *The Handbook of Eyewitness Psychology* (Mahwah, NJ: Lawrence Erlbaum, 2007).

11 The recognition error in which a foil in a police lineup is incorrectly selected is unlikely to lead to charges, trials, and convictions, as the person selected was not a suspect to the police.

12 P.R. Dupuis & R.C.L. Lindsay, "Radical Alternatives to Traditional Lineups" in R.C.L. Lindsay *et al.*, eds., *Memory for People*, vol. 2 of *The Handbook of Eyewitness Psychology* (Mahwah, NJ: Lawrence Erlbaum, 2007); Pozzulo, above note 2; G.L. Wells, "The Psychology of Line-up Identifications" (1984) 14 J Applied Social Psych 89.

13 Nancy Steblay *et al.*, "Eyewitness Accuracy Rates in Sequential and Simultaneous Lineup Presentations: A Meta-analytic Comparison" (2001) 25 Law & Human Behavior 459.

14 Wells, above note 12.

lineup member who best matched their memory of the criminal (was most similar to the criminal), as people trusted that the police have apprehended the culprit and that this person is in the lineup, another example of presumption of guilt. When lineups are target-absent, the relative judgment strategy is dangerous because it leads to relatively high rates of incorrect selections.

6) Sequential Lineups

In order to discourage the use of relative judgments, Lindsay and Wells proposed a sequential lineup method.[15] To reduce relative judgments, several techniques were combined.

1) Lineup members were presented one at a time, thus making comparisons more difficult.
2) People were forced to make yes-or-no decisions for each lineup member before they could see the next lineup member and were not permitted to change a decision once they were shown the next lineup member (to prevent comparisons to previously rejected lineup members).
3) People could not set aside pictures, delay decisions until they viewed other lineup members, or view a previously seen lineup member a second time.
4) People were not informed of the number of lineup members, to prevent them from feeling increased pressure to select someone as the lineup neared the end.

Overall, this procedure works well for reducing incorrect selections by adults (thus increasing correct rejections) though there also is a (smaller) reduction in correct identifications.[16]

B. CHILDREN'S IDENTIFICATION ACCURACY

When correct lineup decisions have been examined in general, five- to six-year-olds and nine- to ten-year-olds provided fewer correct decisions than adults.[17] However, children's accuracy also depends on whether or not the target is present. When a target is present in the identification procedure, children often

15 R.C.L. Lindsay & G.L. Wells, "Improving Eyewitness Identifications from Lineups: Simultaneous versus Sequential Lineup Presentation" (1985) 70 J Applied Psych 556.
16 Steblay *et al.*, above note 13.
17 M.R. Leippe, A. Romanczyk, & A.P. Manion, "Eyewitness Memory for a Touching Experience: Accuracy Differences between Child and Adult Witnesses" (1991) 76 J Applied Psych 367.

provide more correct decisions than when the target is absent,[18] although some researchers have found the opposite.[19] As such, it is not enough simply to compare the overall accuracy of children's lineup decisions against those of adults.

1) Target-Present Lineups

Children's lineup decisions are often as accurate as those of adults when the target is in the lineup. This similarity in correct identifications has been found in a number of studies, for children in kindergarten to Grade 8,[20] and specifically for eight- to eleven-year-olds,[21] eight- to thirteen-year-olds,[22] nine-year-olds,[23] and ten- to fourteen-year-olds.[24] Similarity in correct identifications has also been found when younger children are compared to older ones. Similar accuracy rates have been found in three- to six-year-olds compared to seven- to ten-year-olds (even when the identification decision occurred two weeks after seeing the target[25]), and in six- to seven-year-olds compared to nine- to ten-year-olds[26] and ten- to eleven-year-olds.[27] Notably, while Parker, Haverfield, and Baker-Thomas[28] also found no initial differences across age groups, eight-year-olds were more likely than adults to change a prior lineup decision when presented with a lineup a second time. As well, though Keast,

---

18 D.J. Dekle *et al.*, "Children as Witnesses: A Comparison of Lineup versus Showup Identification Methods" (1996) 10 Applied Cognitive Psych 1; Gross & Hayne, above note 3.

19 J.F. Parker & A. Myers, "Attempts to Improve Children's Identifications from Sequential-Presentation Lineups" (2001) 31 J Applied Social Psych 796.

20 B.V. Marin *et al.*, "The Potential of Children as Eyewitnesses: A Comparison of Children and Adults on Eyewitness Tasks" (1979) 3 Law & Human Behavior 295.

21 J.F. Parker & V. Ryan, "An Attempt to Reduce Guessing Behavior in Children's and Adults' Eyewitness Identifications" (1993) 17 Law & Human Behavior 11.

22 J.D. Pozzulo & J. Balfour, "Children's and Adults' Eyewitness Identification Accuracy When a Culprit Changes His Appearance: Comparing Simultaneous and Elimination Lineup Procedures" (2006) 11 Legal and Criminological Psych 25.

23 J.F. Parker & L.E. Carranza, "Eyewitness Testimony of Children in Target-Present and Target-Absent Lineups" (1989) 13 Law & Human Behavior 133.

24 J.D. Pozzulo & K.L. Warren, "Descriptions and Identifications of Strangers by Youth and Adult Eyewitnesses" (2003) 88 J Applied Psych 315.

25 G.S. Goodman *et al.*, "Effects of Past Abuse Experiences on Children's Eyewitness Memory" (2001) 25 Law & Human Behavior 269.

26 J. Beresford & M. Blades, "Children's Identification of Faces from Lineups: The Effects of Lineup Presentation and Instructions on Accuracy" (2006) 91 J Applied Psych 1102.

27 G. Davies, A. Tarrant, & R. Flin, "Close Encounters of the Witness Kind: Children's Memory for a Simulated Health Inspection" (1989) 80 Brit J Psych 415.

28 J.F. Parker, E. Haverfield, & S. Baker-Thomas, "Eyewitness Testimony of Children" (1986) 16 J Applied Social Psych 287.

Brewer, and Wells[29] found no difference in the correct identification rates of ten- to thirteen-year-olds and adults for one target used in the study, the ten- to thirteen-year-olds made fewer correct identifications with a second target.

Other researchers report correct lineup decisions that differ by age. In particular, correct identifications increase as the age of participants increases.[30] For example, adolescents in Grades 8 and 11 provided more correct identifications than did children in Grade 4,[31] and adults were more accurate than three-year-olds,[32] eight- to ten-year-olds and eleven- to fifteen-year-olds,[33] and ten- to eleven-year-olds.[34] Even when children had extensive interactions with a target (at least ten hours), three- and four-year-olds provided fewer correct identifications than five-year-olds. (In fact, the identification accuracy of the three-year-olds was no different from chance.[35])

One problem with comparing individual studies is that they can provide inconsistent results. For example, Goodman and Reed[36] found six-year-olds to be as accurate as adults, while Lindsay *et al.*[37] found eleven- to fifteen-year-olds less accurate than adults. Because results can vary across individual studies, researchers developed meta-analysis to statistically evaluate the consistency of results across multiple studies.[38] One such meta-analysis of

---

29 A. Keast, N. Brewer, & G.L. Wells, "Children's Metacognitive Judgments in an Eyewitness Task" (2007) 97 J Experimental Child Psych 286.

30 N. Brewer & K. Day, "The Confidence-Accuracy and Decision Latency-Accuracy Relationships in Children's Eyewitness Identification" (2005) 12 Psychiatry, Psychology & Law 119; G.S. Goodman *et al.*, "Children's Memory for Stressful Events" (1991) 37 Merrill-Palmer Quarterly 109–57; Leippe, Romanczyk, & Manion, above note 17; K. Pezdek, I. Blandon-Gitlin, & C. Moore, "Children's Face Recognition Memory: More Evidence for the Cross-Race Effect" (2003) 88 J Applied Psych 760.

31 J.C. Brigham, M. Van Verst, & R.K. Bothwell, "Accuracy of Children's Eyewitness Identifications in a Field Setting" (1986) 7 Basic & Applied Social Psych 295.

32 G.S. Goodman & R.S. Reed, "Age Differences in Eyewitness Testimony" (1986) 10 Law & Human Behavior 317.

33 R.C.L. Lindsay *et al.*, "Simultaneous Lineups, Sequential Lineups, and Showups: Eyewitness Identification Decisions of Adults and Children" (1997) 21 Law & Human Behavior 391.

34 J.D. Pozzulo & R.C.L. Lindsay, "Increasing Correct Identifications by Children" (1997) 5:4 Expert Evidence 126 [Pozzulo & Lindsay, "Increasing Correct Identifications"].

35 W.J. Cain, L. Baker-Ward, & K.L. Eaton, "A Face in the Crowd: The Influences of Familiarity and Delay on Preschoolers' Recognition" (2005) 11 Psychology, Crime, & Law 315.

36 Goodman & Reed, above note 32.

37 Above note 33.

38 R. Rosenthal, *Meta-analytic Procedures for Social Research*, rev. ed., Applied social research methods series, vol. 6 (Thousand Oaks, CA: Sage Publications, 1991).

facial recognition and eyewitness studies showed that six- to eight-year-olds are significantly less likely than either older children or adults to provide correct identifications of adult strangers.[39] A second meta-analysis, by Pozzulo and Lindsay, has indicated that four-year-olds are significantly less likely to correctly identify the target than adults are, while nine- to ten-year-olds and twelve- to thirteen-year-olds are no different from adults.[40] Interestingly, Pozzulo and Lindsay also found that five- to six-year-olds provided more correct identifications than adults did.

2) Target-Absent Lineups

More troublesome is identification accuracy when the guilty person is not in the lineup (target-absent lineups). The general pattern in this circumstance is that children are less likely to correctly reject lineups than adults are.[41] Adults correctly rejected lineups more often than did eight- to eleven-year-olds,[42] eight- to thirteen-year-olds,[43] ten- to thirteen-year olds,[44] and ten- to fourteen-year-olds.[45] Parker and Carranza[46] also found that adults were more likely than nine-year-olds to provide correct rejections, though this difference did not occur when the lineup was shown a second time.

Pozzulo and Lindsay[47] found that four-year-olds, nine- to ten-year-olds, and twelve- to thirteen-year-olds were significantly less likely than adults to correctly reject a target-absent lineup. Children five to six years old were also less likely to correctly reject target-absent lineups than adults, but the difference was not significant. Identification performance with target-absent lineups was particularly poor with four-year-olds and when children saw the target in a slideshow.

Overall, then, a child's ability to make correct lineup decisions depends on whether the target is in the lineup. As indicated by the research, children

39 P.N. Shapiro & S. Penrod, "Meta-analysis of Facial Identification Studies" (1986) 100 Psychological Bulletin 139.

40 Pozzulo & Lindsay, "Identification Accuracy," above note 4.

41 Lindsay *et al.*, above note 33; G.L. Wells & E.A. Olson, "Eyewitness Testimony" (2003) 54 Annual Rev Psych 277.

42 Parker & Ryan, above note 21.

43 Pozzulo & Balfour, above note 22.

44 Keast, Brewer, & Wells, above note 29.

45 Pozzulo & Warren, above note 24.

46 Above note 23.

47 Above note 4.

(except when very young) are as capable as adults of identifying the faces of others, including strangers, when provided with target-present lineups. When the target is absent, however, children are much less able to correctly reject the lineup (i.e., state that the target is not there) than are adults. While these conclusions represent general trends, researchers have also examined specific factors that may influence accuracy as well as factors that may indicate whether a lineup decision is correct.

C. INFLUENCES ON ACCURACY

1) Identification Procedure

Of the identification procedures discussed earlier, the procedures most commonly used by police and researchers are showups, simultaneous lineups, and sequential lineups. As the identification accuracy of adults can be influenced by the identification procedure used,[48] it is important to know whether identification procedure likewise affects children's identification accuracy.

Generally, children have made more correct decisions when presented with showups than when responding to simultaneous lineups, particularly when the target is absent.[49] When the target is present, showups (as compared to simultaneous lineups) sometimes increased children's correct identifications[50] but not always.[51] As well, when three- to six-year-olds were compared to adults, no differences were found in the rates of correct identifications from target-present showups.[52] Overall, children provide more correct decisions for both target-present and target-absent situations when provided with showups rather than lineups, as indicated by Steblay *et al.*'s meta-analysis.[53] Unfortunately, the showup data can be highly problematic, particularly as higher rates of correct rejection do not mean that showups will necessarily lead to lower rates of false identification once the number of photos presented

---

48 Steblay *et al.*, above note 13.

49 C.R. Beal, K.L. Schmitt, & D.J. Dekle, "Eyewitness Identification of Children: Effects of Absolute Judgments, Nonverbal Response Options, and Event Encoding" (1995) 19 Law & Human Behavior 197; Dekle *et al.*, above note 18; Lindsay *et al.*, above note 33.

50 Beal, Schmitt, & Dekle, *ibid.*

51 Dekle *et al.*, above note 18; Lindsay *et al.*, above note 33.

52 Lindsay *et al.*, *ibid.*

53 Steblay *et al.*, above note 13.

is taken into account.[54] Specifically, Lindsay *et al.*[55] show that when the number of photos presented in the identification task is accounted for, children's false identifications rates are much higher for showups (.40) than for either simultaneous (.14) or sequential lineups (.17).

When sequential and simultaneous lineups have been compared, some research has shown that ability to correctly identify the target does not differ. This was true for three-year-olds, six-year-olds, and adults.[56] Yet other research has found that the accuracy of children's identification decisions, especially as compared to adults', depends on the lineup procedure used.

For example, Lindsay *et al.*[57] reported that the correct decisions of adults were very similar to those of three- to six-year-olds and eight- to fifteen-year-olds with simultaneous lineups, but not with sequential lineups. Unlike adults, three- to six-year-olds were as likely to make correct identifications from sequential lineups as from simultaneous ones, and were also more likely to provide correct identifications from sequential lineups than were the adults. However, as with showups, such apparently positive results for the sequential lineup can be misleading. Participants in this study were shown all the members of a sequential lineup, regardless of whether a prior selection had been made (i.e., if a participant identified the second lineup member shown, all subsequent lineup members would still be presented). In this situation, young children were particularly likely to select multiple photos, meaning that while they often selected the target from the lineup, they also often selected other lineup members. In fact, one child selected every single photo, simultaneously ensuring that the target was identified while also mistakenly selecting all of the foils. When only single selections were considered, the data indicated that children provided fewer correct identifications than adults did.

Overall, research indicates that sequential lineups hamper children's identification decisions, due to multiple selections[58] and to a greater likelihood of making incorrect target-absent selections compared to adults.[59] Pozzulo and Lindsay also note that errors in how sequential lineups were administered in the research could have contributed to the lessened effectiveness with children.[60]

---

54 Dysart & Lindsay, above note 10; Lindsay *et al.*, above note 33.
55 Lindsay *et al.*, *ibid.*
56 Goodman & Reed, above note 32.
57 Above note 33.
58 *Ibid.*; Parker & Ryan, above note 21.
59 Pozzulo & Lindsay, "Identification Accuracy," above note 4.
60 *Ibid.*

2) Timing

Two important aspects of eyewitness research are related to timing: how long participants see the target (exposure duration), and how long participants are made to wait between exposure to the target and performance of an identification task (delay). Longer exposures have led to more correct identifications from children, although they have not influenced correct rejections.[61] Delays of ten versus thirty minutes[62] or of one week versus three months[63] did not affect correct identifications. However, a delay of one year resulted in fewer correct identifications than identifications made a few days after the event; this was particularly true for children who were three to four years old during the event (compared to five- to six-year-olds).[64] However, these results should be interpreted in the context of the adult literature, which shows that delays of many months reduce the accuracy of all witnesses, while relatively shorter delays of up to a few weeks have inconsistent effects on the identification accuracy of adults.[65] Thus, while delays may affect children, it is unclear whether they react differently to delays than do adults.

3) Stress

So far, research involving how stress influences children's correct lineup decisions has not been consistent. One study found that children who directly (as opposed to vicariously) experienced stress made more correct identifications, for both a biased and an unbiased lineup, after a delay of one month.[66] A second study found that stress did not affect children's correct identifications

61 Gross & Hayne, above note 3.

62 Marin *et al.*, above note 20.

63 Cain, Baker-Ward, & Eaton, above note 35.

64 Goodman *et al.*, above note 30.

65 J.E. Dysart & R.C.L. Lindsay, "The Effects of Delay on Eyewitness Identification Accuracy: Should We Be Concerned?" in R.C.L. Lindsay *et al.*, eds., *Memory for People*, vol. 2 of *The Handbook of Eyewitness Psychology* (Mahwah, NJ: Lawrence Erlbaum, 2007).

66 M.A. Lindberg *et al.*, "Similarities and Differences in Eyewitness Testimonies of Children Who Directly versus Vicariously Experience Stress" (2001) 162 J Genetic Psych 314. A lineup bias is any factor that would lead a witness to select a lineup member other than by remembering the person from the witnessed event. Lineup biases include poor foils (those who do not resemble the suspect), instructions suggesting that the guilty party is present in the lineup, and clothing bias (clothing only the suspect similarly to the criminal during the crime, as determined by the witness's description).

at all.[67] A third found that children provided fewer correct lineup decisions (target-present and target-absent) when exposed to stress.[68] A substantial issue with the stress used in research, however, is that it is of lower intensity than that elicited in actual criminal events. Thus, how eyewitnesses are affected by stress may not yet be addressed by the research.[69]

4) Target Appearance

Target appearance comprises three factors: the cross-race effect, appearance change, and clothing bias. The cross-race effect is the tendency to be better at identifying people of one's own ethnicity compared to people of a different ethnicity, and it has been found for five-year-olds and eight-year-olds to the same degree as for adults.[70] Notably, some face recognition literature indicates that the cross-race effect exists for older children but not for five- to seven-year-olds.[71] In terms of appearance change, when a target's hairstyle and hair colour changed between the exposure and identification task, children were as likely to correctly reject the lineup (compared to no appearance change), but less likely to correctly identify the target.[72] When a lineup was clothing biased (only the suspect wore clothing similar to the target's at exposure), correct identifications increased, but so did false identifications of the innocent suspect (as compared to in unbiased lineups).[73]

5) Presence of Bystanders

Ross *et al.*[74] found that when a bystander who was seen during the exposure was later present in the identification task, eleven- to twelve-year-olds were more likely to incorrectly identify the bystander as the target than were

67 Goodman *et al.*, above note 30.

68 K.A. Deffenbacher *et al.*, "A Meta-analytic Review of the Effects of High Stress on Eyewitness Memory" (2004) 28 Law & Human Behavior 687.

69 K.W. Alexander, J.A. Quas, & G.S. Goodman, "Theoretical Advances in Understanding Children's Memory for Distressing Events: The Role of Attachment" (2002) 22 Developmental Rev 490.

70 Pezdek, Blandon-Gitlin, & Moore, above note 30.

71 G.S. Goodman *et al.*, "The Development of Memory for Own- and Other-Race Faces" (2007) 98 J Experimental Child Psych 233.

72 Pozzulo & Balfour, above note 22.

73 A. Friere *et al.*, "Lineup Identification by Children: Effects of Clothing Bias" (2004) 28 Law & Human Behavior 339.

74 D.F. Ross *et al.*, "Children's Susceptibility to Misidentifying a Familiar Bystander from a Lineup: When Younger Is Better" (2006) 30 Law & Human Behavior 249.

younger children. Notably, these incorrect selections made by older children did not occur when the actual target was in the lineup (with the bystander). When the target was present in the lineup (without the bystander), the eleven- to twelve-year-olds were the most likely of all groups of children to correctly identify the target. The five- to six-year-olds provided the fewest incorrect identifications of the bystander.

6) Prior Experience with Abuse

Children who had prior experiences with abuse were more likely to identify foils from target-present lineups than were children who had not experienced abuse.[75] This difference was found even though the identification and exposure to the target were unrelated to any abusive experiences (i.e., interactions were innocuous touches).

D. INDICATORS OF ACCURACY

Indicators of accuracy are factors that allow general judgments to be made about the accuracy of an identification, based on knowledge of another measure. Two such indicators have been examined in relation to children's lineup decisions. First, memory for event details examines whether being able to accurately recall other details of the event is related to correct lineup decisions. Second, confidence in the identification decision examines whether greater confidence in decisions is related to greater accuracy.

1) Memory for Events

Correct lineup decisions have been shown to be unrelated to either accurate recall of event details[76] or how many descriptors about a target were provided by eight- to eleven-year-olds,[77] ten- to fourteen-year-olds, and adults.[78] Ability to correctly describe a target's face has also been unrelated to correct lineup decisions for eight- to nine-year-olds.[79] Thus, whether or not a child gave

---

75 Goodman *et al.*, above note 25.

76 Beal, Schmitt, & Dekle, above note 49; Leippe, Romanczyk, & Manion, above note 17.

77 R. Zajac & A. Karageorge, "The Wildcard: A Simple Technique for Improving Children's Target-Absent Lineup Performance" (2009) 23 Applied Cognitive Psych 358.

78 Pozzulo & Warren, above note 24.

79 A. Memon & R. Rose, "Identification Abilities of Children: Does a Verbal Description Hurt Face Recognition?" (2002) 8 Psychology, Crime, & Law 229.

accurate details about other aspects of the event or target (such as colour of clothing) provided no information about that child's ability to make a correct lineup decision. However, these conclusions must be made with some caution, as there has been relatively little research on the topic.

2) Confidence

The relationship between decision confidence and decision accuracy has been extensively studied.[80] Research using apparent confidence (i.e., confidence as rated by others) showed that confidence appeared to be higher in children who made correct lineup decisions than in those making incorrect decisions.[81] When examining self-reported confidence, some research has found no association[82] or no clear association[83] with identification accuracy. Other research has found an association between confidence and accuracy, though it may exist only in certain circumstances. For example, while confidence did not differ between correct and incorrect identifications, it was generally greater for correct than for incorrect rejections.[84] As well, Beresford and Blades found confidence and correct lineup decisions were related for several factors, such as when the lineup was simultaneous, was presented via video, and was presented to six- to seven-year-olds.

Keast, Brewer, and Wells reported that confidence calibration is weak for children,[85] whereas it is generally believed to be at least moderate for adults.[86]

---

80 M.R. Leippe & D. Eisenstadt, "Eyewitness Confidence and the Confidence-Accuracy Relationship in Memory for People" in R.C.L. Lindsay *et al.*, eds., *Memory for People*, vol. 2 of *The Handbook of Eyewitness Psychology* (Mahwah, NJ: Lawrence Erlbaum, 2007).

81 Beal, Schmitt, & Dekle, above note 49; Keast, Brewer, & Wells, above note 29.

82 E. Rassin *et al.*, "Boys Will Be Boys: A Pre-Line-up Gameplay Has Beneficial Effects on Boys' but Not Girls' Identification Performance" (2006) 3 J Investigative Psych & Offender Profiling 157.

83 Leippe, Romanczyk, & Manion, above note 17.

84 Pozzulo & Lindsay, "Increasing Correct Identification," above note 34.

85 Keast, Brewer, & Wells, above note 29. A calibration analysis can be used to analyze confidence measured on a percent scale (e.g., Leippe & Eisenstadt, above note 80). Calibration is good or strong when the percentage of decisions that are correct closely matches the average rated confidence level (e.g., witnesses who state they are 80 percent to 100 percent confident are described as "well calibrated" if 90 percent of their decisions are correct). Witnesses are described as overconfident or underconfident in calibration analyses if the percentage of decisions that are correct is lower or higher than their average confidence, respectively.

86 Leippe & Eisenstadt, above note 80.

Children tend to be overconfident,[87] with this tendency being stronger for eight- to ten-year-old children than for fourteen- to seventeen-year-old adolescents.[88] Age-related research has found that children tend to be less confident than adults (though age-related differences were found for only one of two targets[89]), while other research has found children and adults to be equally confident in correct decisions, with children being more overconfident in incorrect decisions.[90] When only target-present lineups were examined, eight-year-olds[91] and nine- to ten-year-olds[92] reported confidence that was similar to that of adults (although five- to six-year-olds were less confident than adults[93]). As well, when presented with a second lineup, children stated they were more confident in this second decision (adults did not), even though their identification accuracy did not increase.[94] Overall, self-reported confidence appears to change depending on whether or not an identification decision is correct, though the association is inconsistent and appears related to overconfidence. In all, confidence should not be used as an indicator of accuracy for children, due to its unreliability.[95]

E. REDUCING CHILDREN'S TARGET-ABSENT ERRORS

Children (except very young children) perform as well as adults when shown target-present lineups, but are distinctly less accurate when presented with target-absent lineups.[96] One reason for this pattern is that children are simply more likely than adults to guess,[97] which leads them to make more lineup selections,[98] resulting in incorrect decisions when the target is absent.[99] Identification tasks encourage people to make selections, and children are

87 Brewer & Day, above note 30; Keast, Brewer, & Wells, above note 29.
88 Brewer & Day, *ibid.*
89 Keast, Brewer, & Wells, above note 29.
90 Parker & Ryan, above note 21.
91 Parker, Haverfield, & Baker-Thomas, above note 28.
92 Leippe, Romanczyk, & Manion, above note 17.
93 *Ibid.*
94 Parker & Carranza, above note 23.
95 Keast, Brewer, & Wells, above note 29.
96 Pozzulo & Lindsay, "Identification Accuracy," above note 4.
97 Beal, Schmitt, & Dekle, above note 49; Lindsay *et al.*, above note 33.
98 Parker & Carranza, "Identification Accuracy," above note 23.
99 Lindsay *et al.*, above note 33; Pozzulo & Lindsay, above note 4.

less capable of resisting this implicit demand to choose.[100] This demand is reflected in the fact that children are generally more likely than adults to make foil selections, less likely than adults to reject lineups,[101] and less likely than adults to state that they "don't know" if the target is present or not.[102]

The implicit demand on children can also be affected by the social context in which an identification is made, such as whether or not misinformation related to the identification task is given to a child.[103] Children who remembered seeing a target in person — when they did not actually see the target — were just as willing to attempt an identification as were children who did see and remember the target.[104] Of children who saw and remembered the target, 14 percent made correct rejections from the target-absent lineups. Of children who recalled, but never actually saw, the target, only 11 percent made correct rejections.[105] Additionally, biased lineup instructions, which do not specifically state that the target may not be in the lineup (and may feed implicit assumptions that the target is present), increase incorrect target-absent selections in nine- to twelve-year olds, ten- to fourteen-year-olds,[106] and ten- to thirteen-year-olds.[107] Biased instructions also reduced incorrect rejections of target-present lineups. Although adults are also influenced by biased instructions, children are particularly affected, at least for some targets.[108]

F. LINEUP MODIFICATIONS

Researchers have attempted to reduce children's error rates by modifying current identification procedures.[109] These modifications are based on the as-

100 Beal, Schmitt, & Dekle, above note 49; Davies, Tarrant, & Flin, above note 27; Lindsay *et al.*, above note 33; Parker & Carranza, above note 23; Pozzulo & Lindsay, "Identification Accuracy," above note 4; Pozzulo & Warren, above note 24.

101 Pozzulo & Lindsay, "Identification Accuracy," *ibid.*

102 Dekle *et al.*, above note 18.

103 E. Roos af Hjelmsäter, P.A. Granhag, & L.A. Strömwall, "Was the Stranger Alone? On How Different Sources of Social Influence Affect Children's Memory Reports" (2009) 4 Social Influence 155.

104 *Ibid.*

105 *Ibid.*

106 J.D. Pozzulo & J. Dempsey, "Biased Lineup Instructions: Examining the Effect of Pressure on Children's and Adults' Eyewitness Identification Accuracy" (2006) 36 J Applied Social Psych 1381.

107 Keast, Brewer, & Wells, above note 29.

108 *Ibid.*

109 Pozzulo argues that it would be best to find a single procedure that works well for both adults and children because this will assist researchers and police officers

sumption that children's incorrect lineup selections are influenced by social factors, such as demand, and attempt to counteract these influences through practice, explicit instructions, or examples.

1) Practice

When given one practice lineup, as well as feedback on that lineup decision, children's ability to correctly reject target-absent simultaneous lineups improved, though the same improvement was not seen with sequential lineups.[110] When provided with two practice lineups (either one target-present and one target-absent or two target-absent) and with feedback, effects on correct identifications varied based on sex.[111] Girls made significantly more correct identifications with practice, especially when they personally practised (as opposed to watching a video depicting a practice) with two target-absent lineups. In contrast, boys made significantly fewer correct identifications with practice; the only practice condition that was not significantly worse than the control (no practice at all) was when they personally practised with both target-present and target-absent lineups. Generally, practice with two lineups influenced only correct identifications — no effects on correct rejections were found — and this influence was positive for girls but negative for boys.[112] Overall, practice did not improve the rate of correct rejections, though it did increase correct identifications of older children to the extent that they are comparable to the rates seen with adults.[113]

2) Instructions

Modifications to lineup instructions have included strategies such as providing a "don't know" response option (if participants do not know whether or not the target is present), extending instructions by directly emphasizing

---

presenting lineups, who will not have to determine whether a child or an adolescent will produce correct lineup decisions at the same rate as an adult. See Pozzulo & Balfour, above note 22; J.D. Pozzulo & R.C.L. Lindsay, "Elimination Lineups: An Improved Identification Procedure for Child Eyewitnesses" (1999) 84 J Applied Psych 167 [Pozzulo & Lindsay, "Elimination Lineups"]. On the other hand, police and courts are likely to be pleased if researchers can accomplish the less ambitious goal of finding a procedure that reduces children's false identification tendencies, even if the procedure cannot be used with adults.

110 Parker & Ryan, above note 21.

111 Parker & Myers, above note 19.

112 *Ibid.*

113 Pozzulo & Lindsay, "Identification Accuracy," above note 4.

the negative effects of misidentifications, showing a video demonstration depicting the correct decision for target-absent lineups, and providing a reference handout that shows lineups of animals and states the correct decisions for both target-present and target-absent lineups.[114] Of these modifications, only extending the instructions had a significant effect: it increased correct identifications for ten- to eleven-year-olds[115] but also decreased correct identifications for ten- to fourteen-year-olds when compared to adults.[116] No modification affected either correct identifications or correct rejections for twelve- to fourteen-year-olds or adults.[117] Surprisingly, playing a game such as dominoes with a child to build rapport before an identification task could increase correct lineup decisions, though only for boys.[118]

3) New Procedures

Many researchers have devised new lineup techniques explicitly intended to reduce children's incorrect target-absent selections while taking the demand to make a selection into account. These techniques allow children to clearly reject the lineup while still making a positive decision.

a) The Mr. Nobody Lineup

Davies, Tarrant, and Flin[119] tested the Mr. Nobody lineup, for which one of the foils is replaced by a silhouette drawing (Mr. Nobody) that participants should select if they do not see the target. Overall, children were as accurate with a regular simultaneous lineup as with the Mr. Nobody lineup, although any impact of the Mr. Nobody lineup may have been hidden by particularly high accuracy rates. Beal, Schmitt, and Dekle[120] examined a variation of the Mr. Nobody in which a "not here" card was included in the lineup. Although the not here card did not influence children's correct identifications, it did significantly increase the number of correct rejections.

---

114 Pozzulo & Lindsay, "Increasing Correct Identification," above note 34.
115 *Ibid.*
116 Pozzulo & Lindsay, "Elimination Lineups," above note 109.
117 Pozzulo & Lindsay, "Increasing Correct Identification," above note 34.
118 Rassin *et al.*, above note 82.
119 Davies, Tarrant, & Flin, above note 27.
120 Beal, Schmitt, & Dekle, above note 49.

b) Elimination Lineups

Pozzulo and Lindsay[121] tested elimination lineups in which the identification process occurs in two discrete steps. First, all lineup members but one are eliminated, leaving a "survivor." The witness then makes a final decision about whether the survivor is the target. Two versions of the elimination procedure differ in how lineup members are eliminated. With a slow elimination lineup, members are eliminated gradually by taking away the lineup member who looks least like the target one after another until only one lineup member is left. In a fast elimination lineup, the member who appears most similar to the target is selected and all others discarded.

Although Pozzulo and Lindsay found that elimination lineups (when compared to standard simultaneous lineups) did not harm the correct identifications of ten- to fourteen-year-olds, they did decrease the correct identifications of adults. For target-absent lineups, the slow elimination lineup without extended instructions was the least helpful, as it did not significantly reduce false identifications for either children or adults when compared to the simultaneous lineup. With any fast elimination lineup, or when extended instructions were given, children's correct rejections increased to a level similar to that of adults who had simultaneous lineups; adult correct rejections were similar across simultaneous, fast elimination, and slow elimination lineups. Overall, identifications were most informative of guilt when the fast elimination lineup was coupled with extended instructions and were the least informative of guilt when simultaneous lineups were given.

Beresford and Blades[122] found that when broken down by presentation form, fast elimination lineups and simultaneous lineups with extended instructions resulted in more correct rejections (as opposed to incorrect selections), although the pattern of results differed depending on how the lineups were shown. Elimination lineups increased correct rejections only when the lineups were composed of photos, and extended instructions increased correct rejections only when the lineups were presented via video. Simultaneous lineups with extended instructions, but not elimination lineups, also resulted in fewer false identifications, regardless of how the lineups were shown. Correct identifications were not influenced by the type of lineup used, with one exception: the fast elimination lineup decreased the likelihood that children would correctly identify the target, but only when lineups were presented as videos.

121 Pozzulo & Lindsay, "Elimination Lineups," above note 109.

122 Beresford & Blades, above note 26.

For target-present lineups, Pozzulo and Balfour[123] found no difference in accuracy between adults and eight- to thirteen-year-olds and no overall difference between simultaneous and fast elimination lineups. For target-absent lineups, and looking only at correct rejections, children were significantly less likely to reject the lineup than adults and significantly more rejections were found with the elimination lineup than with the simultaneous lineup. Although appearance produced no overall effect on correct rejections — such rejections were not influenced by whether or not the target's appearance had changed between exposure and identification — correct rejections in the elimination lineup were higher when the target's appearance in the lineup matched that in the video. When appearance differed between exposure and lineup, elimination and simultaneous lineups did not differ. Notably, the elimination lineup did not appear harmful to adult identifications in this case.

c) The "Wildcard"

The most recent alternative proposed involves the use of a "wildcard" placed in the midst of the lineup photos, a technique that has similarities with Davies, Tarrant, and Flin's Mr. Nobody lineup.[124] The wildcard depicts a person's head in silhouette and children are told that if they do not see the target in the lineup, they should point to this silhouette.[125] When Zajac and Karageorge tested this alternative with eight- to eleven-year-olds who remembered seeing the target, the wildcard did not affect correct identifications but significantly increased correct rejections (as compared to a standard simultaneous lineup). Overall, if any suspect (either guilty or innocent) was selected from a lineup, the likelihood that the suspect was guilty (i.e., the target) was greater when the wildcard lineup was used than if the simultaneous lineup was used.

G. CONCLUSION

Compared to adults, children are more likely to select a person from a lineup, particularly when shown target-absent lineups. Neither confidence in their decisions nor accuracy for other details is highly indicative of the accuracy

---

123 Pozzulo & Balfour, above note 22.

124 Davies, Tarrant, & Flin, above note 27.

125 Zajac & Karageorge, above note 77.

of children's lineup decisions. Children are particularly susceptible to social influences, which may be why they are more likely than adults to make selections from target-absent lineups, and thus more prone to false identification.

Current alternatives to the traditional lineups show promise, though much more research must be conducted before any of these methods will be ready for the police station and courtroom. Until we find better methods of testing children's memory for strangers, their identification evidence must remain somewhat more suspect than that of adults. Given that adult identifications are somewhat unreliable, the less than trustworthy nature of children's identification evidence presents a serious problem for the investigation and prosecution of cases involving child witnesses to crimes committed by strangers.

Part Two

CHAPTER 6

The Changing Face of Youth Corrections

CARLA CESARONI

A. YOUTH JUSTICE LEGISLATION AND YOUTH CORRECTIONS

Youth justice legislation in Canada has always played a key role in shaping youth corrections. Canada's legislative framework has a direct impact on how many youth are sentenced to custody and for what offences. Under the *Juvenile Delinquents Act* of 1908,[1] notions regarding young people's special needs, their vulnerabilities, and the need to avoid stigmatization were the impetus for the establishment of youth custody facilities.[2] Separate custodial facilities were part of a larger move toward separate courts and a separate justice system.[3] Under the *JDA*, concerns about the corruption or abuse of children placed in correctional facilities with adults was often offered as justification for separate confinement.[4] The Act proposed two different types of custodial dispositions: commitment to the local Children's Aid Society or commitment to an industrial school or "training school" (normally secure

The author gratefully acknowledges the comments of Shahid Alvi on drafts of this chapter.

1 *Juvenile Delinquents Act*, SC 1908, c. 40 [*JDA*].

2 J.S. Leon, "The Development of Canadian Juvenile Justice: A Background for Reform" (1977) 15:1 Osgoode Hall LJ 71.

3 J. Trépanier, "Juvenile Courts after 100 Years: Past and Present Orientations" (1999) 7 European J on Crim Policy and Research 303.

4 Nicholas Bala, *Youth Criminal Justice Law* (Toronto: Irwin Law, 2003).

facilities).[5] Sentences were indeterminate, and once a youth had received a custodial disposition, the case transferred to provincial authorities.[6] The broad, welfare-oriented nature of the *JDA* led to disparities in the use of custodial sentences, and many youth spent long periods in training schools for minor offences such as truancy and "sexual immorality."[7]

In 1984, the *Young Offenders Act* (*YOA*)[8] moved youth justice legislation away from welfare principles and toward criminal law principles.[9] The Act narrowed the scope of federal law pertaining to youthful offenders to include only federal offences. Some of the Act's other important provisions were the standardization of the age of criminalization, definite lengths for all dispositions, the stipulation of maximum sentence lengths, and certain legal protections (e.g., the right to a lawyer, provisions governing statements).[10]

Two levels of custody were defined under the Act: open and secure custody.[11] "Open custody" under the Act meant (1) a community residential centre, group home, child care institution, or wilderness camp, or (2) any other like place or facility. "Secure custody" was defined as custody in a place or facility designated by the Lieutenant Governor in Council of a province for the secure containment or restraint of young persons. Secure custody facilities are generally those in which restrictions are continuously imposed on young persons by physical barriers, close supervision, or limited access to the community. Open custody tends to occupy a mid-range point on the continuum of punishment between complete containment and reintegration, and therefore the restrictions are considered less stringent. Open custody facilities tend to consist of several small residential facilities along with a network of community homes. Youth in open facilities sometimes have access to community schools, recreation in the community, local employment, and treatment.

The lack of clear legislative direction in the general principles of the *YOA* contributed to a number of problems that would later be identified by prov-

5 Anthony N. Doob & Jane B. Sprott, "Changing Models of Youth Justice in Canada" in Michael Tonry & Anthony N. Doob, eds., *Youth Justice: Comparative and Cross-National Perspectives*, vol. 31 of *Crime and Justice* (Chicago: University of Chicago Press, 2004) [Doob & Sprott, "Changing Models"].

6 *Ibid.*

7 Bala, above note 4.

8 RSC 1985, c. Y-1 [*YOA*].

9 Doob & Sprott, "Changing Models," above note 5.

10 Anthony N. Doob & Carla Cesaroni, *Responding to Youth Crime in Canada* (Toronto: University of Toronto Press, 2004).

11 *YOA*, above note 8, s. 24.1(1).

incial governments and advocacy groups.[12] For example, ambiguity in the language of the *YOA* regarding when to impose custody, such as "whenever appropriate" and "reasonable in the circumstance"[13] allowed for enormous latitude in interpretation from judges.[14] In addition, it is generally agreed that under the *YOA*, custodial dispositions were overused for minor and non-violent offences and that the rate of placing youth in custody in Canada was higher than in many other Western countries.[15]

As a response to the perceived inadequacies of the *YOA*, the *Youth Criminal Justice Act* (*YCJA*)[16] was created with the intention of decreasing the use of courts and restricting the use of custody.[17] Indeed, the *YCJA* creates significant hurdles for the use of custody. The *YOA* stated that "[t]he youth court shall not commit a young person to custody . . . unless the court considers a committal to custody to be necessary for the protection of society."[18] Under the *YCJA*, custodial sentences can be imposed only if one or more of four conditions are met: (1) it is a violent offence; (2) the youth has previously failed to comply with non-custodial sentences; (3) the youth has been found guilty of a moderately serious offence and has a history that indicates a pattern of findings of guilt; or (4) "in exceptional cases where the young person has committed an . . . offence, . . . such that the imposition of a non-custodial sentence would be inconsistent with the purpose and principles [of sentencing]."[19]

Custody is now known as a "custody and supervision." Under the *YOA*, a high proportion of young people served their custodial sentences and then were released "cold" back into their home communities, without any kind of probation or community service. Under the *YCJA*, two-thirds of each sentence will be served in custody and the remaining third will be served in the

---

12 Richard Barnhorst, "The *Youth Criminal Justice Act*: New Directions and Implementation Issues" (2004) 46:3 Can J Criminol & Crim Justice 231.

13 *YOA*, above note 8, s. 24(1).

14 Anthony N. Doob & Jane B. Sprott, "Changes in Youth Court Sentencing in Canada" (1999) 11:5 Federal Sentencing Reporter 262.

15 Bala, above note 4; Department of Justice Canada, *A Strategy for the Renewal of Youth Justice* (Ottawa: Department of Justice Canada, 1998); Doob & Sprott, "Changing Models," above note 5; J.B. Sprott & H.N. Snyder, "A Comparison of Youth Crime in the U.S. and Canada, 1991 to 1996" (1999) 10:5 Overcrowded Times 1.

16 SC 2002, c. 1 [*YCJA*].

17 Nicholas Bala, Peter Carrington, & Julian V. Roberts, "Evaluating the Youth Criminal Justice Act after Five Years" (2009) 51:2 Can J Criminol & Crim Justice 131; Barnhorst, above note 12.

18 *YOA*, above note 8, s. 24.(1).

19 *YCJA*, above note 16, s. 39(1).

community. References to open and secure custody have been removed from the law and replaced with a requirement that provinces establish a system with "at least two levels of custody for young persons distinguished by the degree of restraint of the young persons in them."[20] When making a determination about the appropriate level of custody, the *YCJA* suggests that "the appropriate level of custody . . . is one that is the least restrictive" and takes into account (1) the seriousness of the offence; (2) the needs and circumstances of the young person, including proximity to family, school, employment, and social services; (3) the safety of other young persons in custody; and the (4) interests of society.[21] It also suggests that the level of custody should "allow for the best possible match of programs to the young person's needs and behaviour"[22] and assess the likelihood of escape.[23]

Since the enactment of the *YCJA*, there has been a significant decline in the use of courts and custody for Canadian youth.[24] It appears that police, prosecutors, and judges have responded to the Act as intended, reducing the overreliance on custody for youthful offenders.[25] The number of youth held in detention, however, does not appear to have been affected by the *YCJA* and the proportion accounted for by remand of all youth in custodial facilities across Canada appears to have increased.[26] Therefore there has been a shift in the incarcerated population from one comprising (largely) sentenced youth to one comprising a larger proportion of youth being held on remand or pre-trial detention. This change in the proportion of custody to a detention population may have implications for the management of the correctional population not only because of the conditions that generally exist in remand facilities but also because of the types of youths who are held in pre-trial detention.

---

20 *Ibid.*, s. 85(1).

21 *Ibid.*, s. 85(5)(a).

22 *Ibid.*, s. 85(5)(b).

23 *Ibid.*, s. 85(5)(c).

24 Bala, Carrington, & Roberts, above note 17; Anthony N. Doob & Jane B. Sprott, *The Use of Custody under the* Youth Criminal Justice Act (Ottawa: Department of Justice, 2005) [Doob & Sprott, *The Use of Custody*]; Shelly Milligan, *Youth Custody and Community Services, 2005/06* (Ottawa: Juristat Centre for Justice Statistics, 2008).

25 Bala, Carrington, & Roberts, above note 17.

26 *Ibid.*; Donna Calverley, *Youth Custody and Community Services in Canada, 2004/2005* (Ottawa: Juristat Centre for Justice Statistics, 2007); Milligan, above note 24.

B. CHALLENGES OF MANAGING A DETENTION POPULATION

One of the most difficult decisions made in youth court is whether a youth should be detained after arrest.[27] Indeed, the denial of bail for a young person may be one of the most intrusive measures provided for by the *YCJA*. Under pre-trial detention, young people who have not yet been found guilty are detained not in terms of what they have done but on the basis of a prediction of what they might do in the future. Moreover, in many Western jurisdictions, detention facilities are short-term holding facilities for young people and therefore generally have minimal educational programs and services for youth.

Studies of both adults and youth in detention often focus on the negative effect that detention has on the outcome of a case in court. Those who are detained are more likely to plead guilty, to be convicted if tried, and to receive a prison sentence.[28] There is evidence to suggest that in addition to negative legal outcomes, detention may have negative psychological outcomes for young people. Detention is a highly stressful time for most detainees, but especially for youth, because of fear of the unknown (including the uncertainties of charge, conviction, and sentencing), distrust of an authoritative environment, lack of control, and isolation from family and significant others.[29] Youth, who are especially dependent on structure, activity, family support, and staff interaction, may be especially prone to boredom, bullying, a high rate of infractions, and at the extreme — suicide.[30]

Emerging empirical evidence suggests that the diversity of needs and circumstances of youth in remand present several challenges to correctional staff. I conducted a study that illustrates some of these challenges.[31] The research

---

27 Nicholas Bala & Sanjeev Anand, "The First Months under the *YCJA*: A Survey and Analysis of Case Law" (2004) 46:3 Can J Criminol & Crim Justice 251.

28 Jeffrey Fagan & Martin Guggenheim, "Preventive Detention and the Judicial Prediction of Dangerousness for Juveniles: A Natural Experiment" (1996) 86:2 J Crim L & Criminology 415; Gail Kellough & Scott Wortley, "Remand for Plea: Bail Decisions and Plea Bargaining as Commensurate Decisions" (2002) 42:1 Brit J Crim 186; Sharon Moyer & Maryanna Basic, *Pre-trial Detention under the* Young Offenders Act*: A Study of Urban Courts* (Ottawa: Department of Justice, 2006).

29 Lindsay M. Hayes, "Juvenile Suicide in Confinement: An Overview and Summary of One System's Approach" (1994) 45:2 Juvenile and Family Court J 65.

30 Alison Liebling, "Prison Suicide and Prison Coping" in Michael Tonry & Joan Petersilia, eds., *Prisons: Crime and Justice: A Review of Research* (Chicago: University of Chicago Press, 1999).

31 Carla Cesaroni, *The Experiences of Adolescent Males in Secure Detention*. Discussion paper prepared for the Ministry of Children and Youth Services (Ontario), Research and Outcome Measurement Branch (October 2009).

was conducted with adolescent males in detention in five secure detention facilities in the province of Ontario. Study participants were 137 male youths who ranged in age from thirteen to nineteen at the time of the study. Thirty-two percent of respondents identified as white, and the remainder identified as black (48 percent), Aboriginal (4 percent), or other racial/ethnic origins (16 percent). Eighty-five percent of the sample had previously been detained.

The charges associated with the youths in detention included a wide range of offences. Given that the sample was a detention population, it is perhaps not surprising that 70 percent had been charged with violent offences, among them murder, manslaughter, sexual assault, assault with a weapon, aggravated assault, assault, robbery, and various weapon charges. Fifty-one percent of respondents indicated that weapons charges were among their offences. Although many respondents' charges included a violent charge, many (54 percent) also included a property charge and administration of justice offences (50 percent).

The prevalence of psychiatric disorders in incarcerated youth is known to be high.[32] These include, but are not limited to, unipolar and bipolar depression, alcohol dependence, attention deficit hyperactivity disorder, conduct disorder, post-traumatic stress disorder, and separation anxiety disorder.[33] Although prevalence rates for mental disorders are variable across studies, using the most conservative estimates, the rate is approximately four times higher among incarcerated young offenders than in community samples.[34] Research has also demonstrated that up to 75 percent of incarcerated young offenders have learning problems.[35]

I utilized Achenbach's *Manual for the Youth Self-Report and 1991 Profile*,[36] a widely used adolescent behavioural questionnaire, to assess respondents'

32 T. Ulzen & H. Hamilton, "Psychiatric Disorders in Incarcerated Youth" (1998) 16 Youth Update 4–5.

33 C.W. Duclos, "Prevalence of Common Psychiatric Disorders among American Indian Adolescent Detainees" (1998) 37:8 J of Am Academy of Child and Adolescent Psychiatry 866; Ulzen & Hamilton, *ibid.*

34 A.E. Kazdin, "Adolescent Development, Mental Disorders, and Decision Making of Delinquent Youths" in Thomas Grisso & Robert G. Schwartz, eds., *Youth on Trial: A Developmental Perspective on Youth Justice* (Chicago: University of Chicago Press, 2000).

35 Y. Henteleff, "The Learning Disabled Child-at-Risk: Why Youth Service Systems Have So Badly Failed Them" (Paper delivered at the Working Together for Children: Protection and Prevention Conference, Ottawa, September 1999) [unpublished].

36 T.M. Achenbach, *Manual for the Youth Self-Report and 1991 Profile* (Burlington, VT: University of Vermont Department of Psychiatry, 1991).

psychosocial functioning. The reliability and validity of the questionnaire have been extensively documented in school, clinical, and custody settings. According to Achenbach's norms, approximately 16 percent of the general population of young people show worrying levels of internalizing (depressed/anxious/withdrawn) behaviours (defined as falling in the borderline-clinical or clinical range). In two previous studies of youth in custody in the province of Ontario,[37] internalizing behaviours were somewhat overrepresented, at 23 percent and 25 percent, respectively. In contrast, 30 percent of the more recent detention sample were in the borderline-clinical or clinical range. This finding suggests that as a group, youth in detention not only have higher psychosocial needs than youth in the general population but may also have higher psychosocial needs than a custody/sentenced population.

Many indicators of family adversity are associated with incarceration, physical abuse, family breakup, and violence between parents among them.[38] Youth in the detention study reported multiple forms of familial, socio-emotional, and academic disadvantage, including unstable living conditions, difficulties in school, substance abuse, delinquent friends, contact with child welfare authorities, and witnessing of violence. These reports are consistent with previous findings for youth in custody.[39] However, findings from the detention sample also suggest an increased presence of gang violence and gang activity in the respondents' neighbourhoods over the ten-year period over which I have been interviewing incarcerated youth.

Correctional staff have identified the increasing challenge of managing rival gang members within youth facilities. Additionally, interviews with staff and superintendents of youth facilities in Ontario indicate that the reduction of the number of youth with minor, non-violent offences[40] has meant less of a "buffering" effect between staff and high-needs youth. Anecdotal evidence

---

37 The studies sampled custodial facilities and were conducted under the *YOA* in 1999 and in 2002–3. Carla Cesaroni & Michele Peterson-Badali, "Young Offenders in Custody: Risk and Adjustment" (2005) 32:3 Crim Justice and Behavior 251; Carla Cesaroni & Michele Peterson-Badali, "Understanding the Adjustment of Incarcerated Young Offenders: A Canadian Example" (2010) 10:2 Youth Justice: An Int'l J 1.

38 M.A. Bortner & Linda M. Williams, *Youth in Prison: We the People of Unit Four* (New York: Routledge, 1997); Barry Goldson, "Child Imprisonment: A Case for Abolition" (2005) 5:2 Youth Justice 77; Barry Goldson, "Damage, Harm and Death in Child Prisons in England and Wales: Questions of Abuse and Accountability" (2006) 45:5 How J Crim Justice 449.

39 See above note 37.

40 Doob & Sprott, *The Use of Custody*, above note 24.

from staff suggests that this has meant more standoffs between youth and staff, more behavioural incidents/reports, and a greater need for lockdowns. In Ontario, this has led to an increase in the staff-to-youth ratio from one staff for every eight youth to one staff for every five or even three youth.

Changes in federal legislation have had an enormous impact on youth corrections in Canada. This has perhaps resulted in a more challenging correctional population. Though federal legislation determines a list of offences for which youth may be charged, and provides sentencing guidelines, how youths actually do their time is largely shaped by provincial responsibilities. Decisions about the number of facilities, the physical plant, and operational influences on the conditions of confinement largely fall to the provinces. This has meant that management of the population of incarcerated youth has been affected by a range of issues at the provincial or local level rather than solely by federal legislation.

C. PROVINCIAL AUTHORITY AND CORRECTIONS: THE EXAMPLE OF ONTARIO

The recent history of youth corrections in Ontario provides an excellent illustration of how structural changes in the provinces can affect how youths do their time. Several changes took place in the province following the enactment of the *YCJA*. Until August 2003, facilities in Ontario were designated as either Phase I (twelve to fifteen years old at the time of the offence) or Phase II (sixteen to seventeen years old at the time of the offence). This was a remnant of changes that occurred during the enactment of the *YOA*. Sixteen- and seventeen-year-olds were formerly considered adults in Ontario under the *JDA*; Ontario did not agree with setting the uniform age of criminal responsibility higher and therefore left youth custody facilities under the two-tiered system. Until quite recently, some places of maximum security, including detention for the Phase II age group, continued to be housed in adult correctional facilities, though in separate sections known as young offender units. Though the Phase I and Phase II designation no longer formally exists, detention facilities to some degree still attempt to separate younger youth from older youth on an informal basis.

For many years, Phase II facilities and older youth within those facilities fell under the mandate of the Ministry of Community Safety and Correctional Services. Phase I facilities and younger youth fell under the jurisdiction of the Ministry of Community and Social Services. Policies for youth who found themselves in the two ministries often diverged.[41] For example, it has been suggested by groups advocating for youth that Phase II was more correctional in nature and Phase I more youth justice oriented. In August 2003, the government created the Ministry of Children and Youth Services (MCYS) by bringing together programs for children and youth from across the ministries of Community and Social Services, Health and Long-Term Care, and Community Safety and Correctional Services.

All youth facilities now fall under the MCYS. This change has required the development of several new policies and procedures that apply to the entire spectrum of youth ages twelve to seventeen rather than a discrete age bracket within that range.[42] This has included the development of integrated policies regarding the use of restraints and secure isolation, for which different policies previously existed for Phase I and Phase II youth.

The province relied on individually contracted private or not-for-profit agencies to operate several open custody and open detention facilities under the *YOA*. The reduced number of youth in custody and detention across the province since the advent of the *YCJA* has resulted in a process of rationalization by the Ministry.[43] This involved construction of the new, 192-bed Roy McMurtry Youth Centre in the city of Brampton and the closure of roughly 50 percent of youth custody and detention facilities across the province (largely open custody/open detention facilities operated by not-for-profit agencies). Critics have suggested that creating one large central facility in southern Ontario has made it more difficult for youth to stay connected with family and community, thus making rehabilitation and reintegration more difficult.[44]

Ontario's Advocate for Children and Youth has raised questions about the Centre's ability to provide a positive, rehabilitative environment. Since it opened in May, staff have responded to 100 "code blue" emergencies, many related to violence in the facility.[45] Additionally, the youths in custody have complained about the portions of food, sleeping conditions, cancellation of

---

41 Diana Cooke & Judy Finlay, *Open Detention and Open Custody in Ontario* (Toronto: Office of the Child and Family Advocacy, 2007).

42 *Ibid.*

43 *Ibid.*

44 T. Talaga, "Official Fears for Young Offenders Moved out of City to 192-bed Centre" *Toronto Star* (14 October 2009) A18.

45 D. Zlomislic, "Broken Promises" *Toronto Star* (9 November 2009) A1.

family visits, and fears for their safety.[46] In October 2009, just five months after opening, the facility superintendent was replaced, along with several unit managers, and a deputy superintendent was added.[47] Arguably a number of these issues are common to the opening and operating of a new facility. However, they may also be symptoms of a correctional system in transition.

The *YCJA* articulates a general standard of care for youth in custody and detention, noting that the system must provide for "the safe, fair and humane custody and supervision of young persons."[48] Additionally, the *YCJA* recognizes the United Nations *Convention on the Rights of the Child*[49] in its Preamble. However, federal legislation has never included standards of care or guidelines for accountability. Given that correctional staff may be faced with new management challenges and that some provinces, such as Ontario, are undergoing important social, economic, and structural changes, standards of care in terms of conditions of confinement may be essential to ensure that incarcerated youth find themselves in the environment most conducive to rehabilitation and reintegration as prescribed by the *YCJA*.

D. IMPORTANCE OF STANDARDS OF CARE TO CONDITIONS OF CONFINEMENT

Addressing the basic necessities of youth who are detained (food, clothing, health care, education), minimizing their risk while under institutional care, and meeting their special needs are consistent with the rights accorded to all young persons as outlined in the *Convention on the Rights of the Child*. Addressing the basic components of safety, structure, activity, care, and justice can also be considered as matters of best practice for correctional institutions in order for effective rehabilitation and reintegration to take place.[50]

Though youth custody institutions have been designed to care and rehabilitate youthful offenders, they have historically been the target of persistent

46 *Ibid.*

47 *Ibid.*

48 *YCJA*, above note 16, s. 83(1)(a).

49 United Nations, *Convention on the Rights of the Child*, Can. T.S. 1992 No 3.

50 Gaylene J. Styve, Doris L. MacKenzie, Angela R. Gover, & Ojmarrh Mitchell, "Perceived Conditions of Confinement: A National Evaluation of Juvenile Boot Camps and Traditional Facilities" (2000) 24:3 Law and Human Behavior 297.

criticism in both Canada and the United States.[51] It has been argued that such facilities "do not rehabilitate, they do not punish, they are costly, they are abusive, they do not protect the public, and they contribute to future delinquency."[52] The majority of criticism regarding the abusive nature of institutions tends to be in regard to the conditions of confinement.[53] Arguably, youth need to see the behaviour of staff as justifiable, comprehensive, consistent, and fair in order for them to respect the authority and legitimacy of the institution — and hence to be willing to take advantage of available programming.[54]

Canada in the 1990s experienced a nationwide flurry of commissions of inquiry from provincial governments and reports from not-for-profit organizations that advocated for children, all of which expressed concern over the conditions of confinement for youth in custody and detention. The correctional system during this period was being severely taxed by the growing numbers of youth being sentenced to custody, and many institutions were operating above capacity. Several court cases supported the assertion by some youth that their *Charter* rights were being violated due to cruel and unusual treatment or punishment.[55] In the United States in this period, litigation was often used to effect change in juvenile facilities. For instance, *C.J.W. by and through L.W. v. State*[56] held that the state has a duty to protect youth who come under its custody and failure to provide information that results in a child's injury places potential liability on the state.[57]

The Law Commission of Canada's report on child abuse in Canadian institutions, *Restoring Dignity*,[58] provides a historical perspective on the treatment of Canadian children in government-run residential institutions over

---

51 Rolando V. del Carmen, Mary Parker, & Frances P. Reddington, *Briefs of Leading Cases in Juvenile Justice* (Cincinnati, OH: Anderson Publishing, 1998).

52 *Ibid.* at 229.

53 *Ibid.*

54 Alison Liebling, *Prisons and Their Moral Performance: A Study of Values, Quality, and Prison Life* (Oxford: Oxford University Press, 2004).

55 See, for example, *R. v. M.(T)*, 1991 CarswellOnt 107, 4 OR (3d) 203, [1991] OJ No 1382 (Prov Ct), in which King J held that youths were humiliated by the conditions of their holding cells and insensitive treatment by court officers. Additionally, in *R. v. E.T.F.* (2002), OJ No 4497, Weagant J held that conditions at the detention centre and the failure of correctional workers to protect a youth from peer-on-peer violence violated the youth's *Charter* rights.

56 853 P. 2d 4 (Kan. 1993).

57 Del Carmen, Parker, & Reddington, above note 51.

58 Law Commission of Canada, *Restoring Dignity: Responding to Child Abuse in Canadian Institutions* (Ottawa: The Commission, 2000).

seventy years (roughly 1900–70). The report groups institutions into four broad categories: special needs schools, child welfare facilities, youth detention facilities, and residential schools for Aboriginal children. It describes a litany of sexual, physical, and psychological abuse and notes that "it is undeniable that significant harm was done to children in many institutions that were designed for their benefit."[59] Conditions in facilities for Canadian children have vastly improved over the last forty years, but two of the Commission's three main findings undoubtedly remain true.[60] The findings describe conditions that are likely to be an inevitable part of being incarcerated:

- A significant power imbalance existed between the children and those in charge of the institutions and went beyond the obvious power imbalance between a child and an adult in a position of authority. Many staff had the added weight of institutional authority behind them, along with the official power of the government.
- There was little independent monitoring of these institutions. Often the desire to preserve the good name of an institution took precedence over the welfare of children.
- In addition to the vulnerabilities that other children experienced, children in youth custody facilities carried the stigma of conviction.

Before the release of the Law Commission's 2000 report, a 1997 review entitled *Safe and Secure: Eliminating Peer-to-Peer Violence in Ontario Phase II Secure Detention Facilities* attempted to "capitalize on existing knowledge to promote safe and secure detention facilities in Ontario's young offender system."[61] The authors suggest that the concerns of the Ministry of the Solicitor General and Correctional Services (Ontario) came "at a time when civil litigation in the United States has been re-shaping detention practice and when other provinces have already identified peer-to-peer violence as an important issue."[62] This review of reports on conditions in Canadian institutions confirms the high frequency of not only peer-on-peer victimization in youth facilities but also the questionable treatment of youth by some staff.

---

59 *Ibid.* at 4.

60 While the system is still imperfect, monitoring and advocacy for children in youth facilities has improved.

61 A.W. Leschied, A. Cunningham, & N. Mazaheri, *Safe and Secure: Eliminating Peer-to-Peer Violence in Ontario's Phase II Secure Detention Centres* (North Bay, ON: Ministry of Solicitor General and Correctional Services, 1997) at iii.

62 *Ibid.*

The Office of Child and Family Service Advocacy Ontario published a review of an Ontario youth custody facility based on interviews with both staff and youth at the facility.[63] It was instigated as a result of complaints from several youths at the facility regarding their care and treatment. The review identified problems with inadequate furnishings, lack of cleanliness in bathrooms and showers, poor quality and quantity of food, and a lack of programming. One of its findings, consistent with findings from other Canadian reviews and reports on peer-on-peer violence, was that staff were engaged in various forms of inappropriate treatment, including name calling and overuse of force during restraint.

The report also noted that many youths in custody exhibited extremely dysfunctional patterns of interaction, which they had developed as a necessary means of coping within their families of origin. The authors of the report argued that the youths "may be manipulative, and have the ability to provoke rage and aggression on the part of staff. They may set up staff to treat them as perhaps their parents did."[64] As the report emphasized, however, the unique challenges that incarcerated youth present never justify inappropriate treatment by staff, particularly the overuse of force.

The Saskatchewan Children's Advocate Office reviewed issues raised by youth within Saskatchewan custodial facilities between May 1997 and July 1998.[65] Several concerns were raised by the Advocate Office regarding overcrowding; a lack of standards and inconsistency in access to treatment, education, family contacts, and vocational treatment; and frequent transfers between facilities while awaiting sentencing. However, once again the report identified negative staff–resident interactions as the most serious area of concern.

The Ombudsman of British Columbia established the Task Force on Peer Abuse in 1990, which produced its report in 1994.[66] The Task Force was established to assist in the systematic review of peer abuse within British Columbia's youth custody centres. Like the Ontario and Saskatchewan reviews, the BC

63 Office of the Child and Family Service Advocacy, *Care of Youth at Thistletown Regional Centre Syl Apps Campus* (Toronto: The Office, 1992).

64 *Ibid.* at 2.

65 Saskatchewan Children's Advocate Office, *Issues Affecting Youth in Conflict with the Law: A Review of Issues Raised with Saskatchewan Children's Advocacy Office* (Saskatoon: The Office, 1999).

66 Ombudsman of British Columbia, *Building Respect: A Review of Youth Custody Centres in British Columbia*, Public Report No. 34 (June 1994), online: www.ombud.gov.bc.ca/publications/reports/Public_Reports/PR34_Building_Respect/building_respect.html.

review identified verbal abuse by staff and the difficulties of managing peer-on-peer violence in overcrowded facilities, but it did not suggest that staff played a direct role in violence. Instead the focus was on the seriousness of peer-on-peer victimizations and the fact that "bullying" may be a systemic problem. Bullying is only one aspect of institutional life, however, that has been a subject of concern with respect to the experience of incarcerated youth.

The Experiences of Phase II Male Young Offenders in Secure Facilities in the Province of Ontario,[67] a 1999 review, is disturbing not only because of its description of peer-on-peer violence in youth facilities but because of what it revealed about the degree of staff involvement in that violence. The purpose of the survey was to understand the experiences of youth in secure detention and secure custody. It was commissioned by the Canadian Foundation for Children, Youth and the Law during the course of a coroner's inquest into the death of a youth while he was in detention.[68] One hundred youth who had experienced Phase II secure custody in Ontario were interviewed. Isolation from family and friends, distance from home, lack of freedom, and problems with their physical environment were some of the general concerns these youth described. When asked, "What are the bad things about secure custody?" 31 percent mentioned problems with staff, 27 percent mentioned fighting and general security issues, and 19 percent mentioned other inmates.

Doob notes that "From the perspective of those youth who found themselves in secure Phase II facilities in Ontario, there is not only a fair amount of violence, but there is also a fair amount of staff involvement in creating or allowing this violence to occur."[69] According to youth surveyed, staff involvement in violence included putting inmates at risk by "letting bad things happen" (45.9 percent), putting an inmate's safety in jeopardy (46.9 percent), and bribing inmates to "discipline" other inmates (30.9 percent). The use of physical restraint by custodial staff appeared to be the biggest area of concern identified in the report. Physical restraint by staff was seen by youth as being violent, aggressive, and "scary" and also as a means of exercising power and control.[70]

---

67 Anthony N. Doob, *The Experiences of Phase II Male Young Offenders in Secure Facilities in the Province of Ontario* (Toronto: Canadian Foundation for Children, Youth and the Law 1999).

68 Ontario Ministry of the Solicitor General, *Verdict of the Jury at the Inquest in the Death of James Preston Lonnee* (Toronto: The Ministry, 1999).

69 Doob, above note 67 at 30.

70 Office of the Child and Family Service Advocacy, *Voices from Within: Youth in Care in Ontario* (Toronto: Queen's Printer for Ontario, 1998).

A review of the Toronto Youth Assessment Centre (TYAC) was commissioned as a result of a series of events in 2002 at the secure detention facility for Phase II (sixteen- and seventeen-year-old) youths.[71] These events included (1) the suicide of a young person, (2) media reports about conditions at the Centre, (3) judicial requests for the Office of the Child and Family Advocacy to intervene more actively at TYAC, and (4) concerns raised by incarcerated youth at TYAC on the level of peer-on-peer violence. The review identified several concerns, including limited programming and recreational activity, lack of proper clothing, poor food quality, limited physical space, and overcrowding.

The greatest concern raised by the review, however, was over the level of peer violence. Eighty-eight percent of the eighty-five youths interviewed reported witnessing or participating in peer-on-peer violence at TYAC. According to the review, the youths confirmed the presence of various types of peer violence such as soldiering, blowing bubbles, and degrading activity involving bodily fluids.[72]

The review suggested that only a few staff appeared to be complicit in peer violence. Excessive use of force by staff at TYAC did, however, appear to be a serious concern. Forty-two percent of respondents reported situations in which staff kicked, choked, or "smashed" a young person into a wall or threw a young person into a wall, table, or floor. A further 16 percent reported witnessing staff kicking a young person either in the head or the face.

Commissions of inquiry, the courts, and agencies that advocate for children have raised concerns regarding the conditions of confinement for youth in custody and detention in the decade leading up to the advent of *YCJA*. There is evidence to suggest, however, that conditions of confinement remain an issue for youth in Canada.[73] For example, the *Youth Partners Project*,[74] a report by the Canadian Council of Provincial Child and Youth Advocates

---

71 Office of the Child and Family Service Advocacy, *Review of Toronto Youth Assessment Centre (TYAC)* (Toronto: The Office, 2003).

72 Soldiering is defined as one youth demanding that another youth assault a third youth. The weakest youth or new arrivals to the unit are selected as soldiers. Blowing bubbles involves submerging a youth's head in a toilet and making them blow bubbles. Acts of degradation include forcing youth to drink urine or to lick spit or semen off the walls or floors.

73 McCreary Centre Society, *Time Out II: A Profile of B.C. Youth in Custody* (Vancouver: The Society, 2005); Cooke & Finlay, above note 41.

74 J. Finlay, K. Snow, & J. Mirwaldt, *Youth Partners Project* (Saskatoon: Canadian Council of Provincial Child & Youth Advocates, 2005).

(CCPYCA), arose out of concerns regarding the experiences of youth in custody both before and during the implementation of the *YCJA*. One hundred and forty-seven incarcerated youth in seven provinces[75] were surveyed about their experiences in custody from April 2002 to October 2003. The report raises serious concerns about the use of restraints and injuries sustained as a result of restraint, staff–youth relations, and the level of peer-on-peer violence in youth facilities across the country.

Recent incidents at the Roy McMurtry Youth Centre and the death of eighteen-year-old Ashley Smith have also raised serious concerns. Smith, a youth with mental health issues, spent several years in segregation at the New Brunswick Youth Centre before being transferred to an adult facility, where she committed suicide.[76] Given the dramatic changes that have occurred in the correctional system for youth, including the nature of the population itself, correctional staff will continue to face important management challenges. Standards of care and accountability guidelines will become increasingly important during this period of transition.

E. CONCLUSION

Canada has taken an important step with the *YCJA* in reducing the use of custody for youth in conflict with the law. However, ensuring the reduction of the use of custody may not be sufficient for the *YCJA* to fulfil its mandate completely. Some youth will continue to be admitted to custody and detention. Directing how youth will do their time, not just how many will do time, is clearly crucial to the success of the *YCJA*.

The treatment of incarcerated youth is critical. It is not clear that the public would want youths to leave a facility in worse condition than when they entered. In fact, many members of the public believe that assisting in the rehabilitation of a young offender is extremely important.[77] Youth who find themselves in detention or custody require an environment that is the least

---

75 British Columbia, Saskatchewan, Manitoba, Ontario, Nova Scotia, New Brunswick, and Newfoundland and Labrador.

76 The Ombudsman for New Brunswick is now calling for the Youth Centre to be closed down because of its lack of mental health programs for youth, overcrowding, and practice of detaining adults in the same facility.

77 A.N. Doob *et al.*, *An Exploration of Ontario Residents' Views of Crime and the Criminal Justice System* (Toronto: Centre of Criminology, University of Toronto, 1998).

repressive and the most conducive to rehabilitation and reintegration. Arguably, this could best be achieved by clear, enforceable standards of care.

The juvenile custodial population in Canada has shifted, creating a new correctional population. This new correctional reality and the structural transitions it has provoked in some provinces require further attention from the federal government. Steinberg, Chui, and Little[78] argue that a rehabilitative stance toward young offenders provides challenges to both practitioners and policy makers. Ensuring the proper care of the changing youth correctional population is perhaps the next important step for youth justice in Canada, and the next important iteration of the *YCJA*.

78 L. Steinberg, H. Chung Len, & M. Little, "Re-entry of Young Offenders from the Justice System: A Developmental Perspective" (2004) 2:1 Youth Violence and Juvenile Justice 21.

CHAPTER 7

The Last Chance Sanction in Youth Court: The Deferred Custody and Supervision Order

PETER J. CARRINGTON AND JULIAN V. ROBERTS

Reducing the use of custody as a sanction in youth court was a central, stated objective of the *Youth Criminal Justice Act* (*YCJA*),[1] and research has now demonstrated that the Act has achieved this goal. Significant reductions in admissions to custody have been achieved by emphasizing the importance of penal restraint and by creating a number of statutory bars to the imposition of a term of custody in youth court.[2]

With respect to the principle of restraint regarding the use of custody, the Preamble to the *YCJA* makes clear the intent of Parliament that Canada should "have a youth criminal justice system that reserves its most serious interventions for the most serious crimes and reduces the over-reliance on incarceration for non-violent young persons." The *YCJA* provides a detailed set of sentencing principles for youth court judges to apply, including an explicit acknowledgment of restraint with respect to the use of custody as a sanction. Thus section 38(2)(d) states that "all available sanctions other than custody

1 SC 2002, c. 1 [*YCJA*]; see Canada, Department of Justice, "Why Did the Government Introduce New Youth Justice Legislation?" (2009), online: www.justice.gc.ca/eng/pi/yj-jj/ycja-lsjpa/why-pourq.html.

2 For an analysis of trends in the use of custody in youth court, see Nicholas Bala, Peter Carrington, & Julian V. Roberts, "Evaluating the *Youth Criminal Justice Act* after Five Years" (2009) 51:2 Can J Criminol & Crim Justice 131. As with all our writing on the subject of youth justice, this chapter has benefited from the scholarship of Nick Bala, although the views expressed here are solely those of the authors.

that are reasonable in the circumstances must be considered with particular attention to the circumstances of aboriginal young persons." In addition, the Act creates a number of statutory impediments to the imposition of a custodial sentence in youth court. For example, section 39(1) establishes four "gateways" to custody. Unless the case appearing for sentencing conforms to one or more of these criteria, a term of custody may not be imposed.

There is also a final alternative available to courts. If the court has followed all the principles and the case has met the threshold for a custodial sentence, an additional non-custodial sanction is available to the court to avoid committing the defendant to custody: the Deferred Custody and Supervision Order (DCSO). Despite the importance and innovative nature of the DCSO, researchers and youth justice texts have paid scant attention to this sanction — new to youth courts as a result of the *YCJA*. This is surprising, in light of the potential of the DCSO to reduce the use of custody yet also to generate public and professional criticism if it is imposed for a serious crime of violence.[3]

The Deferred Custody and Supervision Order can be fully understood only in relation to the Custody and Supervision Order (C&SO) and the conditional sentence of imprisonment (at the adult level). The relationship between the C&SO and the DCSO is apparent: the latter is a deferred version of the former. But it is also necessary to consider the conditional term of imprisonment because the DCSO shares some features with that sanction (although with differences that will be brought out in the course of this chapter). The C&SO is a blended sentence that incorporates a period in custody, followed by period of community supervision. The components of the CSO conform to a two to one ratio, and combined may not exceed two years.[4] Thus the maximum custodial term that may be imposed is sixteen months, to be followed by eight months of community supervision with conditions.

This chapter explores the theory and practice of this novel youth court sanction, which has been available to youth courts since 2003. The chapter is divided into two parts. Section A discusses the statutory framework of the sanction, noting the parallels between the DCSO and its analogous sanction at the adult level, the Conditional Sentence of Imprisonment (CSI). Commentary to date has simply acknowledged that a DCSO is a youth court ver-

3 Julian V. Roberts, *The Virtual Prison: Community Custody and the Evolution of Imprisonment* (Cambridge: Cambridge University Press, 2004) at 136–38.

4 Or three years for certain serious offences.

sion of a CSI, but with a lower limit to reflect the shorter terms of custody imposed in youth court. In our view this is an oversimplification. Section B presents an examination of recent trends regarding use of the DCSO across Canada since the inception of the youth justice regime in 2003. We conclude by offering some speculations about the evolution of this sanction over the next few years.

A. STATUTORY FRAMEWORK OF THE DEFERRED CUSTODY AND SUPERVISION ORDER

As Bala and Anand note, the DCSO is similar to the adult conditional sentence.[5] The conditional sentence of imprisonment has been available to judges in adult court since 1996, following its introduction by Bill C-41, and has evolved considerably over the past decade, particularly as a result of a number of important decisions from the Supreme Court.[6] Accordingly, the experience with section 742 of the *Criminal Code*[7] provides a good context for an understanding of the application of DCSOs in youth court.

The adult prison population in Canada has been relatively stable over the past decade,[8] and conditional sentencing has played a role in constraining the number of sentenced admissions to custody. Research on the impact of the conditional sentence of imprisonment has revealed a clear decarceration effect.[9] However, this success has not been achieved without some cost to the public image of sentencing in the news media. Courts have been criticized for using the CSI for serious crimes of violence, and this criticism spurred the federal government to restrict the ambit of the conditional sentence at the adult level (see Section A(3) below in this chapter). The DCSO was

5 Nicholas Bala & Sanjeev Anand, *Youth Criminal Justice Law*, 2d ed. (Toronto: Irwin Law, 2009). A number of judgments have from the inception of the new youth justice regime acknowledged as much. For example, in *R. v. M.(H.A.)*, the court described the DCSO as "the youth equivalent to a conditional sentence." *R. v. M. (H.A.)*, [2003] MJ No 147 at para. 43 (Prov Ct), Swail J.

6 Bill C-41, *An Act to Amend the Criminal Code (Sentencing) and Other Acts in Consequence Thereof*, SC 1995, c. 22. For examples of its evolution, see *R. v. Proulx*, [2000] SCJ No 6 [*Proulx*]; see also the discussion in Julian V. Roberts, "Unearthing the Sphinx: The Evolution of Conditional Sentencing" (2001) 80 Can Bar Rev 1019.

7 RSC 1985, c. C-46 [*Criminal Code*].

8 Anthony N. Doob & Cheryl M. Webster, "Countering Punitiveness: Understanding Stability in Canada's Imprisonment Rate" (2006) 40 Law & Soc'y Rev 325.

9 Julian V. Roberts & Thomas Gabor, "Living in the Shadow of Prison: Lessons from the Canadian Experience in Decarceration" (2004) 39:1 Brit J Crim 92.

presumably created in order to provide courts with an additional means to restrain admissions to custody at the youth justice level.

1) Nature of a Deferred Custody and Supervision Order

In light of the negative publicity attracted by certain high-profile conditional sentence cases, it was a surprising (and bold) decision of the previous Liberal government to include an analogous sanction in the new youth justice statute. Perhaps mindful of the negative publicity associated with conditional sentencing, that federal government took steps to avoid some of the image problems associated with the CSI. Thus the *YCJA* equivalent was given a very different name, and was not described as a (conditional) sentence of imprisonment but as a *deferred* custodial order.

From the outset, then, it is important to note differences in the language used in section 742 of the *Criminal Code* and section 41(2)(p) of the *YCJA*. A conditional term of imprisonment is a sentence of custody that the offender purges in the community. The offender is actually sentenced to a term of imprisonment (section 742.1(a)) and then ordered to serve it in the community. The sentence is executed: committal to an institution remains a conditional possibility in the event that the offender fails to comply with court-imposed conditions. An offender who has completed a conditional sentence of imprisonment in the community, but who has not been admitted to custody, is nevertheless deemed to have purged a sentence of imprisonment. No element of a conditional sentence of imprisonment is deferred. In contrast to this, a DCSO is a custodial (and community supervision) order that is imposed, with a *deferred* custodial portion.[10] This sentence also requires the offender to comply with court-imposed conditions while residing in the community.

---

10 The Department of Justice materials describing the DCSO are somewhat confusing with respect to the relationship between the DCSO and the CSI, and indeed whether the DCSO is a sentence of custody. One document notes that the DCSO "should be considered, for most purposes, a type of custodial sentence because a breach of a condition can result in the young person serving the remainder of the sentence as a custody and supervision order." Canada, Department of Justice, "*YCJA* Explained — Youth Sentencing Options" (2005), online: www.collectionscanada.gc.ca/webarchives/20071210191408/http://www.justice.gc.ca/en/ps/yj/repository/3modules/04youth/3040301h.html. This passage raises two questions: first, for what purposes is the DCSO *not* a custodial sanction, and second, how does the possibility of committal to custody for non-compliance make a sanction a custodial disposition? After all, imprisonment is also a possible outcome for non-compliance with a probation order.

In this sense, the DCSO surely conforms more closely than does the CSI to the sword of Damocles model that underlies all conditional, deferred, and suspended sentences. The offender is threatened with a punishment (imposition of a custody and supervision order) more severe than the one initially imposed. Thus committal to custody is a threatened punishment hanging over the head of an offender who is still at liberty in the community, albeit subject to conditions. This is the first significant difference between the statutory frameworks of the DCSO and the CSI. While offenders in both categories are faced with the threat of institutionalization, conditional sentence offenders are deemed to be serving a term of custody. DCSO offenders are not. This said, the difference may be purely theoretical. In practice, courts may regard both sanctions as the most severe alternatives to custody, to be used when custody is warranted but circumstances may justify the imposition of this last possible non-custodial alternative.

Unlike the CSI then, the DCSO is not a term of custody *per se*, although it is subject to the same restrictions on its use as a custodial sentence. This latter requirement does not make it a term of custody but just serves as a filter to ensure that the DCSO is applied to the same offender population as a C&SO. This is a subtle but important difference and may explain why the government eschewed the language of the conditional sentence in favour of an alternative. If the sanction is different, so should be the name. That said, the use of the term *deferred* is surely as inaccurate as *conditional*. A period of open or secure custody is not *deferred* by a DCSO; it is imposed in response to non-compliance with court-ordered conditions. It makes no more sense to use the word *deferred* in this context than to state that students beginning a course receive a deferred failure — which will be imposed in the event that they do not comply with the course requirements and submit a final essay. The DCSO would more accurately be labelled a *suspended* sentence of custody; the custodial element is suspended and is not imposed unless and until the offender fails to comply with the conditions of the order. Why, then, did the government not adopt the language of suspension? In all likelihood because suspended sentences have attracted a negative public image, as a mild sanction without consequences.[11]

11 The poor public image of the suspended sentence is one reason that it fell into desuetude in England and Wales. See Anthony Bottoms, "The Suspended Sentence in England, 1967–1978" (1981) 21 Brit J Crim 1.

The ultimate aim of the DCSO is to confront a serious young offender with his or her offence in a way that holds the offender accountable but also avoids imprisonment and provides an incentive to reform. The incentive lies in the removal of the possibility of imprisonment at the end of the supervisory period. Accountability is achieved by the clear warning issued to the young person: contravention of the conditions of the order may well result in committal to custody. The clarity of the warning is enhanced by the fact that the resort to imprisonment for non-compliance is *relatively* certain and swift.[12] This characteristic distinguishes the DCSO from sanctions such as a traditional suspended sentence with probation used in other jurisdictions, where the consequences of non-compliance are far from certain and not necessarily severe. In short, the DCSO provides the court with the option of a credible threat to the young person; the order constitutes his or her last opportunity to avoid being committed to secure or open custody.

2) Criteria for Imposition of a C&SO and DCSO

a) C&SO

Section 39(1) of the *YCJA* sets out clear criteria that must be met before a young person may be committed to custody:

> A youth justice court shall not commit a young person to custody under section 42 (youth sentences) unless
>
> (a) the young person has committed a violent offence;
>
> (b) the young person has failed to comply with non-custodial sentences;
>
> (c) the young person has committed an indictable offence for which an adult would be liable to imprisonment for a term of more than two years and has a history that indicates a pattern of findings of guilt under this Act or the Young Offenders Act, chapter Y-1 of the Revised Statutes of Canada, 1985; or
>
> (d) in exceptional cases where the young person has committed an indictable offence, the aggravating circumstances of the offence are such that the imposition of a non-custodial sentence would be inconsistent with the purpose and principles set out in section 38.

12 The emphasis here is on "relatively" because the statute permits, but does not require, the conversion of a DCSO to a C&SO upon proven non-compliance with conditions.

b) DCSO

Section 42(1)(p) of the Act states that "subject to subsection (5), [the court may] make a deferred custody and supervision order that is for a specified period not exceeding six months, subject to the conditions set out in section 105(2), and to any conditions set out in subsection 105(3) that the court considers appropriate." In addition to the temporal restriction of six months, section 42(5) contains two additional restrictions on the sanction:

> The court may make a deferred custody and supervision order under paragraph (2)(p) if:
> (a) the young person is found guilty of an offence that is not a serious violent offence; and
> (b) it is consistent with the purpose and principles set out in section 38 and the restrictions on custody set out in section 39.

Before making a DCSO, then, the court must consider the purpose and principles of sentencing, to which we shall shortly turn. First, however, it is worth adding a word about the issue of excluded offences.

3) Statutory Exclusions

One of the most hotly debated issues with respect to conditional sentencing was whether there should be statutory exclusions of an offence-based nature. From the early days of the conditional sentencing regime, the federal government was repeatedly urged to create a statutory bar to the imposition of a conditional sentence for the more serious crimes of violence.[13] Such offences from time to time attract a CSI and with it considerable criticism in the news media. The imposition of a CSI in serious personal injury cases was made possible by the high maximum length threshold set by Parliament: in practice, few crimes in Canada attract a custodial term outside the range of a conditional sentence, even the more serious personal injury offences. Had the federal government set the threshold lower in 1996, these cases could not have resulted in a conditional sentence of imprisonment. On the other hand, a significantly lower ceiling, such as twelve months, would have impaired the ability of the sanction to reduce the volume of admissions to custody. In any

---

13 See, for example, the proposal submitted on behalf of the Alberta Attorney General: Alberta Justice and Attorney General, *The Conditional Sentence of Imprisonment: The Need for Amendment* (Edmonton: Alberta Justice and Attorney General, 2003).

event, Parliament ultimately restricted the ambit of the conditional sentence regime in legislation assented to in May 2007. Bill C-9[14] eliminated the discretion of an adult court to impose a CSI for a "serious personal injury" offence as defined in section 752 of the *Criminal Code*, which is prosecuted by way of indictment and for which the statutory maximum is ten years or more.

The statutory bar for the DCSO is that it may not be imposed for a "serious violent offence." Both statutory exclusions thereby create a penological anomaly: a sentencing court is prevented from imposing a CSI or a DCSO in such cases but not from imposing a lesser sanction, for example, a suspended sentence at the adult level, or an extrajudicial measure or any of a range of non-custodial sanctions in youth court. If the prohibition on a conditional sentence or DCSO is created in the interests of protecting the principle of proportionality, the imposition of a lesser sanction will subvert the intention of the legislation.[15]

4) Maximum Length of a Deferred Custody and Supervision Order

For most offences prosecuted in adult courts, a conditional sentence is available to replace terms of imprisonment up to two years less one day (assuming that the other statutory prerequisites are met). By eliminating federal terms of imprisonment from consideration, Parliament was effectively setting a ceiling (albeit a very high one, in terms of the numbers of custodial sentences within the ambit of the sanction).[16] The most serious offences, which would result in a term of custody of a length that must be served in a federal penitentiary, are excluded from consideration of a conditional sentence. The ceiling for a DCSO is considerably lower: the duration of the order that is deferred may not exceed six months.

By setting a lower maximum length for the DCSO, the government probably hoped to avoid the kinds of headlines attracted by the CSI when it was imposed for a serious crime of violence.[17] The high statutory limit of the adult

14 Bill C-9, *An Act to Amend the Criminal Code (Conditional Sentence of Imprisonment)*, SC 2007, c. 12.

15 This is yet another example of the consequences that may arise when sentencing reform proceeds on an unsystematic basis, with Parliament making decisions about one statutory provision without realizing the consequences for sentencing as a whole.

16 Sentencing statistics reveal that almost all cases of sexual assault, sexual abuse, break and enter, assault with a weapon, and aggravated assault result in sentences of less than two years. See Table 1 in Roberts & Gabor, above note 9.

17 Examples of newspaper headlines included "Mom Put Girl in Freezer, Gets Conditional Sentence"; "Sex Offender Walks Free"; "Law on Sentencing Far Too

sanction permitted courts to impose a conditional sentence for very serious crimes of violence,[18] assuming the other statutory requirements were met. However, as we shall demonstrate in the course of this essay, the *YCJA* ceiling is in reality as permissive as that associated with the conditional sentence.

One justification for a limit on the use of a conditional sentence at the adult level is that the imposition of a conditional sentence instead of a penitentiary term would compromise the fundamental purpose and principle of sentencing, since sentence lengths of two years or longer are imposed only for the most serious offences. The lower youth court level (six months rather than two years less one day) might suggest that the DCSO is intended to be used for a more restricted range of seriousness. (Otherwise the upper limit might have been set higher than six months.) It is important to note, however, that the shorter sentence lengths imposed in youth court mean that the vast majority of sentenced young persons would meet the criterion of six months or less.

In fact, the statutory ceilings for the DCSO and the CSI restrict approximately the same proportion of custodial cases. According to the latest data from Statistics Canada, only 7 percent of custody and supervision orders imposed in youth courts in 2006–7 were in excess of six months and therefore beyond the ambit of a DCSO.[19] Adult court data for the same year demonstrate that 5 percent of custodial terms were two years or longer and therefore above the conditional sentence threshold.[20] The thresholds of the two sanctions therefore filter approximately the same volume of cases, and may be considered functionally equivalent.

Lenient"; and "Cushy Sentence a Miscarriage" (see Roberts, above note 3, Box 7.1, for further examples). It is important to add that although public opinion polls suggested widespread opposition to conditional sentencing, when members of the public are provided with actual cases to consider or are given more information about the nature of a conditional sentence, there is considerable support except with respect to crimes of violence. See Trevor Sanders & Julian V. Roberts, "Public Attitudes toward Conditional Sentencing: Results of a National Survey" (2000) 32 Can J Behavioural Science 199.

18 Such as a manslaughter. See, for example, *R. v. Turcotte*, [2000] OJ No 1316 (CA), where the defendant had strangled his own mother.

19 Jennifer Thomas, "Youth Court Statistics, 2006/2007" (May 2008) 28:4 Juristat 6, online: www.statcan.gc.ca/cgi-bin/af-fdr.cgi?l=eng&loc=/pub/85-002-x/85-002-x2008004-eng.pdf.

20 Michael Marth, "Adult Criminal Court Statistics, 2006/2007" (May 2008) 28:5 Juristat 7, online: www.statcan.gc.ca/pub/85-002-x/2008005/article/10567-eng.htm.

B. TRENDS IN THE USE OF DEFERRED CUSTODY AND SUPERVISION ORDERS

1) Overall Volume of DCSOs Imposed across Jurisdictions

a) Adequacy of Data Sources

It is disappointing — for practitioners as well as scholars — that fully seven years after proclamation of the new statute, comprehensive statistics relating to sentencing in youth courts across Canada are still unavailable. In order to explore the use of the DCSO, researchers need to draw upon *three* separate data sources, each covering a different period and each with different participating jurisdictions.[21] The piecemeal and patchwork nature of the available statistics makes it challenging to draw conclusions about the use of the DCSO across the country, and especially about trends over time in its use. More important, the absence of good data regarding the outcomes of DCSOs means that courts are to a degree sentencing in the dark, unaware of the likely consequences of imposing these orders.[22] It is imperative, we submit, that greater resources be devoted to developing a more adequate database with respect to the youth justice system.

---

21 The three databases are the Youth Court Survey (YCS, online: www.statcan.gc.ca/imdb-bmdi/3309-eng.htm) (later merged into the Integrated Criminal Court Survey, or ICCS), which provides sentencing data; the Youth Custody and Community Services Survey (YCCS, online: www.statcan.gc.ca/imdb-bmdi/3323-eng.htm), which provides data on admissions to community and custodial corrections; and the Corrections Key Indicators Report (CKIR, online: www.statcan.gc.ca/imdb-bmdi/3313-eng.htm), which provides data on average daily counts of young persons who are under the supervision of community and custodial correctional authorities. All are maintained by the Canadian Centre for Justice Statistics, a division of Statistics Canada. At the time of writing (early 2010), the most recent published data were as follows: fiscal 2006–7 for sentencing (Thomas, above note 19), lacking current and historical data for Saskatchewan, and historical data for Newfoundland and Labrador and Manitoba; 2007–8 for admissions (Rebecca Kong, "Youth Custody and Community Services, 2007/2008," online: (May 2009) 29:2 Juristat, online: www.statcan.gc.ca/pub/85-002-x/2009002/article/10846-eng.htm), lacking current and historical data for Prince Edward Island and Nunavut, and historical data for British Columbia; and 2008–9 for average daily counts (Statistics Canada, "Adult and Youth Correctional Services: Key Indicators" (8 December 2009) *The Daily*, online: www.statcan.gc.ca/daily-quotidien/091208/dq091208-eng.pdf), lacking current and historical data for Prince Edward Island, Nova Scotia, and the three territories.

22 See Section B(6), below in this chapter. Once again, there are parallels with the conditional sentencing regime. For many years the only data came from certain jurisdictions and shed no light on critical issues such as breach rates and the judicial response to founded breaches. Even today we still do not have comprehensive, national statistics regarding the success rates of conditional sentences.

b) DCSOs Imposed as a Percentage of Cases Appearing for Sentencing

Some trends are clear, however. Sentencing statistics for 2006–7 from all provinces and territories except Saskatchewan reveal that DCSOs account for a relatively small percentage of all sentences imposed in youth court. In that year, of 31,120 cases appearing in youth court for sentencing 1,080, or 3.5 percent, attracted a DCSO, while 17 percent of cases attracted a custodial order.[23] In contrast, a CSI was imposed in 5.1 percent of cases sentenced in adult court in the same year.[24] Tustin and Lutes conclude that the DCSO "is gaining popularity with the judiciary."[25] The sentencing statistics offer little support for this conclusion. A DCSO was imposed in 3.5 percent of cases sentenced in 2004–5, 3.9 percent in 2005–6, and 3.7 percent in 2006–7.[26] However, more recent data for admissions and for average daily counts provide limited support for this assertion.

From the limited statistical information available, it seems likely that a small number of cases resulting in custody in the first years under the new sentencing regime were in later years attracting a DCSO or a probation order. Over the period 2004–5 to 2006–7, custodial sentences declined slightly as a proportion of *all* sentences imposed (from 13 to 11 percent).[27] The proportion of DCSOs and probation sentences increased slightly over the same period, from 1.8 percent to 2.2 percent and from 39 percent to 40 percent respectively, and the proportion accounted for by all other sentences remained unchanged at 46 percent. If this is the case generally, it parallels developments at the adult level, where, over time, the CSI attracted a wider range of cases.[28]

---

23 Probation accounted for the highest percentage of cases, 59 percent. Multiple sentences were frequent; on average, each case appearing for sentencing received 1.5 different dispositions.

24 In Canada excluding Quebec, for which data were not available. The percentage of CSIs reported by Marth (above note 20 at 15, Table 5) for Canada has been adjusted to account for the missing data for Quebec.

25 Lee Tustin & Robert E. Lutes, *A Guide to the* Youth Criminal Justice Act, *2009/2010 Edition* (Toronto: LexisNexis, 2009).

26 These percentages are based on Canada excluding Newfoundland and Labrador, Prince Edward Island, Manitoba, and Saskatchewan, due to missing data for these jurisdictions for some years. Fiscal 2003–4 is omitted because few jurisdictions have reported DCSO sentences for that year.

27 Percentages cited in this paragraph differ from those in the previous paragraphs because they are percentages of all sentences imposed, rather than of cases sentenced.

28 Roberts, above note 3.

c) Numbers of DCSOs Imposed

In assessing trends over time in the volume of DCSOs, we concentrate on the number of persons admitted to a DCSO, as these data are available for a longer period (2004–8) than sentencing data. In addition, the admissions trends conform closely to the patterns for average daily count data.

The admissions data show a stable pattern of DCSOs from 2004–5 to 2006–7,[29] but a 13 percent increase (to 1,579) in the most recent year for which data are available (2007–8). From 2004–5 to 2007–8, the overall increase in admissions to DCSOs was 11 percent.[30] The Canada-wide trend masks considerable variation between jurisdictions. As can be seen in Table 1, DCSO admissions increased by 40 percent in Manitoba, 32 percent in Saskatchewan, and 26 percent in Quebec, yet decreased by a similar percentage in Nova Scotia (34 percent). Alberta reported a small decline of 8 percent in DCSO admissions over four years. In Ontario, the four-year pattern is one of stability in DCSO admissions, except for a temporary increase in 2004–5.

Table 1: Admissions to DCSO, Canada and Provinces, 2004/05 to 2007/08

Jurisdiction	2004/05	2005/06	2006/07	2007/08	% change, 2004/05 to 2007/08
Canada	1,419	1,472	1,402	1,579	+11%
Nova Scotia	98	92	73	65	−34%
New Brunswick	107	145	91	116	+8%
Quebec	148	132	167	186	+26%
Ontario	502	554	510	490	−2%
Manitoba	121	153	148	169	+40%
Saskatchewan	167	159	187	220	+32%
Alberta	249	206	206	230	−8%

Note: Excludes jurisdictions not reporting or reporting fewer than 20 admissions.

Source: Youth Custody and Community Services Survey, Statistics Canada (www.statcan.gc.ca/imdb-bmdi/3323-eng.htm).

29 For Canada excluding Prince Edward Island, British Columbia, and Nunavut, the numbers of youth admitted to a DCSO were 1,419, 1,472, and 1,402 for 2004–5 to 2006–7, respectively.

30 As noted, these statistics mirror those of average daily counts of young persons on DCSOs (as they should); the average daily DCSO count for Canada (excluding Prince Edward Island, Nova Scotia, and the Northwest Territories) was stable from 2004–5 to 2006–7 and then increased by 12 percent in 2007–8 and by an additional 7 percent in 2008–9.

The numbers of admissions to DCSOs, and by implication of DCSOs imposed, may seem modest but it is important to see them in context. First, 2007–8 is only the fifth year under the new youth justice regime. The conditional sentence of imprisonment accounted for relatively few sentences imposed in the first years of the new adult sentencing regime, before accelerating in volume once the courts became more comfortable with the concept. The same evolution may well occur with respect to the DCSO, as courts become more familiar with the new sanction and more confident in imposing it. On a Canada-wide basis, there was a year-over-year increase of 13 percent in admissions to DCSOs in 2007–8, and a further 7 percent increase in the average daily count data for 2008–9. These increases in admissions and average daily counts for the two past years are the best indication — in the absence of recent sentencing data — that DCSOs are beginning to be more widely used.

Second, custodial sentences are used much less often in youth court than in adult court. In 2006–7, 17 percent of cases sentenced in youth court received a sentence of custody and supervision, versus 34 percent of cases in adult court that received a sentence of imprisonment.[31] If the DCSO and CSI are used as substitutes for custodial sentences, then the pool of cases from which those receiving DCSOs are drawn is only half as large as that for CSIs. If we define the "custodial caseload" as the sum of cases receiving custodial sentences and cases receiving the DCSO (or CSI, in adult court), then in 2006–7, CSIs represented 11 percent of the custodial caseload, and DCSOs represented 18 percent: a much higher percentage. Thus although the DCSO has been available to courts for a shorter period than the CSI, it appears to have already been more successful as a substitute for a custodial sentence than its counterpart in adult court.

2) Variation across Jurisdictions

As noted, across all jurisdictions reporting data, DCSOs represented 3.5 percent of all sentenced cases in 2006–7. This aggregate statistic masks considerable variation. No cases resulted in the imposition of this sanction in the Yukon, Northwest Territories, or Prince Edward Island, while fully 8 percent of sentenced cases in Nova Scotia, 7 percent in New Brunswick, and 6 percent in British Columbia resulted in this disposition being imposed.

---

31 Marth, above note 20 at 15, Table 5.

a) A Digression on Regional Disparities

As in other areas of youth justice, a striking contrast exists between Ontario and Quebec, with courts in the latter province using the DCSO far less frequently. Over the three-year period 2004–5 to 2006–7, 1,534 DCSOs were imposed in Ontario youth courts, compared to only 203 in the province of Quebec. In part this difference is due to the disproportionately low numbers (relative to the rest of Canada) of young people brought to court and found guilty in Quebec, reflecting the province's "unique system of pre-court screening."[32] However, this is not the whole story. The use of DCSOs is much less frequent in Quebec than in Ontario (or in most other provinces) even when expressed as a proportion of cases found guilty: over the three-year period, 1.4 percent of sentenced cases in Quebec resulted in the imposition of a DCSO, compared to 3.5 percent in Ontario. Correctional admissions data from 2007–8 reveal the same pattern: in Ontario, 4.1 percent of youth admitted to community and custodial corrections had received a DCSO, compared to only 1.5 percent in Quebec.[33]

This contrast in the use of the DCSO parallels the relative use of custodial sentences in the two provinces: over the same three-year period, 12 percent of all sentenced cases in Quebec received a community and supervision order, versus 24 percent in Ontario. As Bala and Anand note, "youth court judges in Quebec place an emphasis on *limited* accountability, addressing needs and rehabilitation of adolescent offenders."[34] Of course aggregate differences in custody rates may disappear when specific offences or offence categories are examined, as shown in Tables 2 and 3.

---

32 Bala, Carrington, & Roberts, above note 2 at 141.

33 Since a DCSO may not be imposed in a case that would otherwise not warrant a custodial sentence, and since youth court judges in Quebec are much less likely to find that cases warrant custodial sentences, it follows that they would also impose fewer DCSOs. Consequently, it is surprising that the average daily count of young offenders serving a DCSO during the same period of 2004–5 to 2006–7 was approximately the same in Quebec (149) as in Ontario (155). The explanation for this apparent paradox should lie in the relative lengths of DCSOs imposed and/or actually served in the two provinces. Unfortunately, data on DCSO sentence lengths and time served on DCSOs are not available for Quebec, so this explanation cannot be confirmed. However, data on *custodial* sentence lengths for Quebec and Ontario suggest support for the hypothesis. The median custodial sentence length imposed in youth court for each of these three years was thirty days in Ontario, but ranged from sixty to ninety days in Quebec. The longer custodial (and apparently DCSO) sentences in Quebec appear to reflect the practice of Quebec judges of reserving custodial sentences (and DCSOs) for the most serious cases.

34 Bala & Anand, above note 5 at 175 [emphasis in original].

Table 2 provides comparisons for specific high-frequency offences and offence categories. These data show the same pattern of disparity. For example, in 2006–7, the custody rate (excluding DCSOs) for robbery in Ontario was twice the rate in Quebec (48 percent versus 24 percent). For theft, the Ontario custody rate was almost three times the rate in Quebec (14 percent versus 5 percent). Since the DCSO is considered a form of custody, Table 3 shows the combined DCSO and C&SO rates for the two provinces. This makes the contrast between the provinces even clearer. As can be seen, young persons sentenced in the province of Ontario are generally twice as likely as their counterparts in Quebec to receive a sentence of custody.

Table 2: Custody Rates, Quebec and Ontario, 2006/07

	Quebec	Ontario
Crimes against the person	12%	22%
Robbery	24%	48%
Major assault*	13%	24%
Common assault	5%	14%
Crimes against property	8%	17%
Break and enter	12%	23%
Theft	5%	14%
Other *Criminal Code*	13%	21%

Source: Youth Court Survey, Statistics Canada (www.statcan.gc.ca/imdb-bmdi/3309-eng.htm).

Notes: Percent of sentenced cases that received a custody and supervision order.

* "Major assault" includes assault level 2 (with a weapon or causing bodily harm; *Criminal Code* s. 267), assault level 3 (aggravated assault; s. 268), unlawfully causing bodily harm (s. 269), and assaulting a peace officer (s. 270).

Table 3: "Custody Plus" Rates (C&SO and DCSO), Quebec and Ontario, 2006/07

	Quebec	Ontario
Crimes against the person	15%	27%
Robbery	29%	56%
Major assault*	16%	30%
Common assault	7%	16%
Crimes against property	10%	19%
Break and enter	14%	25%
Theft	6%	16%
Other *Criminal Code*	15%	24%

Source: Youth Court Survey, Statistics Canada (www.statcan.gc.ca/imdb-bmdi/3309-eng.htm).

Notes: Percent of sentenced cases that received a DCSO or a custody and supervision order.

* See notes to Table 2 for the definition of "Major assault."

To conclude this brief diversion into interprovincial disparities in youth court, it is important to acknowledge that the constitutional nature of Canada permits a significant degree of jurisdictional variation in the administration of justice. Nevertheless, to the extent that the differential use of custody and deferred custody reflects factors other than the characteristics of cases being sentenced, this Quebec–Ontario differential is surely very troubling. It means that offenders convicted of the same predicate conduct are treated very differently depending upon the province in which they are sentenced.

3) Offences Resulting in a DCSO

A number of interesting patterns emerge with respect to the specific offences and offence categories resulting in a DCSO. First, almost half (39 percent) of all DCSOs imposed in 2006–7 were handed down for crimes against the person. Property crime accounted for an additional 27 percent and other offences the remaining 34 percent. Within these categories, break and enter accounted for the highest proportion (38 percent) of DCSOs imposed for property offences, while failing to comply with a judicial order[35] accounted for approximately 60 percent of DCSOs imposed for "other" offences, or 19 percent of all DCSOs. It will be interesting to see whether the DCSO increasingly replaces the C&SO as the sentence favoured by courts in response to failures to appear for court and failures to comply with conditions of probation. Historically, youth found guilty of these offences have faced a high probability of receiving a custodial sentence — a probability in the same range as youth found guilty of homicide. The DCSO may prove to be the sentence of choice for these administrative offences, which were considered in the past to warrant a custodial sentence, although such a sentence is grossly disproportionate to their seriousness. On the other hand, a youth who has wilfully breached the conditions of his or her probation order may not be a good candidate for the more stringent conditions of a DCSO.

Table 4 provides a comparison between the DCSO and the CSI caseloads for the year 2006–7. As can be seen, the proportion of DCSOs imposed for crimes against the person is significantly higher than the percentage of CSIs imposed for this category of offending (39 percent compared to 26 per-

---

35 These are mostly failure to comply with a community disposition; that is, breach of probation conditions.

cent). The proportion of DCSO cases involving a property crime as the most serious offence was lower than at the adult level.

Table 4: Offence Category Breakdown, Deferred Custody and Supervision Order and the Conditional Sentence of Imprisonment, Canada, 2006/07

	DCSO	CSI
Crimes against the person	39%	26%
Crimes against property	27%	32%
Other *Criminal Code* (except traffic)	15%	15%
Criminal Code traffic	2%	8%
Other federal statutes	18%	19%
Total	100%	100%

Sources: Adult Criminal Court Survey (www.statcan.gc.ca/imdb-bmdi/3312-eng.htm) and Youth Court Survey (www.statcan.gc.ca/imdb-bmdi/3309-eng.htm), Statistics Canada.

Notes: DCSO data exclude Saskatchewan; CSI data exclude Quebec.

At the adult level, the conditional sentence of imprisonment created considerable controversy when violent offences resulting in a conditional sentence caught the attention of the news media. It is therefore worth examining the application of the DCSO for this category of offending in more detail. Table 5 presents a breakdown of the offences resulting in imposition of a DCSO across the jurisdictions for a violent crime in 2006–7. There will always be exceptional cases of violence for which the "last chance sanction" is appropriate. However, well over 100 cases (28 percent of DCSOs imposed for crimes against the person) involved a major assault conviction, and a similar percentage of DCSOs were imposed for robbery. These are among the most serious offences in the *Criminal Code*. Their presence in this table reflects one of the criteria for this sentence, namely, that the case would call for a sentence of imprisonment were it not for the availability of the DCSO. Although section 42(5)(a) of the *YCJA* prohibits use of the DCSO in a case of a "serious violent offence," and although many of these offences are *prima facie* serious violent offences, the DCSO can still be used as long as there has been no Crown application under section 42(9) leading to a judicial determination that the offence is a "serious violent offence."

This issue calls for more detailed analysis. Many people would find it surprising that an offender could be convicted of a major assault or a robbery and then receive a sanction that is excluded for all convictions of a "serious violent nature." However, the statistical category "major assault" includes several *Criminal Code* offences, namely, aggravated assault, assault with a weapon or causing bodily harm, unlawfully causing bodily harm, and assaulting a peace officer, and these offences in turn cover a broad range of behaviours.[36] Similarly, while "robbery" is defined as a violent offence, a particular instance of robbery may involve minimal violence. Understanding how these cases passed through the statutory provision which precludes the imposition of a DCSO for convictions involving a serious violent offence (s. 42.(5)) would require a closer examination of the case files. To our knowledge, this research has yet to be undertaken. It is also striking that eighty-nine cases of the relatively minor offence of common assault resulted in a DCSO. It would be interesting to know what factors in these cases led to the judicial determination that a custodial sentence was warranted.

Table 5: Breakdown of DCSOs Imposed for an Offence against the Person, Canada, 2006/07

Offence or Offence Category	% of DCSOs with this offence or offence category	Number of Cases
Major assault*	28%	117
Robbery	27%	113
Common assault	21%	89
Sexual assault	8%	35
Uttering threats	8%	34
Other sexual offences	4%	17
Homicide	<1%	1
Other crimes against the person	4%	16
Total	100%	422

Source: Youth Court Survey, Statistics Canada (www.statcan.gc.ca/imdb-bmdi/3309-eng.htm).

Note: Excludes Saskatchewan.

*See notes to Table 2 for the definition of "Major assault."

Table 6 compares the breakdown of DCSO cases involving a crime against the person with conditional sentence cases falling into this offence category. On the whole, the breakdowns are remarkably similar, with the notable exception of robbery. Over one-quarter of DCSOs but fewer than

36 See, for example, the definition of "bodily harm" in the *Criminal Code*, above note 7, s. 2: "any hurt or injury to a person that interferes with the health or comfort of the person and that is more than merely transient or trifling in nature."

one-tenth of CSIs were imposed in cases with robbery as the most serious offence. Once again, the offence of robbery covers a wide range of behaviours. It may well be that many youths tend to commit less sophisticated and less violent robberies than many adults. Indeed, it is not unheard of for a youth to be convicted of robbery for threatening someone or assaulting someone and stealing an item of the victim's clothing: "I like your shoes. Give them to me or else." This type of robbery appears quite rarely in adult court.

Table 6: Breakdown of DCSOs and CSIs Imposed for an Offence against the Person, Canada, 2006/07

Offence or Offence Category	% of DCSOs with this offence or offence category	% of CSIs with this offence or offence category
Major assault*	28% (n = 111)	36% (n = 937)
Robbery	27% (113)	9% (245)
Common assault	21% (89)	26% (661)
Sexual assault	8% (35)	9% (244)
Uttering threats	8% (34)	10% (257)
Other sexual offences	4% (17)	4% (100)
Homicide	<1% (1)	<1% (3)
Other crimes against the person	4% (16)	3% (74)
Total	100% (422)	100% (2,581)

Sources: For DCSO data: Youth Court Survey (www.statcan.gc.ca/imdb-bmdi/3309-eng.htm), Statistics Canada. For CSI data: Michael Marth, "Adult Criminal Court Statistics, 2006/2007," Table 5, online: (May 2008) 28:5 Juristat 7, online: www.statcan.gc.ca/pub/85-002-x/2008005/article/10567-eng.htm at 15.

Notes: DCSO data exclude Saskatchewan; CSI data exclude Quebec.

*See notes to Table 2 for the definition of "Major assault."

4) Length of Orders

As noted, there is a six-month statutory limit on a DCSO.[37] Table 7 shows the lengths of DCSO sentences to be served for youth admitted in 2007–8 — again only for selected jurisdictions. In these provinces and territories,

37 Since the maximum length of a DCSO is six months, it is surprising that according to the Youth Custody and Community Services Survey, some 3 percent of youth admitted to serve a DCSO had sentences of more than six months, and a couple of youth had sentences of more than one year. These anomalies may arise from cases in which the DCSO was to be followed by another sentence, such as probation, and the total length of the combined sentences was erroneously coded. For this reason they have been omitted from Table 6.

just under half (45 percent) of DCSO admissions were for three months or less, and the remainder were for between three and six months. However, the proportions varied greatly between jurisdictions.

As can be seen in Table 7, in Nova Scotia and Manitoba all or almost all DCSOs were for three months or less. In the other provinces for which data are available, sentence lengths reveal a very different distribution. In New Brunswick, Ontario, Alberta, and British Columbia, almost two-thirds or more of DCSOs fell between three and six months. The median lengths of DCSOs also reveal great variation, being lowest in Yukon (8 days) and highest in New Brunswick (182 days). Some of this cross-jurisdictional variation may be explained by variability in the characteristics of cases appearing for sentencing,[38] but it is also likely that it reflects different judicial attitudes to the use of this sanction. If experience with the conditional sentence of imprisonment at the adult level is any guide, the latter explanation is more plausible. Research on the CSI has repeatedly demonstrated wide variation across the country in the use of conditional sentencing.[39]

Although it is hard to make direct comparisons, the sentence length statistics reveal that youth courts are using the entire statutory range of sentence length for the DCSO — more so than adult courts use the conditional sentence. One way of comparing the two distributions is to note that over half the DCSOs are found in the upper half of the distribution (see Table 7). In contrast, conditional sentence orders in the upper half of the range are relatively rare; even for crimes of violence, fewer than one-tenth of CSIs are eighteen months or longer, and fewer than one-fifth are in the twelve months to two years less one day interval.[40]

---

38 It is possible (but in our view, unlikely) that on average the cases appearing for sentencing are systematically more, or less, serious in certain provinces. However, the comparison of sentencing in Ontario and Quebec for specific offences, above in this chapter, Section B(2)(a), suggests that interprovincial variations in the seriousness of cases do not adequately explain variations in sentencing patterns.

39 For example, Avani Barbooram, "The Changing Profile of Adults in Custody, 2006/07" (December 2008) 28:10 Juristat Table 14, online: www.statcan.gc.ca/pub/85-002-x/2008010/article/10732-eng.htm.

40 *Ibid.*

Table 7: Length of DCSOs to Be Served, Selected Jurisdictions, 2007/08

Jurisdiction	% DCSOs of 3 months or less	% DCSOs between 3 and 6 months	Median length, in days	Total Number of Admissions
Newfoundland and Labrador	35%	65%	153	17
Nova Scotia	100%	0%	—	64
New Brunswick	18%	82%	182	102
Ontario	37%	63%	123	486
Manitoba	92%	8%	28	144
Alberta	36%	64%	123	215
British Columbia	30%	70%	120	73
Yukon	100%	0%	8	9
Total	45%	55%	—	1,110

Source: Youth Custody and Community Services Survey, Statistics Canada (www.statcan.gc.ca/imdb-bmdi/3323-eng.htm).

Note: — Not available.

Data do not include jurisdictions reporting fewer than 5 DCSO admissions, or DCSOs with a recorded length in excess of six months.

5) Profile of Offenders Serving a DCSO

There is no systematic evidence that DCSOs are used to a greater or lesser extent for one gender, age group, or ethnic group. Male offenders are slightly more likely than females to receive a custodial sentence and slightly more likely to receive a DCSO; females are more likely to receive other types of sentence. Thus across Canada (excluding Saskatchewan) in 2006–7, 12 percent of male offenders received a custody and supervision order, 2.3 percent a DCSO, and 86 percent some other sentence as their most serious sentence. The pattern for female offenders was little different: 10 percent custody, 1.8 percent DCSO, and 88 percent other dispositions. Offenders aged sixteen or seventeen years were slightly more likely than younger offenders to receive a custodial sentence (12 percent versus 10 percent), and slightly more likely to receive a DCSO (2.3 percent versus 2.0 percent); younger offenders were more likely to receive other sentences. These modest demographic differences may well reflect the fact that young offenders who are male or near the limits of juvenile jurisdiction are more likely to commit more serious offences, and are therefore more likely to meet the criteria for custody.

It is surprising that the DCSO does not appear to be used more often for the younger age group. If the sanction is designed to act as a barrier to custody for those who have met the custodial threshold, the twelve- to fifteen-year-old age group intuitively appears to be the one that should benefit more from the availability of the DCSO. However, not only are the proportions of cases receiving a DCSO similar in the two age groups (2.3 percent of sixteen- and seventeen-year-olds versus 2.0 percent of twelve- to fifteen-year-olds), but the proportion of the total custodial caseload[41] represented by DCSOs is also similar: 17 percent for the younger group and 16 percent for the older group. If substitution of the DCSO for a C&SO were considered more appropriate for younger offenders, the proportion would be considerably higher for the younger group.

Admissions data show that in cases for which the youth's Aboriginal identity was known, those who reported being Aboriginal were slightly more likely than non-Aboriginal youth to be admitted to serve a custodial sentence (17 percent versus 14 percent of non-Aboriginal offenders), and more likely to be admitted to a DCSO (7.8 percent versus 5.5 percent of non-Aboriginal offenders).[42] Non-Aboriginal youth were more likely to have other types of sentence. The higher likelihood of an Aboriginal young offender being admitted to a DCSO may reflect the influence of section 38(2)(d) of the *YCJA*. This provision mirrors section 718.2(e) of the adult sentencing provisions of the *Criminal Code*.[43] It encourages courts to make an additional effort to find a non-custodial alternative for Aboriginal offenders, and the DCSO represents an obvious vehicle by which to put this principle into practice.[44]

These modest associations between the young offender's age, sex, and Aboriginal identity and the probability of receiving a DCSO should not be taken as evidence of discrimination. They could easily be explained by the influence of other factors related to age, sex, and ethnicity, such as the type of offence, the prior record of findings of guilt, or even (in the case of Aboriginal identity) the province, territory, or municipality in which the case was heard.[45]

---

41 Defined as the sum of the number of cases receiving a DCSO or a sentence of custody and supervision.

42 Trends based on self-reported Aboriginal identity should be treated with caution, as Aboriginal identity was unknown in approximately 25 percent of cases.

43 Above note 7.

44 "[A]ll available sanctions other than custody that are reasonable in the circumstances should be considered for all young persons, with particular attention to the circumstances of aboriginal young persons." *YCJA*, above note 1, s. 38(2)(d).

45 Anthony N. Doob & Jane B. Sprott, "The Sentencing of Aboriginal and Non-Aboriginal Youth: Understanding Local Variation" (2007) 49:1 Can J Criminol & Crim Justice 109.

6) DCSO "Failures": Admissions to Custody of Youth Serving DCSOs

Young offenders who breach the conditions of their DCSOs may be apprehended and brought before a judge, who may order that they serve the remainder of the term in a custodial institution. At the adult level, the issue of breach of conditions of a CSI was from the outset a cause for concern. How do the DCSO breach data compare?

Unfortunately, there are no systematic data on the extent of breaches of DCSOs. However, the proportion of young offenders admitted to open or secure custody from a DCSO may be considered an approximate indicator of the "failure rate" of DCSOs. As with adult conditional sentences, if the alleged breach is of a minor nature, or occurs late in the order, probation officers may exercise their discretion not to have the offender arrested and brought to court for a breach hearing. Unlike DCSOs, adult conditional sentence orders may range up to two years less one day in length. With significant numbers of orders in excess of twelve months, the potential for a breach is therefore higher at the adult level than under the DCSO. It seems unlikely that allegations of a breach of a DCSO after four months or more would provoke official action, leaving a much smaller window for the possibility of a breach action. In addition, the official breach rate will always significantly underestimate the true breach rate since it includes only cases in which the breach was apprehended and resulted in an order of custody.

Whatever the reason, the proxy "failure rate" offered here suggests that the vast majority of DCSOs terminate without a founded breach. The raw numbers of youth admitted to custody from a DCSO range from sixty to eighty-five per year over the jurisdictions for which these data are available, with an average of seventy-four admissions over the five years from 2003–4 to 2007–8.[46] The proportion of DCSOs admitted to custody varied between 5 and 6 percent, with an average over the period of 5.3 percent, and no upward or downward trend.

Of the youth who were admitted to custody from DCSOs, the great majority — approximately 80 to 85 percent, except in 2003–4 — were readmitted to open rather than to secure custody. This finding demonstrates that the courts are following the injunctions of the statute to make every effort to keep the young person out of a correctional institution: in this case, even

46 The data exclude Prince Edward Island, British Columbia, and Nunavut for all years, and Saskatchewan for 2003–4.

when the young person fails to comply with the conditions of a "last chance" sanction.

While it is hard to draw firm conclusions, these trends suggest that the failure rate of DCSOs is significantly lower than the breach rate for conditional sentences of imprisonment at the adult level.[47] Limited breach data have been released by Statistics Canada. Overall, the percentage of conditional sentences that resulted in a founded breach was 22 percent in Nova Scotia and 31 percent in Alberta.[48] Roberts, Antonowicz, and Sanders[49] reported breach rates of approximately the same magnitude at an early stage of the conditional sentence regime.

It is also encouraging that the DCSO "failure rate" has remained stable over the past few years when, as noted, the volume of DCSOs imposed has recently risen. These data are important and should be communicated to youth courts. Once again the experience with conditional sentencing is instructive. Judicial apprehension about the adequacy of supervision and public concern about breach rates clearly inhibited the use of such sentences in the early years of the conditional sentencing regime for adults. If concern about the potential breach rate is playing an inhibitory role with respect to the DCSO, the trends reported here will be reassuring.

C. CONCLUSION

This essay has attempted to illuminate the rationale for the new youth sentence called the Deferred Custody and Supervision Order and to trace developments in its use through analysis of the available statistics on sentencing

47 Breach statistics for conditional sentence orders represent yet another gaping hole in the sentencing statistics in this country. A decade after the creation of the conditional sentence a Statistics Canada report noted, "To date, little is known about the rate and extent to which offenders in Canada are breached for violating the conditions of their supervision": Sara Johnson, "Outcomes of Probation and Conditional Sentence Supervision: An Analysis of Newfoundland and Labrador, Nova Scotia, New Brunswick, Saskatchewan and Alberta, 2003/2004 to 2004/2005" (December 2006) 26:7 Juristat 9, online: www.statcan.gc.ca/bsolc/olc-cel/olc-cel?catno=85-002-X20060079521&lang=eng. One wonders how this is possible. The consequence is that courts must employ new sanctions with no systematic knowledge of the probability of successful completion. It is hardly a prescription for best practices. Imagine following such a model with respect to medical treatments or procedures.

48 Johnson, *ibid.* at 13.

49 J.V. Roberts, D. Antonowicz, & T. Sanders, "Conditional Sentences of Imprisonment: An Empirical Analysis of Optional Conditions" (2000), 30 CR (5th) 113.

and corrections. We have compared it with its adult counterpart, the conditional sentence of imprisonment, and attempted to show that the DCSO is not simply a youth court version of the CSI. The purpose of the DCSO is to offer youth courts one last sanction to spare the young person from being committed to custody. While the CSI also represents an alternative to custody (but for adult offenders), the more robust nature of the conditional sentence makes it an appropriate alternative for incarceration in a wider range of cases. The DCSO should contain a package of tailored conditions designed to correct the criminogenic conditions that have given rise to the offending. In addition, the conditions attempt to structure the young person's lifestyle to promote the likelihood of ultimate desistance from crime. In contrast with the CSI at the adult level, the DCSO is not a hybrid sanction, with punitive and restorative elements. Rather it is rehabilitative in nature: the punitive element (committal to open or even secure custody) is merely threatened.

Up to 2006–7, the DCSO was used in only a limited number of cases: less than 4 percent of cases sentenced in youth court, with no evidence of an upward trend. In contrast, the conditional sentence of imprisonment was imposed in approximately 5 percent of cases sentenced in adult court in the same year. Correctional data for 2007–8 and 2008–9 suggest that the use of the DCSO has increased by about one-quarter, to approximately 5 percent of cases sentenced in youth court in 2008–9. This estimate cannot be confirmed until more recent sentencing data are available. Although DCSOs appear to be used currently in approximately the same proportion of cases as their adult counterpart, it should be kept in mind that a sentence of custody is used approximately twice as frequently in adult court as in youth court. Thus, as a proportion of the custodial caseload, the DCSO was used much more than the CSI, even in 2006–7: 18 percent of the custodial caseload in youth court were DCSOs, compared with 11 percent of the adult custodial caseload represented by CSIs.

The use of the DCSO and the length of its term vary enormously among the provinces and territories: far more than could be accounted for by interjurisdictional differences in case seriousness. For example, the proportion of sentenced cases receiving DCSOs was over twice as large in Ontario (3.5 percent) as in Quebec (1.4 percent). This parallels the difference between the two provinces in the use of custodial sentences (C&SOs).

Forty percent of DCSOs were imposed in cases involving a crime against the person, and approximately 20 percent in cases where the most serious crime was an offence against the administration of justice, mainly breach of probation. DCSOs were given in substantial numbers for apparently very serious crimes, such as robbery and major assault. There appears to be little or no relationship between the use of the DCSO and the offender's age, gender, or Aboriginal identity. It is surprising that DCSOs are not used more frequently as a substitute for a term of imprisonment for serious cases involving younger and/or Aboriginal offenders.

The scant information available suggests that the vast majority of DCSOs are completed successfully, without a founded breach. Youth admitted to secure or open custody from a DCSO (presumably as a result of a breach) represent 5 to 6 percent of DCSOs in a given year, and there is no trend over time. This compares favourably with published estimates of breaches of the CSI — admittedly based on fragmentary data — in the range of 20 to 30 percent.

Within a year of their entry into the *Code*, the conditional sentence provisions were amended, and approximately a decade after the sanction was created, the ambit of the sanction was circumscribed by Parliament.[50] The first amendment was an appropriate reminder to courts about the importance of considering the purpose and principles of sentencing when deciding whether to impose a conditional sentence. The second amendment smacks far more of penal populism. However, in both cases an argument can be made that the original legislation was flawed or that the government had failed to promote the benefits of the new sanction to a sceptical public. The consequence was Bill C-9. It is important that the DCSO not fall prey to the same populist pressures.

The experience with conditional sentencing has shown that a sanction may attract the wrong kinds of headlines, with consequences for the legal framework. To date, the DCSO has not attracted the same level of adverse publicity as the CSI, possibly on account of the smaller number of serious crimes resulting in the youth court sanction.

The evolution of the conditional sentence was characterized by a debate over whether it represented the equivalent of a term of custody — as claimed by its name — or whether it was a sanction falling somewhere on a scale of severity between probation and imprisonment. Critics argued that it could never be the equivalent of custody and particularly not in the early years, when the jurisprudence suggested that the duration of a conditional sen-

---

50 See the discussion in Roberts, above note 3.

tence should not exceed that of the term of imprisonment it replaced. All that changed with the *Proulx*[51] decision, in which the Court took the position that as a term of custody, a conditional sentence had to have a punitive element, usually meaning a strict curfew or even house arrest. No such judgment has emerged at any level regarding the DCSO. This suggests there is a distinction between the two sanctions, with less emphasis in the youth court version on punishment, and more on preventing re-offending.

Finally, we return to the parlous state of youth justice statistics. It is surely unreasonable to expect courts to impose sentences in the absence of comprehensive statistics relating to the frequency and effectiveness of these sanctions. This is particularly true in the case of youth courts in Canada, where judges can draw upon a wider range of dispositions than any other common law jurisdiction. With respect to the DCSO, many research priorities can be identified; in conclusion we offer but one. It concerns the conditions crafted for young persons on whom a DCSO is imposed. Courts need to know which kinds of conditions are most effective in achieving compliance and encouraging desistance, yet little is known about the conditions imposed or their relative effectiveness.[52] In addition, conditional and suspended sentences (including the DCSO) are hard to locate on a scale of severity because their penal value is so dependent on the number and nature of conditions imposed upon the offender. Both the conditional sentence and the DCSO

---

51 Above note 6.

52 The little that we do know is a result of original data collection by the Department of Justice and/or individual researchers. See, rather than Statistics Canada surveys, the following: Sharon Moyer, *A Comparison of Case Processing under the* Young Offenders Act *and the First Six Months of the* Youth Criminal Justice Act, Report to the Department of Justice Canada (2005), online: www.justice.gc.ca/eng/pi/yj-jj/res-rech/moyer/p1.html; Sharon Moyer & Maryanna Basic, *Crown Decision-Making under the* Youth Criminal Justice Act, Report to the Department of Justice Canada (2005), online: www.justice.gc.ca/eng/pi/yj-jj/res-rech/moyer_basic/decision/toc-tdm.html; Jessica E. Pulis, "Understanding Failure to Comply Convictions with Young Offenders: A Snapshot of One Canadian Courthouse" (2007) 19:1 Forum on Corrections Research 28; Jessica E. Pulis & Jane B. Sprott, "Probation Sentences and Proportionality under the *Young Offenders Act* and the *Youth Criminal Justice Act*" (2005) 47:4 Can J Criminol & Crim Justice 709; Jane B. Sprott, *Understanding Cases of Failure to Comply with a Disposition*, Report to the Department of Justice Canada (2004), online: www.justice.gc.ca/eng/pi/yj-jj/res-rech/sprott/toc-tdm.html; Jane B. Sprott, "The Use of Custody for Failing to Comply with a Disposition Cases under the *Young Offenders Act*" (2006) 48:4 Can J Criminol & Crim Justice 609.

carry minimal compulsory conditions — the action is all in the optional conditions attached to the order. These may be relatively minor or very intrusive, restricting the offender's lifestyle to a significant degree. A database that simply records the volume of DCSOs imposed and their duration fails to provide any idea of the true impact of these sanctions on the offender.

CHAPTER 8

The Youth Criminal Defence Office: A Model Approach to the Right to Counsel

CATHY LANE GOODFELLOW, QC

It is appropriate to start by saying a word about Nick Bala. Actually, I would like to say many words about Nick. I first learned his name in 1984, when I entered the practice of law. I had attended the first seminar offered by the Legal Education Society of Alberta on the topic of representing young people under the newly proclaimed *Young Offenders Act* (*YOA*)[1] and began a career in this area by accepting certificates from the Legal Aid Society to conduct duty counsel services in youth court. Today I am the Associate Senior Counsel of the Youth Criminal Defence Office in Calgary, Alberta, and have practised exclusively in youth criminal justice since 1993.

One cannot read anything about youth justice — any case, case commentary, or textbook — that was not either written or influenced by Nick Bala. His work has been quoted and applied by the Supreme Court of Canada innumerable times. However, it is not even the prolific nature of his writing that is the most striking — it's that he thinks so holistically about it. He sees the entire picture; he sees it with principled and good-natured objectivity and he does this at the speed of light. He has been the man with the answer, the wise man sitting on the top of the mountain, for a very long time. We've wanted him to be wrong. Although Nick is always child and youth focused in his analysis of the law, as an office we didn't like what he had to say to the

1 RSC 1985, c. Y-1 as amended [*YOA*].

Nunn Commission[2] about changing the criteria for the detention of youth. So, we have sometimes wanted to push him off that mountain top. Knowing him only a little I think he enjoys being pushed — revels in the intellectual challenge and would happily concede defeat and pass the torch — if it was the logically right thing to do. That makes him a true and honest teacher. I have been taught by Nick from afar for my entire career, largely without his knowing. Thank you, Nick.

Part of being a career advocate for youth is that you become philosophical about why you do the work. I have been asked that question countless times, often by laypeople at social functions. There is no answer. However, I have come to understand that, as individuals, we are profoundly affected by both the blessings and the hardships of life. That impact informs how we think, live, love, form relationships and move through space. Fatalists might say that our response to experience "is what it is," but for me, that rationale fails utterly. Why? Because some rise above profoundly negative experiences to become better, more ethical, kinder, gentler human beings. Others become disdainful of and in life. Belief in the rightness of goodness helps us, as individuals, decide which camp to join. Viktor E. Frankl wrote, "We who lived in concentration camps can remember the men who walked through the huts comforting others, giving away their last piece of bread. They may have been few in number, but they offer sufficient proof that everything can be taken from a man but one thing: the last of the human freedoms — to choose one's attitude in any given set of circumstances, to choose one's own way."[3]

This may seem an unusual way to start an article about youth justice but it reflects the philosophy of my advocacy practice. It is a profound privilege to hear the stories of youthful clients but that privilege comes at a very

---

2 Nova Scotia, Nunn Commission of Inquiry, *Spiralling Out of Control: Lessons Learned from a Boy in Trouble — Report of the Nunn Commission of Inquiry* (Halifax: Nunn Commission of Inquiry, 2006) (Chair: Merlin Nunn) [Nunn Inquiry]. This landmark public inquiry into Canada's youth criminal justice system was chaired by Merlin Nunn, a retired justice of the Supreme Court of Nova Scotia. The Commission examined the events of 14 October 2004, in which Theresa McEvoy, of Halifax, Nova Scotia, a fifty-two-year-old teacher's aide and mother of three boys, was killed when the car in which she was travelling was broadsided by another vehicle. The car was stolen and was being driven at high speed by a serial young offender who had been mistakenly released from jail just two days previously. See page 232 of the Report and onward, where it is reported Professor Bala suggested changes to the *Youth Criminal Justice Act*, SC 2002, c. 1 [*YCJA*] that would lower the threshold for custody.

3 Viktor E. Frankl, *Man's Search for Meaning* (New York: Pocket Books, 1985) at 86.

personal price. Their lives are more often than not a constellation of horrific events that shock and enrage even the most callous. As advocates for these incredibly vulnerable members of our society, we are often asked to solve, fix, help, ameliorate, offer cure, and especially, offer a guarantee of successful rehabilitation. It should not be a surprise to anyone that this is the last thing we are capable of doing. We have to believe in the rightness of goodness. We are compelled to hope that youth will "choose their way" and to stop judging their behaviour against our own past. From the front line, this seems to be the essence of youth advocacy. Bryan Stevenson distilled this notion down to its most basic when he said that "people are more than their worst act."[4]

I would like to elaborate on what I have come to understand as the twelve truths of practising in the area of youth criminal justice. They are my own value assumptions:

1) Youth are worth paying attention to, and an advocate should devote enough time to understand the context of their lives.
2) Youth can smell fear in others, so own up to yours and dispel the public myth about teenagers.
3) We should be cautious about applying any psychological label from the *Diagnostic and Statistical Manual of Mental Disorders* (DSM IV)[5] to a youth unless it means the difference between some resources or none.
4) Don't be such an egoist as to believe your help has resulted in a youth making a long-term positive change. They own their own stories, not you. Instead, believe in serendipity.
5) Criminal lawyers who use youth justice court as a training ground, where mistakes don't matter, should be outlawed and reported to the Law Society.
6) A specifically trained youth justice court bench and bar is needed that appreciates adolescent development but does not enable bad behaviour or dismiss it because of the age of the youth. You can get to "meaningful consequences"[6] by imposing a sanction that fits the crime and the con-

---

4 Bryan Stevenson, executive director of the Equal Justice Initiative, Keynote address to the 13th Annual Juvenile Defender Leadership Summit, Denver, CO, 15 October 2009.

5 *Diagnostic and Statistical Manual of Mental Disorders*, 4th ed. (Washington, DC: American Psychiatric Association, 1994) (DSM IV). The manual is the most widely used psychiatric reference in the world.

6 The word "meaningful" and the term "meaningful consequence" are found in several sections of the *YCJA*, above note 2: in the Preamble, ss. 3(1)(a)(iii), 3(1)(c)(iii), and 38(1). The Alberta Court of Appeal discussed this concept in *R. v. M.L.M.*, 2008 ABCA 212 at

text of the youth's life. We should all strive for the goal of youth taking ownership in any manner possible.

7) Many youths are smart enough to know exactly what they want without our help.
8) Those who advocate for youth should not be put off by clothing, piercings, or colourful language unless it presents an issue of personal safety — yours or theirs. Sometimes it is their only way to communicate.
9) Youths are incredibly resilient and it is good to look that word up in the dictionary now and then.
10) Make sure the youthful client understands the legal process enough to exercise some kind of control within it. This fosters personal ownership.
11) Have a community conference[7] whenever you can.
12) It is all right to say "no" to judges who don't understand the twelve truths. It is your job to persuade them to a better "yes."

It has been a sad truth that very few legal academics write in the area of youth justice in Canada, even though social interest in the area has for many years been extremely high. In my short twenty-five-year practice, the law has dramatically changed, from the *Juvenile Delinquents Act* (*JDA*) of 1908 to the *Young Offenders Act* (*YOA*) of 1984 and to the *Youth Criminal Justice Act* (*YCJA*) of 2003.[8] The philosophical changes alone have been profound, yet they do not reflect the "get tough on youth crime" rhetoric that we have heard. In fact, the legislative changes have moved steadily toward recognition that it is better to be circumspect when prosecuting youths and, that when they are involved in the criminal justice process, they deserve to have the goal of

---

para. 14, stating,

> While the term "meaningful consequences" is notionally similar to the concept of specific deterrence, there is a distinction between these two concepts. "Meaningful consequences" seemingly requires that a sentence be based on the young person's past conduct, while specific deterrence is intended to discourage future conduct considered to be inappropriate. Although there may only be a thin line between imposing a "meaningful consequence" and creating a deterrent effect, a sentence will be appropriate so long as it is intended to ensure the long-term protection of the public by focussing on the rehabilitation of the young person, without regard to any consequential deterrent effect such a penalty may have.

7 We are privileged in Calgary to have access to the Calgary Community Conferencing program. According to its website, www.calgarycommunityconferencing.com, the program "brings together a young person and their victim(s), their respective families and supporters, other key people affected by the conflict and relevant community members to address what's happened and find solutions beneficial to all."

8 *Juvenile Delinquents Act*, SC 1908, c. 40 [*JDA*]; *YOA*, above note 1; *YCJA*, above note 2.

rehabilitation as the primary focus. This philosophy values children, understands their social, emotional, and developmental differences from adults, and brings détente to the historical war waged against youth crime.

I will offer some examples of this evolution. From 1908 to 2003, the number of youths who could potentially have been prosecuted was significantly and purposely reduced, simply by increasing of the age of criminal responsibility. The *JDA* allowed for the prosecution of children under the age of sixteen (although provinces were given the option of choosing either seventeen or eighteen as the demarcation point[9]). Because the *Criminal Code* at that time prescribed the age of criminal responsibility to be seven,[10] children between the ages of seven and the day before their eighteenth birthday could theoretically be prosecuted under the *JDA*. By contrast, under the *YOA* and *YCJA* only youths aged twelve to seventeen can be prosecuted.[11]

Further, the legislation has evolved toward limiting the duration of its effect on a youth's life. Section 20(1) of the *JDA* set out the courses of action a judge could take once the youth was adjudged to be a delinquent: suspending the final disposition; adjourning the hearing for a definite or *indefinite* period; imposing a fine; committing the child to the care of a probation officer or other suitable person; reporting to a probation officer; placing the child in a foster home; committing the child to a children's aid society; or committing the child to an industrial school. Once the child was adjudged to be a delinquent, the discretion of the court seemed thereafter unlimited. Section 20(3)[12] of the *JDA* allowed the court to give notice to, summons, or

---

9 *JDA, ibid.*, s. 2(2).

10 RSC 1970, c. C-34, s. 12.

11 See *YOA*, above note 1, s. 2(1) for the definition of "young person" and s. 5, and *YCJA*, above note 2, s. 2(1) for the definition of "young person" and s. 14.

12 Section 20(3) reads:

> Where a child has been adjudged to be a juvenile delinquent and whether or not such child has been dealt with in any of the ways provided for in subsection (1), the court may at any time, before such juvenile delinquent has reached the age of twenty-one years and unless the court has otherwise ordered, cause by notice, summons, or warrant, the delinquent to be brought before the court, and the court may then take any action provided for in subsection (1), or may make an order with respect to such child under section 9, or may discharge the child on parole or release the child from detention, but in a province in which there is a superintendent, no child shall be released by the judge from an industrial school without a report from such superintendent recommending such release, and where an order is made by a court releasing a juvenile delinquent from an industrial school or transferring such delinquent from an industrial school to a foster home or from one foster home to another under

issue a warrant for a juvenile delinquent *any time before the age of twenty-one* and, in effect, re-sentence them. Re-sentencing included the possibility of an adult sentence. According to section 20(5), the court was required to take the kind of action "that the child's own good and the best interests of the community require." By contrast, the *YCJA* codifies a youth's right to "timely intervention"[13] and to a sentence that is the "least restrictive" but capable of achieving the purpose of the Act.[14] Section 29 of the *YCJA* creates a presumption against custody that speaks to the Act's overarching philosophy, as stated in its Preamble: "Canadian society should have a youth criminal justice system that commands respect, takes into account the interests of victims, fosters responsibility and ensures accountability through meaningful consequences and effective rehabilitation and reintegration, and that reserves its most serious interventions for the most serious crimes and reduces the over-reliance on incarceration for non-violent young persons."

In order to achieve the lofty objectives found, *inter alia*, in the *YCJA* Preamble, in its Declaration of Principle,[15] or in its Purpose and Principles of sentencing,[16] the youth justice system must be supported by personnel willing to advocate to make the statute meaningful. It is not a simple task to interpret the intention of legislators in using terms such as "accountability" and "meaningful consequences" but excluding "specific" or "general deterrence."[17]

> this subsection, it is not necessary for such delinquent to be before the court at the time that such order is made.

13 *YCJA*, above note 2, s. 3(1)(b)(iv).

14 *Ibid.*, s. 38(2)(e)(i).

15 *Ibid.*, s. 3.

16 *Ibid.*, s. 38.

17 See *R. v. B.W.P.*, 2006 SCC 27. The Supreme Court held, at para. 24, that

> [h]ad Parliament intended to make deterrence part of the [new] regime, one would reasonably expect that it would be expressly included in the detailed purpose and principles set out in the statute. Yet the words "deter" and "deterrence" are nowhere to be found in the *YCJA*: the words do not appear in the "Declaration of Principle" under s. 3, nor in the "Purpose and Principles" listed under s. 38 and not even in the list of particular sanctions found in s. 42. This omission is also of considerable significance.

Further, the Summary states as follows:

> Nor can general deterrence, or some equivalent concept, be implied from the wording of ss. 3 and 38. Rather, the focus throughout remains on the young person before the court. Since no basis can be found in the *YCJA* for imposing a harsher sanction than would otherwise be called for to deter others from committing crime, general deterrence is not a principle of youth sentencing under the new regime. The *YCJA* also does not speak of specific deterrence. Parliament has sought preferably to promote the long-term protection of the public by addressing the circumstances

It is also surprisingly difficult to conceptualize the need to narrow the definition of "violent offence" in order to meet the objective of the statute to reduce overreliance on incarceration.[18] The purpose of this discussion is to emphasize the role of counsel in this very specialized criminal justice milieu. I have always taken the position that lawyers are ethically obligated to be competent in the area of youth justice if they intend to practise in the area.[19] Later I will review the history and development of the staff lawyer model for youth in conflict with the criminal law in Alberta, now known as the Youth Criminal Defence Office, a program of Legal Aid Alberta. However, I would first like to review what the law says about the right to counsel in youth justice court and how that has been interpreted in other provinces. That will serve to highlight the uniqueness of the two staff lawyer offices in Alberta.

To start, it helps to compare the relevant sections in the *YOA* and the *YCJA*. Sections 11 and 25, respectively, entrench a young person's right to be informed of the right to retain and instruct counsel and to be given an opportunity to do so. The import of this should not be understated. Sherri Davis-Barron comments that "[p]rocedural issues aside, the scope of the right to counsel for a young person under the *YCJA* also distinguishes it and elevates it above the right to counsel guaranteed to all accused persons under s. 10(b) of the *Charter*."[20]

> underlying the offending behaviour, by rehabilitating and reintegrating young persons into society and by holding young persons accountable through the imposition of meaningful sanctions related to the harm done. Undoubtedly, the sentence may have the effect of deterring the young person and others from committing crimes, but Parliament has not included deterrence as a basis for imposing a sanction under the *YCJA*. [para. 4] [paras. 22–30] [paras. 39–40]

18 See *R. v. C.D.; R. v. C.D.K.*, 2005 3 SCR 668.

19 See Cathy Lane Goodfellow, *The Philosophy of the* Young Offenders Act *and Its Impact on the Formal Legal Education and Practice of Advocates for Youth* (LLM thesis, University of Alberta, 1995) [unpublished].

20 Sherri Davis-Barron, *Canadian Youth & the Criminal Law: One Hundred Years of Youth Justice Legislation in Canada* (Markham, ON: LexisNexis, 2009) at 286. This is not the first time this comment was made. The same was said about s. 11 of the *YOA*, above note 1. See A.W. Leschied, P.G. Jaffe, & W. Willis, eds., *The* Young Offenders Act: *A Revolution in Canadian Juvenile Justice* (Toronto: University of Toronto Press, 1991) at 115:

> The drafters of the *Young Offenders Act* were not, however, content to rely solely on the right to counsel declared in the *Charter*. They were determined to give even more vitality to the right of accused young persons to legal representation. Section 11 of the *YOA* not only provides that a young person has the right to retain and instruct counsel without delay, at any stage of proceedings against him or her, but also requires arresting police officers and judicial officers at every stage of the process to advise the young person of his or her right to be represented by counsel and to give the young person a reasonable opportunity to exercise that right. The act goes well

However, issues have arisen over the two-step process involved in the practical application of these sections. Therefore, I will focus on the relevant subsections of *YOA* and *YCJA*, which are virtually identical. The *YOA* reads:

> 11(3) Where a young person is not represented by counsel
> (*a*) at a hearing at which it will be determined whether to release the young person or detain him in custody prior to disposition of his case,
> (*b*) at a hearing held pursuant to section 16,
> (*c*) at his trial,
> (*c.1*) at any proceedings held pursuant to subsection 26.1(1), 26.2(1) or 26.6(1),
> (*d*) at a review of a disposition held before a youth court or a review board under this Act, or
> (*e*) at a review of the level of custody pursuant to subsection 28.1(1),
> the justice before whom, or the youth court or review board before which, the hearing, trial or review is held shall advise the young person of his right to be represented by counsel and shall give the young person a reasonable opportunity to obtain counsel.
>
> (4) Where a young person at his trial or at a hearing or review referred to in subsection (3) wishes to obtain counsel but is unable to do so, the youth court before which the hearing, trial or review is held or the review board before which the review is held
> (*a*) shall, where there is a legal aid or an assistance program available in the province where the hearing, trial or review is held, refer the young person to that program for the appointment of counsel; or
> (*b*) where no legal aid or assistance program is available or the young person is unable to obtain counsel through such a program, may, and on the request of the young person shall, direct that the young person be represented by counsel.
>
> (5) Where a direction is made under paragraph (4)(*b*) in respect of a young person, the Attorney General of the province in which the direction is made shall appoint counsel, or cause counsel to be appointed, to represent the young person.[21]

The *YCJA* reads:

---

beyond the constitutional minimum mandated by the *Charter* and seeks to attach special significance to legal representation in *YOA* proceedings.

21 *YOA*, above note 1, ss. 11(3)–(5).

25(3) When a young person is not represented by counsel

(*a*) at a hearing at which it will be determined whether to release the young person or detain the young person in custody prior to sentencing,

(*b*) at a hearing held under section 71 (hearing — adult sentences),

(*c*) at trial,

(*d*) at any proceedings held under subsection 98(3) (continuation of custody), 103(1) (review by youth justice court), 104(1) (continuation of custody), 105(1) (conditional supervision) or 109(1) (review of decision),

(*e*) at a review of a youth sentence held before a youth justice court under this Act, or

(*f*) at a review of the level of custody under section 87,

the justice or youth justice court before which the hearing, trial or review is held, or the review board before which the review is held, shall advise the young person of the right to retain and instruct counsel and shall give the young person a reasonable opportunity to obtain counsel.

(4) When a young person at trial or at a hearing or review referred to in subsection (3) wishes to obtain counsel but is unable to do so, the youth justice court before which the hearing, trial or review is held or the review board before which the review is held

(*a*) shall, if there is a legal aid program or an assistance program available in the province where the hearing, trial or review is held, refer the young person to that program for the appointment of counsel; or

(*b*) if no legal aid program or assistance program is available or the young person is unable to obtain counsel through the program, may, and on the request of the young person shall, direct that the young person be represented by counsel.

(5) When a direction is made under paragraph (4)(*b*) in respect of a young person, the Attorney General shall appoint counsel, or cause counsel to be appointed, to represent the young person.[22]

The *YCJA* added two subsections to this section that reflect a notion of fiscal restraint or responsibility:

(10) Nothing in this Act prevents the lieutenant governor in council of a province or his or her delegate from establishing a program to authorize

22 *YCJA*, above note 2, ss. 25(3)–(5).

> the recovery of the costs of a young person's counsel from the young person or the parents of the young person. The costs may be recovered only after the proceedings are completed and the time allowed for the taking of an appeal has expired or, if an appeal is taken, all proceedings in respect of the appeal have been completed.
>
> (11) Subsections (4) to (9) do not apply to a person who is alleged to have committed an offence while a young person, if the person has attained the age of twenty years at the time of his or her first appearance before a youth justice court in respect of the offence; however, this does not restrict any rights that a person has under the law applicable to adults.[23]

I do not plan to review that which has been exhaustively covered in Chapter 6 of Nicholas Bala and Sanjeev Anand's *Youth Criminal Justice Law.*[24] However, two issues do need to be identified here. The first is at what point in the process the right to be referred to a legal aid program crystallizes, and the second is what happens either if there is no legal aid program to which to direct the youth or if the existing program declines to appoint counsel.

A. THE RIGHT TO BE REFERRED TO A LEGAL AID PROGRAM

YOA section 11(3) and *YCJA* section 25(3) list a number of procedural steps that may or may not be taken in a criminal proceeding against a youth. Conspicuously absent are first appearances at which pleas are to be made or referrals to diversion programs (under the *YOA* called "alternative measures" and under the *YCJA* called "extrajudicial sanctions"). This is important because in both section 11(4)(a) and section 25(4)(a), the list is repeated and the right to be referred to legal aid for counsel seems to occur at the time the youth is facing the discrete procedural step. Therefore, how the word "trial" has been interpreted has greatly affected the ability of a youth to obtain counsel. The Alberta and Ontario courts have come to very different conclusions about when the right to be referred under sections 11(4)(a) and 25(4)(a) is engaged. Justice Russell of the Alberta Court of Queen's Bench in *S.T.C. v. Alberta (Attorney General)* found as follows:

---

23 It is important to note that none of the provinces has enforced s. 25(10) or (11) presumably because provincial politicians recognize their problematic nature.

24 Nicholas Bala & Sanjeev Anand, *Youth Criminal Justice Law*, 2d ed. (Toronto: Irwin Law, 2009).

> The Crown argues that section 11(3) of the Act which lists the legal situations where a positive duty is imposed upon the Youth Court to apprise a young person of his right to counsel, one of which is "at his trial", does not include situations of guilty pleas and disposition hearings, and that the Act contemplates situations where the young offender will not have counsel. It is implicit in that argument that the duty of the court to appoint counsel is therefor constrained. However, The Encyclopedia of Words and Phrases: Legal Maxims (Canada) 3rd ed. Vol. 4 p. 328 defines "trial" as including the entry of a guilty plea and sentencing. Furthermore, section 11(4) only applies if ". . . the young person wishes to obtain counsel . . ." so is clearly not intended to impose counsel on a young person against his wishes.[25]

It is interesting to note that this case was decided during the very first year the Youth Criminal Defence Office was in existence and has clearly affected the way in which counsel have been appointed ever since — an inclusive rather than an exclusive approach. As a further aside, and apart from the obvious financial issue, one may wonder at the rationale for *not* appointing counsel when the same is requested. In *R. v. C. (S.T.)*, the Court of Queen's Bench noted with disfavour the comments Catonio J made in the lower court decision before declining the original application for a section 11 order: "[O]ne of the greatest things about teaching young people responsibility, is when they get into trouble, they should fend for themselves or have their parents look after them. And for that reason, I will not sign these certificates, and I refuse to do so in this case."[26]

In diametric contrast, and after the *YCJA* had been proclaimed, the Ontario Court of Appeal held in *R. v. L.S.* that

> . . . it is clear from a plain reading of sections 25(3) and 25(4) that it is only when the youth is at a certain stage of proceedings and unable to obtain legal counsel through legal aid that the young person may apply for publicly funded counsel. Parliament has specifically provided that it is only when there is a hearing related to the custody of the young person, including sentencing or when the young person is engaged in a trial that the youth may apply for publicly funded counsel. While a young person may require legal advice at the stage when he or she is considering whether to partake in EJS, that advice would be available through duty counsel.[27]

---

25 *S.T.C. v. Alberta (Attorney General)* (1993), 140 AR 259 at 264 (QB).

26 *Ibid.* at 261.

27 (2006), 218 OAC 49 at para. 9.

This case was followed, reluctantly, in *R. v. R.K.S.*, a later decision of Kukurin J.[28] However, Kukurin J does spend a considerable amount of time talking about the impact of the Court of Appeal decision that is relevant to this discussion and to the work done by the Youth Criminal Defence Office:

> As a general rule, my preference is to have a lawyer assisting any young person charged with offences in the youth justice court. This does not mean necessarily that all young persons should invariably have their own private counsel. It matters but little whether the legal assistance comes from a counsel retained privately, or retained on a legal aid certificate, or from a legal aid duty counsel, or from a public defender, or from a pro bono counsel. My main concern is that the young person have someone competent in law who can advise and represent him or her adequately in matters arising out of the charges before the court. From my experience, if not from common sense, the earlier such "legal representation" comes on board, the better for all concerned — the young person, the court and the administration of justice. Young persons have no legal training. They are acknowledged by Parliament to be subject to developmental challenges [preamble to *YCJA*], greater dependency, [section 3(1)(b)(ii) *YCJA*] and reduced level of maturity [section 3(1)(b)(ii) *YCJA*]. Even adults find some aspects of criminal procedure somewhat incomprehensible. The criminal justice system is historically an adversarial one. This has been imported into the youth criminal justice system despite its many differences and safeguards. The contest between a trained, professional Crown counsel, especially an experienced one, with the resources of the state to draw upon, pitted against the typical unrepresented teenager is, in my experience, a mismatch.[29]

After a lengthy discussion of the practical and negative repercussions of the appointment of counsel late in the legal process, he concludes by saying:

> It takes only a little imagination to foresee how this will tax the system. The concept of no right to apply for a section 25(4)(b) order until an accused young person is "at trial" combined with a legal aid policy of no certificate if no probability of incarceration in the climate of the 2003 *YCJA* has great implications for not only the duty counsel system but also the

---

28 2007 ONCJ 139 [*R.K.S.*].

29 *Ibid.* at para. 11.

> Crown counsel, for the defence bar, for the judiciary, for court personnel and for the administration of justice.[30]

B. DIRECTION FOR COUNSEL

Under *YOA* section 11(4)(b) and *YCJA* section 25(4)(b), if the preconditions have been met and the young person is unable to obtain counsel through a legal aid program then, upon application, the court should direct one be appointed. The result is, pursuant to sections 11(5) and 25(5), that the provincial government is to fund the appointment. Again, Russell J in *S.T.C. v. Alberta (Attorney General)* held that

> In my view, the only interpretation that can be placed on the provision is that the court has no discretion to decline to direct the appointment of counsel where the young person has been unable to obtain legal aid. The Youth Court need only be satisfied that the young person wishes to obtain counsel but has been unable to do so because legal aid is not available for any reason. An affidavit to that effect, or in the alternative a simple inquiry into those facts alone should suffice. The court has no discretion to determine whether a young person should be provided with a lawyer out of public funds. An attempt to exercise such discretion is an error of law going to jurisdiction.[31]

The Ontario Court of Appeal in *R. v. J.H.*,[32] again in contrast, found that there is a positive onus on the court to launch an inquiry into a young person's inability to obtain counsel as the phrase "unable to obtain counsel" is found in section 11(4)(b).[33] At paragraph 24 of that decision, the court said:

> In the final analysis, this case is about the simple matter of the proper administrative process to be followed before a youth court judge is required to order state-funded counsel for a young offender. Before the state pays for counsel, the inability of the young person to obtain counsel must be established. This question cannot completely be answered without reference to the finances of the young person's parents.

30 *Ibid.* at para. 37.

31 Above note 25 at 267.

32 (1999), 28 CR (5th) 129 (ONCA).

33 *YCJA*, above note 2.

In a subsequent case from the Ontario Court of Justice, *R. v. E.R.B.*,[34] McKerlie J declined to conduct an inquiry when the twelve-year-old accused's parents refused to provide their financial information to Legal Aid. Even though the youth's father swore an affidavit attesting to being unable and unwilling to provide financial assistance, the court sent the assessment of "inability" back to the Legal Aid Plan as it was better able to make the assessment. The court was obviously concerned that the youth and his parents were trying to circumvent the established protocols of the Ontario Legal Aid Plan. However, the practical result is that the young person would have then been forced to somehow convince his parents to be forthcoming to Legal Aid before having counsel appointed for his trial. There was nothing in the written decision that suggests the young person's position on plea was any different than that of his parents. If they were averse then the youth is put into exactly the situation that the words found in both *YOA* section 11(1) and *YCJA* section 25(1) were included to prevent: that the young person is entitled to exercise his right to counsel "personally."

Since 1993, the Youth Criminal Defence Office[35] (formerly called the Legal Aid Youth Office) has been in operation in both Calgary and Edmonton. The offices exclusively deliver services to young people in conflict with the criminal and quasi-criminal law. That means the offices represent youth charged with anything from bylaw violations (graffiti and transit tickets) to homicide. The program has two primary objectives: (1) to provide quality, effective, and efficient legal services to those young persons; and (2) to develop and provide legal services that reflect and are responsive to the special legal needs of young persons. The pilot project for the program was evaluated in 1996 by RPM Planning Associates.[36] Sanjeev Anand, in his case comment on the conflicting judgments of two Toronto youth court judges concerning the appointment of counsel for youth, argued in favour of the delivery of youth justice advocacy through a staff lawyer model. He asserted that when the project was evaluated, it was "found to provide more economical and effective legal representation than did the pre-existing judicare model. The pilot project resulted in savings of more than one million dollars a year compared to the judicare system of delivery. The staff lawyers developed an expertise in

34 [2003] OJ no 3738 (Ct J).
35 A program of Legal Aid Alberta.
36 RPM Planning Associates Ltd., *Evaluation of the Staff Lawyer Pilot Project* (Edmonton: Legal Aid Society of Alberta, 1996).

young offender law, and this was complemented by the paralegals' knowledge of community resources that could be utilized by the young offenders."[37] What began as a pilot project is now an entrenched part of the youth justice system with local, regional, provincial, and national acknowledgment.

It is my view that the Alberta staff lawyer model experience has answered the concerns expressed by Kukurin J in *R.K.S.*,[38] discussed above. It has also always been able to respond to those who argue that there is a threat to legal independence, that a staff lawyer model limits choice of counsel, and the quality of representation will be reduced. We operate in an environment in which the young person is required to apply for counsel, to establish a certificate, but invariably receives legal assistance. No young person has had to wait for his or her trial to have counsel appointed, and inquiries are never made by the court into the financial resources of the parent. To be clear, it is not a perfect world; however, this service delivery model meets our ethical obligations to be competent advocates to a vulnerable population in an exemplary fashion, and we have developed an expertise that is relied upon by the judiciary. We provide the services described in the following sections.

1) Telephone Contact with Counsel upon Arrest

When a young person is arrested he or she is entitled to speak to a lawyer for advice pursuant to both the *Canadian Charter of Rights and Freedoms*[39] and the *YCJA*.[40] During business hours, these calls are patched to each office. Outside of business hours, an office cell phone is staffed by an office lawyer, on a rotation basis, every night of the week. On occasion, the on-call lawyer will conduct a bail hearing via telephone conference with a justice of the peace. If the charge is very serious, and for homicides particularly, counsel will attend at the police station where the youth is being held.

2) Duty Counsel

Both Calgary and Edmonton courthouses have docket courtrooms where young people make appearances for judicial interim release and plea. Law-

37 Sanjeev Anand, "Does the Staff Model Offer a Solution to the Issue of Court Ordered Youth Legal Aid" (1998), 18 CR (5th) 328 at 334 [footnotes excluded].

38 See above note 28.

39 Enacted as Part I of the *Constitution Act, 1982*, being Schedule B to the *Canada Act* 1982 (UK), 1982, c. 11.

40 Above note 11.

yers from the offices appear each day in a duty counsel capacity in each of these courtrooms. As each office has a minimum of two youth or social workers, at least one such worker attends court for the purpose of offering support to youth, developing case plans for judicial interim release hearings, conducting liaison with representatives from Child and Family Services if the youth has status, and offering assistance and legal information to parents and other supporters. Duty counsel act as an important part of the continuum of representation for a youth, as information is passed from the duty counsel to the assigned counsel easily and efficiently. Technologies are being developed within the offices to assist further with this process. The motivation to create seamless and consistent representation meets one of the principles in the Declaration of Principles of the *YCJA*, that "the criminal justice system for young persons must be separate from that of adults and emphasize the following: (v) the promptness and speed with which persons responsible for enforcing this Act must act, given young persons' perception of time."[41]

3) Assigned Files

Each lawyer is required to fill the on-call role and the duty counsel role and to carry a caseload. Caseloads are monitored so that equal distribution is the gold standard. Young people have choice of counsel within the offices and that choice is honoured whenever possible. Of course, in the event of conflicts with co-accused or adverse witnesses who have or are currently represented by the office, young people have the right to be assigned a lawyer from the private bar. Each youth or social worker is also assigned files in which the young person has specific needs that require addressing or support. Often the relationship between the worker and the client is the key to the youth's engaging in rehabilitative services as sometimes, the worker is the only adult supporter. These relationships sometimes linger past the closing of the file and workers are encouraged to continue offering the services of the office.

Our assigned files have taken us to the Supreme Court of Canada on two occasions. In *R. v. C.D.; R. v. C.D.K.*,[42] Charles Seto and Patricia Yuzwenko from the Edmonton office were counsel for the appellants, and in *R. v. B.W.P.*,[43] Patricia Yuzwenko and I intervened on behalf of the Youth Criminal Defence Office. Our offices also handle adult sentencing hearings and

41 *YCJA*, above note 2, s. 3(1)(b)(v).

42 [2005] 3 SCR 668.

43 Above note 17.

conviction and sentence appeals and were the first law firm in Alberta to received an intensive rehabilitative custody and supervision sentence for a client under section 42(2)(r) of the *YCJA*.

4) Youth/Social Workers

What really sets us apart is the invaluable work accomplished by our youth and social workers. They do their best to work with youths with the life context in mind. They advocate with Child and Family Services for assistance, they drive youths to appointments, they buy them lunch, they take them to the hospital, they take them to the airport or bus stations when they are from out of town, they pick them up when they are in danger, they show up when others won't — because they take the task of rehabilitation to heart. One worker in the Calgary office is specifically assigned to assist youth who have been referred to the extrajudicial sanctions program, whether or not they are clients of the office. From January to November 2009, she dealt with approximately 650 youth, including explaining the extrajudicial sanctions program, doing follow-up contact, and advocating for extensions to complete when necessary.

5) Work Environment and Commitment to Growth

Lawyers employed by the Youth Criminal Defence Office currently enjoy a salary commensurate with that of the Crown prosecutor's office. This parity ensures that quality staff are not only employed but will stay at the office. Traditionally, representatives from each of the two offices attend the annual National Criminal Law Conference, and there is a thoughtfully developed budget for training opportunities that include updating substantive law knowledge, honing advocacy skills, and developing managerial skills. Professional development plans are created by each staff person and monitored by the leadership team, which is made up of the senior counsel, the two associate senior counsel from each office, and the senior administrative assistant. The offices have engaged in strategic planning that hopes to ensure growth and longevity.

6) Community Impact

In my opinion, one of the essential elements to the success of the two offices has been our investment in the community we serve. Although this list is by no means exhaustive, our community outreach has included the following:

- Providing sessional instruction at the University of Calgary in the area of disabilities and the law and alternative dispute resolution.
- Membership on the Criminal Trial Practice and Practice Review committees of the Law Society of Alberta.
- Membership with the Calgary Bar Association, Edmonton Bar Association, Criminal Trial Lawyers Association, and Canadian Bar Association.
- Membership on the organizing committee and teaching faculty of the National Judicial Institute[44] for conferences delivered by them on the *Youth Criminal Justice Act* for members of the judiciary in Canada.
- Guest-speaking on the topic of youth justice to junior and senior high school students when requested to do so throughout the year.
- Providing volunteer services with Calgary Legal Guidance, an organization that provides free legal advice for individuals with low incomes.
- Board membership with the Elizabeth Fry Society, an organization that works with women and teenaged girls in conflict with the law.
- Membership as a Bencher of the Law Society of Alberta.
- Developing and delivering a training module called "*YCJA* in a Nutshell" to members of the private bar when requested and to staff of Legal Aid Alberta.
- Guest-speaking on the topic of legal service delivery for young people at conferences hosted by the Public Legal Education Network of Alberta.[45]
- Guest-speaking on issues concerning the legal representation of youth with Fetal Alcohol Spectrum Disorder (FASD) at national conferences.[46]

---

44 Based in Ottawa, Ontario, the National Judicial Institute (NJI) is "dedicated to the development and delivery of educational programs for all federal, provincial and territorial judges. The Institute's programs stimulate continuing professional and personal growth and reflect Canada's cultural, racial and linguistic diversity, as well as the changing demands on the judiciary in a rapidly evolving society. The programs focus on the three major components of judicial education: substantive law, skills training and social context issues." For more information go to www.nji.ca.

45 The Public Legal Education Network of Alberta (PLENA) is a grassroots network of members and partners united by a shared interest in law, justice, and democracy. PLENA is committed to improving access to legal education and justice resources for all Albertans. See online: http://plena.org [currently under construction].

46 The conferences took place in Banff, Alberta, on 21–24 May 2008; in Victoria, British Columbia on 11–14 March 2009; and in Vancouver, British Columbia, on 12–15 April 2010.

- Volunteering with the FASD Justice Support Project for Youth.[47]
- Partnership in the Urban Games initiative.[48]
- Partnership in the development of the Youth Restorative Action Project (YRAP), a youth justice committee sanctioned under the *YCJA*. It was the first committee of its kind mandated to work, in youth court, with young people who have caused harm as a result of racism, intolerance, and significant social issues. It is also the world's only youth justice committee made up entirely of youth members (ages fifteen to twenty-four). The members come from diverse ethnic, social, and economic backgrounds and share a common wish to make a positive impact on their community.
- Board membership of the Children's Legal Education Resource Centre, Calgary, Alberta (CLERC).[49]
- Membership with the Youth Sector of the Calgary Homeless Foundation.[50]
- Membership with the Edmonton Inter-agency Youth Service Association (EIYSA).[51]
- Partner in the Just Us Girls initiative, the first gender-specific youth justice committee in Canada, designed to help mothers between the

---

47 The FASD Justice Support Project for Youth, in Edmonton, Alberta, is described as follows:

> Beginning in 2004, a Steering Committee representing members from various Alberta government departments (e.g., Alberta Justice and Attorney General, Youth Criminal Defence, Edmonton Police Service, etc.) and community agencies was formed to assist youth with FASD (both suspected and diagnosed) involved with the criminal justice system. The Steering Committee develops a comprehensive case plan for each youth with the goal of having them succeed in the community. Youth are linked with various community agencies. The project can assist up to 24 youth per year and in 2007 the project served 10 youth. There is no funding requirement for this project as the employers permit the Steering Committee members to work on this project as part of their regular employment duties. An evaluation is planned for 2008.

See online: www.justice.gc.ca.

48 The games are a two- or three-day competition that gives participants $500 in educational bursaries for each event they enter. Events include unconventional activities such as skateboarding, graffiti, poetry, and Hacky Sack. See "Group Hopes to Launch 'Urban Games' in Edmonton" online: www.canada.com/edmontonjournal/news/story.html?id=5dc58408-9834-4378-b023-81c003993b1f.

49 CLERC's mission is "to provide legal support and services for children and youth and to engage in related education and research." See www.clerc-calgary.ca.

50 See www.calgaryhomeless.com.

51 The EIYSA (eiysa.blogspot.com) meets once a month to present topics relevant to youth-serving agencies in Edmonton and surrounding areas.

ages of twelve and twenty-four who have committed crimes or who have had their children apprehended by Children's Services.

- Volunteering with ihuman. The program's mission is "to work with high-risk youth and to promote their re-integration into the community through a program involving crisis intervention, arts mentorship, and life skills development programs."[52]
- Partnership in the development of the Kids in the Hall program in Edmonton. The program was developed to provide opportunities for at-risk youth sixteen to twenty-four years old to learn life and employment skills while they operate a food outlet.
- Membership on the organizing committee for the annual Youth Gear Up in Calgary. Gear Up for Winter is a joint project between the Boys and Girls Clubs of Calgary, the City of Calgary, AADAC, Inner City Resource Centre, Red Cross, and Youth Criminal Defence Office. The purpose of this one-day event is to prepare homeless youth for the winter months by providing them with resources and the necessities that will help them to survive.
- Volunteering with the Alberta Adolescent Recovery Centre, an addiction treatment facility in Calgary, by providing legal information.
- Membership at Youth Justice Court roundtable meetings held at the Calgary Court Centre. The purpose of these meetings is to air practical issues that face participants of the youth justice process and to resolve them, if possible.
- Providing input to the 2009 Alberta Child Intervention System Review Panel.

I hope to have given a useful, albeit brief, outline of the depth of expertise the Youth Criminal Defence Office has developed over the last sixteen years. Advocating for youth is meaningful, relevant, and socially important. We understand that the right to counsel under the *YCJA*, and previously under the *YOA*, must include the right to quality and independent representation. The experiences of each Youth Criminal Defence Office in Alberta prove that this type of representation can be delivered effectively and efficiently through a staff lawyer form of service delivery — a model of service delivery that I hope will be used more and more frequently across Canada.

---

52 See online: www.ihuman.org.

CHAPTER 9

Understanding the Principled Arguments for Criminalizing Misbehaviour by Youths under Twelve

ANTHONY N. DOOB AND JANE B. SPROTT

In our everyday lives — perhaps especially for those of us who study the youth justice system in Canada — we expect to run into people whose views on something important differ from our own. When a minister of justice implies that by dropping the word "deterrence" into the *Youth Criminal Justice Act* youth crime will be decreased, one can smile politely, being quite confident that he doesn't have the slightest idea what he is talking about.[1] More important, one is not challenged by his assertion. Few of those who are knowledgeable about youth crime and youth justice toward the end of the

The preparation of this paper was aided by grants from the Social Sciences and Humanities Research Council of Canada to each of us.

1 This is not, of course, a hypothetical example. On 19 November 2007, the Department of Justice news release coinciding with the introduction of Bill C-25, *Youth Criminal Justice Act*, 2d Sess., 39th Parl., 2007, stated that the "The Honourable Rob Nicholson, Minister of Justice and Attorney General of Canada, today introduced legislation that will provide new measures to protect communities from young offenders who pose a significant risk to public safety. The provisions include: [a]mending the *Youth Criminal Justice Act* . . . to allow courts to consider deterrence and denunciation as objectives of youth sentences" (at 1). In fact, had the bill become law, sentences under the *Youth Criminal Justice Act* "*may* have [had] the following objectives . . . [to] deter the young person and other young persons from committing offences" [emphasis added]: Bill C-25, *ibid.*, s. 38(2)(f). However, even that provision was subject to the proportionality requirement. Said differently, the sentence would still have to be proportionate to the seriousness of the offence and the youth's responsibility for the offence, and the judge would still be required to hand down, within proportionality, the most rehabilitative sentence possible.

first decade of the twenty-first century would be surprised to find a political statement that is in clear contradiction with almost all empirical evidence about youth crime. But when one finds that one disagrees with Nick Bala on as important a youth justice issue as the determination of the age of criminal responsibility, then there is a problem that deserves some serious intellectual work.

That is the situation that many of us found ourselves in when the long promised review of the *Young Offenders Act*[2] got underway in mid-1994 in response to a request from the then minister of justice, the Honourable Allan Rock. Nick Bala — a person we and most others who have worked on youth justice matters have respected and learned from for years — did what at first blush was the unmentionable: he recommended to the committee that under certain circumstances, the minimum age of criminal responsibility be lowered from twelve (which it had been since 1984) to ten.

When he appeared before the committee and made this recommendation, Nick joined a group of criminal justice organizations that he generally did not agree with fully about youth justice policy. These included Victims of Violence, Citizens against Violence, the Edmonton Police Service, Crime Responsibility and Youth (founded by Chuck and Dona Cadman after their sixteen-year-old son had been killed by another sixteen-year-old), as well as the minister of justice of Alberta in Ralph Klein's government, the Conservative minister of justice of Manitoba, and Ontario Conservative Premier Mike Harris's solicitor general. Together they apparently agreed that under certain circumstances the age of criminal responsibility for some youths should be reduced to ten, though many of them probably did not have as nuanced a recommendation as Nick did. But in the list of those who supported the recommendation contained in the report of the Standing Committee on Justice and Legal Affairs, Professor Nicholas Bala stands out as the only *individual* (speaking as a person) listed as having supported this view. Certainly no other academic experts appeared to take this position.

Though other individuals have certainly expressed the view that those under twelve should be subject to the criminal law, Nick, of course, was cited by the Committee not only because of his importance in the field but because, in the end, he persuaded them to adopt his position. Nick Bala and the solicitor general of his province, Bob Runciman, probably agreed on little

2 *Young Offenders Act*, RSC 1985, c. Y-1, repealed SC 2002, c. 1, s. 199 [*YOA*].

else, especially in youth justice matters. This agreement was puzzling — or perhaps more accurately astonishing — and it probably reflects poorly on us that we did not fully understand Nick's position until about a decade later.

In any event, the proposal was a modest one.[3] The Committee recommended that the attorney general of a province, in consultation with appropriate child welfare and other authorities, would have to consent to such a prosecution personally. It further required that a youth court judge consider whether it was appropriate to deal with the youth in the youth (criminal) court system. Finally the parliamentary committee that made this suggestion was obviously concerned about how it would be implemented: it recommended that the government report back to Parliament in three years on how the proposal was working. To some extent, it seems that the idea of a discretionary inclusion of ten- and eleven-year-olds into the youth justice system acknowledges that there are few absolutes and that the determination of any fixed age is arbitrary. But there are other complex issues to consider when thinking about the age of criminal responsibility.

Nick's *Youth Criminal Justice Law*[4] is unambiguously the gold standard for authoritative and thoughtful interpretations of the *Youth Criminal Justice Act*. In the 2003 edition of this book, after spending seventeen pages presenting a thoughtful and interesting discussion of the minimum age issue, Nick allowed himself the licence granted to book authors and used four of the 613 pages to present an interesting, gentle, and balanced answer to the question contained in the heading of this section: "Offending Behaviour by Youths under Twelve: Is Law Reform Needed?" A careful reader can see that Nick's view — between his mid-1990s appearance before the late Shaughnessy Cohen's parliamentary committee and his writing of that chapter — had not changed. Nick favoured the *possibility* of criminal justice intervention in the lives of those who had committed serious offences.

To be clear, however, Nick was unambiguous in his belief that criminalizing the behaviour of youths under twelve years old should be the exception, not the rule:

> Although most children under twelve who commit offences should be dealt with informally, or under child welfare or mental health legislation,

---

3 Canada, House of Commons, Standing Committee on Justice and Legal Affairs, *Renewing Youth Justice* (April 1997) (Chair: Shaughnessy Cohen, MP).

4 Nicholas Bala, *Youth Criminal Justice Law* (Toronto: Irwin Law, 2003).

> there is a strong argument that present child-welfare and institutional arrangements are not totally adequate. For some cases it may be inappropriate to have an approach that focuses solely on the "best interests" of the child and appears to give no weight to accountability, the concerns of victims, or the protection of society. The present responses may be seen as failing to meet the needs of victims .... Further, the criminal law has an important symbolic value for society in general and the victims of crime in particular. The public's sense of injustice at the lack of accountability of offenders under twelve may have some negative implications for the entire justice system and certainly frustrates victims, the police, and in some cases the parents of child offenders as well.[5]

Nick's position puzzled us for a long time, for a number of reasons, including the fact that he cited a couple of our papers in support of his argument. Although we could see the logic of the various arguments he made — a few of which are quoted above — our overriding concern with his recommendation related in large part to the fact that the Canadian youth justice system, did not, at that point, have a very good record of screening out all but the most serious youth court cases involving the very young. Hence our concern was in part that the prosecution of those under twelve would open up the youth justice system to increasing numbers of youths whose offences were best dealt with by other means.

Our concerns were not entirely theoretical. In the last year in which those under twelve could be charged criminally (under the *Juvenile Delinquents Act* in 1983), a disproportionately high number of the cases brought to youth court involved ten- and eleven-year-olds who had committed minor thefts or mischief.[6] Twelve-year-olds under the *Young Offenders Act* were also relatively unlikely to be brought to court, but if they were, it was much more likely to be for minor property offences than for serious (or even minor) violence.[7] And, although Nick's own research has shown that with the implementation of the *Youth Criminal Justice Act*, Canada has dramatically improved its ability to screen out less serious offences from the youth justice system, it needs

5 *Ibid.* at 180–81.

6 *Juvenile Delinquents Act*, SC 1908, c. 40 [*JDA*]; Anthony N. Doob & Carla Cesaroni, *Responding to Youth Crime in Canada* (Toronto: University of Toronto Press, 2004) at 58.

7 Doob & Cesaroni, *ibid.* at 53; *YOA*, above note 2.

to be remembered that under the *Young Offenders Act* large numbers of minor cases had been brought to court.[8]

Clearly this kind of "net widening" would have been very unlikely to occur if the 1997 parliamentary committee's recommendation had been strictly followed. It seems very unlikely that anyone would seek the provincial attorney general's permission to charge an eleven-year-old for shoplifting even if it were a case of serial shoplifting. Our concern at the time with the recommendation was that provincial attorneys general would make the decision to charge those ten- or eleven-year-olds largely on the basis of the number of decibels of public outcry. Furthermore, we were concerned that if the absolute ban of prosecuting those under twelve was relaxed at all, relaxing it a bit more each time some high-profile event occurred would be too easy for governments more interested in appearing to be responsive to public opinion than in showing leadership in promoting sensible youth justice policies. After all, there is a history, in *Criminal Code*[9] amendments, of adding to a list of toughening factors once one has been provided. One only has to look at the history of factors that lead to a "reverse onus" on release on bail to know that such lists have a tendency to get longer as politicians find it necessary to demonstrate their abhorrence of certain kinds of crime. In a similar vein, in the list of aggravating factors in sentencing it seems strange that the Parliament of Canada thought it necessary, in the early part of this century, to tell judges that "evidence that the offence was a terrorism offence shall be deemed to be aggravating circumstances"[10] In the area of youth justice, the attempts to expand on the meaning of a "violent offence" in section 39(1)(a) suggest that when a door is open wide enough to let a mouse through, some attorney general will argue that elephants are really only larger versions of mammals.

One can therefore easily imagine that a limited list that someone like Nick Bala could construct of offences (or types of offenders or offences) for which ten- or eleven-year-olds might, under specially defined circumstances,

8 Nicholas Bala, Peter J. Carrington, & Julian V. Roberts, "Evaluating the *Youth Criminal Justice Act* after Five Years: A Qualified Success" (2009) 51:2 Can J Crim 131; Peter J. Carrington, "Trends in Youth Crime in Canada, 1977–1996" (1999) 41 Can J Crim 1; Doob & Cesaroni, above note 6; Anthony N. Doob & Jane B. Sprott, "Changing Models of Youth Justice in Canada" in Michael Tonry & Anthony N. Doob, eds., *Youth Crime and Youth Justice: Comparative and Cross-National* Perspectives, vol. 31 of Crime *and Justice: A Review of Research* (Chicago: University of Chicago Press, 2004) at 216, table 3.

9 RSC 1985, c. C-46 [*Criminal Code*].

10 *Ibid.*, s. 718.2(a)(v).

be brought into court would be both short and reasonable. However, such a list in the hands of a justice minister looking for a majority government could be viewed as an election resource. Few opposition politicians would, we suspect, be willing to argue against adding an offence or a circumstance to the list of eligible ones in the wake of a highly publicized disturbing offence apparently committed by a ten- or eleven-year-old. The worry is not that the government might want to include ten- and eleven-year-olds suspected of involvement in terrorism to the list. Rather, it is easy to imagine that the eleven-year-old described in the media as "spinning out of control" who participates in a robbery with an older sibling might fall within the gaze of a pre-election minister.

Canada has seen variation in both the recommendations and legislated age of criminal responsibility. We have lived under two different minimum ages: seven under the *Juvenile Delinquents Act* and twelve under the *Young Offenders Act* and the *Youth Criminal Justice Act.*[11] In addition, there have been serious proposals for two other minimum ages: ten, as recommended by the Standing Committee in 1997; and fourteen as recommended in the 1975 report *Young Persons in Conflict with the Law.*[12] But in addition are various other age-related, and arbitrary, demarcations. Youths older than fourteen, but not those younger than fourteen, can be sentenced as adults. And youths older than sixteen who are sentenced as adults are liable to somewhat harsher sentences for murder than are youths under sixteen.

European countries also vary dramatically in the ages at which children can be held responsible for criminal acts. In Scotland, the minimum age is eight, whereas in England and Wales it is ten. At the other extreme, in New Zealand it is fourteen, and in Sweden and Denmark it is fifteen. We see similar variation across the United States. Although apparently many states rely on common law decisions rather than statutory law to determine the minimum age, legislated minimums vary from six (in North Carolina) to ten in a number of states (e.g., Minnesota, Mississippi, and Texas).

We argue that Canada has survived quite well for the past quarter century with a lower age of twelve. At the same time, looking historically and internationally, we fully understand that these demarcations are necessarily

---

11 *JDA*, above note 6; *YOA*, above note 2; *Youth Criminal Justice Act*, SC 2002, c. 1 [*YCJA*].

12 Canada, Ministry of the Solicitor General, *Young Persons in Conflict with the Law: A Report of the Solicitor General's Committee on Proposals for New Legislation to Replace the* Juvenile Delinquents Act (Ottawa: Ministry of the Solicitor General, 1975).

arbitrary. Different people at different times in different places would draw an arbitrary line in different places. The question that we wrestled with was how one could justify making this line flexible.

The most obvious way to think about the "age" issue is to think about research on the immaturity of youths. This research aligns with Nick's proposals suggesting flexibility. Although focused on the maximum age and adult court processing, rather than on the minimum age, recent research by Laurence Steinberg and others[13] finds that logical reasoning abilities in structured situations and basic information-processing skills develop during adolescence at different rates. One does not need to be a psychologist to know that ten-, twelve-, fourteen-, or sixteen-year-old children do not think like adults. Research suggests that by the age of fifteen or sixteen, most adolescents display adult levels of competency to stand trial (e.g., understanding facts about a court proceeding and reasoning with those facts in a rational manner). However, when looking at psychosocial maturity (e.g., impulsivity, sensation seeking, future orientation, and susceptibility to peer pressure) adolescents appear to be quite different from adults. Adolescents appear to display much higher levels of impulsivity and susceptibility to peer pressure and much lower levels of consideration for consequences. Indeed, psychosocial maturity appears to continue to develop well into the twenties.[14] Thus, risky behaviours tend to be much more common in adolescence and early adulthood. These results have led some to argue for added protections for youths (such as extending youth court jurisdiction beyond age sixteen in various states in the United States and/or having age as a mitigating factor in adult criminal law, and so forth). More generally though — and back to Nick's argument about flexibility in age ranges —

> the notion that a single line can be drawn between adolescence and adulthood for different purposes under the law is at odds with developmental science. Drawing age boundaries on the basis of developmental research cannot be done sensibly without a careful and nuanced consideration of the particular demands placed on the individual for "adult-like" maturity in different domains of functioning.[15]

---

13 Laurence Steinberg *et al.*, "Are Adolescents Less Mature Than Adults? Minors' Access to Abortion, the Juvenile Death Penalty, and the Alleged APA 'Flip-Flop'" *American Psychologist* (October 2009).

14 *Ibid.*

15 *Ibid.* at 583.

Clearly these arguments are based on the maximum age — but similar nuanced arguments can be made for the minimum age as well.

When thinking about flexibility in the age ranges, many think only of the offence. In starkest terms, for such people, the question is how one can justify responding to serious offending by ten- and eleven-year-olds under the criminal law but less serious offending outside of the criminal law. Said differently, what is it about the most serious cases that they can have the effect of instantly maturing a youth sufficiently to hold that youth criminally responsible? That, after all, was what Nick and the 1997 Parliamentary Report appeared to be telling us would make good youth justice policy.

In this context, American juvenile justice expert Barry Feld reproduces, apparently with approval, Scott and Steinberg's summary of "the current developmental psychological research on adolescent reasoning and maturity of judgment":[16]

> Using the tools of developmental psychology, we examine two important dimensions of adolescence that distinguish this group from adults in ways that are important to criminal culpability. First, the scientific evidence indicates that teens are simply less competent decision makers than adults . . . . Second, adolescence is a developmental period in which personality identity and character are in flux and begin to take shape through a process of exploration and experimentation. Youthful involvement in crime is often a part of this process, and, as such, it reflects the values and preferences of a transitory stage, rather than those of an individual with a settled identity. Most young violators do not become adult criminals . . . .[17]

At that time, then, Nick's more flexible position on the "minimum age" issue appeared to make little sense in the context of passages such as this. Why would one want to consider a child mature or competent enough to be worthy of criminal justice prosecution *only* if that child had committed a serious, in contrast with a less serious, offence? We now understand that we did not fully appreciate Nick's position. Fortunately or unfortunately, Nick never needed to address these sorts of questions because the general proposals from the late 1990s never went anywhere. Because the government did not accept the

---

16 Barry C. Feld, *Cases and Materials on Juvenile Justice Administration*, 2d ed. (St. Paul, MN: Thomson West) at 85.

17 Elizabeth S. Scott & Laurence Steinberg, "Blaming Youth" (2003) 81:3 Texas L Rev 799 at 801, quoted in Feld, *ibid*. at 86.

Committee's recommendation, Nick and others were not encouraged to develop full and formal proposals on what such a scheme would look like. We have no doubt that if Nick had had to develop the recommendation further, however, he would have created principled arguments and detailed, nuanced proposals. Indeed, as discussed below, Nick's identification of the goals of the youth justice system was an important beginning to this process.

Nine years after Nick's appearance before the parliamentary committee, he ensured that one of us (Tony Doob) would have to think more clearly about this issue. Nick arranged that Tony would be invited to participate in a policy meeting (including giving a formal talk) on the manner in which the age issue had been dealt with in Canada. This policy meeting took place in Macau, a country Tony knew nothing about. Macau was thinking about changing the age at which youths became adults for criminal justice purposes. In its case, the focus was largely on what we would consider to be the age at which youths were considered adults for the purpose of criminal justice processing. But the issues — upper and lower age ranges for youth court processing — are not very different. In addition, by thinking of this issue in part in terms of an upper age, one is forced to consider that Canada from 1908 until 2003 had a flexible upper age limit for youths. After all, a high proportion of youths fourteen and older were liable to be transferred to adult court. And after 2003, a somewhat smaller proportion of youths were subject to the possibility of being sentenced as adults.[18] In all cases, few youths were ever transferred or (apparently) sentenced as adults. But the possibility was, and is, there. In other words, at the top end of the age distribution for the youth justice system, we have always allowed for the possibility of treating youths as adults. There has been no serious principled objection to this. It is often seen as a safety valve, and like most safety valves, it is important when it is needed but the assumption is that it should be needed infrequently.

18 Under the *YOA*, above note 2, s. 16(1), a youth fourteen and over could be considered for transfer to adult court only if that youth were charged with an indictable offence other than one in the absolute jurisdiction of a provincial court judge (those offences listed in *Criminal Code*, above note 9, s. 553). Under the *YCJA*, above note 11, a youth is liable to an adult sentence if the young person has been found guilty of an offence for which an adult is liable to imprisonment for a term of *more than* two years (see, for example, s. 64(1)). There are a non-trivial number of indictable offences carrying maximum sentences of two years that are not under the absolute jurisdiction of a provincial court judge. These cases are therefore not eligible for adult sentences but would have been eligible for transfer.

The unanswered question, however, was Nick's support for flexibility of the minimum age. The two of us discussed this issue in the context of a paper we had each recently read in connection with an information service that we help produce for those interested in criminal justice policy (*Criminological Highlights*).[19] In that paper, David Smith did not address the minimum age issue *per se* but instead gave a broad framework for thinking about what we mean by "effectiveness" in youth justice.

Smith pointed out that there are various ways in which a youth justice system can be defined as effective and "not all are primarily concerned with using juvenile justice to bring about change in young offenders or in the wider social world."[20] Indeed, the first four he listed were not consequentialist:

1) responding in a morally and legally appropriate manner to offending ("The emphasis is on retribution out of a sense of justice"[21]);
2) communicating to the general public "through appropriate symbolic gestures,"[22] often, in the case of serious crimes, simply to indicate that certain types of behaviour are not to be tolerated;
3) satisfying victims of crimes committed by youths;
4) responding in a "caring" fashion to the needs of young people who offend;
5) deterring youth crime;
6) controlling and supervising troublesome youths; and
7) changing the behaviour of young offenders so that they will not offend when they are no longer under the control of the youth justice system.

Smith notes that "many of the conflicts and tensions, both within the juvenile justice system and in public debate, arise because we want the system to do many different things that may be incompatible, or at least hard to reconcile."[23]

This framework for thinking about the legitimate goals of the youth justice system made us go back to Nick's discretionary approach to the age of criminal responsibility. Assuming that youths age ten and eleven passed the test of knowing that something was wrong and criminal, why would one

---

19 David J. Smith, "The Effectiveness of the Juvenile Justice System" (2005) 5:2 Criminology and Criminal Justice 181.

20 *Ibid.* at 183.

21 *Ibid.*

22 *Ibid.*

23 *Ibid.* at 184.

want to have the age of criminal responsibility arbitrarily set at a single point in the development of a child?

In this context, then, it also makes enormous sense that relatively similar Western countries have different ages of criminal responsibility. Why, after all, would one expect that different jurisdictions, at different times, would weigh the various purposes that David Smith listed in a similar fashion?

We realized, after reading David Smith's paper, that Nick's own statement was quite logical. It could not be dismissed on the basis that his logic correlated "being an adult" with the severity of the crime that a youth was alleged to have committed.

Obviously David Smith was talking about the various dimensions on which one might evaluate a youth justice system. But thinking instead about how one might respond to certain offences or offence categories, the appropriateness of a hard and fast rule by which a youth can be charged on his or her twelfth birthday but not the day before might be reconsidered. It may be that it would be seen as unseemly and morally and legally inappropriate to respond to a case of theft by a ten-year-old by invoking the criminal (or youth criminal) law. However, in the case of a brutal assault or a murder, it may be that values like those listed above (e.g., retribution, denunciation, responding to victims' wishes) would be given more weight in the decision whether to consider the case "criminal."

Perhaps because Nick talked of the "needs" of victims and protection of society, we had not considered carefully some of his other justifications for breaking through the age twelve barrier. Nick, after all, said that "the criminal law has an important symbolic value for society in general and the victims of crime in particular. The public's sense of injustice at the lack of accountability of offenders under twelve may have some negative implications for the entire justice system and certainly frustrates victims, the police, and in some cases the parents of child offenders as well."[24]

If we accept this interpretation (or perhaps this elaboration) of the position that Nick and the 1997 parliamentary committee took with respect to age, we need to ask whether this kind of thoughtful weighing of alternatives — the kind of thoughtful weighing that Nick himself would make — would be likely to flow from legislation that allowed attorneys

24 *Ibid.* at 180–81.

general to decide which serious crimes by ten- and eleven-year olds would be dealt with under the criminal law.

We do not have very good data on the frequency with which youths under age twelve are involved in very serious offences, but it does happen. A study in 1992[25] using data from twenty-seven police forces that were collecting detailed information about criminal incidents suggests that very few of those identified by the police as offenders were under age twelve (about 1.2 percent). This 1.2 percent constituted 4,757 youths, the majority of whom were ten or eleven years old. Only 8 percent involved violence, the majority of which was classified by the police as the lowest level of assault. Three of these 4,757 incidents were described as aggravated assaults. A 1997 study listed four aggravated assaults (of 5,169 incidents involving youths) and one case of a youth under twelve being named as a suspect in a homicide. Not surprisingly, most of the victims of the assaults were either acquaintances or members of the offender's family or close friends. Clearly, under child welfare law, the most serious cases would not be ignored; indeed, they would be very likely to result in rather substantial amounts of (institutional) control.

Though these data are obviously dated, the point we want to make is that exceedingly few cases would be likely to involve those under twelve being eligible for criminal prosecution *if the threshold were kept high* for treating young violence in the youth justice system.

Indeed, our assessment of the scope of the problem at this point is that it is so small that to open up the possibility of prosecutions of this small group may in the end create more problems than it solves. But like all things, this is the weighing of different approaches. We differ, perhaps, in how we see the relative harm of not prosecuting those cases "deserving" of criminal prosecution with the alternative: prosecuting cases that should not be prosecuted. We might differ from Nick over how we weigh the benefits and costs of these two choices, but we are unambiguously thankful to him for forcing us to understand our differences. In the end, Nick's challenge to us, and to others, led us to a better understanding of one aspect of youth justice. This, of course, is what Nick has always done. Whether his audience consists of public servants, legislators, students, or other academics, he continues to challenge and teach us in his usual thoughtful and gentle manner.

---

25 Summarized by Doob & Cesaroni, above note 6 at 60–61.

Part Three

CHAPTER 10

Judicial Interviews of Children in Custody and Access Cases

DAN L. GOLDBERG

In 1991, Canada ratified the United Nations *Convention on the Rights of the Child*.[1] This agreement enshrined into international law the inalienable rights of children. Pursuant to Article 12 of the *Convention*, a child who can form views in a matter affecting him or her can, either directly or through a representative or an appropriate body, have those views placed before any judicial or administrative proceeding. This provision theoretically allows a child to communicate his or her views directly with a judge or other judicial officers. In Canada, children who are involved in custody/access proceedings and whose views and preferences are ascertainable are also, at least symbolically, entitled under international law to have their own counsel to serve as their representative.

Under Article 12, the opportunity for a child to be heard in any judicial and administrative hearing is to be provided in a manner consistent with the procedural rules of *Convention* signatory countries. In regard to the methods of ascertaining children's views, the statutory provisions and regulations of

---

The views expressed in this article are those of the author and do not necessarily represent the views of the Office of the Children's Lawyer. The author gratefully acknowledges the research assistance of Philippa Geddie, 2009–10 Student-at-Law, Office of the Children's Lawyer. The author gratefully acknowledges, with fondness and admiration, the enormous contribution to family law in Canada and internationally by Queen's University Professor of Law Nicholas Bala.

1 Can. T.S. 1992 No 3.

the Canadian provinces and territories vary, both as to whether judicial officers have the discretion to interview children and with respect to the systematic provision of children's counsel.

In the past several years, the issue of judges conducting forensic interviews with children for the purpose of eliciting their custodial and visitation preferences has resurfaced and generated a debate in many Western jurisdictions regarding the appropriateness of this practice. This chapter discusses the issue and describes the many significant concerns about judicial preference interviews. At the same time, it describes some circumstances in which it may be appropriate for a judge to have a conversation with a child without discussing that child's preferences regarding custody and visitation.

There are several ways to place children's views and preferences in evidence before the court without directly involving them as witnesses or subjecting them to judicial interview. An assessor's report, a therapist's evidence, a parent or another's statement, and, in Ontario, evidence of a clinical investigator/social worker assisting the child's counsel can all be used as vehicles for ensuring that a child's wishes are placed before the court.

A. EXCEPTION TO THE RULE AGAINST HEARSAY EVIDENCE

The traditional rule about hearsay statements is that they are not admissible in evidence. However, an exception in both criminal and family law proceedings is that children's statements to third parties are admissible.

The decision in *R. v. Khan*[2] established the hearsay exception for children's statements to third parties on the basis of the dual test of necessity and reliability. The Supreme Court of Canada applied its decision in *Ares v. Venner*[3] and held that "necessity" should be interpreted as "reasonably necessary." If a child's *viva voce* evidence would be inadmissible, then hearsay evidence is necessary. A psychological assessment that the child's testimony in court might be traumatic or harm the child can also establish necessity.[4]

In *R. v. Khan*, the Supreme Court of Canada held that "reliability" may be determined by evidencing the "timing, demeanour, the personality of the child, the intelligence and understanding of the child, and the absence of any reason to expect fabrication in the statement. . . . The matters relevant to reli-

2 [1990] 2 SCR 531.
3 [1970] SCR 608.
4 Above note 2 at para. 30.

ability will vary with the child and with the circumstances, and are best left to the trial judge."[5] The Supreme Court also held that courts must be more flexible in accepting children's hearsay evidence, especially in cases in which the children may have been victims of sexual abuse.

In *Khan v. College of Physicians and Surgeons of Ontario*,[6] the Ontario Court of Appeal held that the test of necessity and reliability set out by the Supreme Court of Canada in the *R. v. Khan* criminal proceedings also applied in civil proceedings:

> The reliance in *Khan* on *Ares v. Venner*, ... a civil case, indicates that the necessity and reliability criteria identified in *Khan* have equal applicability whether the child's out-of-court statement is tendered in a civil or criminal proceeding. That is not to say that the determination of whether those criteria have been met will be the same regardless of the nature of the proceedings, but only that both factors will have to be addressed in both types of cases.[7]

In *R. v. Khelawon*,[8] the Supreme Court of Canada widened the scope for admitting children's hearsay evidence: trial judges may now properly consider, at the threshold reliability stage, evidence of the circumstances under which the statement was made, including the presence or absence of any corroborating evidence.

In custody and access proceedings, courts tend to admit into evidence statements made by children to third parties. *J.K.F. v. J.D.F.*[9] concerned a five-year-old child who had told a daycare worker, a social worker, and a psychologist that her father had poked her in the genital and rectal areas. The mother applied to suspend the father's access on the basis that he had sexually abused the child and, at trial, sought to introduce the child's hearsay statements into evidence. The court commented that the rules of evidence must be more flexible in both child protection and custody cases. The court applied the *Ares v. Venner* decision and held that the reception of hearsay evidence is justified on the grounds of necessity and reliability. The court stated that reliability depended on whether the statements were spontaneous, whether the child

---

5 *Ibid.* at 547.
6 [1992] OJ No 1725 (CA).
7 *Ibid.* at 34.
8 [2006] 2 SCR 787 at paras. 92–100.
9 [1988] BCJ No 278 (CA).

was coached, whether the questions suggested an answer, and whether the child's disclosures were consistent over time.

In *Gillies v. Gillies*,[10] counsel for the father sought to introduce into evidence statements made by the children to various third parties, including the father's current wife. The children were not called to testify directly because they were only six and seven years old and because the atmosphere in the court was too intimidating. The court held that the statements were admissible and would determine after hearing the evidence whether they were reliable and what weight they would be given. Justice Fortier stated:

> In normal situations, hearsay is prohibited unless it is hearsay that fits into one of the numerous categories considered to be exceptions to the hearsay rule. Utterances of children to third parties have not, until recently, been considered to be an exception to the hearsay rule.
>
> It is my experience that a practice has evolved that children's utterances to the third parties be admitted in evidence in custody and access cases because it is useful to assist the judge at least in determining issues of credibility.[11]

In *P.V. v. D.B.*,[12] the mother, in the context of a custody and access case, alleged that her ten-year-old daughter (M.) was at risk of violence when she was with her father. The British Columbia Supreme Court addressed the issue of the admissibility and weight of a child's hearsay statements in a custody case. Justice Russell stated:

> Much of the evidence relied on by the defendant in this case consists of statements made by M. to other persons, particularly the defendant and professionals engaged by the defendant to counsel M. Both parties agree . . . that a child's hearsay evidence may be admissible in a child custody case, provided that it is both necessary and reliable. However, P.V. asserts that M.'s statements should be viewed as unreliable and given limited weight by the Court, because the statements to her mother are the product of improper influence. Further, he submits that statements to other third parties may be influenced by M.'s need to please her mother, her anxiety

10 (20 May 1993), Owen Sound 1105/89 (Ont Ct J).
11 *Ibid.* at para. 3.
12 [2007] BCJ No 343 (SC).

about her mother's safety and her mother's continued hostility to the father that has been communicated to M.

In this case, the child did not testify and, therefore, the admission of her hearsay evidence is necessary in order to fully consider the question of her best interests. The bigger issue is the reliability of these statements. A list of the indicia of reliability of a child's hearsay statements was given by Dillon J. in *S.F.R. v. E.C.R.* [(1997), 41 BCLR (3rd) 239] at [paragraph] 43:

> The indicia of reliability have been established in *R. v. Khan, supra,* and in the cases that have applied *R. v. Khan*. They include: timing of the statement; demeanour of the child; personality of the child; intelligence and understanding of the child; absence of motive of child to fabricate; absence of motive or bias of the person who reports the child's statement; spontaneity; statement in response to non-leading questions; absence of suggestion, manipulation, coaching, undue influence or improper influence; corroboration by real evidence; consistency over time; and statement not equally consistent with another hypothesis or alternative explanation . . . .[13]

In *Neuberger v. Connors*,[14] a professional's testimony about a child's disclosure of sexual abuse was held to be admissible to prove the truth of the statement. The court held that custody and access litigation is not the same as ordinary litigation because the only issue is the best interests of the child. The court stated that the rules of evidence should therefore be more flexible where the court's only mandate is to act in the child's best interests and thus admitted the professional's testimony based on the criteria of necessity and reliability.

Allowing expert testimony of a child's views and preferences by an individual such as an assessor or therapist permits the child's wishes to be heard while protecting the child from being directly involved in the dispute. This approach ensures that the best interests of the child remain the focal point of the proceeding in terms of both the desired outcome and the procedure that is followed.

---

13 *Ibid.* at paras. 17–18.

14 (4 July 1990), Napanee, 7796/89 (Ont Ct Gen Div), aff'd [1994] OJ No 3612 (CA), leave to appeal to SCC refused, [1994] SCCA No 420.

B. WHY CHILDREN SHOULD NOT BE CALLED TO GIVE DIRECT EVIDENCE

Despite the provisions of the Ontario *Evidence Act*,[15] which allow the testimony of children in custody/access proceedings, there is a general reluctance on the part of the judiciary to have children called as witnesses, believing that it is undesirable to have children openly and publicly declare a parental preference in a courtroom.

Regrettably, in a custody/access case when it is suggested by a parent or their counsel that a child testify or speak to a judge, it is often as a result of the child being aligned with one parent due to inappropriate influence and/or pressure by that parent. This circumstance alone should give pause to judges in determining whether to allow a child to testify or whether they should conduct an interview with the child.

It is important to note that in criminal cases, a child's testimony may be necessary. There, an accused whose liberty may be at stake, is entitled to have the child's evidence tested on the *beyond a reasonable doubt* standard of proof. This is to be contrasted with a custody/access case, in which the issue is to be decided in the best interests of the child and based on the *balance of probabilities* standard of proof. In this latter instance, the direct testimony of a child is not only unnecessary but may well be harmful to the child.

Even in a resource-strapped environment, it is not the responsibility of children to solve adult disagreement over their custody. Children should not be made to feel burdened by the weight of a perception that where they live is a decision they get to make. Nor should children be made to feel omnipotent — that their view will be determinative. Both of these perceptions have much greater traction with children when a judge, as opposed to child's counsel or a mental health professional, conducts an interview for the purpose of obtaining that child's preferences. For a child, the judge's position of authority alone significantly magnifies the importance of the circumstances to make that child's perceptions feel even more real.

Professionals in two major categories think that judges should interview children. First are those who operate in a resource-strapped environment in which lawyers for children are not involved in every custody/access case and who believe they have no credible, independent third party to provide information to the court regarding a child's views and preferences. This cat-

15 RSO 1990, c. E.23.

egory includes situations when no mental health professional, *amicus curiae*, or guardian *ad litem* is available at least to advise the court about the child's wishes. Second are those who are ideologically committed to the notion that they are well suited to elicit the child's views and preferences, even if those wishes are before the court through a recent assessment or child's counsel. While the former instance may be more justifiable than the latter, judges are not in a good position to conduct interviews of children for the purpose of eliciting their views and preferences.

It is important to establish the purpose of the judicial interaction with a child. Is it a get-acquainted meeting, or a forensic interview designed primarily or exclusively to elicit the child's custodial or visitation preferences? The debate in this controversial area revolves largely around the latter.

In Canadian caselaw, most judges express a great reluctance to interview a child because of their lack of training in both child development and conducting child interviews, a judge's chambers being an inappropriate setting, as well as their concern for the potential parental loyalty bind in which they believe a child may be placed.

In Ontario, child's counsel, through the Office of the Children's Lawyer, receives training on child development and interviewing skills. Significantly, unlike a judge, child's counsel conducts multiple interviews over time, in a neutral setting such as a school, which is a familiar and comfortable place for most children. As a result, counsel has the opportunity to establish a rapport and trust that will, in time and in most cases, yield reliable information regarding the strength, consistency, and independence of a child's views and preferences. By also interviewing the child's parents (or other litigants) and collateral sources such as teachers, therapists, and important extended family members, child's counsel can also gain a crucial understanding of the context or circumstances surrounding those views and preferences.

In its *Working Paper 13 — Divorce*, the Law Reform Commission of Canada commented on the practice of having children testify or be judicially interviewed:

> Where a custody dispute goes to trial, some judges attach significance to opinions and preferences expressed by the children but others do not. We think the children should have their opinions taken into account. We recommend that, where custody is being contested in divorce proceedings, the court should be statutorily required to ascertain the views of the children. We do not propose that the children be called as witnesses and asked

> direct questions respecting their preferences. Nor do we propose that the judge should speak to the children informally in his chambers.[16]

Most of the literature regarding child witnesses involves children who have been victims of sexual abuse and the re-victimization they may experience were they to testify about the event. Many children, however, find the experience of testifying to be traumatic in itself. This point is made by lawyer Bryan Finlay and Supreme Court of Canada Justice Thomas Cromwell (then of the Nova Scotia Court of Appeal):

> . . . [T]here is a good deal of expert evidence reported in the cases supporting the view that testifying in the particular circumstances of those cases will or is likely to be damaging to the child. Moreover, counsel knows that many adults find testifying a difficult experience and it seems unlikely that children would find it less so . . . . [C]ounsel should therefore consider very carefully whether it is essential for the child to testify.[17]

As the author of one American study observed:

> It seems clear that putting a child on the witness stand in a custody case, and expecting him to express a preference or reveal damaging facts about one or both of his parents, is almost certain to make a bad situation worse. As observed by the New York Court of Appeal in *Lincoln v. Lincoln*:
>
> > It requires no great knowledge of child psychology to recognize that a child, already suffering from the trauma of a broken home, should not be placed in the position of having its relationship with either parent further jeopardized by having to publicly relate its difficulties with them or be required to openly choose between them.[18]

Heino Lilles has commented on the difficulty for children of being witnesses and how, consequently, the information they provide may not be very accurate or helpful:

---

16 Law Reform Commission of Canada, *Working Paper 13 — Divorce* (Ottawa: Information Canada, 1975) at 50.

17 Bryan Finlay, QC, & T.A. Cromwell, *Witness Preparation Manual,* 2d ed. (Aurora, ON: Canada Law Book, 1999) at 95–96.

18 Lisa Carol Rogers, "Comment: Child Custody: The Judicial Interview of the Child" (1987) 47 La L Rev 559, quoting from *Lincoln v. Lincoln*, 24 NY (2d) 270 at 272 (CA 1969).

> ... [T]he court appearance, can also be the most confusing, strange and traumatic for the child witness. The memory of the child may already be partially disabled due to the passage of time and exposure to extraneous facts; his memory organization techniques are underdeveloped; he may not fully understand the language of the court and certainly its purpose must be a mystery to him; often he is asked to recall traumatic events or to accuse a parent, relative or friend; and then he must cope with cross-examination of defence counsel, an exercise which is highly verbal and demanding of developed cognitive skills. In these areas, young children are clearly at a disadvantage. Furthermore, "[c]hildren are less likely than adults to have the cognitive skills necessary to organize the experience" for recall purposes.[19]

The authors of a Canadian study commented on the differences in the cognitive abilities between children and adults in the context of the legal system, and the impact on a child's testimony:

> Children are not just short adults; they have different reasoning and communication skills. For them, words and ideas often have different meanings. Children also have more limited life experience than adults and often do not understand the reasoning or motives of adults. Additionally, they do not understand the legal system. For example, some children believe that they can go to jail if they give the wrong answer or do not answer a question. Further, children do not have the same language skills as adults. As a result, complex questions are often beyond children's ability to comprehend. These factors affect how they understand the questions they are asked as witnesses.[20]

As young children grow older, their capacity to reason increases. Nevertheless, the stress and possible trauma of testifying in a courtroom may have a bearing on the ability of a child to do so. Another Canadian study commented on this point:

> When these abilities are beginning to emerge, they may not always be correct and may regress under conditions of physical or emotional stress.

---

19 Heino Lilles, "Children as Witnesses: Some Legal and Psychological Viewpoints" (1986) 5 CJFL 237 at 250.

20 John Philippe Schuman, Nicholas Bala, & Kang Lee, "Developmentally Appropriate Questions for Child Witnesses" (1999) 25 Queen's LJ 251 at para. 5.

> Under such conditions more immature ways of thinking and reasoning may re-emerge and persistent questioning may not be fruitful.[21]

If counsel or a party seeks to compel a child to testify by issuing a subpoena, then the court must deal with the matter as part of its duty to control its own process. D.A. Rollie Thompson has addressed this very issue:

> The court is able to enforce its own views of the propriety of children being called as witnesses through its control over the court's process, including subpoenas. While counsel and not the court have the right to determine who they wish to call as witnesses, this right is not unfettered. The trial judge retains a discretion to vacate or set aside a subpoena directed to a child, as part of any court's ability to control its own process and also as part of its legislated mandate to act in the best interests of the child.
>
> . . . The discretion must be exercised judicially which means, it is submitted, that a judge should have some evidence as to the child's condition, circumstances and interests before ruling on the propriety of the subpoena. Because of counsel's general control over the calling of witnesses, the onus of calling such evidence should be upon the party seeking to have the subpoena vacated or refused.[22]

In custody/access matters, courts in Canada have generally discouraged parties from calling children as witnesses. In *Taberner v. Taberner*[23] each parent sought to call one child as a witness. In deciding not to hear the children's testimony, Wright J held that unless it is necessary for the court to make its decision, children should not be placed in the position of deciding disputes between their parents.

In *Wakaluk v. Wakaluk*,[24] the Saskatchewan Court of Appeal affirmed the trial judge's decision not to allow the two children, aged twelve and almost eleven years, to testify. The court held that the trial judge had the discretion to quash a subpoena and that the possibility of further destruction to the family unit as a result of the child testifying was an important factor in deciding whether to quash the subpoena. Justice Brownridge stated: "I agree

---

21 Marcellina Mian *et al.*, "The Child as Witness" (1991), 4 CR (4th) 359 at 362.

22 D.A. Rollie Thompson, "Taking Children and Facts Seriously: Evidence Law in Child Protection Proceedings — Part I" (1988) 7 CJFL 11 at 40.

23 (1971), 5 RFL 14 (Ont HCJ).

24 (1976), 25 RFL 292 (Sask CA) [*Wakaluk*].

with the view that, in general, children ought not to be encouraged to give evidence for or against either parent."[25]

Justice Bayda commented on the issue of whether the trial judge had been wrong in refusing to hear the children testify as to their views and preferences and on the topic of judicial interviews of children:

> Whether to allow a child to express his own wishes in a custody proceeding is a matter for the discretion of the trial judge. The age and maturity of the child are two important factors to consider in making that decision. There are, of course, other factors. Each individual case will reveal those other relevant factors . . . .
>
> To call the child as a witness and ask direct questions to establish his preferences is a procedure that should be discouraged. It is generally, but not always, inappropriate . . . .
>
> The procedure involving a judge speaking to a child, informally, in his chambers, also is not particularly satisfactory to me. To expect a child in such a short period and abnormal atmosphere (from child's point of view) to choose between parents, and to expect to obtain from that child an accurate insight into the reasons for the child's feelings and preferences is ordinarily to expect too much . . . .
>
> A procedure involving a trained and competent third party independent of the parents, charged with the responsibility of ascertaining the child's opinions and preferences using such techniques as are most likely to yield genuine feelings and wishes, and be least harmful to the child, over such period of time as may be necessary, and thereafter reporting to the court, by giving testimony or otherwise, is the procedure to be looked upon with most favour.[26]

In *Blaschuk v. Blaschuk*,[27] counsel requested that the judge meet with the seven-year-old child. In rejecting the request, the court relied upon the decision in *Wakaluk*. In *Schweigert v. Schweigert*,[28] Foran J relied upon both *Wakaluk* and *Blaschuk* when he declined to meet an eight-year-old girl. Similarly, in *Pang v. Pang*,[29] Trainor J relied upon *Wakaluk* in refusing to meet with a ten-year-old

25 *Ibid.* at 298.
26 *Ibid.* at 304.
27 [1980] OJ No 788 (HCJ).
28 [1981] OJ No 1711 (Prov Ct (Fam Div)).
29 [1980] OJ No 1254 (HCJ).

girl. Citing *Wakaluk*, Wittmann J of the Alberta Court of Queen's Bench, in *Howard v. Sandau*,[30] stated that there are obvious policy concerns regarding the testimony of children in family law cases and, as such, special regard to the exercise of a court's discretion must be had concerning minor children.

In *Thur v. Thur*,[31] the court found that allowing a six-year-old boy to testify directly in court was not the appropriate means of ascertaining his views and preferences:

> I believe that the child's wishes can be ascertained in ways other than that provided for in section 65, e.g. through expert witness evidence, the evidence of the parties. It is possibly dangerous to allow a child of age nine to attend in court to express his or her wishes by reason of the fact that if the wishes cannot be followed in light of other evidence to which the child was not privy, it might well be looked upon by the child as yet another in a long string of rejections to which it has been subject.[32]

The court went on to say that notwithstanding section 65 of the *Children's Law Reform Act*[33] (*CLRA*) (now section 64(2)), which allows the court to interview the child to determine views and preferences, the comments of the trial judge cited by Brownridge JA in his decision in *Wakaluk* are still valid: "What weight can properly be given to statements on the part of the immature children not under oath, who have been caught in a tug-of-war for their entire lives. I think very little, if any, and this is why I refused to see or hear them at trial."[34]

In *Uldrian v. Uldrian*,[35] the Ontario Court of Appeal held that section 64(2) of the *CLRA* did not impose a *duty* upon a trial judge to interview the child. In *Hamilton v. Hamilton*, the Saskatchewan Court of Appeal affirmed the position in *Uldrian* and stated, "[W]hile the advisability of holding . . . [a judicial] interview is a matter properly left to the discretion of the trial judge, we agree that its use should be limited and not seen as an opportunity to obtain vital information shielded from the knowledge of and challenge by the litigants."[36]

---

30 [2008] AJ No 742 at para. 56 (QB).
31 [1982] OJ No 1029 (Prov Ct (Fam Div)) [*Thur*].
32 *Ibid.* at para. 4.
33 RSO 1990, c. C.12.
34 *Thur*, above note 31 at para. 4, quoting *Wakaluk*, above note 24 at 297.
35 (1988), 14 RFL (3d) 26 (Ont CA).
36 [1989] SJ No 687 at para. 3 (CA).

Some may see judicial interviews as a preferable alternative to a child testimony, better shielding a child from the court process. However, such an interview still involves the child in the proceedings and, due to the unnatural circumstances, lack of training of judges in child interviewing skills, and the fact that usually only a single child interview is conducted, the procedure has the concomitant risk of yielding inaccurate information. In *Baxter v. Benoit*, the court commented on the practice of judicial interviews of children: "The judicial interview has the advantage of being less intimidating than the courtroom. It has the disadvantage that few judges have the skill to conduct the interview and interpret the evidence."[37]

As some cases have recognized, if a judicial interview is conducted in private, outside the presence of the parties and/or their counsel, then the information obtained by the judge may be prejudicial, to varying degrees, to one or both of the parties. This is another example of why the evidence of a child is best introduced by way of a third party.

In the child protection case of *C.A.S. for the County of Prince Edward v. S.H. and B.H. and E.F.*,[38] Kirkland J ruled, in opposition to counsel's request, that he would not conduct an interview of the child in chambers for a number of reasons. First, he did not have the training to determine the wishes of the children or to determine if they were putting forth their own views. Second, evidence had come before the court that it would be very stressful for the child to come to court and participate. Third, Kirkland J did not know what criteria to use to determine the questions to be asked. Finally, he determined that interviewing the child privately and off the record would be unfair to the parties and their counsel.

Similarly, in *Jandrisch v. Jandrisch*,[39] the Manitoba Court of Appeal commented negatively on the trial judge's interview of four children in chambers with no one else present. Justice Monin stated:

> I honestly do not think that it is a wise or sound practice and this case seems to prove it. Such a conduct leaves the trier of fact with information, evidence or call it what you wish, that the parties, counsel and members of the appellate tribunal have no knowledge of and absolutely no possibility of finding out what happened. It may be of use in exceptional circumstances, but not in a hotly contested matter such as this one. In this bitter dispute

37 [2004] YJ No 107 at para. 58 (SC).
38 (23 March 1993), Picton, (Ont Prov Ct (Fam Div)).
39 [1980] MJ No 6 (CA).

> where the views of the children have taken such exaggerated prominence, it was in my view, unwise to question them in camera and then to use this information to question fairly severely one of the spouses only.[40]

In declining either to allow the testimony of or to interview twelve- and thirteen-year-old children, Van Rensburg J expressed concerns about the desirability and appropriateness of judicial interviews for the purpose of ascertaining the children's custodial preferences:

> This process, with Wesley and Shawn confronting their parents in open court and being examined and cross-examined by them, might well be upsetting and even traumatic, and wouldn't necessarily elicit their real views. A private interview of each child . . . was also not an option . . . . A "behind closed doors" consultation with the judge alone, about such an important matter, is inconsistent with the appearance of justice.
>
> . . . It was inadvisable for the reasons I have noted to obtain such evidence directly from the children. In the circumstances I would also be concerned that the stressful environment of the trial, together with the necessity of confronting both parents about the sensitive matter of which parent a child would prefer to live with might inhibit Wesley and Shawn from accurately expressing their views in court. Communication of each child's views in a comfortable environment to an impartial third party with appropriate professional skills, in my view provides some assurance that his true preferences will be before the court.[41]

In *S.J.M. v. D.F.M.*,[42] the Nova Scotia Family Court cited *Jandrisch* and also commented on the ability of judges to conduct interviews of children. Justice Daley held that "the judiciary are, with rare exceptions, not trained in the human behaviour sciences nor have specialized training or experience with children who are undergoing possibly the most traumatic experience a child can face in its young life."[43]

In *L.E.G. v. A.G.*,[44] the British Columbia Supreme Court cogently addressed the issue of conducting judicial interviews of children. Justice Martinson held:

---

40 *Ibid.* at para. 13.

41 *Ali v. Williams*, [2008] OJ No 1207 at paras. 52 and 54 (SCJ).

42 [1985] NSJ No 489 (Fam Ct).

43 *Ibid.* at para. 39.

44 [2002] BCJ No 2319 (SC) [*L.E.G.*].

> Concerns about the judge interview have been raised that go beyond procedural safeguard questions. Judges usually are not trained to interview children in a way that allows them to accurately assess the real wishes of the child. Judges lack knowledge about developmental differences in cognitive, language and emotional capacities in children. From a clinical perspective, being interviewed in chambers can be far from a relaxing experience for children. Rather, it can be a formidable and inherently stressful experience for most children . . . .
>
> . . . A judge may not be able to obtain accurate information in one relatively short meeting . . . . There is an added concern that the judge may think that he or she has received accurate information when the information is not, in fact, accurate.[45]

In the custody case of *Palumbo v. Palumbo*,[46] Eberle J declined to conduct a preference interview with twelve- and fourteen-year-old children, stating that although he had done so on some occasions, he did not find it satisfactory:

> I have no magic in dealing with children.
>
> And the situation is worsened by the fact that an interview by a judge, even in chambers, with no one else present, is an interview, by a child, with a complete stranger in strange surroundings. And these children are certainly at an age where I am sure both of them are aware that the trial is going on today between their parents, and I am sure both children will be fully aware of the great pressures and stresses that are upon everybody who participate in a trial.
>
> And so, it seems to me that interviewing a child, or children, in an attempt to determine their real wishes in those circumstances is to do so in entirely false circumstances, unreal circumstances, and circumstances in which, if one were to arrive at the right answer, it would be only by luck and good fortune, and not for any other reason. So I am not inclined to interview the children.[47]

Wayne D. v. Christina D.[48] was an access case in which a father issued and served a subpoena to his ten-year-old child to testify whether the child wanted to see his father's common law partner. The child was fearful about

45 *Ibid.* at paras. 25–26.

46 [1982] OJ No 1576 (HCJ) [*Palumbo*].

47 *Ibid.* at paras. 4–6.

48 (11 April 1990), North York, D.620/82 (Ont Prov Ct (Fam Div)).

attending court. The court declined to have the child testify and accepted the submissions of counsel for the child about the child's wishes. Judge Felstiner thought that bringing the child to court to express an opinion might be traumatic to the child and that any answers given to questions in court would be those that the child felt would please the parent or the court.

In *S.E.C. v. G.P.*,[49] the court refused to allow a thirteen-year-old girl to testify. Justice Perkins stated:

> I . . . find that having to testify would likely be traumatic for her, and while it might not cause long lasting damage, it would nevertheless cause her real harm that could last for some time . . . . It would be ironic in the extreme on a custody and access issue, where the only factor is what is in the best interests of the child, if the litigation process were used so as to cause harm to the child for the ostensible purpose of ascertaining her wishes or even shedding light on her best interests.[50]

In *T.W. (Re)*, Schmaltz J quashed a subpoena for T.W., an eleven-year-old boy, to testify at a child protection hearing as oppressive and not in his best interests:

> Subjecting a young child to court procedures, examination, cross examination, is not a reasonable way to ascertain a child's views or preferences. Court procedures and the adversarial system were not designed with children in mind . . . . The legislators have recognized that requiring a child to attend court in what can only be described as a highly emotional situation for adults, is more than likely a confusing, frightening, stressful, and potentially traumatizing situation for a child.[51]

In *Mamchur v. Mamchur*,[52] notwithstanding that both counsel wanted the judge to interview a twelve-year-old boy in chambers regarding his views and preferences in a custody/access proceeding, the court declined to do so. The court stated:

> Counsel for each of the parties, with somewhat different degrees of enthusiasm, invite me to question Bryce privately to ascertain the sincerity or otherwise of his expressed desire to live with his mother. I have indi-

49 [2003] OJ No 2744 (SCJ).
50 *Ibid.* at para. 32.
51 [2006] NWTJ No 25 at para. 26 (Terr Ct).
52 (1987), 11 RFL (3d) 66 (BCSC).

> cated informally to counsel, and repeat, that I am at least ambivalent as to the value of such an interview, in a situation such as this, where so youthful a person expresses a preference . . . and thus to exhibit a maturity which I simply think not possible. There is a traumatic factor, with possible adverse effect upon Bryce, in the conduct of such a proposed interview. I consider this undesirable.[53]

McCartney v. McCartney was a custody/access case involving a ten-year-old girl whose father wanted the judge to speak with her in chambers; the girl's mother opposed this request.[54] Justice Mullally declined to interview the child and said, "I have decided not to see the child. I am strongly of the opinion that children at this age want and expect these decisions to be made for them . . . . This burden should never be with a child. It must be assumed by adults and in this case the court must make the decision."[55]

Similarly, in *Mannila v. Mannila*,[56] Stach J commented on a request from one of the parents' counsel for His Honour to conduct an interview with the eleven-year-old girl who was the subject of the litigation over which of her parents should have custody:

> . . . I have grave doubts as to the value of an interview, specifically with a shy child. I am reluctant to subject Ashley to this unnecessary trauma, and to the risk that she may feel "responsible" for the ultimate decision which in any event must be made by me alone. I adopt the rationale of another judge who said that this burden should never be imposed upon a child and that it must be assumed by adults. In this case, this court must make the decision.[57]

In *S.R. v. C.S.*,[58] a father of two girls, aged ten and eleven, asked the court to interview his children after the mother had cut off his access to them. Justice Skilnick reluctantly met with the children because the parties' positions were polarized and there was no independent evidence of the children's views. However, the judge neither asked the children to state a potential preference nor reported on any direct statements they had expressed. Justice Skilnick stated:

---

53 *Ibid.* at 67.

54 [1985] MJ No 36 (QB (Fam Div)).

55 *Ibid.* at para. 7.

56 [1992] OJ No 2145 (Gen Div).

57 *Ibid.*

58 [2006] BCJ No 8 (Prov Ct).

> As a general rule, it is my view that parties should be discouraged from involving children directly in court proceedings. In a case such as this, where there is acrimony between the parents, it is generally unfair and emotionally cruel to do something which might make a child feel responsible for the making of a decision which will so fundamentally affect his or her future relationship with the parents. Whatever decision this court reaches will likely be unsatisfactory to at least one of the parties. Under no circumstances should this child be brought to appear or feel responsible for a decision that may add to discord in the home. Children in this position generally ought to be sheltered and protected from any emotional fallout from the break-up of their parents' relationships and should be free from any subsequent guilt or blame that may be placed upon them, either spoken or otherwise.[59]

In *British Columbia (Superintendent of Family and Child Service) v. S.H.*,[60] the court addressed both the issue of a child's testifying in court and being the subject of a judicial interview in chambers. Justice Stansfield held:

> Certainly in theory either event should provide an opportunity to assess the child just as one does any other witness, but I doubt it is very realistic to expect that with a young child who is for a brief period asked to speak to a number of strange persons in an intimidating environment that one will find the child sufficiently outspoken and articulate to permit reliable insight or penetration beyond whatever programming may have occurred over a protracted period.
>
> I heartily endorse the view that young children should not be put in the position of "choosing" between proposed caregivers.[61]

C. JUDICIAL INTERVIEWS IN QUEBEC

In Quebec, there is a markedly different attitude toward the practice of judicial interviews and the issue of children's evidence. Article 34 of the *Civil Code of Quebec* states: "The court shall, in every application brought before it affecting the interest of a child, give the child an opportunity to be heard if his age and power of discernment permit it."[62]

59 *Ibid.* at para. 18.
60 [1995] BCJ No 932 (Prov Ct (Fam Div)).
61 *Ibid.* at paras. 52–53.
62 SQ 1991, c. 64.

As several authors have noted, this is a "rights-based approach to the involvement of children,"[63] as opposed to a best interests approach. The underlying belief is that children should be able to express their views about their future, even to the point of testifying in open court.

In some cases, Quebec judges have "deliberately sought out children"[64] to have conversations about their wishes. In *L.L. c. R.H.*,[65] the court decided, apparently on its own initiative, to interview two children, aged seven and nine, in a custody dispute.

One aspect of the Quebec approach is that children may testify in court or participate in a judicial interview even if their views could have been put before the court in other ways. A recent case involved two children, aged seven and thirteen, in a custody dispute.[66] They wished to reside mainly with their mother, and made their wishes very clear through their lawyer. Nevertheless, Sévigny J interviewed both children, and discussed their stated views and preferences in her judgment.[67]

In another recent case, the applicants sought access to their two teenaged grandchildren.[68] The grandchildren did not want to see their grandparents because of intense family conflict that followed the death of their mother. The children were represented by counsel, who informed the court of their wishes. The court noted that the stress and tension of the litigation was affecting the children's well-being.[69] Regardless, the children gave testimony in open court, in the presence of all parties. The court noted: "Hearings were a difficult period for the girls. They skipped school as they were exhausted. X is sleepless [*sic*]. But they were eager to be heard and to speak out."[70]

D. JUDICIAL ROLE

By conducting interviews of children, the role of a judge is brought into issue. In the adversarial system, the judge's role is to be an impartial trier of fact. Yet

63 Nicholas Bala, Victoria Talwar, & Joanna Harris, "The Voice of Children in Canadian Family Law Cases" (December 2005) 24 CFLQ 221.

64 Claire Bernard, Robin Ward, & Bartha Maria Knoppers, "Best Interests of the Child Exposed: A Portrait of Quebec Custody and Protection Law" (1992) 11 Can J Fam L 57.

65 [1989] JQ no 891 (CS).

66 *Droit de la famille 082460*, [2008] QJ No 9426 (Sup Ct).

67 *Ibid.* at para. 16.

68 *Droit de la famille 08544*, [2008] QJ No 1886 (Sup Ct).

69 *Ibid.* at para. 58.

70 *Ibid.* at para. 54.

by intervening to conduct child interviews, the judge becomes a participant in the evidence gathering process by assuming an inquisitorial role. This latter role is considered by some to be a violation of the judge's position as an impartial adjudicator in the Anglo-American legal tradition. A thoughtful observation about the practice of judicial interviews of children was published in 1983 by a committee comprising Abella, L'Heureux-Dubé, and Rothman JJ. The committee was critical of judicial preference interviews of children and concerned about judges assuming the role of an inquisition in questioning children and thereby possibly compromising their impartiality:

> The practice of interviewing children in chambers by a judge is not an ideal way to ascertain a child's wishes. The interview is conducted in an intimidating environment by a person unskilled in asking questions and interpreting the answers of children. In the relatively short time these interviews take, it is difficult to investigate with sufficient depth and subtlety those perceptions of a child which explain, justify or represent the child's wishes. Moreover, the interview may be perceived as a violation of the judge's role as an impartial trier of fact who does not enter the adversarial arena. The impartiality may also be compromised by the judge assuming the role of the inquisitor in questioning children.
>
> ... With the increasing use of independent legal representation for children, the judicial interview is likely to be replaced by a more expert and skilful assessment of a child's wishes arranged with the assistance of counsel for the child. Where other methods appear to be unavailable, the judge's interview is an appropriate last resort, provided it is conducted in a manner which does not violate the rights of the parties to due process.[71]

In *Richie v. Harkness-Gehle*,[72] Pugsley J addressed the mother's request for him to interview an almost fourteen-year-old girl to ascertain her views and preferences:

> In my view, such a personal meeting runs the risk of the judge's entering the fray between the parties and the practice should be used very rarely and only where all other means of ascertaining the child's views are ab-

71 Judge R.S. Abella, Justice C. L'Heureux-Dubé, & Justice M.L. Rothman, "A Code of Recommended Procedure in the Resolution of Family Law Disputes" in Rosalie S. Abella & Claire L'Heureux-Dubé, eds., *Family Law — Dimensions of Justice: Selected Papers Presented at the Judicial Conference on Family Law, 1981* (Toronto: Butterworths, 1983) at 329.

72 [2008] OJ No 4050 (Ct J).

> sent. Indeed, in my view, this was one of the founding reasons for the creation of the . . . Office of the Children's Lawyer.[73]

Justice Eberle, in *Palumbo v. Palumbo,* commented on the position in which he could have found himself if he had decided (which he did not) to interview the twelve- and fourteen-year-old children:

> If, as a result of that, I were to conclude that they wanted to be with one particular parent, if I were to conclude that they had strong feelings one way or another, what is the situation that I would be faced with? It would either be a situation in which I, in effect, abrogate the responsibility (a responsibility that I do not seek but which is put upon me) in deciding what I think is in the best interests of the children. I abrogate that responsibility to simply ascertain their wishes or, having ascertained their wishes, go against them.[74]

This blurring of roles should be of concern even to those who have a broad view of the role of a judge. Many judges are concerned about legislation that places them in the position of being investigators. Yet at the same time, some of the same judges are seemingly open to becoming, in effect, investigators, when they conduct forensic interviews with children.

Recently retired Martinson J of the British Columbia Supreme Court has provided some insightful commentary on the misconceptions some generalist judges hold regarding their ability to deal with difficult family law matters. Justice Martinson's observations have applicability to judges who seek to conduct forensic interviews with children:

> Judges sometimes think that because of their life experience as a child, a partner, a parent and a lawyer, they can figure out the right result in any family law case they face. They were, after all, selected as judges because they were viewed as having what it takes to make decisions. However, being able to identify these cases, determine the nature of the problem and devise the necessary solutions is not intuitive. Nor is the information and expertise required learned from day-to-day life experience. Yet, making the wrong choices can be harmful to children.[75]

73 *Ibid.* at para. 26.

74 Above note 46 at para. 7.

75 Hon. Donna J. Martinson, "One Case — One Specialized Judge: Why Courts Have an Obligation to Manage Alienation and Other High Conflict Cases" (2010) 4 Fam Ct Rev 180 at 187–88.

Most judges who have conducted judicial interviews of children or are contemplating doing so are no doubt motivated by a desire to act in the children's best interests by seeking their input or, as judges may perceive it, as giving a voice to children who are the subjects of litigation. However, instead of relying on their intuitive belief that they may be able to obtain reliable information from such children, judges would, in my respectful opinion, be wise to consider the social science literature describing how most qualified mental health professionals view the effects on children of participating in judicial preference interviews. Psychologist Joan B. Kelly provides a clinical perspective that judges would be well served to consider when determining whether to conduct such interviews:

> Interviewing a youngster can bring the child into sharp focus for a judge, particularly when parents and their attorneys describe the child's needs in widely divergent ways. On the other hand, from a clinical perspective, being interviewed in chambers is a formidable and inherently stressful experience for most school-aged youngsters. Except for youngsters who are pathologically alienated from a parent, and who often want and enjoy the power of the judges' attention, the majority of children are in untenable psychological positions in interviews with judges. Assuming that their discussions are not confidential, they may simultaneously experience intense loyalty, conflict, guilt and fears of retribution or serious damage to the parent–child relationship. Further, judges are not trained in child interviewing skills, and generally lack knowledge about developmental differences in cognitive, language, and emotional capacities. Thus, it is hard for even the most experienced judge to place children's responses in an appropriate context and evaluate the weight that should be given to their wishes.[76]

Indeed, courts are now far more willing to consider and rely upon social science literature in family law cases, whether or not it has been formally introduced into evidence.[77]

---

76 Joan B. Kelly, "Psychological and Legal Interventions for Parents and Children in Custody and Access Disputes: Current Research and Practice" (2002) 10:1 Va J Soc Pol'y & L 129 at 153–54.

77 *Warcop v. Warcop*, [2009] OJ No 638 at para. 47 (SCJ); *Young v. Young*, [1993] 4 SCR 3 at paras. 103–9.

Judges sitting in family courts have an extremely challenging job determining child custody and access cases. It is made far more difficult when, in increasingly high numbers, the litigants appear without counsel, usually because they do not qualify for legal aid. In addition, the cost of obtaining custody/access assessments is for many people prohibitive. The Office of the Children's Lawyer in Ontario offers both legal and clinical services to children but is unable to be involved in every case before the courts. Most other Canadian provinces and territories offer few or no legal services to children in these areas. In addressing all these concerns (in the context of government restraint in British Columbia in 2002), Martinson J commented that it has become more difficult to determine what a child's wishes are, in a neutral way, through a third party:

> The effect of these cutbacks may be to deny access to justice to families and to deny children the individual justice to which they are entitled. It would be unfortunate if the courts find themselves in the position where judges are resorting to a judge interview because it is the only option available, rather than because it is the method that is in the best interests of the child whose future is at stake.[78]

E. CIRCUMSTANCES IN WHICH IT MAY BE APPROPRIATE FOR A JUDGE TO MEET A CHILD

Under some circumstances it may be useful for a judge, ideally having received some formal training on child development and how to talk to children of various ages, to meet and have a conversation with the child who is the subject of the litigation. As long as this get-acquainted meeting is contained and does not devolve into a forensic interview seeking the child's preferences, it may, in fact, humanize the case for the judge. In *Stefureak v. Chambers*,[79] Quinn J addressed this perspective: "[S]ome judges have held that meeting with the child is not necessarily a matter of attempting to determine the wishes of the child, but may better serve simply to come to a fuller understanding of who the child is for the purposes of determining best interests."[80]

---

78 *L.E.G.*, above note 44 at para. 59.

79 [2004] OJ No 4253 (SCJ).

80 *Ibid.* at para. 67.

Similarly, the British Columbia Court of Appeal commented on judicial interviews:

> [T]hose private interviews are often undertaken not for the purpose of obtaining statements of preference from the child, but to obtain a better idea of the nature of the child. It is helpful to a judge considering the difficult question arising in custody cases to know the child as well as he can.[81]

Finally, in *More v. Primeau*,[82] Blair J interviewed an eight-year-old boy in his chambers and stated, "Before doing so I advised counsel that I did not intend to question him about his wishes about the outcome of this trial. I also had no illusions about my ability to determine the true wishes of a child in such a short discussion conducted under all the emotional pressures surrounding this trial. I simply wanted to see what kind of a boy he was."[83]

Although courts use the term *interview* in the context of a "get-acquainted" interaction, it is probably more useful in this debate to characterize this contact as a *meeting* or a *conversation*, as opposed to a *forensic interview*, which has as its primary purpose to elicit the views and preferences of a child. This process allows children to feel that they have been heard but does not burden them with the feeling that it is their responsibility to resolve their parents' disputes.

A judge may want to meet with a child at a preliminary stage of the proceedings to explain what may happen as the case progresses. For example, a judge may want to talk to a child to explain that an assessment was ordered and that the child and his parents (and possibly others) will be meeting with a social worker, psychologist, or psychiatrist who will then be making recommendations to the judge about various issues, including custody and access.

A judge may also want to explain to a child and both parents a court order that she or he has made and express the expectation that the order be followed. In *Reeves v. Reeves*,[84] Mossip J dealt with a severe alienation case in which she transferred custody of thirteen- and sixteen-year-old boys from their father to their mother. In proposing to meet the children, Her Honour stated, "I intend to advise them of my Court order and what is going to happen immediately following my discussion with them."[85] Given the dramatic

81 *Jespersen v. Jespersen*, [1985] BCJ No 2440 at para. 31 (CA).
82 [1977] OJ No 913 (HCJ).
83 *Ibid.* at para. 22.
84 [2001] OJ No 308 (SCJ).
85 *Ibid.* at para. 42.

nature of a reversal of custody order, especially with older children, it is of some benefit, albeit probably minor, for a judge to assume responsibility for the decision, relieving some of the burden from the new custodial parent.

Finally, a judge may have a case involving exigent circumstances. It may be necessary to ascertain the preferences of a child when time is of the essence and the quick intervention of a mental health professional or child's counsel is not possible or practical. One example of this occurred in Ontario in September 2009, when a judge interviewed a child as the school year was about to start and the parents were proposing two different and credible school options. The judge believed that an immediate decision was necessary and that the fifteen-year-old child was capable of communicating a preference on this issue, independently of her parents.[86]

One must be careful, however, not to label all high-conflict cases as exigent simply because they are high conflict. Most cases do not need an immediate decision requiring the direct involvement of the child.

F. CONCLUSION

Although some judges might want to interview children, it is the experience of children's counsel in Ontario that the vast majority of children have no interest or desire to be interviewed by a judge. Of course, it is acknowledged that these children are already having their views placed before the court by child's counsel. However, many older children understand that their counsel also has the responsibility to inform the court of the context or circumstances surrounding these views and that these may not support the views expressed, yet they are still not interested in attending court or speaking to a judge. The very few cases in which children have expressed to their counsel a desire to speak to a judge have typically involved severe parental alienation, in which a parent motivated the child to do so and thus to advise the judge of that child's (influenced) wishes.

The lack of strong social science research on judicial interviewing of children should not be filled by an emerging mythology that many or most children actually want to talk to a judge about their preferences and that this is a desirable and sound practice.

86 *Davies v. Aldcroft*, (3 September 2009), Toronto, D29015/05 (Ont Ct J).

Judges also need to be alert to the unintended consequence that if a preference interview is conducted with a child who is legally represented, there is a risk that the child will be empowered to the point of then refusing to talk to his or her counsel, wanting to talk only with the judge.

Quite apart from the issue of interview training, without fundamentally altering a judge's role as an adjudicator, judges simply cannot, as a practical matter, conduct multiple interviews and do so in a place familiar to a child, such as a school. The result is that it is difficult, in most cases, for a judge to develop a genuine rapport and trust with a child, which would be likely to yield more accurate and reliable information regarding the strength, consistency, and independence of the child's views, along with the significant circumstances surrounding those views.

I suggest that the issue of judicial interviewing of children for forensic purposes should be revisited only when a majority of credible, empirical, peer-reviewed studies by mental health experts conclusively demonstrate that, in their currently defined role as adjudicators, judges can obtain reliable information from children without visiting harm upon them. The legal community should pay serious attention to lessons learned from qualified psychologists, social workers, and psychiatrists, who, I believe, are far more knowledgeable in this area than people trained in the law.

In many Western jurisdictions family law has evolved positively from the former practice of interviewing children in chambers to elicit their preferences to the use of well-trained mental health professionals or child's counsel. While there is always room for improvement, this has been a marvellously progressive and successful development, both expressly and tacitly acknowledged as such by the courts.

Well-meaning and renewed efforts to provide children with input into the decision-making process about their custodial placement and visitation schedules by conducting judicial interviews about their preferences have been posited by some as progressive. I respectfully disagree with this characterization and submit that, save for very limited exigent circumstances, this approach is a backward step. Instead, efforts should be directed at establishing guidelines to which judges can refer when considering whether to have a meeting or conversation with a child, a preference interview, or neither. These guidelines should, of course, be drafted by judges, who could benefit from the input of qualified mental health professionals and experienced child's counsel. Although judges in many jurisdictions will still have the authority and discretion to conduct judicial interviews, following guidelines derived with broad and multidisciplinary input is the optimal way to deal with a debate that has resulted in polarized and entrenched positions. We owe such an effort to children who, through no fault of their own, find themselves in high-conflict cases in the family justice system. We must develop a sensible approach to judicial interviews and meetings that serves children's interests and is grounded in sound social science literature and research.

CHAPTER 11

Speaking for Themselves: A Pilot Program Balancing Children's Rights and Best Interests in High-Conflict Families

DALE HENSLEY, QC AND JEAN DUNBAR

Children exposed to their parents' custody and access/parenting[1] disputes, particularly in a context of domestic violence, experience significant trauma, including high stress, depression, social isolation, acting out, school failure, suicidal tendencies, aggressive behaviour, self-harm, and sometimes death at the hand of a parent.[2] Decisions about these children's residency, custody and access/parenting, or visitation are frequently made in the context of the family law system and therefore involve lawyers, the courts, and judges. Often, such decisions are made with insufficient information about, and few resources supporting the children. They are made in the context of a contest between parents and with insufficient focus on the circumstances of the children. Judges are faced with "he said/she said" situations. Often, the resulting

1 This chapter uses the terms *custody and access/parenting*, or simply *custody and access*. The term *parenting* is the language of Alberta's *Family Law Act*, SA 2003, c. F-4.5. *Custody and access* is used in Canada's divorce legislation and caselaw.

2 We have directly observed these consequences in Alberta. Additional evidence is found in the following: Victoria Bream & Ann Buchanan, "Distress among Children Whose Separated or Divorced Parents Cannot Agree Arrangements for Them" (2003) 33 Brit J Social Work 227; Clare Dalton, Susan Carbon, & Nancy Olesen, "High Conflict Divorce, Violence, and Abuse: Implications for Custody and Visitation Decisions" (Fall 2003) Juvenile and Fam Ct J 11; P.G. Jaffe, C.V. Crooks, & S.E. Poisson, "Common Misconceptions in Addressing Domestic Violence in Child Custody Disputes" (Fall 2003) Juvenile and Fam Ct J 57; J.B. Kelly & R.E. Emery, "Children's Adjustment Following Divorce: Risk and Resilience Perspectives" (2003) 52 Fam Relations 352.

decisions are not beneficial to children. One young person told our evaluators, "I felt like my parents weren't listening to me. They were too caught up in their battle."

Professionals working with these cases experience challenges and frustrations. Counsellors are at a loss to provide adequate support, guidance, information, and advocacy to solve the children's problems and to end the harm and pain caused by the conflict. Lawyers working with these children do not have sufficient resources, reliable information, or appropriate skills to provide them with adequate legal and social support. Typically, children's best interests are lost in the rhetoric of parents' statements and positions and consequently receive insufficient attention within the legal system. Limited knowledge about the depth of harm caused to children by their parents' conflicts, the particular nature of the conflicts and children's real circumstances all compound the barriers to addressing children's needs and best interests. In addition in Alberta, where this program was conducted, the child protection system tends to ignore the needs of these children as such disputes are commonly characterized as custody and access conflicts and therefore perceived by these officials not to be their responsibility.

Solutions to these conflicts are neither obvious nor straightforward, and tension arises in many jurisdictions as to the best approach. Should services for children take a best interests approach, reflecting an adult's opinion of conditions that will promote a child's development, well-being, and safety but not necessarily incorporating consultation with the child or the child's perspective? Or should an advocacy approach prevail, whereby a child's perspectives, opinions, interests, and right to be heard are respected and promoted, but that may not reflect the child's best interests and, some argue, could harm the child? Can both objectives be served?

This chapter describes the *Speaking for Themselves Program*, which integrated bests interests and rights-based approaches by combining therapeutic counselling and legal representation for children caught in their parents' high-conflict disputes. During development and implementation, the partners who provided services through the program learned more about the impact of such conflicts on children, identified processes and procedures that worked well or poorly, and discovered effective means for the two professions to work together.

A. THE PROGRAM

In 2004–5, two agencies in Calgary — the Children's Clinical Services department of the YWCA of Calgary (YWCA) and the Children's Legal and Educational Resource Centre (CLERC) — created the *Speaking for Themselves Program* (*SFT*), targeting children whose parents engaged in domestic violence before, during, or after separation and who then engaged in high-conflict custody and access/parenting disputes. The program was designed to respond to and ameliorate the harm caused to children when their parents engaged in such conflict, and specifically to

1) end or reduce the conflict the children experienced;
2) increase children's safety and reduce their risk of victimization;
3) ensure children's needs, experiences, and views were heard and considered; and
4) inform "best interests" decisions with evidence of children's interpretation of their experience.

The three-year pilot project (2005–8), funded by Alberta Children's Services (now Alberta Children and Youth Services) and externally evaluated, offered children therapeutic trauma counselling provided by the YWCA and legal support provided by CLERC. The YWCA provides free services to women, children, and men, including domestic violence programming, with staff knowledgeable in child development and specialists in domestic violence and children's trauma. Services were offered to *SFT* children at the YWCA's women's shelter. CLERC is a rights-based organization founded on and guided by the principles of the United Nations *Convention on the Rights of the Child*.[3] CLERC provides free legal support in civil law matters, including representation and education for children and youth. CLERC meets with children at locations of their choosing.

While designing the program, we recognized that children's problems and needs are multidimensional and require multidimensional, multidisciplinary responses. The combination of mental health and legal support, with neither service dominating, was intentional and perceived by the partners as fundamental and a strength of the program.

We were guided by several common beliefs. We recognized the importance of listening to children and accepting what they have to say while not

3 Can. T.S. 1992 No 3.

imposing decision-making responsibility on them. Other programs offer assessment and legal counsel, but to our knowledge no other program offered therapeutic counselling and legal counsel to children. Furthermore, we sought to address children's needs and not simply to use children to solve problems that adults themselves had been unable to manage or resolve. We knew, based on our respective expertise and professional literatures,[4] that resolution — an end to the conflict between the parents — serves the best interests of children. By supporting young people and providing mental health and legal support together, we intended to develop one means of providing safe solutions for children trapped in these conflictual conditions. We expected that by listening to young people, helping them to cope with their circumstances and be aware of their experiences, helping them to understand what was happening in their lives and families, ensuring their circumstances and perspectives were understood by others, and helping them learn what they could and could not control or be responsible for, the program would enhance their well-being and improve their lives.

1) Operations and Protocols

A synopsis of the protocols and operations adopted by the program follows.

1) Screening criteria were used to identify eligible children.
2) Therapists obtained parental consent for children to participate in the program and its evaluation;[5] lawyers obtained the children's consent.
3) With a few exceptions, therapists provided therapy first and formed opinions about a child's circumstances and condition. Therapists used a variety of strategies such as cognitive behaviour, play, and art therapy to

---

4 M.F. Whiteside & B.J. Becker, "Parental Factors and the Young Child's Postdivorce Adjustment: A Meta-analysis with Implications for Parenting Arrangements" (2000) 14 J Fam Psych 5; Bream & Buchanan, above note 2; Kelly & Emery, above note 2; K. Adamsons & K. Pasley, "Coparenting Following Divorce and Relationship Dissolution" in M.A. Fine & J.H. Harvey, eds., *Handbook of Divorce and Relationship Dissolution* (Mahwah, NJ: Lawrence Erlbaum, 2006); J.H. Grych, "Interparental Conflict as a Risk Factor for Child Maladjustment: Implications for the Development of Prevention Programs" (2005) 43 Fam Ct Rev 97; P.R. Amato & B. Hohmann-Marriott, "A Comparison of High- and Low-Distress Marriages That End in Divorce" (2007) 69 J Marriage & Fam 621.

5 This procedure was used because we considered that a child's therapist would be less threatening to parents than would a child's lawyer. Consent included permission for the partners to share information with each other.

assist young people with coping, relieving anxiety, safety planning, and exploring and recognizing feelings. Later during the therapy, lawyers developed their own relationships with the children.

4) At the conclusion of therapy, therapists wrote a report to inform decision makers of their findings, outcomes, and recommendations.
5) The report was first reviewed with the young person and the child's lawyer and then presented individually to parents and guardians. Most files were settled shortly thereafter.
6) If the legal dispute between the parents continued, the lawyer managed the file and advocated for resolution relying on the therapeutic report and the child's interests and viewpoint.

Screening primarily verified that the families were engaged in high-conflict custody and access/parenting disputes and that domestic violence was known or suspected. Family violence was defined as

> the abuse of power within relationships of family, trust or dependency that endangers the survival, security or wellbeing of another person. It can include many forms of abuse including spouse abuse, senior abuse and neglect, child abuse and neglect, child sexual abuse, parent abuse, and witnessing abuse of others in the family. Family violence may include some or all of the following behaviours: physical abuse, psychological abuse, criminal harassment/stalking, verbal abuse, sexual abuse, financial abuse, and spiritual abuse.[6]

A high-conflict custody and access/parenting dispute was defined as a dispute characterized by a lack of trust between the parties, a high level of anger, engagement in repetitive litigation, and the use of power and control by one or both parties to advance their position, with little or no consideration of the risks to or impact on the children.[7]

Further screening criteria were adopted, some of which were implemented after the program started. Specifically, a young person was admitted to the program only if

---

6 Alberta Roundtable on Family Violence and Bullying, *Finding Solutions Together*, (2004), online: www.child.alberta.ca/home/documents/familyviolence/rpt_opfvb_finding_solutions_high.pdf. We use the terms *domestic violence, domestic abuse*, and *family violence and abuse* interchangeably.

7 Adapted from S.H. Ramsey, "The Wingspread Report and Action Plan" (2001) 39 Fam Ct Rev 146.

- his or her experience could be revealed as a result of receiving the program's services (e.g., could a two-year old's experiences be identified through the program?);
- the young person did not suffer from a physical or mental disability outside the expertise of the therapists;
- the child was not a victim of sexual abuse (such files were referred to the specialized Child Sexual Abuse team at the Alberta Children's Hospital);
- the young person consented to involvement in the program (when the young person had capacity to do so);
- the young person and both parents/guardians resided in Calgary or the immediate vicinity and the legal action was in the Judicial District of Calgary; and
- the young person was not the subject of a child-protection investigation.

A comprehensive and lengthy screening tool was developed.[8] In most cases, the YWCA screened for domestic violence and CLERC screened for high-conflict custody and access/parenting. Both agencies had to agree that the family met the screening criteria before it would be accepted into the program. Either agency, or any other source, could refer a child or family to the program. No court order was required for a child to be accepted into the program, but both parents had to consent to the child's involvement. Further information was exchanged with parents during intake interviews with YWCA staff. Parents met with therapists approximately three times while a child was in therapy. Counselling for parents was offered by the YWCA. Throughout the program, therapeutic and legal staff held monthly case-review meetings. The therapist and lawyer constituted a team and worked together to produce results meeting a child's interests and best interests.[9]

2) Participants

Twenty-five families with forty-one children aged two to sixteen received service. The mean age of the children was ten. Forty-eight percent were from single-child families, 28 percent from two-child families, and 12 percent each from three- and four-child families. Of those from single-child families and

8 Available from either Jean Dunbar, YWCA Calgary, or Dale Hensley, CLERC.

9 For the disctinction between interests and best interests, see Dale Hensley, "Role and Responsibilities of Counsel for the Child in Alberta: A Practitioner's Perspective and a Response to Professor Bala" (2006) 43 Alta L Rev 871.

in the program overall, 58 percent of the children were male, 42 percent female. Parents of twenty-four of the children reported on their children's involvement with the child-protection system. Of those, 42 percent had had involvement. Of the fifty parents, 66 percent had legal counsel, including 22 percent with counsel appointed by the provincial legal aid program.

3) Implementation

The program designers planned for equal involvement of therapists and lawyers, with services available incrementally at half-time involvement for both practitioners during the first year (18–20 hours/week), 0.7 time during the second year (26–28 hours/week), and full-time during the third year (37.5 to 40 hours/week). However, we soon learned that more therapeutic than legal support was required for these families and attempted to hire 1.3 therapists (more were needed), whereas the lawyers' involvement never exceeded approximately 0.7 time. Why this unexpected imbalance in use of the two services?

a) Elevated Need for Therapy

Children generally entered the program highly traumatized. Two standardized test instruments were used to measure their trauma symptoms: the *Angie/Andy Trauma Cartoon Scales* (*ACTS*)[10] and the *Trauma Symptom Checklist for Children* (*TSCC*).[11] At pre-testing with *ACTS*, twenty-one of the *SFT* children (who had been screened for both high-conflict and domestic violence) scored 14 percent higher than children from another YWCA program who had been screened for domestic violence alone. Although mental health and/or addiction were not formally measured or assessed in the *SFT* program, evaluators noted a high incidence of these problems and a higher incidence of these conditions was reported by *SFT* parents than by those in the other YWCA program. Children required more therapy than had been expected initially: on average 18 to 20 one-hour weekly sessions.

b) Reduced Need for Legal Support

The legal aspects of most of these files were settled or litigation terminated at a rate higher than expected when we designed the program. Only two of the

10 F. Praver, D. Pelcovitz, & R. DiGiuseppe, *Angie/Andy Cartoon Trauma Scales* (Toronto: Multi-Health Systems, 1998).

11 John Briere, *Trauma Symptom Checklist for Children (TSCC), Professional Manual* (Odessa, FL: Psychological Assessment Resources, 1996).

twenty-five families continued to trial, both of which were truncated based on the therapists' evidence or negotiations led by child's counsel. The litigation then ended for one family and eventually ended for the other family after several further brief court appearances. An additional five families required one or two further contested chambers applications and then litigation ended. The custody and access/parenting issues of thirty-five of the forty-one children who received *SFT* services were resolved either without court or with minimal further litigation. The dispute status of two families is unknown. Given the history of these families, we had expected much higher usage of the legal system.

Further explanations are offered below for the unequal use of the two services, along with additional suggestions for improving operation and implementation of *SFT*-like programming.

B. OUTCOMES

By providing children with both therapy and legal support, *SFT* was very successful in assuring that children's needs, experiences, and views were heard and considered, which in turn led to cessation of family conflict and enhanced the safety of these children. As a result of the therapists' reports and meetings with parents and of the lawyers' presentations, children's views, interests, and best interests were made known to decision makers, whether to parents or the courts, in 97.5 percent of cases.[12] As noted, files settled at an unexpectedly high rate, ending conflict between parents about the children. No consistent mode of termination of legal disputes emerged. File dispositions included referral to parenting coordinators, uncontested or contested chambers applications, trial (with the therapist as the child's lawyer's witness), negotiated settlement led by the child's lawyer, and judicial dispute resolution. In 63 percent of cases, future decisions about access or "parenting time," as it is known in Alberta legislation, will occur only after consultation with and the agreement of the children. Furthermore, legal outcomes reflected children's opinions of desired solutions in 80.5 percent of cases. Eighty-three percent of outcomes also reflected the therapist's opinion of the child's best interests, indicating considerable congruence between the perspectives of children, their therapists, and decision makers. These outcomes brought children psychological peace and enabled them to focus on activ-

12 The views and best interests of one child were not presented due to concerns for her safety.

ities more typical for children. Therapeutically, the ten children who were both pre- and post-tested with the *ACTS* showed an overall 24 percent reduction in trauma, and the seven children pre- and post-tested using the *TSCC* showed improvement in all six clinical subscales of that test, with statistically significant improvement in three. While we attribute these improvements to the *SFT* intervention, it is possible that the children might have improved over time without counselling, but this would be likely only if the legal dispute between the children's parents was otherwise resolved. Without intervention, these disputes can persist and had persisted for years.

These outcomes reveal that *SFT* provided a means of balancing a child's best interests with a child's rights. Specifically, therapists were responsible for addressing a child's best interests, which were made known to decision makers through their reports, their evidence, the therapist's and lawyer's presentations, and the lawyer's advocacy of the reports. The lawyer's role was to advocate for the rights, interests, and views of a competent child. Although *SFT* policy required that the lawyer present the therapist's report and position in all cases, even when the child's and therapist's views were not congruent, in 89 percent of cases children and therapists agreed on the best outcome. In most cases, best interests were consistent with rights advocacy. In other words, most children have a very good sense of their own best interests. Furthermore, by providing children with the services of both therapists and lawyers, decision makers become fully aware not only of children's best interests but also of their position, permitting their needs, views, experiences, rights, and interests to be taken into account in a best interests decision.

1) Family Perspectives

To assess the perspectives of participants in *SFT*, the evaluators conducted independent interviews with fifteen families, comprising seventeen children, twelve mothers, eight fathers, and one step-parent. Below is a small sample of the responses and summary of the perspectives expressed.

Children viewed their *SFT* experience positively. In general, they reported that they could talk to the lawyers, lawyers understood their needs and made them feel safer, and they believed that the lawyers had the power to change things. Children also reported that the counselling helped them understand themselves and the dispute between their parents and that it, and the breakdown of their parents' relationship, was not their fault and that they could not have prevented it. Children told our evaluators:

> [The program helped me] get a voice to help me talk to my dad about how I feel . . . to talk to him about things I don't talk about . . . . Sometimes he used to blame us for everything, now I can tell him what actually happened, instead of staying in the corner and taking all the blame.

> . . . [T]hey don't fight as much on the phone as they used to . . . . [M]y dad does not talk badly about my mom as much.

> [My lawyer's job] is to help me have a relationship with my Dad — he did that . . . . I wanted my dad to be nicer and now he is nicer.

> [The therapist] did more than just talk to me. She taught me how to say my feelings.

> [The therapist] took time to get to know me as a person without a rush to "fix" me.

Without exception, residential mothers and fathers reported that their children benefited from therapy and from the program. As the following comments indicate, they also reported that the program positively influenced the custody and access/parenting dispute:

> The fact that [the therapist] was able to provide consistent contact over such a lengthy period of time was ultra helpful.

> My kids can communicate and express themselves now, they are not "locked" up any more.

> As a result of the lawyers' participation, the children really felt that they were heard.

Non-residential mothers and fathers were reported by the evaluators to have participated reluctantly in the program, and some suggested that the legal and therapeutic aspects of the program be separated. Overall they had little positive to say about the program. Their comments reflected a lack of understanding of the program, particularly the therapy:

> [The program allowed my daughter] to be brainwashed against me . . . .

> [The program] just placed a big responsibility on the shoulders of a 12-year old . . . . [The child] does not use this responsibility [well].

> [*SFT*] could be extremely biased towards the residential parent, who has much influence over the child. Children tend to tell the parents exactly what they want to hear.

These quantitative and qualitative results suggest that the goals of the program were met: the conflict ended for most of the children involved, their trauma was reduced, their well-being improved, their voices were heard, their experiences made known, and their views considered.

C. CHALLENGES AND LESSONS LEARNED

1) Low Service Numbers, High Program Cost

Forty-one children received service during approximately 2.25 years of service spread over 3 years at a cost of approximately $708,000, a relatively high cost per client. A broader analysis of the protocols established for *SFT* is required to determine why this was the case and to assist others to achieve improved service delivery. Significantly in this context, therapy preceded the involvement of the lawyer, so that the elevated need for therapy and other complications, created caseflow problems and a bottleneck in service delivery, creating a waiting list throughout the program. Indeed, some families waited more than a year before the therapists were ready for a new client. Planners should consider whether lawyers could begin work on files even if the young person might require therapy later.

2) Impediments to Caseflow

a) High Demand for Therapy, Insufficient Numbers of Therapists

As noted earlier, the program experienced higher than expected demand for therapeutic support. The program needed more therapists but could not acquire them due to insufficient funds, therapist burnout, and unavailability of qualified personnel. More therapists than lawyers must be planned for in future to enable more children to receive service.

b) Imbalance in Workload

We erred in assuming equivalent demand of the two service professionals. In addition to the lower than expected need for legal involvement, therapists and lawyers address cases differently. For therapists, each child represents a file and requires individual therapy and therapists must write individual reports for every child (with some repetition when working with siblings). In contrast, generally for lawyers and the courts, the whole family is a single file. Given this fact alone, planners must anticipate higher time demands for therapists. However, if conflict between parents persists, lawyers will deal much more extensively with files: at least two adults, the child client, and other lawyers. On average, however, at least 3 or 3.5 therapists to 1 lawyer is recommended.

c) Demanding Files and Personalities

Without documenting reasons, the program evaluators noted that therapists found *SFT* files extremely demanding. Unlike in typical domestic violence cases, *SFT* files required engagement with both parents, who might both have extremely high needs and expectations. In addition, grandparents or new partners/step-parents can often be significantly involved.

As well, the work is volatile, emotionally demanding, and taxing. Parents in high conflict have great animosity to each other, are deeply entrenched in their positions, and often have personality disorders and/or mental health and addiction issues. The stakes are extremely high. Parents are highly anxious about what their children tell the therapist and are motivated to recruit therapists to their "side," to convince therapists of their own good capacity to parent, and to vilify the other parent. This behaviour can create an almost impossible burden for some therapists as they attempt to manage parents while trying to treat the children effectively. Any lawyer who works in custody and access is familiar with these pressures, which cause many family lawyers to abandon this area of practice early in their legal careers. Despite their years of experience in domestic violence, the nature and intensity of the stress associated with high-conflict custody and access disputes was new and overwhelming for some domestic violence/trauma therapists. The therapists, rather than the lawyers, absorbed the stress that typically accompanies these files. Good professional supports for therapists must be built into such programs.

Although parents were offered counselling through the YWCA, and some accepted, therapists suggested that in retrospect, these parents should have received more attention because they are a root cause of the problems for young people and often created considerable difficulty and extra work for the children's therapists. Access for parents to more support (parent managers or coordinators) could ease the burden for therapists and enhance their work with children. *SFT* lawyers were largely unaware of these difficulties, or greater assistance might have been provided. When parents have lawyers, a word to their counsel by child's counsel can alleviate interference problems. Full communication between service providers, therapists who understand family law dynamics and are able to manage them, and referral options for parents would all be beneficial in building a program.

d) Consents and Inefficient Use of Therapists?

SFT did not require court orders for children and families to receive service, and therefore consent to participate had to be acquired from all participants. The program planners decided against requiring a court order as *SFT* was to provide an alternative means of resolving disputes. However, therapists reported higher compliance and cooperation from parents when a court order was in place and because therapists expended much time in acquiring consent from parents, especially non-referring parents, an inordinate time could elapse between a child's acceptance into the program and commencement of therapy. Different protocols may be required, such that referring parents can be asked to acquire a court order to facilitate their children's involvement in programming. Other solutions are having different personnel acquire consents, acquiring consents earlier, and/or closer relations with courts to facilitate court orders.

e) Consents and Caseload Management

A further difficulty associated with therapists' acquiring consents is the impact on their willingness to accept new files. Therapists were well aware of their caseloads and the number of clients from whom they were seeking consent. Even if they were not working at full capacity, therapists would often refuse new files for fear that they would be unable to manage more files once all consents were acquired. Solutions mentioned immediately above and a broadened referral base to include more than one counselling agency could improve caseflow.

f) Communication and Professional Differences

SFT evaluators proposed that professional differences and resulting communication problems and interpersonal tensions increased program costs. However, relations between management and service delivery personnel of the two agencies were good from our perspective, but tensions did arise over the challenges of the work itself, such as report writing, and limitations imposed by the dynamics and nature of family law. Contrary to the evaluators' assessment, we believe the partnering of the two groups enhanced rather than diminished the energy and enthusiasm of the professionals.

g) Therapists' Reports

Therapists' reports are a key element of this programming. They are the concrete manifestation of therapeutic work with a young person and direct parents and other decision makers to potential solutions. Reports are also essential in negotiations between lawyers and are relied upon by judges. However, writing reports can be a major stumbling block for some therapists, contributing to burnout and seriously compromising the smooth progress of clients through a program. Although *SFT* children attended an average of eighteen to twenty weekly therapy sessions, they often remained on a therapist's caseload much longer, in some cases for up to a year, until the report was written and distributed. Some reports were never written.

Reasons for difficulty with report writing included confusion about overall program goals and the therapist's role; insufficient articulation of therapeutic treatment goals for individual clients; limited expertise and experience in report writing, particularly for a highly critical audience of parents, lawyers, and judges; and insufficient experience with the legal context of custody and access disputes. These problems resulted in much staff time spent reviewing and revising reports.

The required style of report writing can also contribute to the need for review and revision. In *SFT*, some therapists had misgivings about relying on and including their professional judgment and assessment in their reports. In retrospect, we suggest that therapists may not have understood their role in and the goals of the program, owing perhaps to insufficient training. The program name itself, *Speaking for Themselves*, probably contributed to confusion. The program did not intend that children "speak for themselves"; rather, young people were to speak through the therapy, their therapists, and their lawyers. To serve this objective, therapists must understand they are speaking for the children and be firm in their professional opinions of what will contribute to children's best interests. Reports need to state the therapist's opinions explicitly, rather than quote children's words or describe in detail what happened in therapy.

During the latter half of *SFT*, a further difficulty arose over the crafting of recommendations. An analysis conducted by an interim coordinator suggested the existence of risk in the program and to therapists if they made recommendations concerning custody and access/parenting. The analyst accurately observed that *SFT* therapists did not conduct assessments concerning these matters and determined that they should not make such recommendations. Although the therapists faced no serious challenges in this regard during *SFT*, the concern added stress and further complicated the report writing process. From the lawyers' perspective, this risk can be ameliorated by framing recommendations in the context of the actual work done by therapists; that is, the therapy provided to the children.[13] From a systems perspective, the risk arises partly because of insufficient development and recognition of expertise in domestic violence and the impact of exposure to domestic violence on children.

In summary, because efficient and effective report writing is vital to smooth caseflow, therapists must be comfortable with and knowledgeable about the custody and access/parenting context to avoid case-management bottlenecks due to problems in writing reports.

3) Other Causes of High per Client Cost

SFT was a pilot program, and the combination and equality of therapeutic and legal services was unique. Developing and maintaining a pilot program is costly: the number of clients tends not to be the focus; creation and development of the program is paramount and can result in a top-heavy structure with few individuals involved in service delivery relative to the time and personnel committed overall; and development is planning intensive. A program needs to function long enough to progress to the service-focused operational phase. In *SFT*, the processes for program organization, management, and maintenance were cumbersome: joint agreement of admissions, time-consuming screening and consent processes, joint management of waiting lists, inefficient document exchange, inefficient information exchange and file review procedures, and numerous committees. The evaluation process was also difficult and time consuming, in part because the evaluators had little knowledge of custody and access/parenting disputes and did not acquire independent legal expertise.

---

13 One such challenge occurred during the program but was dismissed by the court. In addition, part of the role of the *SFT* lawyer is to argue for the credibility of the report and the author.

SFT partners speculate that caseflow could be improved with a looser partnership and less emphasis on a formal program; however, cooperation between agencies would still be required. We suggest that the two agencies maintain greater autonomy and refer files to one another; determine the appropriateness of each file for themselves; and conduct their own work with the understanding that the child has both a therapist and a lawyer and that information must be shared. In contrast to the recommendation of the *SFT* evaluators, neither agency can select or supervise professionals from the other agency, their work, or the two services, as neither organization has the capacity to do so.

4) Additional Lessons

a) Informational Needs of Parents

SFT therapists met approximately three times with parents during a young person's therapy. However, we learned that parents need more information about what is happening with their child. The program partners attempted to address this need through an interim reporting letter to parents, but what occurs in therapy is between the child and therapist, at least until release of the final report. For some parents, no one would have been able to provide enough information. For example, some demanded weekly reports. Such a demand cannot be met. Good communication with lawyers and the courts might assist with unreasonable parental expectations.

b) Therapy First

As noted above, *SFT* therapists engaged first with the children accepted into the program; the children did not meet their lawyers until much later. Therapy first is logical, but a complete disengagement of the lawyer from the young person is problematic, as a therapist can control the lawyer's access to a child. The young person can become overly anxious about meeting "the lawyer." We revised the protocol so that lawyers met children immediately after admission to the program to acquire the young person's consent to participate in *SFT*.[14] With this protocol, lawyers must be highly respectful of boundaries and careful that the young person understands the lawyer is not the child's therapist. With the revised procedure, the lawyer is a known en-

---

14 Consent from the young person to participate in the evaluation was acquired by the lawyer later.

tity to the young person from the outset and the prospect of a future meeting is not intimidating.

c) Staffing Expertise

SFT evaluators suggested that the primary criterion for hiring staff for such a program should be expertise working with children and that on-the-job training would suffice for other required areas of expertise. Unquestionably, therapists must be experienced with and understand children, especially those exposed to domestic violence and who have experienced trauma. However, therapists must also have experience with the legal context of custody and access disputes; otherwise, report writing and management and control of parents and their demands can be problematic. Without this knowledge, therapists can also be frustrated and challenged by cautions from lawyers over the need to maintain high boundaries with respect to their involvement with either parent, particularly with the mother, who is typically the victim of domestic violence.

Without understanding of the legal context, therapists can feel that the strictures imposed compromise their treatment approaches and their capacity to learn and meet their clients' needs. However, given the context of custody and access litigation, which was usually suspended while the child underwent therapy, there is no choice but for therapists to be hypervigilant of the need for even-handed treatment of both parents, particularly at the outset of a file. Even greater vigilance is necessary if service is delivered from a location that also houses a women's shelter because this fact alone can pose a barrier to fathers.

We therefore suggest that therapists need expertise and experience in at least three areas: (1) child development and the impact on children of exposure to domestic violence; (2) domestic violence in and of itself and its inherent dynamics; and (3) custody and access, including the dynamics of these disputes in the legal context.

d) Service from a Women's Shelter

The *SFT* evaluators recommended that *SFT*-like programs be housed in neutral community locations and commented on the difficulty of engaging fathers in the process when therapeutic service was delivered from a women's emergency shelter because many *SFT* fathers tended to see women's shelters as biased against men. Although *SFT* programming was completely distinct from the shelter programming and *SFT* accepted no referrals from the shelter, simply because the service was delivered from the same building that also housed a women's shelter caused deep suspicion in some fathers that the program was "against" them from the outset. However, the reality is that women's shelters are the primary locus of expertise in domestic violence. Offering *SFT* programming from a women's shelter may offer an early opportunity to learn about parents' potential biases as well as their insight into the dynamics of domestic violence and their respective roles in it.

D. ADDITIONAL RECOMMENDATIONS BASED ON LESSONS LEARNED IN *SFT*

In addition to other recommendations already noted, we suggest that future program designers incorporate the following elements:

- If frequent court applications are used as an indicator of high-conflict disputes and a criterion for acceptance into a program, direct evidence of the number of prior court appearances must be acquired. Parents tend to be poor historians of legal processes.
- The services must be free, to eliminate barriers to participation and promote balanced involvement of all affected individuals.[15]
- Cross-disciplinary training should be provided at the outset of collaborative endeavours.
- No therapist should have a full-time caseload of *SFT*-type clients and, if possible, multiple therapists should be hired to provide service. Therapeutic goals need to be clear, with regular case management, review, and supervision, and support should be provided to therapists. Timely reports must be written for every child.
- Effective means of engaging non-residential parents must be developed.
- The judiciary must be engaged, so that they are informed about and understand the program.
- Other legal or litigation-related processes involving the parents (such as mediation and assessments) must be halted while a child is in therapy.

---

15 A fuller statement supporting this position is available on request.

E. DISCUSSION

From the perspective of the *SFT* partners, the program was a success, even though fewer young people received service than expected, which in turn created a high cost per client. As a pilot program, *SFT* tested both a principle and a particular implementation: evidence supports the success of the principle; an alternative implementation may be needed for its effective application. But treatment of children who are victims in family conflict *is* expensive and time consuming. Many agencies will not involve themselves in custody and access work, let alone when it involves domestic violence, because of the resource demands. Expense, however, cannot justify ignoring these children. In the absence of effective solutions, children suffer significant consequences and are much less functional later in their lives: society simply pays a higher price.

One major reason for *SFT*'s positive results was the effectiveness of the team approach in meeting program goals and assisting young people. The combination of a lawyer and a therapist working together was key to assisting these children because although these are essentially legal files, neither the legal system, lawyers, nor therapists can resolve them effectively alone. The therapist's report is crucial to conflict resolution. Advocacy of and power accompanying the report are equally essential. The lawyer empowers the therapist's perspectives and the report through advocacy, in part because most lawyers representing parents seek confirmation of a child's circumstances not solely from a therapist but also from one of their own, the child's lawyer. The child's counsel evens the playing field for the child client. The child's therapist addresses the child's best interests; the child's lawyer advocates the child's rights, interests, and views. The partnership respects and supports children, ensures that reliable information about the perspectives and experiences of children is known, and provides the court with insight into the reality of the affected families.

The outcomes reflect the success of the program: participation in *SFT* improved the lives and circumstances of 83 percent of the children involved in that the changes recommended by therapists were implemented in 83 percent of cases. With changes in custody and access/parenting arrangements, children's experiences and behaviour changed. They were no longer suicidal, they no longer faced hair pulling, beating, harassment, and bullying at the hands of parents or step-parents, and they no longer guarded their deep-seated anxieties and traumas. These children found understanding of themselves, their parents, and their experiences; they could begin to believe in themselves and to learn to trust again. These developments were achieved by listening to children and believing in them, giving them respite from conflict and trauma so they could begin to be themselves. One child poignantly summarized the impact as follows: "The counsellor talks to me, he tells the lawyer what I say and then the lawyer goes to court and my dad is nicer since this started and I like that."

Resolution of these legal actions has one dominant characteristic: taking power that is being misused and causing trauma for children away from one or both parents and putting it in the hands of children's therapists and lawyers. This power transfer is fundamental to success but poses a threat to societal norms; effective application of this power therefore requires steadfast focus on the objective of assisting children and on creating space for their authentic voice and perspectives.

The high closure rate of the legal aspects of highly contentious files provides the strongest evidence that combined therapeutic and legal services are effective in resolving these custody and access disputes. Access to the true voice of the young person through the therapy, the therapist, and the lawyer works. It causes litigation to end so fewer demands are placed on lawyers and the legal system. More important, once a child's story is known and told, or sometimes with just the prospect of the story being told or of the child having a lawyer, positive results follow for the child's physical and mental health. When credible evidence is heard by someone with the power and capability to do something significant with the information, disputants withdraw their claims, legal actions by parents are resolved, and solutions meeting children's best interests and respecting their rights are the result. Children can begin to heal.

The evidence provided by *SFT* demonstrates that providing children with a combination of mental health and legal support in high-conflict custody and access/parenting disputes is a best practice and it is possible to meet both objectives of respecting children's rights and serving their best interests.

CHAPTER 12

An Evaluation of Alberta's *Family Law Act*

LESLIE D. MacRAE, SHANE D. SIMPSON, JOANNE J. PAETSCH, LORNE D. BERTRAND, SHERYL PEARSON, AND JOSEPH P. HORNICK

Historically, family law has been inherently complicated in Alberta. Not only are the issues dealt with sensitive, but the processes to deal with them have also been challenging. Federal–provincial jurisdictional distinction has meant that some issues have proceeded in the Court of Queen's Bench and others in Provincial Court, causing much confusion and frustration among members of the public.[1]

In addition to procedural issues, a number of pieces of legislation addressed family law issues in the province, and there were many inconsistencies and much overlap among provisions. In the early 1990s, Alberta Justice recognized that family law reform was necessary, and the Alberta Law Reform Institute (ALRI) was contracted to address these shortcomings in provincial family law. ALRI worked to recommend a sound legislative framework that would "modernize, rationalize, and consolidate Alberta family law."[2] The *Family Law Act* (*FLA*)[3] came into force on 1 October 2005 to address non-divorce matters in Alberta family law.

The Act was intended to improve the family law system in Alberta in a number of ways:

---

1 Michelle C. Christopher, "Alberta's New *Family Law Act*" *LawNow* (June–July 2006).

2 Alberta Law Reform Institute, *Family Law Project: The Conclusion*, Final Report No. 93 (Edmonton: The Institute, 2004).

3 *Family Law Act*, SA 2003, c. F-4.5 [*FLA*].

- simplifying the law;
- improving accessibility for all, particularly self-represented litigants;
- supporting non-adversarial approaches to resolving family conflict in the best interests of children and families;
- supporting alternatives to court for resolving issues; and
- streamlining court procedures so that Provincial Court and Court of Queen's Bench share the ability to hear most matters under the Act and follow the same application forms and procedures.[4]

Substantively, the *FLA* also updated the language of family law in Alberta, replacing concepts of "custody" and "access" with "guardianship," "parenting time," and "contact." Further, while the Act addressed many family law issues, fundamental changes were made in a number of specific substantive areas, including the best interests of the child, guardianship, custody and access/parenting orders, contact orders, child support, and adult interdependent relationships.

Though a number of procedural and substantive changes were made to Alberta family law with the introduction of the *FLA*, it was unknown whether these changes had the desired effect. With funding from the Alberta Law Foundation, and the support of Alberta Justice and the Alberta Law Reform Institute, the Canadian Research Institute for Law and the Family (CRILF) conducted a two-year evaluation of the legislation in order to determine whether the procedural and substantive changes introduced by the *FLA* were fair, effective, and efficient.[5]

A. METHODOLOGY

The primary purpose of this project was to evaluate the impact of the procedural and substantive changes to family law in Alberta introduced by the *Family Law Act*, and inform recommendations for change. To achieve these ends, the project was divided into two phases: (1) a development phase, from April 2007 to March 2008, producing a detailed evaluation framework that

4 Alberta Court Services, *Alberta's* Family Law Act*: An Overview*, online: www.albertacourts.ab.ca/cs/familyjustice/FLAOverview.pdf.

5 L.D. MacRae *et al.*, *An Evaluation of Alberta's* Family Law Act (Calgary: Canadian Research Institute for Law and the Family, 2009), online: http://people.ucalgary.ca/~crilf/publications/FLA_Final_Report_May_2009.pdf.

included measurement tools and instruments; and (2) an evaluation phase, from April 2008 to March 2009, implementing the evaluation framework.

The evaluation framework incorporated four research methodologies.

1) Legislative Review

A legislative review examined the changes made to family law in Alberta with the enactment of the *FLA* and compared the Act with family law legislation in other jurisdictions. A supplemental caselaw review was also conducted. The strengths and weaknesses of the Act were highlighted and possible areas for change were identified.

2) Caseflow and Outcomes Analysis

A caseflow and outcomes analysis was conducted using data from the Justice Online Information Network (JOIN), the Alberta Court of Queen's Bench database (CASES), and relevant family court programs and services. JOIN and CASES data were examined to determine the impact of the enactment of the *FLA* on the flow of cases through Alberta's family courts, and the consequent effect on workload and human resources. Outcome data (i.e., case resolutions) were collected and analyzed to examine the effectiveness of the alternative dispute resolution programs and services supported by the *FLA*.

3) Survey of Professionals

A survey of professionals examined the opinions of professionals who have had direct experience with the Act, providing information about its effectiveness, efficiency, fairness, and accessibility. The professional groups included Provincial Court judges, Court of Queen's Bench justices, family lawyers, mediators, dispute resolution officers, child support resolution officers, mental health professionals, First Nations Legal Services staff, Family Justice Services (FJS) staff,[6] conflict resolution instructors, judicial clerks, and court administrators. Surveys were administered by email and mail, resulting in a total of 152 completed surveys. The surveys yielded both quantitative and qualitative data.

---

6 Family Justice Services is a group of programs and services offered by Alberta Justice in collaboration with the courts in order to assist people in obtaining appropriate solutions for their family law issues.

4) Interviews with Self-Represented Litigants

Telephone interviews with self-represented litigants (SRLs) were conducted to gain insight into the simplicity, accessibility, fairness, and efficiency of the *FLA* for those proceeding without legal counsel. With the aid of FJS, SRLs were provided with study information packages at the courthouse and asked to complete and return a contact information sheet if they were interested in participating. A total of sixty-four contact information sheets were obtained, and thirty-three interviews completed out of fifty-eight eligible participants.

B. RESULTS

1) Legislative Review

The legislative and caselaw review analyzed the substantive differences between pre- and post-*FLA* Alberta family law, and compared the *FLA* to similar legislation in other jurisdictions in six major areas: guardianship; the best interests of the child; parenting orders; contact orders; child support; and spousal/adult interdependent partner (AIP) support. In doing so, the legislative review addressed two research questions:

1) Is the *FLA* effective in serving the best interests of children and families?
2) Have the substantive changes introduced by the *FLA* made family law more fair and effective?

The treatment of guardianship in the *FLA* saw several changes to the former regime, with the review revealing that it essentially modernized the guardianship regime in Alberta. In doing so, it reversed the previous practice of defaulting guardianship to the mother by providing that both the mother and father will be guardians unless they fall within noted exceptions. This change eliminated the former gender bias of the guardianship provisions whereby the mother was sole guardian unless the father satisfied one of the relationship requirements. Additionally, the *FLA* enumerates the powers, responsibilities, and entitlements of guardians, enabling courts to parcel out the various components, as required, if the parents or guardians cannot agree on how to share them.

The standard of "best interests" that is commonly used for determining applications involving children in family law disputes was also examined.

Though the application of the test is not substantially different from under the previous legislation, the *FLA* codified the best interests test and, in doing so, made it clear which factors must be considered when determining the best interests of the child and the contexts in which those factors are applicable. It also specifies the degree to which past conduct may be considered and clarifies that only conduct related to family violence may be considered when determining the best interests of the child, an aspect that makes the *FLA* unusual among family law legislative instruments in Canada.

A third notable change reflected in the *FLA* is the elimination of the custody and access regime and its replacement with a shared parenting model. By replacing the concepts of custody and access with the non-equivalent, non-traditional concepts of parenting and contact orders, the *FLA* adopted a more functional approach to parenting arrangements. In contrast to the concepts of custody and access, which represent a deterministic approach to post-separation parenting, parenting orders assume meaningful involvement of all guardians unless otherwise provided by agreement or order. The adoption of a shared parenting model is arguably the most progressive and noteworthy change reflected in the *FLA*, Alberta being the first jurisdiction in Canada to abandon the concepts of custody and access and the only jurisdiction to employ the term *parenting time*.

The adoption of contact orders as an alternative to access orders is also a unique aspect of the *FLA* as it functions to distinguish third parties and non-guardian parents from guardians vis-à-vis their role with children. Whereas the concept of access previously applied to any party, guardian or not, who did not have care and control of a child, parenting orders are now used exclusively by guardians, while contact orders are used exclusively by non-guardians. This change had significant implications for grandparents in some situations, who no longer have a presumptive right to apply for access but instead have a qualified right to apply for contact under the *FLA*.

Another significant change in the *FLA* is the establishment of comprehensive child support provisions. Although child support orders under the *Divorce Act*[7] are still determined by the *Federal Child Support Guidelines*,[8] these provisions eliminate any distinction between the treatment of children of married and unmarried parents. They also establish clear parameters for child support obligations, including (1) the threshold for the exemption

7 RSC 1985, c. 3 (2nd Supp.).

8 *Federal Child Support Guidelines*, SOR/97-175.

of children under eighteen, which includes children who are married or in an AIP, or who have voluntarily withdrawn from their parents' charge and are living independently; (2) a cap on the obligation for adult children being full-time students between eighteen and twenty-two years of age; (3) a presumption that adult children will make a reasonable contribution to their education; and (4) a definition of persons standing in the place of a parent and the corresponding obligation of those persons.

Finally, the *FLA* provides for equal support obligations of both spouses and adult interdependent partners and eliminates all references to traditional fault-based doctrines. Now, the support obligation in the provincial context mirrors the spousal support obligations under the *Divorce Act*.

Since coming into effect, the *FLA* has been judicially considered on a number of occasions and, for the most part, its application and interpretation by the courts has been uniform.[9] Perhaps the consistency with which the *FLA* has been applied can be attributed to the simplicity and cohesiveness of its drafting. However, a handful of specific issues that may warrant legislative attention did surface in the analysis.

First, in the course of reviewing the best interests test, it became evident that the caselaw is unclear with respect to the application of the "fitness" test as compared to the "best interests" test in the context of the *FLA*. The fitness test is a higher threshold test that must be met when a legal stranger is attempting to unseat a current guardian. While this issue was judicially considered in the former context of guardianship, custody, and access, the place of the fitness test is not obvious in the new regime of guardianship and parenting orders.

A second notable issue arises in the context of support obligations. With the enactment of the *FLA* came the repeal of the general support provisions for adults who were destitute or unable to work for "other causes" (other than being a full-time student). It is unclear whether the repeal of these provisions has created a gap in the social safety net for vulnerable adult children, or whether the general support provision for spouses and adult interdependent partners sufficiently compensates for the gap arising in the context of child support. If a gap does in fact exist, it may be necessary to consider whether

9 See full project report for a comprehensive review of the caselaw: L.D. MacRae *et al.*, *An Evaluation of Alberta's* Family Law Act (Calgary: Canadian Research Institute for Law and the Family, 2009), online: http://people.ucalgary.ca/~crilf/publications/FLA_Final_Report_May_2009.pdf.

the scope of the child support provision should be broadened to include this group or whether a general support provision, discretionary or not, should be adopted providing for the support of dependent adults.

The review ultimately concluded that, in spite of the few outstanding issues, the *FLA* clearly provides a comprehensive, equitable, and progressive approach to family law issues that may well serve as a model for the development and amendment of family law legislation in other jurisdictions across Canada and internationally. Alberta's *Family Law Act* was the response to the need for a simpler, more effective, efficient, and accessible provincial family law system, one that took into consideration the best interests of children and families, minimized the negative impact of family breakdown, and modernized Alberta family law.

2) Caseflow and Outcomes under the *FLA*

To assess the impact of the implementation of the *FLA* on workload and human resources in the courts, family law caseflow through Provincial Court, Court of Queen's Bench, alternative dispute resolution processes, and court services was examined, as was the number of SRLs applying in the family law system. Due to the data available, time periods and units of analysis differed for the various courts and processes. The following research questions were addressed by this analysis:

1) How have procedural changes under the *FLA* affected workload and human resources in Alberta's courts and affiliated services?
2) How has the use of alterative dispute resolution programs and processes affected cases, processes, and outcomes under the *FLA*?

The *FLA* was enacted with the hope of increasing the effectiveness and efficiency of the family law system in Alberta and decreasing the number of cases heard in Provincial Court and Court of Queen's Bench. Though data on the number of cases reaching resolution prior to being heard in court were not available, overall caseflow on the number of family law issues before the courts provides a picture of how many *FLA* files are being processed in each level of court. Figure 1 shows new family law issues before Alberta's Provincial Court from 1 January 2005 to 31 December 2007[10] and *FLA* claims filed in

10 Family law orders requested prior to October 2005 were filed under the *Provincial Court Act*, RSA 2000, c. P-31, and the *Domestic Relations Act*, RSA 2000, c. D-14.

Court of Queen's Bench from 1 October 2005 to 31 December 2007.[11] Family law issues before the Provincial Court increased steadily across the province during this period, representing a 73 percent increase between January 2005 and December 2007 and nearly a 40 percent increase since the enactment of the *FLA*.[12] Various explanations are possible, including the tremendous increase in Alberta's population in recent years (10.7 percent between 2001 and 2006), the fact that changes to process and procedure introduced by the *FLA* made it easier for SRLs to apply, and the increased jurisdiction of Alberta's Provincial Court since the enactment of the *FLA* — an important development. However, given the increasing availability of, and support for, alternative dispute resolution programs since the enactment of the *FLA*, it is possible that a substantial number of family law issues before the Provincial Court are resolved prior to reaching formal courtroom proceedings.

Although pre-*FLA* data are not available for Alberta Court of Queen's Bench, the number of *FLA* claims filed there has remained relatively stable. The overall number of *FLA* claims filed in the province increased in the years following the enactment of the *FLA*, peaking at a 45 percent rise in June 2007; however, between October 2005 and December 2007, *FLA* claims increased by only 31 percent.

---

11 For Provincial Court, JOIN data were analyzed by family law issue, which refers to applications for specific orders (i.e., child support, custody/access, guardianship, etc.) under the pre-*FLA* legislation and each type of relief sought in a claim (e.g., guardianship, parenting, contact) under the *FLA*. Family law issue was used as the unit of analysis for several reasons. First, it allowed pre- and post-implementation of the *FLA* to be compared when possible. Second, the JOIN data did not contain information on individual files or *FLA* claims. Available CASES data provided aggregate information on the *FLA* forms filed; therefore, comparisons between the two courts could not be accurately drawn.

12 Court and program statistics often see a noticeable drop in December of each year. This pattern is due to service closures and court not being in session over Christmas holidays.

Figure 1: Family Law Caseflow, Alberta Provincial Court and Court of Queen's Bench, January 2005–December 2007

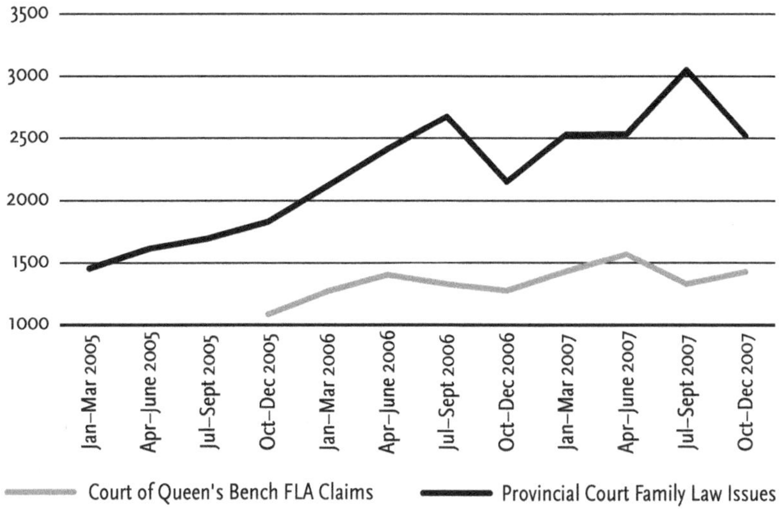

Data Sources: Justice Online Information Network (JOIN); CASES

The enactment of the *FLA* stressed the use of available programs and services to provide information and resolve issues so that fewer cases would be dealt with in the courtroom, creating greater efficiency. The Caseflow Conference Program, introduced by Family Justice Services in Edmonton Provincial Court in 2001 and Calgary Provincial Court in 2006, was put in place as a method of dispute resolution to increase the efficiency of the court process. The *Intake and Caseflow Management Regulation*,[13] permanently implemented in July 2005, made it mandatory for SRLs to have a caseflow conference scheduled on filing an application. Caseflow conference is unique in that it is one way in which an agreement can be reached *within the court process* without being facilitated by a judge in a courtroom. Caseflow coordinators use mediation techniques to explore areas of agreement, and when possible, agreements can be drafted into consent orders and forwarded to a judge for approval. Caseflow coordinators may also inform clients of alternative dispute resolution options and resources and provide information about the next step in the process should clients choose to proceed to a courtroom. Figure 2 illustrates the number of applications to the Edmonton Caseflow

13 Alta Reg 150/2005.

Conference Program from December 2003 to November 2007. Though the program was well used even prior to the *FLA*, the introduction of the regulation in July 2005 and the enactment of the *FLA* in October 2005 saw a noticeable increase in applications, followed by a more modest increase in the following years. By November 2007, the number of applications proceeding to caseflow conferences since December 2003 had increased by 131 percent.

Figure 2: Applications to Caseflow Conference Program, Edmonton Provincial Court, December 2003–November 2007

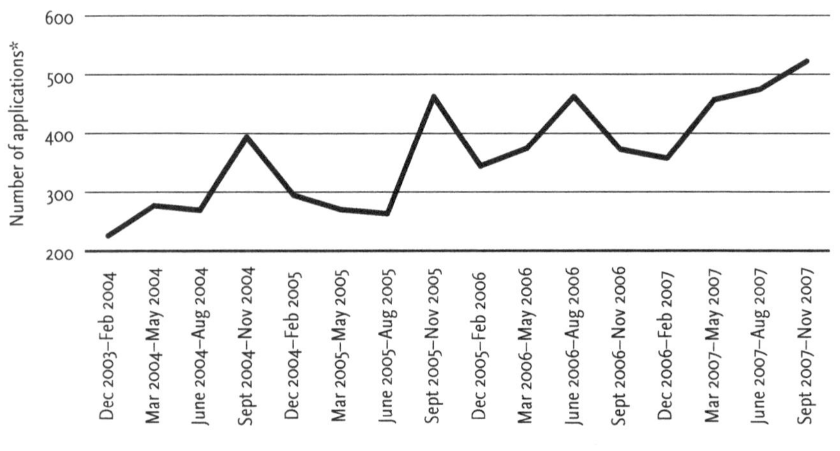

Data Source: Edmonton Family Justice Services
* Number of applications includes all applications that could be concluded in caseflow.

Outcome data for the Edmonton Caseflow Conference Program revealed that only 23.7 percent of cases that entered a caseflow conference from 1 October 2005 to 31 December 2007 proceeded to docket court following the conference. Just over 10 percent reached a full consent order after the conference, and 43.9 percent were adjourned so that the parties could get access to services such as mediation, legal aid, family court counsellors, and so forth. The remaining conferences were withdrawn/abandoned or adjourned *sine die* or to trial.

The Family Justice Services Family Court Counsellor Program (FCC) also witnessed a noticeable increase in caseload. FCCs perform various functions, including orientation and intake when a self-represented litigant is proceeding in Provincial Court, mediation, and in-court support. FCC intake and brief mediation are also potential points at which to resolve issues and reach consensus. Figure 3 shows the intakes performed by family court counsellors from January 2004 to December 2007.[14] A notable rise in intakes occurred across the province with the enactment of the *FLA*, followed by a steady increase to December 2007—a 62 percent increase from January 2004. This trend speaks to the importance of family court counsellors as both a dispute resolution mechanism and a support for SRLs.

Figure 3: FJS Family Court Counsellor Intake Alberta, January 2004–December 2007

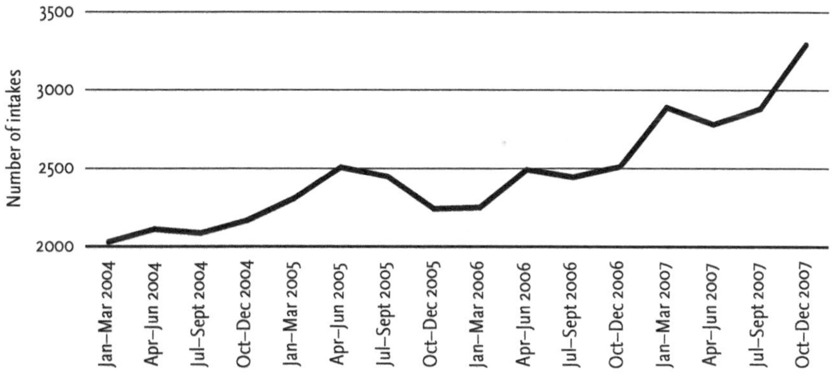

Data Source: Family Justice Services
Due to administrative staff changes, intake statistics for regions other than Calgary and Edmonton were not kept from November 2005 to March 2006. Therefore, data were interpolated for this period by averaging the intakes from October 2005 and April 2006.

One aspect of Family Justice Services for which caseflow has declined is the Mediation Program. Though mediation experienced an increase in referrals with the enactment of the *FLA*, and despite some fluctuation over the years, mediation numbers throughout all regions in Alberta have, on average, remained relatively consistent with those prior to the *FLA*. This may be due to the availability of the Caseflow Conference Program in Calgary and Edmonton and possible underutilization of Family Justice Services Mediation in other regions. Family Justice Services Mediation is offered at no cost only to those with children under eighteen and when at least one party earns less than $40,000 per year. Parties who do not fit these criteria must hire a private mediator. Despite this decrease in caseflow, however, provincial program outcome data revealed that nearly 90 percent of cases that proceeded

14 The *Intake and Caseflow Management Regulation, ibid.*, of July 2005 made intake sessions mandatory for self-represented litigants proceeding in Provincial Court. Thus, this regulation is applicable only to Calgary and Edmonton.

through the FJS Mediation Program from 1 October 2005 to 31 December 2007 (n = 2,558) reached either full or partial agreement.

Though caseflow has increased since the enactment of the *FLA*, the processing time for family court files has dropped. As shown in Figure 4, the average number of days between an applicant's opening a file and a final order being made began to decrease after the *FLA* was enacted in October 2005, and has continued to decrease, from roughly ninety days in September 2005 to approximately forty days in December 2007. Thus, it is apparent that overall, efforts to improve the efficiency of the family law system in Alberta Provincial Court have succeeded in this respect.

Figure 4: Average Processing Time for Family Court Files, Provincial Court, January 2005–December 2007

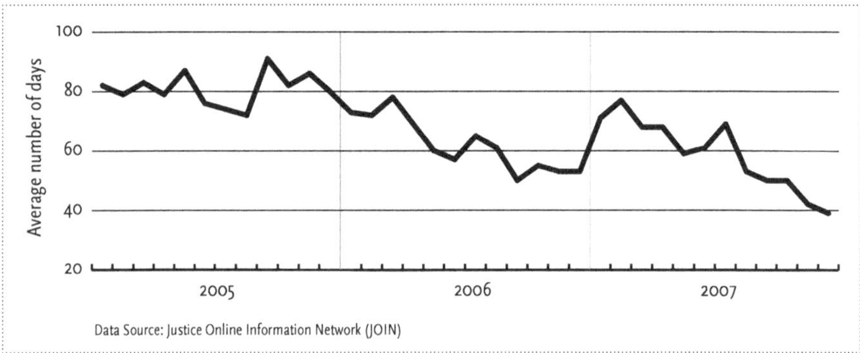

3) Survey of Professionals

The intent of the survey of professionals was to discover the opinions and experiences of family law professionals in Alberta regarding processes and procedures under the *FLA*, its various substantive areas, and the language of the legislation. The survey addressed the following research questions:

1) How has the response process affected procedures and outcomes under the *FLA*?
2) Have procedural changes under the *FLA* made processes more efficient?
3) Have procedural changes under the *FLA* made processes simpler and more accessible for self-represented litigants?
4) Is the *FLA* effective in serving the best interests of children and families?
5) Have the substantive changes introduced by the *FLA* made family law more fair and effective?

6) Is the language of the *FLA* more appropriate, easier to understand, and more effective?

A total of 152 professionals completed the survey. Similar proportions of respondents indicated that they conducted most of their work in Edmonton (32 percent), Calgary (27 percent), or other cities (30 percent), while the remaining respondents worked primarily in rural Alberta. The largest proportion of respondents (41 percent) worked in areas related to court administration (family court counsellors, caseflow coordinators, judicial clerks/court clerks, and FJS staff). Almost one-third of respondents were judges or justices (32 percent), and 21 percent were lawyers. The remaining 7 percent were psychologists/psychiatrists/social workers and others, including mediators and consultants. Over two-thirds of the respondents (68 percent) reported working in family law for more than five years. A further 11 percent had three to five years experience, 17 percent had one to three years experience, and only five (3 percent) had worked in family law for less than one year. When asked if they were familiar with Alberta's *Family Law Act* and/or its associated processes and procedures, almost all respondents (98 percent) reported that they were. The three respondents who were not familiar with the *FLA* were asked to end their surveys at that point.

Figure 5: Respondents' Opinions on Whether Efforts to Improve Processes and Procedures under the FLA *Have Been Successful, by Profession*

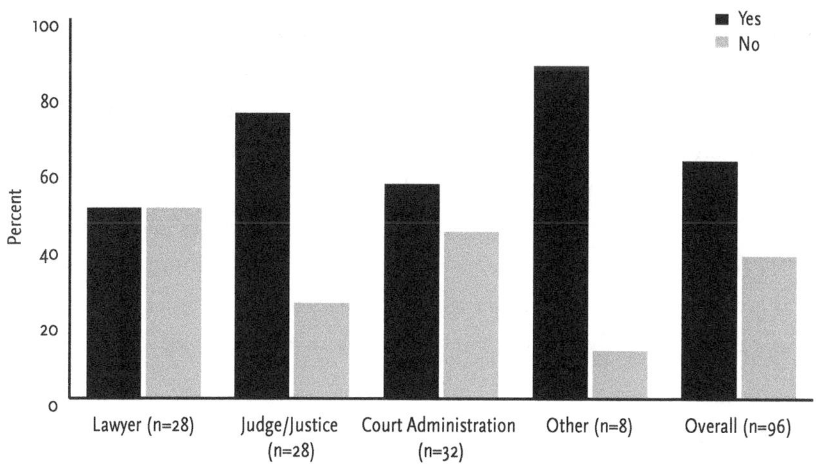

Data Source: Survey of Professionals
Total n=116; total missing or invalid responses=20

Survey respondents were asked a number of questions about the procedural and substantive changes introduced by the *FLA*. Among them, respondents who had experience with the previous family law legislation (79 percent; n = 116) were asked to draw comparisons to the family law system under the *FLA*. The first question asked if, in their experience, the efforts to improve processes and procedures under the *FLA* have been successful. Of the surveys with valid responses (n = 96), 63 percent said yes and 38 percent said no. There were interesting differences, however, when the data were analyzed by profession. As shown in Figure 5, lawyers and court administration personnel were less positive than were judges/justices and other professions. Only 50 percent of the lawyers thought the efforts were successful, compared to 56 percent of court administration staff, 75 percent of judges/justices, and 87.5 percent of other professions.

Survey respondents were also asked to explain why they thought the efforts to improve the processes and procedures under the *FLA* were successful, or not. A total of 76 respondents made 125 comments. The most common (n = 33) was that there are too many forms, or that the forms are too restrictive, redundant, inappropriate, or complicated:

> [There are] too many forms. A simple motion and affidavit as previously used in QB was significantly much more efficient. The attempt to make everything into forms to streamline the process for the general public has not been successful. There is also the fact that QB and Provincial Court have different procedures that never were and are still not congruent. Provincial Court has tried so hard to make itself user friendly that it results in little or no structure and application of the Rules of Court are non-existent. The result is that I try to stay out of Provincial Court. I feel my clients are better served in Queen's Bench because of more predictable processes and more uniform application of the Rules of Court . . . .
>
> The consolidation of legislation under the one Act has been positive. The forms — less so. They are often unduly restrictive, redundant, and inappropriate when counsel uses them, and lay people find them confusing, and are legitimately worried about filling them out incorrectly.

On the other hand, the next most common comment (n = 15) was that the processes and procedures are more user friendly for SRLs and more client focused. For example, one respondent said,

> The forms have been simplified, which makes it easier for laypeople to make applications. The procedures are standardized in both courts, making the system appear fair, and making both courts equally accessible to the parties. I especially approve of the fact that the filing fee was removed.

The same group of professionals were then asked how the implementation of the *FLA* has affected their workload. Most telling, perhaps, is that none said their workload had decreased. Of those with valid responses (n = 108), 63 percent of respondents said that their workload had increased, and 37 percent said that it had stayed the same. The vast majority of court administration staff (94 percent) reported that their workload had increased. Lawyers and other professionals were more likely to report that their workload had increased than that it had stayed the same. Only judges/justices were more likely to report that their workload had stayed the same than that it had increased; 60 percent said their workload had stayed the same. Provincial Court judges, however, were more likely to report that their workload had increased (60 percent), whereas Court of Queen's Bench justices were more likely to report that it had stayed the same (57.6 percent).

The professionals were asked if the *procedural* changes introduced with the *FLA* better serve SRLs than those that existed before. The responses (n = 96) were mixed; 55 percent said yes, and 45 percent said no. These data were analyzed to examine differences by profession, and the results are presented in Figure 6. All professions except court administration staff had a greater proportion of positive responses than negative responses. Almost three-quarters of the judges/justices (73 percent) thought the procedural changes better served SRLs, compared to 57 percent of other professions and 56 percent of lawyers. Almost two-thirds (63 percent) of the court administration staff, however, did not agree.

When asked to explain their answers to this question, seventy-eight respondents made ninety-six comments. The most common (n = 31) was that there is too much paper and the forms are too confusing. As one respondent said,

> A large number of people who come to our counter have never had contact with the courts before, therefore they do not have any idea of how to fill out the overwhelming amount of forms or understand the terminology. Neither this legislation nor the paperwork is user friendly for the self-represented litigants. Even a lot of learned counsel have a hard time understanding the paperwork.

Another respondent said,

> The part that I do like is that the respondent now has the ability to file a Response and get their side out there, where in the past they didn't really have that opportunity. But I'm also finding that some people are not understanding that they are supposed to be filing a Response and then it delays the process to get the Response in. And what is not helping is that the forms are confusing for the average person with no legal experience/court knowledge.

The second most common comment (n = 22) was that the procedural changes are more user friendly for SRLs, and that the caseflow process is now more efficient and allows more comfort and input from clients. One respondent said, "Certainly, the previous system of documents was a significant bar to self-represented litigants commencing an application, and the forms have made it easier for them to seek relief."

Figure 6: Respondents' Opinions on Whether the Procedural Changes Introduced with the FLA *Better Serve Self-Represented Litigants, by Profession*

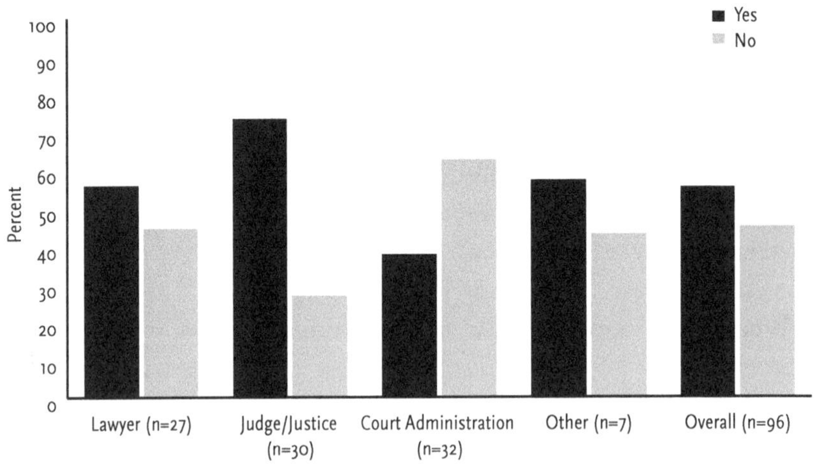

Data Source: Survey of Professionals
Total n=116; total missing or invalid responses=20

The professionals were then asked if the *substantive* changes introduced by the *FLA* better served SRLs than previous family law legislation in Alberta. Overall, respondents (n = 98) were more positive about the substantive changes than they were the procedural changes. Some 68 percent agreed that the substantive changes better served SRLs, and 32 percent disagreed. When the figures are examined by profession (see Figure 7), we see that 86 percent of other professions and 80 percent of judges/justices thought that the substantive changes to the *FLA* better served SRLs. The majority of court administration staff and lawyers agreed, but the proportion of positive responses was smaller (62 percent of court administration staff and 59 percent of lawyers).

Respondents were asked to explain their answers, and fifty-seven respondents made sixty-seven comments. The most common comment (n = 12) was that consolidating the legislation was greatly needed. As one respondent put it, "The previous morass of unconnected and diffuse legislation must have been a nightmare for unrepresented litigants." The next most common comment (n = 8) was that SRLs still do not understand the law. As one respondent put it, "The underlying problem of a lack of understanding of substantive law cannot be overcome with procedural changes."

Figure 7: Respondents' Opinions on Whether the Substantive Changes Introduced with the FLA *Better Serve Self-Represented Litigants, by Profession*

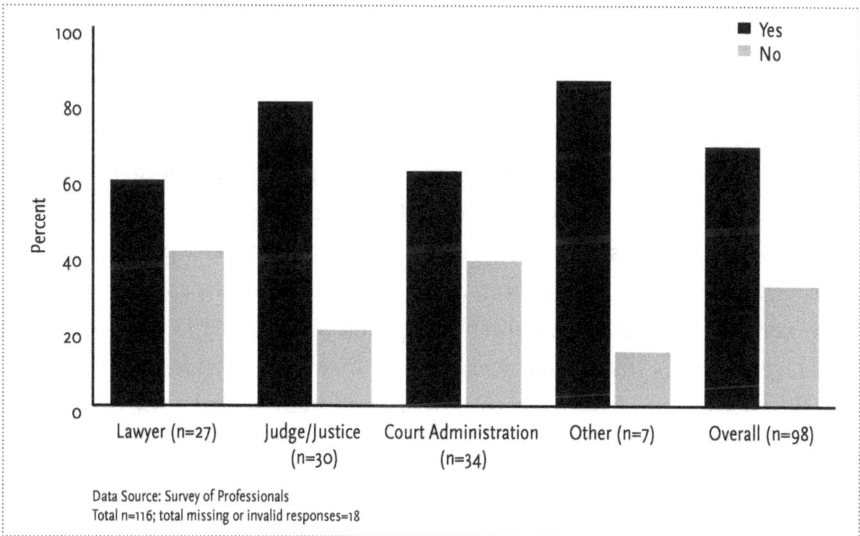

4) Interviews with Self-Represented Litigants

Self-represented litigants (SRLs) were interviewed in order to gain an understanding of whether the changes introduced by the *FLA* to make the system more accessible to individuals without representation have been effective. The following research questions were addressed:

1) Have procedural changes under the *FLA* made processes simpler and more accessible for self-represented litigants?
2) Is the *FLA* effective in serving the best interests of children and families?

A total of thirty-three SRLs were interviewed for the study, 61 percent of them female and 39 percent male. Participants ranged in age from twenty-one to fifty-seven. The majority (60.6 percent, n = 20) were between the ages of thirty and forty-nine, and the remainder were twenty to twenty-nine (27 percent) or fifty to fifty-nine (12 percent). Over half (52 percent) resided in Calgary, 18 percent in Edmonton, and 30 percent in other cities or towns in Alberta. About half the participants (52 percent) identified themselves as single, 18 percent were separated, nearly 25 percent were married or common law, and approximately 6 percent were divorced. Every participant had at least one child. Nearly half (46 percent) of the children lived solely with their mother and 21 percent lived solely with their father; the rest lived jointly with both parents (15 percent), with their grandparents (6 percent), or on their own (12 percent). Participants who stated that their children lived on their own were involved in cases in which a contact order had been made by a grandparent or spousal support was involved. All but two of the participants proceeded in Alberta Provincial Court.

Participants were asked a number of questions about their experience with the response process under the *FLA*, in particular about the forms they are required to complete. A majority (79 percent) reported that they had to complete forms, and nearly all of them (96 percent) reported that the instructions were easy to understand and the forms were easy to complete. However, just over half (54 percent) required assistance in completing the forms from Family Justice Services, duty counsel, or a friend.

The enactment of the *FLA* arose from an intent to make the family law court process less intimidating and more accessible for SRLs. To achieve this goal, support services have been made available. SRLs were asked about their experience with court support services, including Family Justice Services, Family Law Information Centres (FLIC), and duty counsel. Just under half (42 percent) of the participants accessed a FLIC, which offers assistance to those making a family law application and provides information about Child Support Guidelines and other areas of family law; 86 percent of these participants found that the information they received improved their understanding of court procedures and the options available to them. A large majority of participants (88 percent) indicated that they had completed an intake with Family Justice Services, where they were provided with various supports such as information on the family court process and the options available, referral to services, and assistance with forms. Three-quarters of these participants indicated that the intake had helped them better understand court procedures and the options available to them. For the few who received support from Legal Aid Family Duty Counsel (n = 6), available in the courts to provide information on courtroom process as well as legal advice, all found the support helpful.

Of those who had to attend court (n = 23), 57 percent were greeted by Family Justice Services staff; 69 percent found this helpful. A majority (83 percent) met with an FCC in Provincial Court caseflow, and just over two-thirds found that this helped them better identify issues concerning their application. As one participant articulated,

> They were very helpful and told me how everything is going to go . . . gave me a play by play on what to expect, and she stood by me when we started talking [in court] . . . . I knew it was going to be difficult being self-represented and having a person there that was knowledgeable was extremely helpful.

Of those who had to attend docket court (n = 15), when asked whether they felt prepared for what they experienced, 80 percent indicated they did.

Another goal of the new processes and procedures under the *FLA* was to support dispute resolution mechanisms outside the courtroom. The SRLs interviewed were asked about two such mechanisms: caseflow conferencing and mediation. Though only nine participants had attended a caseflow conference, two-thirds found the discussion helped them to understand the issues regarding their application, and all but one reached consent orders, either full or interim. For those who attended mediation (n = 12), two-thirds reached an agreement without having to proceed to court.

At the conclusion of the interview, SRLs were asked to rate their experience with *FLA* processes and procedures. Overall, participants were positive. On a scale of 1 to 10, with 1 being the lowest and 10 being the highest possible rating, participants were asked about the accessibility, fairness, efficiency, and their overall experience with the processes and procedures of the *FLA*. On average, participants rated accessibility at 7.3, fairness at 6.6, efficiency at 6.3, and overall experience at 6.9. The majority of participants also indicated that the *FLA* met (55 percent) or somewhat met (24 percent) their family's needs.

C. DISCUSSION

1) Family Law Procedure in Alberta

The evaluation set out to examine whether the new processes and procedures introduced with the *FLA* simplified family law, improved accessibility for SRLs, supported alternatives for resolving separation issues, and streamlined court procedures, providing for a more efficient, effective, and accessible provincial family law system. These factors were explored using analyses of caseflow and outcome data, a survey of professionals, and interviews with SRLs.

Overall, the data suggest that the *FLA* has resulted in an increased workload and human services demand for Provincial Court, Court of Queen's Bench, and associated services (e.g., Family Justice Services). Trends illustrated by the caseflow data demonstrate an increase in the amount of family law activity in the courts since the introduction of the *FLA*, particularly for Provincial Court and its associated services (Family Justice Services caseflow conferencing, mediation, and so forth). The Provincial Court data also suggest that an increasing number of individuals are proceeding under the *FLA* without legal representation. These trends indirectly point to a rising demand for staff and resources in the services that support SRLs. Information provided by professionals working with the *FLA* confirm these hypotheses. A majority of professionals (particularly court clerks) stated that their workload had increased; only judges/justices were more likely to state that their workload had stayed the same. Though Alberta's substantial population growth may account for some of these increases, it is likely that greater family law jurisdiction for the Provincial Court as a result of the *FLA* and improved accessibility of the system for SRLs are also factors.

In the spirit of supporting a more efficient and effective court process, procedures introduced with the *FLA* acknowledged the importance of dispute resolution programs and services, and information and supports for SRLs. Though many of these options existed prior to the implementation of the Act, initiatives such as intake and caseflow management (family court counsellor intake and caseflow conferencing) assist applications in reaching resolution prior to proceeding to the courtroom. As demonstrated by the program outcome data, dispute resolution programs and services are effective means of reaching resolution prior to the application proceeding to the courtroom (i.e., docket court or Chambers) or trial. Information provided by SRLs also points to the effectiveness of dispute resolution options. Sources of information such as Family Law Information Centres and Family Justice Services also proved important for SRLs in that they improve understanding of court procedures and the options available. Thus, the findings of the evaluation clearly point to the importance of alternative dispute resolution programs and court supports in improving procedural effectiveness and efficiency under the *FLA*.

The extent to which efforts to streamline court procedures have been successful is unclear, and the evaluation produced mixed findings. Though overall, professionals believe the claim and response process under the *FLA* is simpler and more efficient, many think there are too many forms, and that the forms are too restrictive, redundant, and complicated, particularly for SRLs who lack knowledge of the law. Further, though professionals think the *FLA* procedures are more client focused, they differ over whether the process better serves SRLs; judges/justices are quite positive and court administration staff more negative. In contrast, SRLs report little difficulty in completing and filing forms on their own, or indicate that they have enough information and support in case of difficulty.

With regard to court procedures, specifically, SRLs are generally positive about their experience, particularly with regard to the support and information they received from Family Justice Services staff, family court counsellors, and duty counsel. A large majority of SRLs felt prepared for what they experienced in docket court, pointing to the likelihood that the supports available to them are enabling a more efficient process. This is particularly positive given the number of SRLs proceeding on family matters since the implementation of the *FLA*. However, as most SRLs interviewed for the evaluation proceeded in Provincial Court, experiences in Court of Queen's Bench remain relatively unknown.

Results from analyses of Provincial Court processing-time data suggest that overall, the implementation of the *FLA* has resulted in a more efficient system, as the average time from the opening of a file to final order has steadily decreased.

2) Substantive Areas of the *Family Law Act*

The evaluation also examined the substantive changes to family law introduced by the *FLA*. The legislative review and interviews with professionals contributed to this body of knowledge. The substantive changes are intended to consolidate and modernize family law in Alberta, to adopt a child-centred perspective to ensure the best interests of children in matters of separation, and to reduce the financial and emotional costs to children and families to the greatest extent possible. Results from both the legislative review and the survey of professionals are clearly positive with regard to the consolidation of family law. A majority of professionals thought this was clearly needed, and the legislative review pointed to the important difference that simplifying the law has made to Albertans. Professionals were more positive about the substantive changes introduced by the *FLA* than about the procedural changes.

D. CONCLUSION

Evaluation of Alberta's *Family Law Act* suggests that overall, the implementation of the legislation has been of great benefit. The consolidation of previous legislation has simplified family law in the province, making it more accessible for professionals and SRLs alike. The procedural changes introduced with the legislation have improved the overall efficiency of the family law process, making it easier for SRLs to proceed under the *FLA*, though opinions differ among professionals and litigants over the simplicity of the claim and response process. The introduction of services and supports and new forms of alternative dispute resolution, as well as the continued use of those that existed prior to the introduction of the *FLA*, has improved the efficiency of the application process and outcomes for cases. Substantively, the *FLA* has made great strides in protecting the best interests of children and families, modernizing family law in Alberta and addressing important issues such as family violence.

CHAPTER 13

No Presumptions: Joint Custody in the British Columbia Court of Appeal

SUSAN B. BOYD

Descriptions of Canadian family law trends are disproportionately influenced by developments in Ontario, simply because that province produces a large amount of both family law and commentary on family law. For example, most Canadian family law books are written by Ontario lawyers and law professors, such as Nicholas Bala.[1] Much of this work is excellent, and it is certainly relied on in other jurisdictions. It can, however, generate a skewed view of developments in other provinces. Accordingly, this chapter offers a study of joint custody trends in the British Columbia Court of Appeal compared to those in Ontario.

In 2007, Martha Shaffer published two excellent articles on joint custody.[2] Her review of Ontario caselaw focused on contested joint custody after the

---

This project was funded by the Foundation for Legal Research. Cynthia Poblador, Eiad el Fateh, and Bree Makohn provided excellent research assistance. Former Justice Donna Martinson of the British Columbia Supreme Court, recently retired, kindly commented on a draft, as did Vancouver family law practitioner John-Paul Boyd. All errors remain my own.

1 Citing examples of books alone, one finds Nicholas Bala *et al.*, eds. *Canadian Child Welfare Law: Children, Families, and the State*, 2d ed. (Toronto: Thompson, 2004); Berend Hovius, *Family Law: Cases, Notes and Materials*, 6th student ed. (Scarborough, ON: Thomson Carswell, 2005); Mary Jane Mossman, *Families and the Law in Canada: Cases and Commentary* (Toronto: Emond Montgomery Publications, 2004); and Julien Payne & Marilyn Payne, *Canadian Family Law*, 2d ed. (Toronto: Irwin Law, 2006). If one were to cite articles, Nicholas Bala's name would, of course, feature prominently.

2 Martha Shaffer, "Joint Custody since *Kaplanis and Ladisa* — A Review of Recent Ontario Case Law" (2007) 26 Can Fam LQ 315. [Shaffer, "Joint Custody since *Kaplanis*"];

important 2005 Ontario Court of Appeal decision in *Kaplanis v. Kaplanis*,[3] which reiterated that court's cautious approach to ordering joint custody in contested cases (taken earlier in *Baker v. Baker*[4] and *Kruger v. Kruger*[5]). Specifically, it held that joint custody should not be ordered in such cases unless there is clear evidence that the parents are able to communicate effectively with one another, despite animosity and personal differences. One parent's opposition to joint custody would not on its own suffice to block such an award.[6] However, the message to Ontario judges was clear: joint custody will seldom be in a child's best interests if the parents are not capable of effective communication, as they will not be able to act jointly in their children's best interests. Although Shaffer identified some problems in post-*Kaplanis* case law, she found that, overall, Ontario courts take a cautious approach to joint custody in contested cases and make such orders sparingly.

Shaffer's article made me wonder to what extent trends were similar in British Columbia and whether the cautionary approach in *Kaplanis* is followed by BC judges, especially given that anecdotal evidence indicates joint custody is now the *de facto* starting point at custody hearings. Although a 1994 decision of the British Columbia Court of Appeal in *Stewart v. Stewart*[7] adopted a very cautious approach to joint custody in the face of communication difficulties, stating that such awards should be made rarely and only under circumstances in which the parties are totally in agreement and for all intents and purposes do not need the assistance of the court, a later decision in *Robinson v. Filyk*[8] came out strongly against the use of presumptions in custody decisions, negating the force of *Stewart*.

Martha Shaffer, "Joint Custody, Parental Conflict and Children's Adjustment to Divorce: What the Social Science Literature Does and Does Not Tell Us" (2007) 26 Can Fam LQ 286 [Shaffer, "Joint Custody, Parental Conflict"].

3 *Kaplanis v. Kaplanis* (2005), 10 RFL (6th) 373 (Ont CA) [*Kaplanis*]. A November 2009 review of Ontario Court of Appeal cases on joint custody reveals no significant departure from the rulings in *Kaplanis* and its sister case *Ladisa v. Ladisa* (2005), 11 RFL (6th) 50 (Ont CA) [*Ladisa*].

4 *Baker v. Baker* (1979), 8 RFL (2d) 236 (Ont CA) [*Baker*].

5 *Kruger v. Kruger* (1979), 11 RFL (2d) 52 (Ont CA) [*Kruger*].

6 *Ladisa*, released the same day as *Kaplanis*, both above note 3, made this clear. The Court of Appeal upheld a joint custody order despite the mother's opposition and the fact that high-level conflict existed between the parents. Evidence established that the parents could, nevertheless, communicate effectively and put the children's interests ahead of their own.

7 *Stewart v. Stewart* (1994), 2 RFL (4th) 53 (BCCA) [*Stewart*].

8 *Robinson v. Filyk*, [1996] BCJ No 2519 (CA) [*Robinson*].

In 2008, I undertook a review of judicial decisions dealing with joint custody in the British Columbia Court of Appeal. A search for "joint custody" cases using LexisNexis Quicklaw yielded ninety-nine cases falling between 11 December 1996, when the Court of Appeal decided *Robinson v. Filyk*, and spring 2008.[9] Forty-five of these dealt with custody as a significant issue on appeal, and these cases were studied for the purposes of this chapter.[10] Although I will offer some figures, this analysis is of course not statistically significant, nor does it give an accurate picture of all custody cases that go to court; it simply gives a sense of trends within the British Columbia Court of Appeal over a little more than a decade, based on cases that involved a claim for joint custody at some point. My overall conclusion is that the Ontario and BC courts may not depart radically from one another, but the jurisprudence of British Columbia's appellate court reveals some significant differences in emphasis that may be of concern.

A. NO PRESUMPTIONS: *ROBINSON v. FILYK* (1996)

In December 1996, the British Columbia Court of Appeal rendered an important judgment in *Robinson v. Filyk*.[11] On appeal, a non-custodial mother sought an order of joint guardianship or joint custody, having been denied sole custody at trial. The trial judge had found little to choose between the parents, who had made consensual shared parenting arrangements until each moved away from British Columbia, the father to London, Ontario, and the mother to Calgary, Alberta. The father was a university professor who had remarried. The mother was a medical student in Calgary, who was living with her mother in the maternal family home. Each parent originally sought joint or sole custody and primary residence. The trial judge found it inappropriate to grant joint physical custody because that was the point on which the parents had

9 This study differs from Shaffer's "Joint Custody since *Kaplanis*," above note 2, because it is both broader (hers focused on *Kaplanis* and on joint custody in close proximity to communication, cooperation or conflict) and narrower (because it focuses only on appellate level decisions). I have also conducted a review of BC trial decisions on joint custody for the years 2000 and 2007, in an effort to gauge any shift in approach over time: Susan B. Boyd, "Joint Custody and Guardianship in the British Columbia Courts: Not a Cautious Approach" (2010) 29:3 Can Fam LQ 223 [Boyd, "Joint Custody"].

10 Of the other fifty-four BCCA cases turned up on the search, the vast majority involved a joint custody award that was not questioned on appeal; instead, the issue on appeal was child or spousal support or matrimonial property, a jurisdictional issue, contempt of court, child protection, or criminal law.

11 *Robinson*, above note 8.

been unable to agree. He went on to conclude, reluctantly, that given the geographical separation, a joint order of custody and guardianship was unworkable, citing the cautious approach of the Ontario Court of Appeal in *Baker v. Baker*,[12] suggesting that joint custody is an exceptional disposition appropriate only when two parties will be able to cooperate. He awarded the mother only reasonable and generous access, but expressed the "hope and expectation that Mr. Robinson will consult with Ms. Filyk on all major decisions concerning the development of Pascale."[13] When the father moved to Norway, the mother appealed, asking for joint guardianship and joint custody. The father did not disagree that joint guardianship would be in the daughter's best interests.

The Court of Appeal followed the Supreme Court of Canada decisions in *Young v. Young*[14] and *Gordon v. Goertz*[15] in making a strong statement that the only consideration in custody cases is the best interests of the child and that there is no legal presumption in favour of either sole or joint custody. Is is important to note that Huddart JA distanced herself from her earlier opinion (when a County Court judge) in *Anson v. Anson* that a joint custody and joint guardianship order would be appropriate "where both parents are excellent parents, there is a history of co-operation with respect to the parenting of the child and there is no valid reason to exclude a parent from having significant input into the raising of the child."[16] She now saw such an opinion as being as much of a legal or factual presumption as had been seen in the early Ontario Court of Appeal decisions in *Baker* and *Kruger*.[17] Justice Huddart also stated that the

> essence of [the mother's] argument is that the trial judge in effect applied a presumption in favour of sole custody . . . when he adopted the cautious approach to joint custody taken . . . by the Ontario Court of Appeal in *Baker v. Baker* . . . and *Kruger v. Kruger* . . . , approved by this court in *Stewart v. Stewart* . . . , rather than making the enquiry into Pascale's particular circumstances.[18]

She then made a key statement:

---

12 *Baker*, above note 4.

13 *Robinson*, above note 8 at para. 8.

14 *Young v. Young*, [1993] 4 SCR 3.

15 *Gordon v. Goertz*, [1996] 2 SCR 27 [*Gordon*].

16 *Anson v. Anson* (1987), 10 BCLR (2d) 357 at 370 (Co Ct) [*Anson*].

17 *Baker*, above note 4; *Kruger*, above note 5.

18 *Robinson*, above note 8 at para. 20.

> It is now clear that legal and factual presumptions have no place in an enquiry into the best interests of a child, however much predictive value they may have. The Supreme Court of Canada has stated absolutely clearly that such presumptions detract from the individual justice to which every child is entitled.[19]

In other words, any indication in a judgment of a presumption in favour of (or against) either joint or sole custody is inappropriate. Instead, the only issue is a child's best interests, to be "found within the practical context of the reality of the parents' lives and circumstances."[20]

Although Huddart JA affirmed the principle that appellate courts should interfere with trial decisions only rarely,[21] she added:

> If the reasons [of a trial judge] reveal a mindset with a pre-ordained default position, then the decision must be reviewed as if that mindset were not there. The trial judge who brings presumptions to the enquiry is not considering the best interests of the particular child in the particular circumstances and will have erred.[22]

In the case at hand, Huddart JA did not interfere with the award of sole custody to the father, even though she said that the trial judge could be read as having endorsed the cautious approach of Ontario courts, which suggests a threshold test before joint custody would be ordered.[23] The reason for her deference to the trial decision was that joint decision making would not be workable because the geographical separation would continue to exacerbate the communication difficulties that had emerged after the parents' respective relocations.

Somewhat contradictorily, however, Huddart JA did vary the order to provide for joint guardianship, in order to ensure that (1) the mother would have decision-making authority when the child was with her, and (2) should the father die, guardianship would pass directly to the mother without a court order being necessary.[24] In addition, she noted that the *Family Relations Act* contains a provision permitting a joint guardian to ask for directions on vari-

19 *Ibid.* at para. 22.
20 *Ibid.* at para. 29, quoting from *Gordon*, above note 15 at para. 46.
21 *Ibid.* at para. 16.
22 *Ibid.* at para. 30.
23 *Ibid.* at para. 32.
24 *Family Relations Act*, RSBC 1996, c. 128, s. 29.

ous issues rather than applying for a change of custody[25] and that this inquiry "would remove some of the threat implicit in the more adversarial application for a change of custody."[26] She added:

> Geographical separation may make a joint custody order unworkable, but it makes a joint guardianship order desirable when a child spends considerable periods of time with the non-custodial parent and that parent is the obvious person to assume the care-giving of the child upon the death or incapacity of the custodial parent.[27]

This award raises the thorny question — somewhat peculiar to British Columbia — of the difference between joint custody, which Huddart JA refused to order, and joint guardianship, which she did order.

B. TERMINOLOGY: THE BC DIFFERENCE

Terminology is generally a problem in the custody field, as Shaffer notes: some courts use the term *joint custody* to connote arrangements giving both parents shared decision-making authority over significant child-rearing issues, and others use it to mean shared physical care.[28] When *shared parenting* is used by the British Columbia Court of Appeal, it is usually in relation to physical care of the child or to describe access arrangements, when the child lives with each parent alternately.[29] The term *shared custody* is used occasionally, generally to connote roughly equal shared time with a child and sometimes when joint custody is already in place, implying that the terms may mean something different.[30]

Terminology is further complicated in British Columbia, in a way that it is not in Ontario, by the concept of guardianship, which co-exists, not always peacefully, with the concept of custody. Under section 27 of the *Family Relations Act,* married parents and parents who cohabit are joint guardians of the child. If they separate, they remain joint guardians of the child's estate but

25 *Ibid.*, s. 32.
26 *Robinson*, above note 8 at para. 14.
27 *Ibid.* at para. 16.
28 Shaffer, "Joint Custody since *Kaplanis,*" above note 2 at 321.
29 For example, *Nunweiler v. Nunweiler*, 2000 BCCA 300 [*Nunweiler*].
30 For example, *Parker v. Parker*, 2002 BCCA 299. The father wanted one week on, one week off, but the court found insufficient evidence to warrant increased contact. The parents already had joint custody and guardianship.

the parent who has the usual care and control of the child is the sole guardian of the child, *unless otherwise agreed or ordered*.[31] Section 34 then outlines who may exercise custody over a child in terms that are generally parallel to those in section 27. These sections do not assist very much in defining the ambit of guardianship and custody or the relationship between them. Indeed, in 1990 the Court of Appeal stated in *Lennox v. Frender* that the terms *guardianship, custody,* and *care and control* are "often used without precision" but "may, in some circumstances, have different meanings from each other."[32] The court added that these terms may have different meanings for the purposes of the *Divorce Act*[33] than for the *Family Relations Act,* and suggested that it would be better if parties and/or courts spelled out what is intended, for instance, in minutes of settlement, rather than relying on legal jargon. It reviewed earlier British Columbia Supreme Court cases[34] indicating that joint guardianship normally meant that each parent would have a full and active role in providing a sound moral, social, economic, and educational environment for the children, and that they should consult one another in planning religious upbringing, educational programs, athletic and recreational activities, health care (excluding emergency), and significant changes in the social environment. Neither party should exercise this power and authority to frustrate or unduly affect the life of the other, and each should exert best efforts to cooperate in plans consistent with the children's best interests.

The Court of Appeal went on in *Lennox* to review definitions of joint custody in the Ontario cases *Baker* and *Kruger,* indicating that joint custody gave equal parental control over, and equal ultimate parental responsibility for, the care, upbringing, and education of the child, but that the child might nevertheless be ordered to reside with one parent who had immediate direction and guidance, while the other parent enjoyed access. The court "accept[ed] these descriptions of joint custody when it is not distinguished from guardianship" as saying essentially the same thing: "That is, that parents with joint custody continue to act as parents and continue to have the right to share in the making of important decisions respecting the child."[35] For instance, in *Lennox* the mother, who had care and control of the child,

31 *Family Relations Act,* above note 24, ss. 27–28 [emphasis added].

32 *Lennox v. Frender* (1990), 27 RFL (3d) 181 (BCCA) [*Lennox*].

33 RSC 1985, c. 3 (2nd Supp.).

34 Quoting especially from Gansner LJSC in *Charlton v. Charlton* (1980), 19 BCLR 42 at 45 (SC).

35 *Lennox,* above note 32 at para. 32.

but shared joint custody with the father, did not have the authority to decide unilaterally to send the child to private school.[36]

Anson v. Anson, an oft-cited 1987 decision by Huddart J when she sat on the British Columbia County Court, defined the "ancient" concept of guardianship as the full bundle of rights and duties assumed by an adult in respect of a child and stated that under both federal and BC legislation, custody has come to hold a similar wide meaning, going beyond a narrower conception of physical care and control.[37] As a result, an award of custody would give a full bundle of rights and responsibilities to the custodial parent, apart from those reserved to a guardian. *Anson* also stated that a joint custody order should not be viewed as a finite disposition but a broad range of post-separation custodial arrangements, the details of which are to be worked out. The key is where the residual authority lies: "Joint guardianship and joint custody orders grant both divorced or separated parents an equal voice in the upbringing of their children."[38] Neither is given final decision-making authority and normally, the parties must confer with each other and decide what is best for the child. If they cannot agree, either guardian can consult a professional third party or seek directions from the court under the *Family Relations Act*.[39]

As it was discussed in *Lennox* and *Anson*, joint guardianship seems strikingly similar to what scholars would typically call joint legal custody and what many courts refer to as simply joint custody. Shaffer similarly uses "joint custody" to refer to "arrangements in which parents share the authority to make significant decisions over their children's lives — that is, on matters relating to their children's education, health care and religious upbringing."[40]

---

36 See the later case *J.B.R. v. A.M.R.*, 2003 BCCA 135, where the BCCA remanded a case back to the BCSC. The trial court had awarded joint custody and joint guardianship with primary residence to the father, but also allowed the father to determine the children's schooling and terms of the mother's access. The question was whether these terms were consistent with a joint custody and joint guardianship award.

37 *Anson*, above note 16.

38 *Ibid.* at para. 27.

39 In the *Anson* case, the parents often disagreed on questions of the health care and education of their son, but Huddart Co Ct J nevertheless overturned the Provincial Court decision, which had awarded sole custody to the mother with joint guardianship, but not joint custody. I wonder whether the Provincial Court judge had resisted joint custody precisely because of the history of disagreement on health care and education. Justice Huddart instead emphasized the history of cooperation with regard to parenting. Recall that this decision is one from which Huddart JA distanced herself in *Robinson*, above note 8.

40 Shaffer, "Joint Custody since *Kaplanis*," above note 2 at 322.

Yet *Robinson* indicates that a joint guardianship order might be made in circumstances in which joint decision making is not workable, for reasons to do with the passing of guardianship after death of the custodial parent and exercise of authority while the child is with the non-custodial parent. It appears that pragmatic reasons led Huddart JA to distinguish between joint custody and joint guardianship in *Robinson*. She also signalled that an award of joint guardianship might avert adversarial proceedings in the future. As the British Columbia Court of Appeal indicates in *Falvai v. Falvai*, an award of joint guardianship can ameliorate the broad concept of custody, which normally entails the full bundle of rights relating to both physical care and control and decision-making authority.[41] It is possible that joint guardianship may be ordered in some cases, or suggested in settlement conferences,[42] in order to encourage parents to stop contesting custody and get on with post-separation parenting. Note that joint guardianship is awarded not only in non-divorce scenarios in which the provincial *Family Relations Act* is the governing statute but also in claims for custody in divorce scenarios.

As we have seen, joint guardianship and joint custody are not always awarded together. In fact, BC decisions generally indicate an "unbundling"[43] of the rights and responsibilities associated with custody, with a perhaps surprising variety of orders. Joint guardianship is sometimes ordered in tandem with a sole custody award and sometimes with a joint custody award. A "Master Joyce" model of joint guardianship is sometimes used to clarify what is meant.[44]

41 *Falvai v. Falvai*, 2008 BCCA 503 [*Falvai*].

42 Justice Donna Martinson suggested in 2007 that there is a growing trend among judges in family law cases, particularly in the context of pre-trial settlement conferences, to emphasize the importance of shared parenting so that children have the benefit of contact with both parents. Donna Martinson, "Post-Separation Parenting — Submerged Gender Issues" (Paper for Why Gender Equality Still Matters, the National Judicial Institute Conference on Emerging Gender Issues, Toronto, 28–30 November 2007). Full evidence about issues such as conflict or abuse is not typically available at pre-trial settlement conferences, which raises concerns about any trend toward emphasizing joint arrangements.

43 The term *unbundling* is more commonly used in relation to legal services, offering parties who cannot afford full legal representation the option to choose legal services à la carte rather than having to opt between full and no legal services. Franklin R. Garfield, "Unbundling Legal Services in Mediation: Reflections of a Family Lawyer" (2002) 40:1 Fam Ct Rev 76. A special issue of the *Family Court Review* covering issues of unbundled law was published in January 2002.

44 Family Law in British Columbia, "Guardianship," online: www.familylaw.lss.bc.ca/resources/fact_sheets/guardianship.asp. Other models include the Charlton model, which emphasizes the importance of cooperation, and the Master Horne model, which is similar to the Master Joyce model but has no clause giving one parent final decision-

Under this model, which is premised on one parent having primary care, each parent has the obligation to discuss with the other matters and decisions of a significant nature concerning the child, including those about health (except emergency decisions), education, religious instruction, and general welfare. In the event the parents cannot reach agreement despite best efforts, the primary care parent has the right to make such decision. The other parent may seek a review under section 32 of the *Family Relations Act*.[45] Each parent has the right to obtain information about the child from third parties.

Having identified the terminological minefield in British Columbia (which may or may not be resolved when the *Family Relations Act* is revised), I turn now to examine the trends in the British Columbia Court of Appeal cases relating to joint custody.

C. APPELLATE TRENDS IN BRITISH COLUMBIA 1996–2008

The Court of Appeal made some strong statements in *Robinson*, and a key question is whether the court has followed its directives in favour of deference to trial judgments and against the use of presumptions of any sort. Another question is how the court deals with difficulties in communication and cooperation, given its distancing from the cautious approach of the Ontario Court of Appeal and from the use of any presumptions. Prior to addressing these questions, an overview of the decisions reveals the unbundling of the rights and responsibilities associated with custody that characterizes BC decisions, as well as the gender dynamics.

1) Unbundling of Custody

Perhaps the most interesting finding in this study is the need to examine carefully the actual orders under the labels *sole custody* or *joint custody* and the unbundling of custody that is revealed. Orders that appear on their face to be for sole custody might involve aspects commonly associated with joint custody,

---

making authority; guardianship is described primarily in terms of a parent's right to get information about the child and participate in decision making. The Master Joyce model is used more often in orders and agreements, according to J.P. Boyd (BC Family Law Resource, "Children > Guardianship," online: www.bcfamilylawresource.com/03/0302body.htm), but my study does not indicate it is used in a majority of joint guardianship awards.

45 *Family Relations Act*, above note 24.

such as joint decision making (often via a joint guardianship order). By the same token, orders for joint custody might relegate physical custody and/or decision-making authority primarily to one parent. This unbundling of custody relates to a trend that I have previously referred to as the enlargement of access and a diminishing of the authority associated with custody.[46] As D.M. Smith J has said, this narrower concept of custody has become increasingly prevalent.[47] The trend to unbundle custody may lend support to those who argue that the language of "custody" and "access" is outmoded and should be removed in law reform processes. On the other hand, the fact that so many joint custody awards reserve primary residence or decision making to one parent speaks to some degree of caution that BC courts signal about awarding "equal" rights to parents. Moreover, in a not insignificant number of cases, courts still decide that sole custody orders are warranted.

a) Sole Custody

About 58 percent of the cases reviewed involved trial orders for sole custody that were usually appealed by the non-custodial parent who argued for sole custody, joint custody, or, often, one of those orders in the alternative. In some cases, joint custody was barely discussed by the court, the implication being that it was inappropriate. These decisions were made on the basis of the best interests of the child and/or a finding that the parents could not communicate or were not cooperative.[48] There was little evidence in these decisions of any presumption against joint custody when there is an inability to communicate; rather, evidence of inability to communicate was usually assessed and taken into account, albeit sometimes briefly.

Sole custody awards were not always traditional in form, although the majority were. A few cases awarded sole custody to one parent (more often, but not always, the mother) but then varied its exclusivity by awarding an aspect of custody such as joint guardianship, or even primary care, to another party. *Ness v. Ness*, for instance, awarded the mother sole custody but granted

---

46 Susan B. Boyd, *Child Custody, Law, and Women's Work* (Don Mills, ON: Oxford University Press, 2003) at 130.

47 *Falvai*, above note 41 at para. 37.

48 For example, *Pratap v. Pratap*, 2005 BCCA 71, where the trial judge found that it would not be in the best interests of the children to disrupt their lives by removing them from the situation (sole custody with the mother, generous access with the father) in which they had been comfortably settled for 2.5 years. The father's "controlling personality" was also a factor, but only one factor.

joint guardianship to the father.[49] Joint custody was viewed as inappropriate because the parents lacked the proper degree of mutual deference and respect to create a harmonious environment for the children. A very unusual award was affirmed in *Metzner v. Metzner*, with sole custody to the father but primary care to the mother. Joint custody, on the other hand, was viewed as inappropriate because "the parties could not agree on anything."[50] In two cases involving Aboriginal children, sole custody was granted to one parent, with joint guardianship to the other parent.[51] This unbundling of the rights and responsibilities associated with traditional awards of sole custody dilutes the exclusive and primary control that sole custody connotes, often making the award more palatable to the other parent.[52]

b) Joint Custody

Joint custody awards were made at trial in about 42 percent of the cases reviewed, usually combined with joint guardianship. Only two of these were successfully appealed, and not on the joint custody award itself. Problems of communication rarely seemed to be the key issue in these appeals, which is not to say that problems of communication or about access did not exist.[53] In one case, evidence of ability to communicate under a joint guardianship model worked against a mother's appeal against a joint custody award. A Master Joyce model of guardianship was involved under which the mother, who held the responsibilities of primary parent, had to consult the father about significant decisions concerning the children.[54] The mother's argument that the joint custody award should be overturned in favour of sole custody to her (to reflect the respective roles she and the father now played in the children's lives) failed because she was agreeable to extensive parental consultation

---

49 *Ness v. Ness*, 1999 BCCA 51 [*Ness*].

50 *Metzner v. Metzner*, [1997] BCJ No 904 at para. 58 (CA) [*Metzner*].

51 *A.L. v. D.K.*, 2000 BCCA 455, additional reasons in *A.L. v. D.K.*, 2000 BCCA 633; *B.L.M. v. G.T.M.*, 2003 BCCA 381.

52 This was clearly not the case in the unusual *Metzner* decision, above note 50, given that the mother appealed on the grounds that the award of sole custody to the father was not workable and went against the children's best interests. This award also generated various questions with regard to child support, since the payor parent was also the custodial parent.

53 For example, *McLean v. Russell*, 1999 BCCA 440 (communication problems) [*McLean*]; *Ebrahim v. Ebrahim*, 2000 BCCA 398. (Joint custody had been awarded in order to permit the mother to "enforce" access! The appeal was about contempt of court.)

54 *Skrivanek v. Pow*, 2006 BCCA 239.

(joint guardianship), plus her children were of an age (nine to eighteen) at which, the Court of Appeal said, custody had little significance.[55] A few appeals reflected a challenge by a parent who sought sole custody on the basis that the joint custody scheme was not workable,[56] or that the trial court did not give weight to the status quo.[57] In one case, the parents had joint custody of two elder children but sole custody of a younger child was awarded to the father; the mother applied unsuccessfully for an extension of time to adduce fresh evidence about how joint custody had (or had not) worked out.[58]

The vast majority of joint custody awards were modified by an award of primary residence or primary care to one parent and, notably, more appeals arose on these details rather than on the joint custody itself. In one case, the mother appealed, unsuccessfully, a variation order specifying that each parent had primary residence for one child.[59] Sometimes the parents had initially agreed on the terms in a separation agreement, but often they were judicially imposed at some stage. Most of these "detail" appeals related to a relocation. For instance, one parent might want to overturn a primary residence order to the other parent to prevent that parent from moving with the child. Or one parent might seek a primary residence order in his or her favour in order to be able to move with the child.

The preponderance of appeals on collateral issues such as primary care rather than on joint custody itself, even if problems related to communication or access existed or if relations seemed acrimonious,[60] indicates a certain acceptance of the normativity of joint custody — which had sometimes been agreed to by the parents themselves rather than judicially imposed. It also illustrates that awarding joint custody in an effort to diffuse adversarial stances between parents may not always succeed; the disputes simply shift to the details such as primary residence and relocation.[61]

---

55 *Ibid.* at para. 5. The father now saw the children for some hours every other weekend, on both Saturday and Sunday. In other words, the mother clearly had the primary responsibility.

56 *Carr v. Carr*, 2001 BCCA 415 [*Carr*]. It was specified that the children should live with each parent alternately.

57 *M.F.A. v. R.D.A.*, 2002 BCCA 210; additional reasons at *M.F.A. v. R.D.A.*, 2002 BCCA 477.

58 *Pharaoh v. Brace*, 2000 BCCA 385.

59 *Rail v. Rail*, [1999] BCJ No 2283 (CA) [*Rail*].

60 For example, *McLean*, above note 53 (communication); *C.L.R. v. R.A.R.*, 2006 BCCA 209 (acrimonious relations).

61 Similarly, research in Australia, which eradicated the terms *custody* and *access* in the mid-1990s in an effort to diffuse acrimony, shows that litigation did not diminish but

2) Gender and Appeals

All the cases reviewed involved opposite-sex parents, which is not surprising given how few custody disputes between same-sex parents have, as yet, reached the courts. In a majority of cases (about 71 percent), the father was the appellant and, as we will see below, most appeals failed. His appeal often reflected his wish to alter an award of sole custody to the mother (mothers received the vast majority of such awards) in favour of either sole custody to him or joint custody. Fathers also appealed orders of primary care or residence to mothers, who received a majority of such awards. Sometimes they challenged relocations by mothers or wanted to alter a joint custody award to a sole custody award in his favour.[62] Fathers successfully appealed three cases. Two fathers succeeded in having the trial judgment of sole custody to the mother overturned and in gaining custody.[63] The third father succeeded in having the case remanded to trial to determine whether sole custody to the mother was warranted or whether the separation agreement providing for joint custody, with primary residence to the father, should have been reflected in the order.[64]

Mothers generally appealed orders for sole custody to the father (sometimes related to relocation); awards of primary residence to the father or a refusal of relocation; or a Hague Convention return of a child to another jurisdiction. In one case, a mother succeeded in having an interim award of sole custody to the father overturned in favour of interim joint custody.[65] In another she was able to obtain sole custody on appeal.[66]

---

instead increased on questions such as contact. It also became more difficult to protect the interests of vulnerable parties, particularly abused women and children. Helen Rhoades, "Posing as Reform: The Case of the *Family Law Reform Act*" (2000) 14 Austl J Fam L 142; John Dewar & Stephen Parker," The Impact of the New Part VII *Family Law Act 1975*" (1999) 13 Austl J Fam L 96.

62 *Carr*, above note 56, involved the latter scenario.

63 *Van de Perre v. Edwards*, 2000 BCCA 167 [*Van de Perre*]; *Struck v. Struck*, 2003 BCCA 623. The decision in *Van de Perre* was overruled by the Supreme Court of Canada, 2001 SCC 60.

64 *M.L.H. v. T.R.H.*, [2006] BCJ No 521 (CA). Separation agreements were by no means always simply confirmed by the courts.

65 *Testawitch v. Farquhar*, [1997] BCJ No 2866 (CA) [*Testawitch*].

66 *Nunweiler*, above note 29, discussed further below: see below footnote 80 and related text. Other successful appeals by mothers resulted in remands to the trial court.

Although the gendered dynamics in these appeal cases might be seen as feeding the fire of the fathers' rights movement,[67] awards of sole custody and primary care to mothers must be seen against the backdrop of evidence that in most opposite-sex parenting scenarios, parenting remains gendered. Mothers still assume more primary responsibility for children and most of the responsibility dimension that involves the planning, scheduling, orchestrating, and coordination of family activities. The time that mothers devote to child care actually increased between 1986 and 2005, even as fathers become more involved in child care. Women also account for 89 percent of stay-at-home parents.[68] It should be no surprise that these patterns often continue after separation or divorce. Nevertheless, fathers did receive several awards of primary residence or care, in addition to the numerous joint custody awards.

It must also be noted that in some cases, a father's behaviour (e.g., substance abuse, assaults) accounted for judicial resistance to awarding him joint (or sole) custody rather than any predetermined bias against paternal custody. For example, in three cases, (self-represented) fathers had actually refused to exercise access with their children because they had not been awarded custody. In *Dhaliwal v. Beloud*, joint custody had been ruled out by the trial judge due to the inability of the parents to communicate. Although the mother had shown a more amenable and flexible attitude in the later stages of proceedings, the parties continued to have a "high degree of antipathy" at appeal.[69] The father was also found to have terminated his access with his son in an attempt to gain custody. The father had been self-represented, which had clearly presented the court with difficulties, but he could well afford counsel and the court advised that he consider retaining a lawyer to assist with negotiations.[70] Somewhat similarly, in *E.J.P. v. E.A.K.*, the father had refused to exercise his supervised access. One of the orders he sought was "[f]or the judge to be held responsible for his actions in forcefully remov-

---

67 Richard Collier & Sally Sheldon, eds., *Fathers' Rights Activism and Law Reform in Comparative Perspective* (Oxford: Hart, 2006); Jocelyn E. Crowley, *Defiant Dads: Fathers' Rights Activists in America* (Ithaca & London: Cornell University Press, 2008).

68 Katherine Marshall, "Converging Gender Roles" in Statistics Canada, *Perspectives on Labour and Income*, vol. 7, no. 7 (Ottawa: Ministry of Industry, 2006) at 11; Kerry Daly, *The Changing Culture of Parenting*, Contemporary Family Trends series (Ottawa: Vanier Institute of the Family, 2004).

69 *Dhaliwal v. Beloud*, [1998] BCJ No 1152 at para. 53 (CA).

70 *Ibid.* at para. 54.

ing a loving father from the son's life, slandering the father in the son's eyes, and having this published on the internet, and violating the state's obligation to help parents protect their children."[71] Justice Southin called him on his strategy: "[Y]ou told us this morning that you do not propose to attempt to implement the order because your position is that either there should be joint custody or you do not want this access."[72] Given that he agreed, the court decided that his mission was to retry the question of the sole custody award to the mother and dismissed the appeal. In *Green v. Millar*, a father who challenged the constitutionality of the statutory provisions concerning custody and access, in addition to wanting to set aside the order of sole custody and guardianship to the mother, refused to exercise access because it was supervised (due to the fact that the father imposed conflict on the child during access visits). He asked that "the parties be recognized in full equality at law as the parents" of their child, which the court took to mean joint guardianship and joint custody.[73] He had left the mother after he kicked down a bedroom door (she had locked herself in with the child), after which a restraining order was made and then varied to permit him supervised access. In the last two cases at least, the discourse of the father appellants resembled that used in the fathers' rights movement, which often takes a stance quite antagonistic to mothers.[74]

3) Deference to Trial Judges: Only Occasional Reversals

The British Columbia Court of Appeal generally appears to apply the principle of deference to trial judges: in only about 15 percent (seven) of the forty-five cases did the Court of Appeal reverse the trial decision or remand the case back for further hearing. As Huddart JA put it in *Bain v. Bain*, "this Court rarely interferes with a child care regime put in place by a trial judge. It may do so only when there is a material error, a serious misapprehension of the evidence or an error in law."[75] The scope of appellate review regarding

---

71 *E.J.P. v. E.A.K.*, 2003 BCCA 520, [2003] BCJ No 2379 at para. 1 (CA), leave to appeal to SCC refused (2004), 328 NR 396.

72 *Ibid.* at para. 8.

73 *Green v. Millar*, 2004 BCCA 590 [*Green*], leave to appeal to SCC refused, [2005] SCCA No 22.

74 See Susan B. Boyd, "'Robbed of Their Families'? Fathers' Rights Discourses in Canadian Parenting Law Reform Processes" in Richard Collier & Sally Sheldon, eds., *Fathers' Rights Activism and Law Reform in Comparative Perspective* (Oxford: Hart, 2006).

75 *Bain v. Bain*, 2008 BCCA 49 at para. 21 [*Bain*].

interim orders is even narrower,[76] and the court should maintain the status quo in the absence of reasons to the contrary.[77] Moreover, since appeals will be generally unsuccessful because of the narrow scope of appellate review, the court has said that, provided parents have a long history of cooperating, it is usually in the best interest of the child that their disagreements be dealt with through an application for variation before the trial court.[78]

Given its strong statement against presumptions, one might have expected that the Court of Appeal would be inclined to overturn trial decisions that ventured too close to a legal or factual presumption. But rarely did it do so, reflecting the dominance of the principle of deference to the orders of trial judges. The reasons for overturning mostly related to a lack of sufficient evidence to ground the order, or to improper weight given by trial judges to material evidence. An example of the latter was the well-known decision overturning a sole custody award to the (single) biological mother, Kimberley Van de Perre, with joint guardianship to the biological father Theodore (Blue) Edwards, who was married to a third party. In a controversial decision subsequently overturned by the Supreme Court of Canada,[79] the British Columbia Court of Appeal overturned the trial judge because it found that the judge had relied excessively on negative factors related to the father. The appellate court not only added Edwards' wife as a party but granted joint custody to her and to Edwards, with joint guardianship and access to the mother. The court also laid some emphasis on the fact that the child was mixed race and might benefit from living with the father, who was African American.

In one case, *Nunweiler v. Nunweiler*, involving a mother's relocation, the Court of Appeal did address problematic presumptions in its finding of reversible error in the trial judge's (mis)apprehension of the facts and evidence. Justice Saunders noted that an approach that considers the status quo to be the preferred position should a convincing case for a move not be made re-inserts a presumption (in favour of the status quo) into custody discussions. The court also found this approach to be contrary to the instruction in *Gordon*

76 *J.G.F. v. C.L.B.*, 2003 BCCA 382 at para. 11, Huddart JA in chambers; see also *Testawitch*, above note 65.

77 *Leung v. Leung*, [1998] BCJ No 2614 at paras. 11–12, and 14 (CA). The court also noted that the status quo can be defined in different ways, such as where the children have resided versus which parent had day-to-day care. Moreover, once parents separate, ideal arrangements are not always possible (MacFarlane JA).

78 *B.L.M. v. G.T.M.*, 2003 BCCA 381.

79 *Van de Perre*, above note 63.

v. Goertz to respect the view of the parent wishing to relocate, barring an improper motive.[80] The trial judge had attempted to determine the mother's residence by awarding her joint custody and primary residence only if she were to move back to the town where the father lived. Otherwise the father would be awarded sole custody. The Court of Appeal found that the trial judge had not fully considered the child's best interests and took the rare step of substituting an order rather than ordering a new hearing. Taking into account that the trial judge had recognized the appropriateness of the child residing primarily with her mother, the court substituted an order of sole custody with the mother, without geographical restriction, combined with generous access to the father and joint guardianship to confirm his legal responsibility.[81]

4) No Presumptions

The strong statement by the British Columbia Court of Appeal against presumptions either in favour of or against sole or joint custody has not been challenged at the appellate level. Indeed the Court of Appeal applauded a trial judge for not relying "upon any presumption in favour of the mother as a primary caregiver."[82] In a dissent in *Rail v. Rail,* however, Prowse JA indicated some push-back on Huddart JA's reiteration for the majority that "[o]ne cannot begin with presumptions with articulated premises."[83] The issue in this case was not joint custody *per se,* but rather whether the son should have his primary residence with the father instead of the mother. (Permanent residence with the mother had been agreed under a joint custody and guardianship arrangement for the two children.) Justice Prowse found two errors made by the chambers judge and would have retained the status quo. While she stated clearly that it could not be disputed "that the court must not commence a best interests analysis with presumptions in favour of the status quo or of the primary parent, that is not to say that those factors are not entitled to significant weight in determining where the best interests of the child lie."[84] She emphasized that the seven-year-old son had lived primarily with

80 *Nunweiler,* above note 29 at para. 30, citing *Gordon,* above note 15.

81 See also *Falvai,* above note 41 (a case that falls outside the time frame of our study), in which a mother succeeded in appealing a condition of a sole custody order requiring her to reside in the community where the father lived.

82 *Langtry v. Langtry,* [1997] BCJ No 264 at para. 7 (CA), Goldie JA.

83 *Rail,* above note 59 at para. 19.

84 *Ibid.* at para. 34, Prowse JA in dissent.

his mother and his sister since he was ten months old and that, although the relationship with his father was a good one, it had not been put to the test on a day-to-day basis.[85] In a prefiguring of the Supreme Court of Canada warning in *Van de Perre v. Edwards*, Prowse JA also stated that she could not see how the fact that the father could offer a two-parent home, while the mother could not, could tilt the balance in favour of moving the son out of his mother's home, given the strong support network the mother had in place involving grandparents and other competent caregivers.[86] The majority decision by Huddart JA acknowledged that factors such as maintenance of the status quo, the tender years doctrine, and the premise that courts should avoid splitting siblings were not rules of law but considerations to be taken into account in the context of all the factors that must be weighed when determining best interests of a child whose parents cannot agree.[87]

Some appellate cases implicitly referenced the dangers of presumptions, but rarely were they explicitly addressed. In *M.J.D. v. J.P.D.*, the court emphasized a trial judge statement that a lack of cooperation does not always lead to a refusal of an order of joint custody, but affirmed the trial holding that when cooperation on any controversial matter appears unlikely, joint custody might be unwise.[88] In *Cross v. Cross*, Hall JA affirmed a variation of a joint custody award with alternating blocks of time with each parent in favour of sole custody to a mother, citing "an unfortunate history of controversy over the care and custody of their child."[89] Although he had found that both husband and wife were loving and worthy parents, he noted that it "has been observed in other cases that joint custody is usually only feasible where there is a fairly high level of agreement between the parents" and in this case, it had been demonstrated that there was "a quite low level of agreement."[90] Some might see a hint of a presumption in this language.

5) Communication and Cooperation

The Ontario Court of Appeal decision in *Kaplanis* had not yet been cited by the British Columbia Court of Appeal as of November 2009, which may

85 *Ibid.* at paras. 38 & 39.
86 *Ibid.* at para. 49. See also *Van de Perre*, above note 63.
87 *Ibid.* at para. 18, Huddart JA.
88 *M.J.D. v. J.P.D.*, 2001 BCCA 155.
89 *Cross v. Cross*, [1997] BCJ No 2758 at para. 3 (CA).
90 *Ibid.* at para. 4.

not be surprising given that, as we saw above, the BC court earlier distanced itself in *Robinson* from the cautious approach to joint custody endorsed by the Ontario court when there is evidence of inability to communicate. In one case in our study, *Carr v. Carr*, the appellant father challenged an award of joint custody, with children living with each parent during alternate weeks. He invoked the 1994 British Columbia Court of Appeal decision in *Stewart v. Stewart*, standing for a cautious approach to joint custody.[91] The court did not state that *Stewart* had been altered by *Robinson* but dismissed the appeal because a new custody and access report reported only relatively minor difficulties in communication, whereas the children had adjusted well to the routine and appeared to be benefiting from the schedule.[92] Arguably this approach reflected the spirit of *Robinson*, which directs that the evidence must be looked at carefully, rather than making assumptions based on the quality of communication.

Despite its strong position against presumptions, the BC court has paid attention to the ability or inability of parents to communicate or cooperate. Sometimes a determination of inability to communicate was based on evidence that one parent has an anger management problem or has assaulted the other. For instance, in *Javid v. Kurytik*, the trial judge found that an order for joint custody would not be in the children's best interests. The father had organized his time in order to be able to be with the children as much as possible but had not dealt with his anger management problems, and he attributed all problems to the mother or others rather than himself. The Court of Appeal found that "the evidence . . . is overwhelming that joint custody is not appropriate for them."[93] It also stated, "Whatever reasons underlie their parents' inability to communicate sensibly and to co-operate in caring for Emma and Maxwell, the parents' conflict is real and continuing."[94] In *Bain*, the court stated that the evidence was overwhelming that the parents could not com-

91 *Stewart*, above note 7.

92 *Carr*, above note 56 at para. 10. Somewhat troubling is that the second custody and access report stated that "[w]hatever strain the children may experience could be attributed to the ongoing tensions between their parents, rather than arising from the custodial schedule," apparently ignoring studies indicating that such strain can pose risks for children in joint custody arrangements if their parents are in high conflict: Shaffer, "Joint Custody, Parental Conflict," above note 2 at 309.

93 *Javid v. Kurytik*, 2006 BCCA 565 at para. 28, leave to appeal to SCC refused, [2007] SCCA No 80.

94 *Ibid.* at para. 26.

municate sufficiently to permit them to co-parent the two young daughters.[95] The court did not state specifically why, but a restraining order prohibiting the father from having contact with the mother and entry on the property where she was residing was kept in place. The mother was not concerned that the father would be physically violent with the children, but there were references to the volatility of his behaviour and "the nasty difficulties during some access visit exchanges."[96] The trial judge had found that the father had threatened and intimidated the mother. In *Ness*, the trial judge had found that the mother expressed a continued fear about Mr. Ness and referred to an earlier restraining order, although the Court of Appeal simply referred to a lack of the requisite degree of mutual deference and respect to warrant joint custody.[97]

In her Ontario study, Shaffer found that in their focus on communication and cooperation, some post-*Kaplanis* decisions tend to lose sight of the point that joint custody should be considered only when both parents have a strong claim to custody based on the relevant statutory factors speaking to children's best interests, and should not be ordered if it is clearly in the children's best interest to be in the custody of one parent.[98] Problematic parental conduct can be overlooked in the focus on communication and cooperation that *Kaplanis* generated. Possibly the last three BC cases discussed reveal a similar tendency. However, in another case involving abuse, *Narayan v. Narayan*, the Court of Appeal dismissed the appropriateness of joint custody/guardianship without making communication the key. The court referred back to the trial judge's rejection of Mr. Narayan's claim for joint guardianship, stating:

> This is not an appropriate case for an order for joint custody or joint guardianship. The defendant has admitted assaulting the plaintiff in the past, he has an obvious animosity to her and blames her without justification for his problems and he has a demonstrated lack of reliability . . . .[99]

The British Columbia Court of Appeal found no basis for interfering with this decision, although it left it open to the parties if they wished later to agree to joint guardianship.

---

95 *Bain*, above note 75 at para. 18.

96 *Ibid.* at para. 19.

97 *Ness*, above note 49 at para. 17, Lambert JA.

98 Shaffer, "Joint Custody since *Kaplanis*," above note 2.

99 *Narayan v. Narayan*, 2006 BCCA 561 at para. 18.

Other cases on (in)ability to communicate include *Green*, in which the trial judge had found that the father's attitude made it impossible for the parties to cooperate as joint custodial parents. The father had also alleged that the mother was psychotic, which was unfounded in the eyes of the trial judge.[100] In *Chan v. Chan*, the trial judge had found that poor communication between the parties was clearly in evidence and likely to continue in the future.[101]

D. CONCLUSION

It appears, then, that the Ontario and the British Columbia courts of appeal differ somewhat in their approaches to joint custody, with the Ontario court being more cautious and the BC court more neutral as to what evidence might ground a determination of whether joint custody was in the best interests of a child. Both courts — of necessity, given governing legislation and Supreme Court of Canada precedents — accept that the only consideration in custody and access cases is the best interests of the child, and neither court applies presumptions *per se*. However the Ontario court has come closer to an approach that says that without clear evidence of ability to cooperate, a joint custody award is inappropriate.

One could argue that without a strong cautionary statement in a case such as *Kaplanis*, and with a strong directive to look carefully at the evidence in each case in determining an individual child's best interests, the BC courts are more able to dispense individual justice. After all, Huddart JA's instruction to find a child's best interests within "the practical context of the reality of the parents' lives and circumstances"[102] comes close to suggestions from many law reform–minded scholars who seek to ground decision making about children in their familial and social realities, including the history of care, any abusive relationships, and so on.[103] However, in a society and legal system that increasingly favours shared parenting, the lack of a cautionary precedent in relation to joint custody can equally lead to complacency about its appropriateness in circumstances that either generate risk (to a parent or

100 *Green*, above note 73 at para. 29.

101 *Chan v. Chan*, [1997] BCJ No 1105 at para. 4 (CA), Hollinrake JA.

102 Justice Huddart in *Robinson*, above note 8 at para. 29, quoting from *Gordon*, above note 15 at para. 46.

103 For one example, see Carol Smart & Bren Neale, *Family Fragments* (Cambridge: Polity Press, 1999) at 192ff.

a child) or are simply not conducive to consensual decision making. Some parents, unfortunately, require clear direction from courts in order to avoid ongoing disputes and court applications. It must be remembered that the minority of parents who appear before judicial panels are, of necessity, in some degree of conflict — sometimes high conflict — and that some of these cases involve spousal abuse. As we know from Shaffer's social science review, children do not fare better after divorce in joint custody arrangements than they do in sole custody and some children may fare worse, including those in high-conflict families.[104] In addition, parental conflict significantly increases the risk of reduced well-being on the part of children who experience their parents' divorce. Joint custody awards should therefore be awarded only when the evidence shows that they are appropriate.

On the whole, it appears that joint custody awards that have reached the British Columbia Court of Appeal thus far are more about joint decision making than about equally shared time with children.[105] As such, the question of what conditions are requisite for reasonably consensual decision making is key. The awarding of joint guardianship in some cases where joint custody was deemed inappropriate is somewhat puzzling in this regard, to the extent that joint guardianship is, for most purposes, very similar to joint custody. This pattern means that the proportion of joint custody awards is higher than might be thought, although apparently not the proportion of shared parenting. Perhaps the existence of joint guardianship in British Columbia, with the potential for orders on the Master Joyce model, makes it possible for judges to craft arrangements that at least to some degree control any potential for inappropriate wielding of control via the power given through joint guardianship or joint custody. A review of BC trial decisions sheds more light on how joint custody (and guardianship) is being dealt with in the BC courts and whether adequate attention is being paid to whether such orders are appropriate, including the ability to communicate and cooperate.[106]

---

104 Shaffer, "Joint Custody, Parental Conflict," above note 2.

105 This finding sheds some light on what lies beneath the increasing rate of joint custody awards in Canadian divorce courts. 2003 statistics indicate that in 44 percent of court-determined custody cases in the Canadian divorce context, the outcome is an order for joint custody, which is more than double the number from the mid-1990s and four times the figure when compared to the late 1980s: Statistics Canada, *Women in Canada: A Gender-Based Statistical Report*, 5th ed. (Ottawa: Target Group Project, 2006) at 40.

106 Boyd, "Joint Custody," above note 9.

Whereas in 2000, a majority of BC trial awards were for sole custody, in 2007, the majority had shifted in favour of joint custody. This evidence supports an argument that British Columbia has indeed departed from the more cautious approach in Ontario.

Contributors

Lorne D. Bertrand is the senior research associate for the Canadian Research Institute for Law and the Family (CRILF). Dr. Bertrand obtained his BA (First Class Honours), MA (with Distinction), and PhD degrees in Social Psychology from Carleton University in Ottawa. Prior to coming to CRILF in 1993, he completed a three-year postdoctoral fellowship in the Psychology Department at the University of Calgary, followed by research positions at Calgary Health Services and the Alberta Lung Association.

Michelle I. Bertrand is a PhD candidate in Social-Personality Psychology at Queen's University and has earned her MA in the same program. Her research, in the area of psychology and law, has included testing the effectiveness of new lineup presentation methods, surveying Canadian and American police officers on their identification procedures, and examining methodological issues in psychology and law research. She has held scholarships from the Social Sciences and Humanities Research Council of Canada during her MA and PhD, as well as an Ontario Graduate Scholarship during her PhD. She has articles in refereed journals as both first and co-author, has presented a talk at a conference for the Society for Applied Research in Memory and Cognition, and had multiple poster presentations at conferences for the American Psychology-Law Society, the Canadian Psychological Association, and the American Psychological Association.

Susan B. Boyd is a professor of law at the University of British Columbia, where she holds the chair in Feminist Legal Studies. She teaches courses on family law as well as feminist legal studies. Her research lies primarily in the fields of child custody law and legal parenthood. Her books include *Child Custody, Law, and Women's Work* (Don Mills: Oxford University Press, 2003), *Reaction and Resistance: Feminism, Law, and Social Change* (Vancouver: UBC Press, 2007), and *Law and Families* (2006), a volume of the International Library of Essays in Law and Society.

Peter J. Carrington is professor of Sociology and Legal Studies at the University of Waterloo and editor of *Canadian Journal of Criminology and Criminal Justice*. His current research project, the Canadian Criminal Careers and Criminal Networks Study, combines his long-standing interests in social network analysis and in the development of crime and delinquency. His other research interests include police discretion and the impact of the *Youth Criminal Justice Act*. His recent articles appeared in *Criminology*, *Canadian Journal of Criminology and Criminal Justice*, and *Criminal Justice Policy Review*. He is co-editor of *The SAGE Handbook of Social Network Analysis* (London: Sage Publications, 2011) and *Models and Methods in Social Network Analysis* (New York: Cambridge University Press, 2005).

Mark Carter is a professor at the College of Law, University of Saskatchewan where he teaches constitutional law and legal theory. He is a member of the Manitoba and Saskatchewan Bars.

Carla Cesaroni received her PhD from the Centre of Criminology, University of Toronto. She is currently an associate professor at the University of Ontario Institute of Technology (UOIT). For the past decade, Professor Cesaroni has explored the experiences and adjustment of incarcerated adolescent males. She is currently conducting a comparative study on the experiences of girls and boys in detention.

Professor Cesaroni is an associate researcher with the Scottish Centre of Criminal Justice Research.

Anthony N. Doob is a professor of Criminology at the Centre of Criminology, University of Toronto and a Fellow of the Royal Society of Canada. He has been at the University of Toronto since 1968, first in the Department of Psychology and later at the Centre of Criminology. He graduated from Harvard in 1964 and received his PhD (in psychology) from Stanford University in 1967. He served as director of the Centre of Criminology from 1979 to 1989 and was one of the members of the Canadian Sentencing Commission from 1984 until 1987. He has written on a wide range of topics related to the youth and adult justice systems and Canadian imprisonment policies including *Responding to Youth Crime in Canada* (Toronto: University of Toronto Press, 2004, with Carla Cesaroni); *Justice for Girls? Stability and Change in the Youth Justice Systems of the United States and Canada* (Chicago: University of Chicago Press, 2009, with Jane Sprott); and "Punitive Trends and Stable Imprisonment Rates in Canada" in Michael Tonry, ed., *Crime and Justice: A Review of Research*, Vol. 36 (Chicago: University of Chicago Press, 2007, with Cheryl Marie Webster).

Jean Dunbar is the associate director of Intervention Services at the YWCA of Calgary and oversees upwards of fifteen domestic violence intervention programs with 200 clinical staff, which include a women's emergency shelter, visitation programming, and treatment programs for men, women, and children. She has worked in the domestic violence field for over seventeen years in both group settings and individual play therapy with children and families exposed to domestic violence.

Dan L. Goldberg is senior counsel with the Office of the Children's Lawyer, an independent law office within the Ministry of the Attorney General of Ontario. Since 1984, Dan has represented children in custody/access and child protection cases. He has organized and presented at numerous legal educational programs and has been a guest lecturer on family and children's law at his alma mater, McGill University, as well as Queen's University, University of Toronto, University of Ottawa, Osgoode Hall Law School (both LLB and LLM programs), and at the former bar admission course (Ontario). Dan has appeared before the Supreme Court of Canada, successfully arguing on the issue of relocation rights of custodial parents (*Gordon v. Goertz*), and has authored articles on parental alienation, relocation rights, grandparent-grandchild access, the impact of religion in custody/access disputes, and the legal representation of children in child protection cases, as well as custody/access disputes.

Dale Hensley, QC, is a founding member and executive director of the Children's Legal & Educational Resource Centre (CLERC) in Calgary, Alberta.

CLERC provides legal advice, information, education, and representation to children and youth in civil law matters and was incorporated in 2002. Dale has worked with young people confronting civil law issues for twenty years.

Joseph P. Hornick is the executive director of the Canadian Research Institute for Law and the Family (CRILF). Since completing his PhD at the University of Waterloo in 1975, Dr. Hornick has worked in academic, government, private sector, and social service settings. He became the founding director of CRILF in 1987, and since that time has focused on applied research, particularly program evaluation, legislative evaluation, and policy research, and has co-authored over 100 publications. His major areas of interest and expertise are family policy, young offenders, child sexual abuse, domestic violence, victimization, and community policing.

Natalie Kalmet is currently a PhD candidate at Queen's University and holds an MS, also from Queen's University. She conducts research on eyewitness identification techniques, including the utility of presenting multiple views of faces in lineups and the impact of photo size on identification accuracy. She has presented posters at conferences for the American Psychology-Law Society, as well as a talk at a conference for the Society for Applied Research in Memory and Cognition. She has received two Joseph-Armand Bombardier Canada Graduate Scholarships from the Social Sciences and Humanities Research Council of Canada (SSHRC) — she currently holds the SSHRC Doctoral Scholarship, and held the SSHRC Master's scholarship during her MS.

Cathy Lane Goodfellow, QC, graduated from the University of Alberta Law School in 1983 and practised law in Edmonton from 1984 to 1991 in the areas of family law and youth criminal defence. In 1992, she relocated to Calgary and has been in continuous employment with the Youth Criminal Defence Office since October 1993 and became the associate senior counsel in 2008. Cathy obtained her LLM in 1995 and her thesis focused on the *Young Offenders Act* and the ethical and legal obligation for specialized advocacy for young people. She has guest-lectured numerous times for a variety of community or social agencies, been a lecturer for the Legal Education Society of Alberta, and a sessional instructor at both the University of Calgary and University of Alberta in Edmonton. She was the recipient of the 2005 Distinguished Service Award from the Law Society of Alberta and Canadian Bar Association, Alberta Branch.

Kang Lee is currently a professor in the Dr. Erick Jackman Institute of Child Study, University of Toronto. He received his PhD from the University of New Brunswick in 1994. For over fifteen years, Dr. Lee has been studying children's moral understanding of honesty and dishonesty, and their actual lying or truth-telling behaviors in various social and cultural contexts.

Rod Lindsay is a professor of Psychology at Queen's University where he has been studying eyewitness issues since 1982. Dr. Lindsay has testified as an expert on eyewitness issues in both criminal and civil cases and consulted with individual police identification officers and departments regarding identification procedures. He consulted on and was called to testify in one of the United Nations war crimes (genocide) trials for Rwanda. As a member of the Technical Working Group for Eyewitness Evidence (US National Institute of Justice), Dr. Lindsay co-authored the American national guidelines for obtaining and preserving eyewitness evidence (published in 1999 as *Eyewitness Evidence: A Guide for Law Enforcement*). Dr. Lindsay co-edited and co-authored several chapters of the *Handbook of Eyewitness Psychology* (London: Psychology Press, 2007), the most comprehensive collection of scientific views on eyewitness issues to date. In 2002, the Canadian Psychological Association bestowed a career award on Dr. Lindsay for his Distinguished Contributions to the Application of Psychology.

Leslie D. MacRae holds a BA (First Class Honours) in Sociology from the University of Calgary and an MA in Sociology from Queen's University. Ms MacRae has been a member of the staff at Canadian Research Institute for Law and the Family (CRILF) for six years, first as a research associate, then as Coordinator of Alberta-Based Research Projects. With the CRILF team, she has conducted numerous studies relating to law and family during her time at CRILF, among them the evaluation of Alberta's *Family Law Act*.

Jamal K. Mansour earned her PhD from Queen's University in July 2010 and is currently an assistant professor at Simon Fraser University. She has published her research in journals such as *Applied Cognitive Psychology* and *Legal and Criminological Psychology* and has presented her research at the American Psychology-Law Society, the Society for Applied Research in Memory and Cognition, and the Society for Personality and Social Psychology. Dr. Mansour's research focuses on how people make decisions about faces. She is particularly interested in how eyewitnesses make decisions about police lineups and the mechanisms of basic face recognition. Recent work includes eyewitness decisions when viewing conditions vary or lineups are biased, the relationship between confidence and accuracy in lineup decisions, theories of eyewitness lineup decisions, and how face recognition varies with encoding conditions.

Anne McGillivray is a professor of law at the University of Manitoba. Her research centres on childhood, children's rights, and the right to live free from all forms of violence. Her publications include *Black Eyes All of the Time: Intimate Violence, Aboriginal Women and the Justice System* (Toronto: University of Toronto Press, 1999) *Governing Childhood* (Hants: Dartmouth Publication Company, 1997), and over fifty chapters, scholarly articles, and reports on childhood, rights, corporal punishment, *parens patriae*, Aboriginal childhood, child protection, violence against women, and the child in literature. She serves on the boards of the International Journal of Children's Rights, the Canadian Journal of Human Rights, and Mosaic: A Journal for the Interdisciplinary Study of Literature. She served on the 1997 CIDA Children's Rights Delegation to Cuba and the Health Canada Steering Committee for the Canadian Incidence Study on Child Abuse and Neglect Part II.

Joanne J. Paetsch has been the administrator for the Canadian Research Institute for Law and the Family since its establishment in 1987. Ms Paetsch obtained her BA in Psychology (with Distinction) from the University of Calgary in 1996. In addition to her administrative duties, she is also a research associate, spending approximately half her time on project development and research activities.

Sheryl Pearson is a lawyer and a social worker who practises as an independent law and policy consultant. She has expertise in the areas of legal representation of children, family law, child protection, vulnerable adults and the law, lobbying legislation, and administrative processes. Formerly a lawyer with Emery Jamieson LLP and legal counsel for the Alberta Law Reform Institute, she now assists clients by designing and implementing consultation processes, reviewing legislation, engaging in policy and data analysis, drafting policy, and designing and leading training sessions on specific topics.

Julian V. Roberts is a professor of criminology in the Faculty of Law, University of Oxford, and a member of the Sentencing Council of England and Wales. He is editor-in-chief of the *European Journal of Criminology* and associate editor of the *Canadian Journal of Criminology and Criminal Justice.* He has been a visiting scholar in the Department of Justice Canada, a visiting professor at the Catholic University of Leuven and visiting international professor, Faculty of Law, Université Libre de Bruxelles.

Gerald B. Robertson, QC, is a professor in the Faculty of Law at the University of Alberta, having obtained his LLB from the University of Edinburgh and his LLM from McGill University. He is also a practising barrister and solicitor in Alberta. His main research interests lie in the fields of health law and tort law. His textbooks include *Legal Liability of Doctors and Hospitals in Canada*, 4th ed. (Toronto: Carswell, 2007, with Madam Justice Ellen Picard), and *Mental Disability and the Law in Canada* (Toronto: Carswell, 1994). He has published numerous articles in legal and medical journals in Canada, the United States, and the United Kingdom.

Shane D. Simpson is currently a research analyst in the Office of Institutional Analysis and Planning at Mount Royal University. He received a BA (Honours) in Sociology and a BS in Psychology from the University of Ottawa, and an MA in Sociology from Queen's University. Prior to Mount Royal, he held a research position at the Canadian Research Institute for Law and the Family, where he worked on the evaluation of Alberta's *Family Law Act*.

Jane B. Sprott received her PhD from the Centre of Criminology at the University of Toronto. She is currently an associate professor in the Department of Criminal Justice and Criminology at Ryerson University. Her research interests include the operation of the youth and adult criminal justice systems, pretrial detention, and perceptions of crime and criminal justice policies. Professor Sprott has published work on a variety of issues related to youth justice including, most recently, *Justice for Girls? Stability and Change in the Youth Justice Systems of the United States and Canada* (Chicago: University of Chicago Press, 2009, with Anthony N. Doob); "Punishing Processes in Youth Court: Procedural Justice, Court Atmosphere and Youths' Views of the Legitimacy of the Justice System" (2010) 52:5 Canadian Journal of Criminology and Criminal Justice, with Greene, Madon, and Jung; and "Gendered Treatment: Bail Conditions Placed on Youths" (2010) 52: 4 *Canadian Journal of Criminology and Criminal Justice*, with Anthony N. Doob.

Victoria Talwar is an associate professor in the Educational & Counselling Psychology Department at McGill University. She received her PhD from

Queen's University in 2003. Her research has investigated issues related to child witness testimony, including child witness credibility and competence. She has also studied children's verbal deception, lie detection, and children's moral and cognitive development.

MIX
Papier | Fördert gute Waldnutzung
FSC® C083411

Kolibri 360 GmbH
Ferdinand-Jühlke-Straße 7
99095 Erfurt, Deutschland
produktsicherheit@kolibri360.de